BTOOOM!

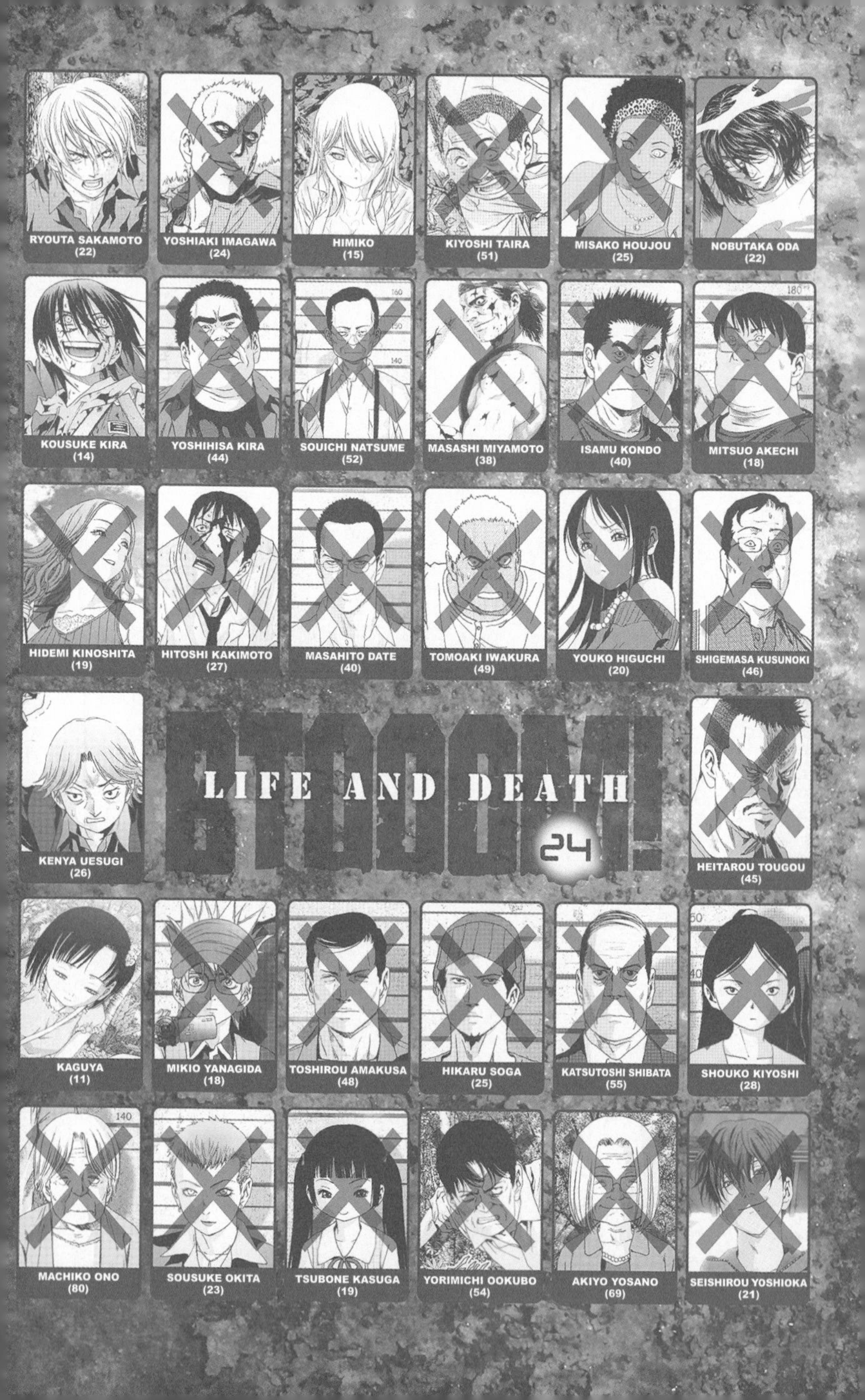
RYOUTA SAKAMOTO (22)
YOSHIAKI IMAGAWA (24)
HIMIKO (15)
KIYOSHI TAIRA (51)
MISAKO HOUJOU (25)
NOBUTAKA ODA (22)
KOUSUKE KIRA (14)
YOSHIHISA KIRA (44)
SOUICHI NATSUME (52)
MASASHI MIYAMOTO (38)
ISAMU KONDO (40)
MITSUO AKECHI (18)
HIDEMI KINOSHITA (19)
HITOSHI KAKIMOTO (27)
MASAHITO DATE (40)
TOMOAKI IWAKURA (49)
YOUKO HIGUCHI (20)
SHIGEMASA KUSUNOKI (46)
KENYA UESUGI (26)
BTOOOM!
LIFE AND DEATH
24
HEITAROU TOUGOU (45)
KAGUYA (11)
MIKIO YANAGIDA (18)
TOSHIROU AMAKUSA (48)
HIKARU SOGA (25)
KATSUTOSHI SHIBATA (55)
SHOUKO KIYOSHI (28)
MACHIKO ONO (80)
SOUSUKE OKITA (23)
TSUBONE KASUGA (19)
YORIMICHI OOKUBO (54)
AKIYO YOSANO (69)
SEISHIROU YOSHIOKA (21)

BTOOOM!

JUNYA INOUE

CHARACTER

NOBUTAKA ODA

GENDER: Male
AGE: 22
BLOOD TYPE: AB
JOB: Restaurant manager
HOME: Tokyo

Sakamoto's biggest rival and an old classmate of his from high school. His elaborate plans and surprisingly daring athleticism have helped him procure chips at a rapid pace as he plans for his own departure from the island. Engaging in life-or-death battles with his former best friend Sakamoto, he has demonstrated himself to be an unequaled master at combat.

HIMIKO

GENDER: Female
AGE: 15
BLOOD TYPE: B
JOB: High school student
HOME: Tokyo

A foreign high school girl who has teamed up with Sakamoto. She harbors a deep resentment against men after a sordid experience in her past, but after surviving some battles thanks to Sakamoto, she begins to trust him. Her character in the online version of "BTOOOM!" is actually married to Sakamoto's character, and she has fallen in love with the real Sakamoto too.

RYOUTA SAKAMOTO

GENDER: Male
AGE: 22
BLOOD TYPE: B
JOB: Unemployed
HOME: Tokyo

After spending every day cooped up in his home gaming online, he suddenly finds himself forced to participate in "BTOOOM! GAMERS," a killing game taking place on a mysterious uninhabited island. As a world ranker in the online third-person shooter "BTOOOM!", he uses his experience and natural instincts to survive and concoct a plan to get off the island with his comrades, only for it to end in failure. At the Sanctuary, he teams up with Kaguya and Soga to beat Torio.

KAGUYA

GENDER: Female
AGE: 11
BLOOD TYPE: AB
JOB: Grade schooler
HOME: Tokyo

A mysterious little girl who came across Sakamoto when he washed ashore. She doesn't speak and uses a tablet to communicate. She's the figurehead of the Order of Moonlight, a religious cult, and can see dead people. In the Sanctuary, she worked with Sakamoto and Soga to defeat the real villain behind the tragedies, Torio.

KENYA UESUGI

GENDER: Male
AGE: 26
BLOOD TYPE: AB
JOB: Office worker
HOME: Tokyo

A cowardly and easily flattered young man who used to dream of becoming an actor. He was almost killed by Kira, but he escaped thanks to Higuchi's lie-detecting ability. He was previously a part of Tougou's team.

KOUSUKE KIRA

GENDER: Male
AGE: 14
BLOOD TYPE: AB
JOB: Junior high student
HOME: Tokyo

This junior high student harbors a dark, brutal, murderous past. On the island, he blew up his own father and is genuinely enjoying this murderous game of "BTOOOM!". He's always been a big fan of the online version of the game, and his dream is to defeat "SAKAMOTO," a top world ranker. Unfortunately, he keeps failing at it. Tougou's death makes him realize for the first time ever how precious life is.

BTOOOM! 24

LONGER SCHWARITZ

GENDER: Male
AGE: 77
BLOOD TYPE: O
JOB: Capitalist
HOME: New York

A descendant of European aristocracy, he is a man of power who controls the world behind the scenes with his considerable capital. In order to more thoroughly control the online realm, he founds the THEMIS project and has high hopes for "BTOOOM! GAMERS."

XAVIERA FRANCISCA

GENDER: Female
AGE: 22
BLOOD TYPE: O
JOB: Freelancer
HOME: Washington

The operator of the drone that dropped the medicine case down on the island. Instead of BIMs, she attacks the players with a machine gun. Her skill is universally acknowledged, and in the online version of "BTOOOM!", she is the reigning world champion. However, she's never beaten Sakamoto, so she's obsessed with doing so.

TAKANOHASHI

GENDER: Male
AGE: 45
BLOOD TYPE: AB
JOB: Game planner
HOME: Hokkaido

An executive staff member at Tyrannos Japan, he is the leader behind all the development of the online and real-life versions of "BTOOOM! GAMERS." He considers Sakamoto a valuable player and debugger. As a result of Sakamoto's plan to hijack the helicopter, Takanohashi's precious game was almost forced to come to a premature end.

HISANOBU

GENDER: Male
AGE: 55
BLOOD TYPE: A
JOB: Unemployed
HOME: Tokyo

Yukie's new husband and Sakamoto's stepfather. He's worried about how much time his stepson spends up in his room and scolds him, only to be attacked. Having just been laid off, he racks up debt because of his praiseworthy efforts to preserve his family's lifestyle. However, Yukie is frail in body and mind and attempts to kill herself. Fate has dealt him an unfair card in life.

TSUNEAKI IIDA

GENDER: Male
AGE: 24
BLOOD TYPE: A
JOB: Programmer
HOME: Tokyo

An employee at Tyrannos Japan and Sakamoto's senpai from college. He's an excellent programmer and works under Takanohashi on the development of "BTOOOM! GAMERS." But he doesn't agree with the inhumane nature of the game and approached Sakamoto with the proposal and strategy to put a stop to the game's development, only for the plan to fall apart.

MATTHEW PERRIER

GENDER: Male
AGE: 27
BLOOD TYPE: O
JOB: Ex-NSA programmer, political refugee
HOME: Washington
(location unknown after exile)

A former programmer with the NSA (U.S. National Security Agency), he's a capable hacker and curbed a number of cyber-crimes while with the NSA. But after learning about the government's darker side, he made off with sensitive data about the THEMIS project — in a way, the evidence of their nefarious plans — and defected to another country.

THE SITUATION AS OF VOLUME 23

SITUATION

BATTLES ERUPT EVERYWHERE— ON THE ISLAND, BACK IN JAPAN, AND EVEN OVER ELECTRONIC NETWORKS!!

MENTAL BATTLE

PSYCHOLOGICAL WARFARE

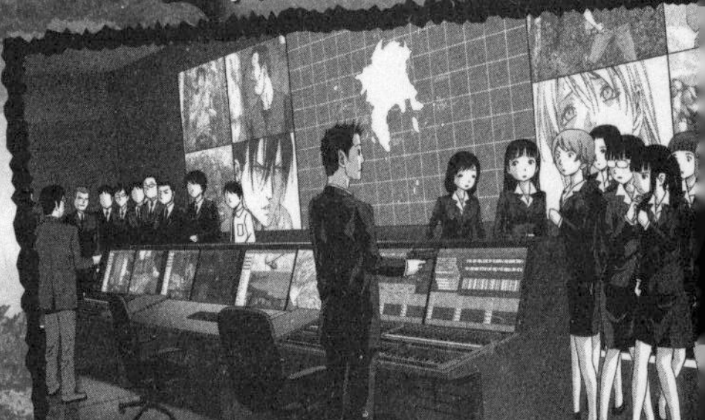

IIDA VS TYRANNOS JAPAN

IIDA AND HISANOBU HAVE TAKEN CONTROL OF THE OFFICE'S MAIN CONTROL ROOM. IN ORDER TO SAVE SAKAMOTO AND THE OTHERS, IIDA MUST HOLD A GUN AGAINST HIS FORMER COWORKERS.

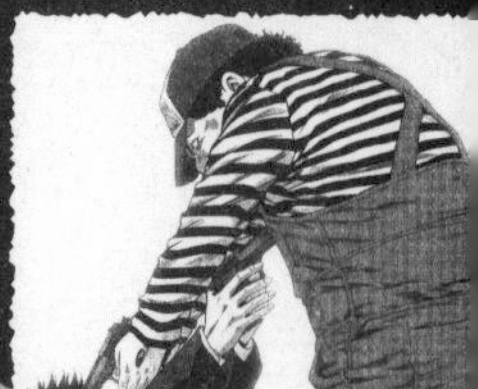

REAL BATTLE

RAID WARFARE

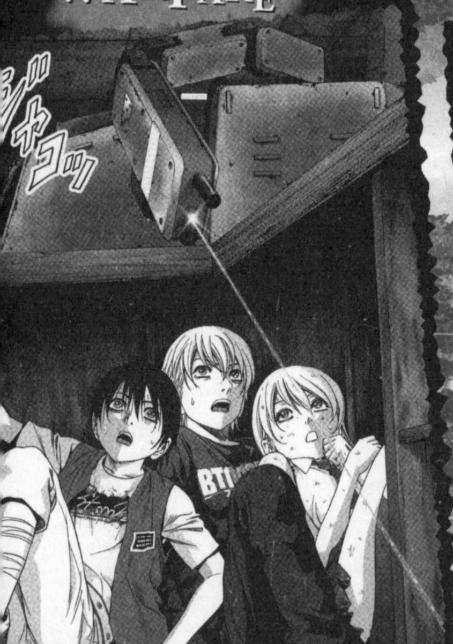

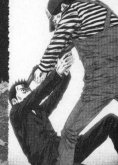

PLAYERS VS DRONE UNIT

TWO KINDS OF DRONES—A BIG BISON AND GUN FLYERS—DRIVE SAKAMOTO AND HIS TEAMMATES INTO A TIGHT CORNER. DO THEY STAND ANY CHANCE AGAINST THEM!?

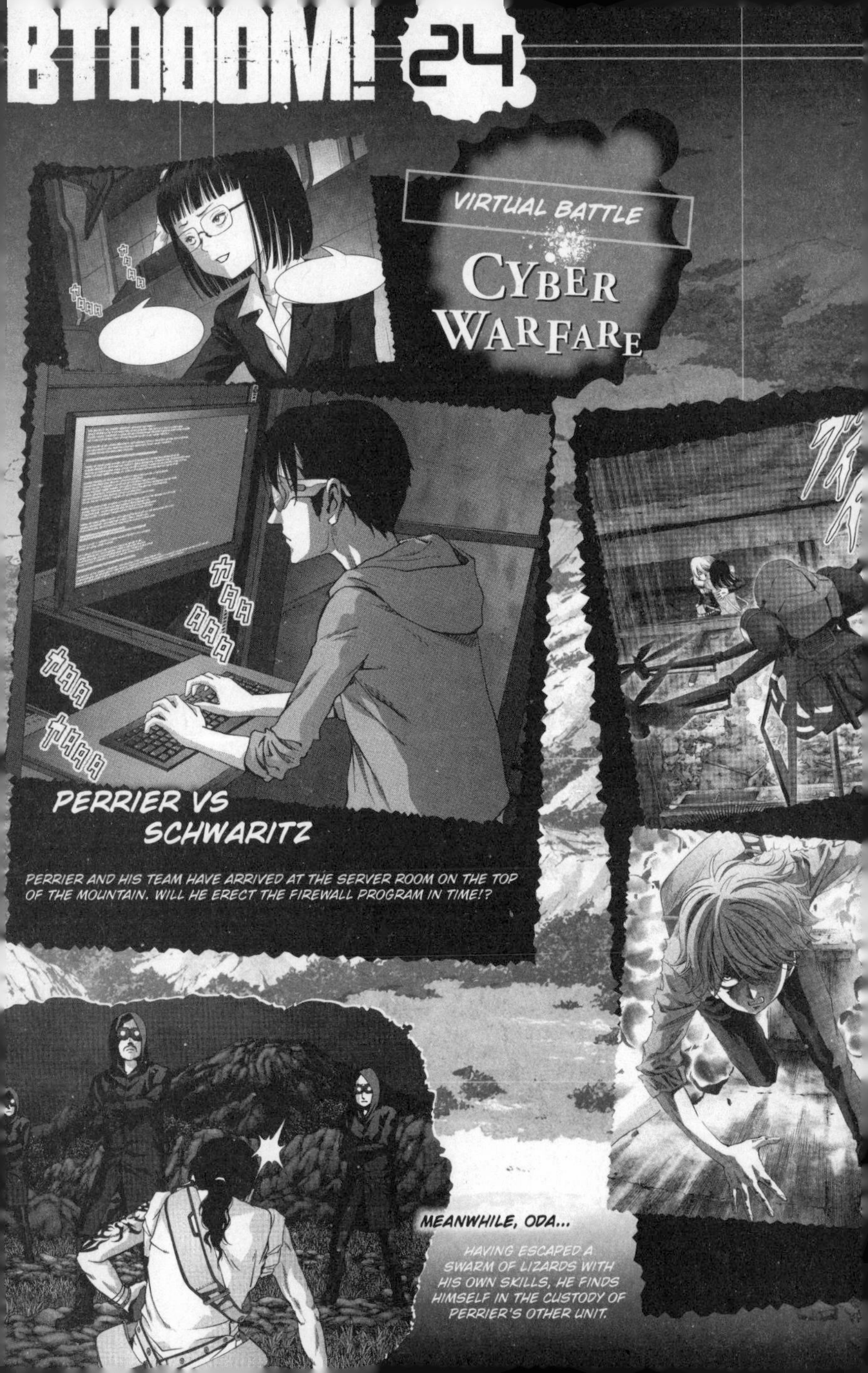
BTOOOM! 24
VIRTUAL BATTLE
CYBER WARFARE
PERRIER VS SCHWARITZ
PERRIER AND HIS TEAM HAVE ARRIVED AT THE SERVER ROOM ON THE TOP OF THE MOUNTAIN. WILL HE ERECT THE FIREWALL PROGRAM IN TIME!?
MEANWHILE, ODA...
HAVING ESCAPED A SWARM OF LIZARDS WITH HIS OWN SKILLS, HE FINDS HIMSELF IN THE CUSTODY OF PERRIER'S OTHER UNIT.

CONTENTS

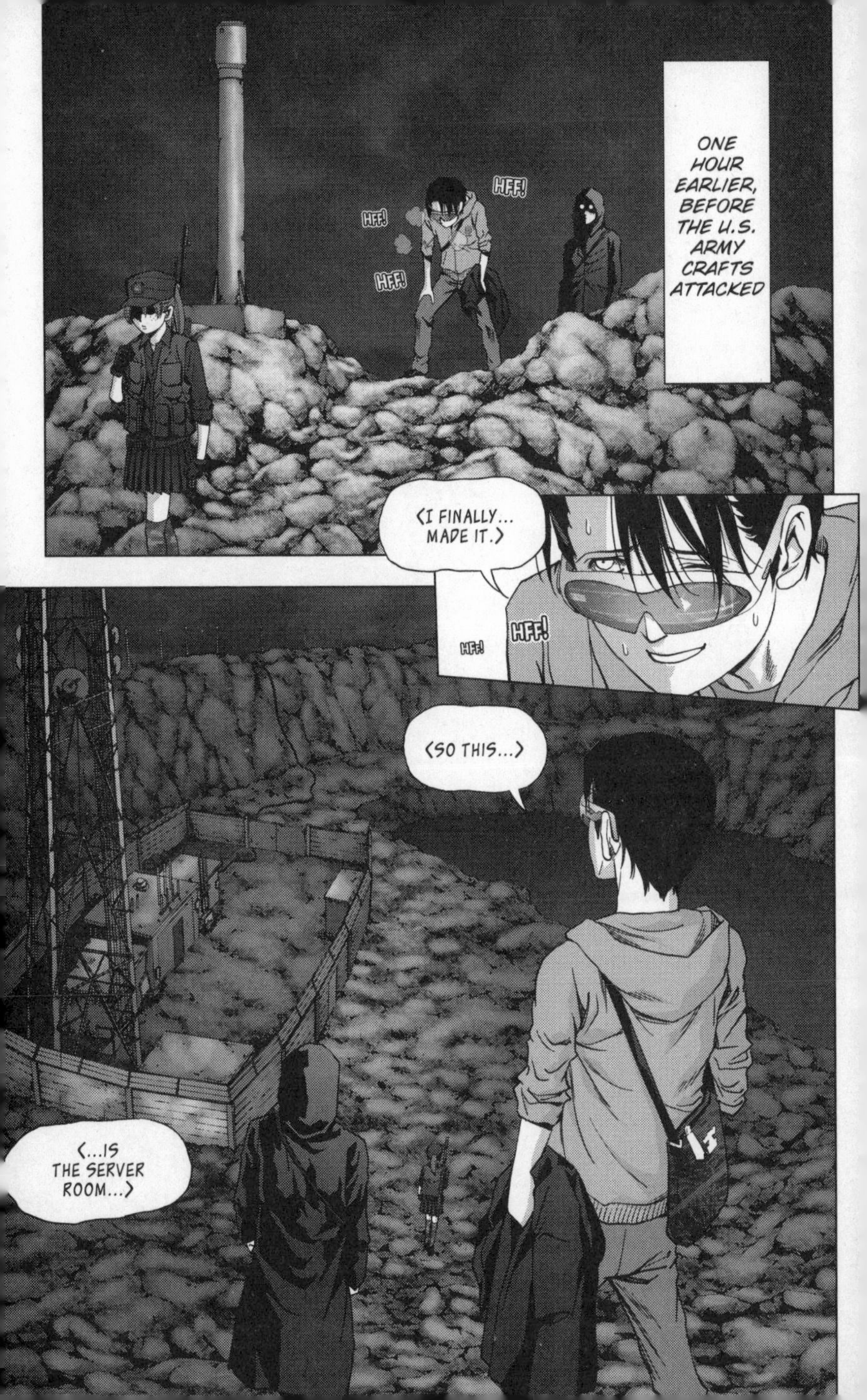
ONE HOUR EARLIER, BEFORE THE U.S. ARMY CRAFTS ATTACKED
HFF!
HFF!
HFF!
<I FINALLY... MADE IT.>
HFF!
HFF!
<SO THIS...>
<...IS THE SERVER ROOM...>

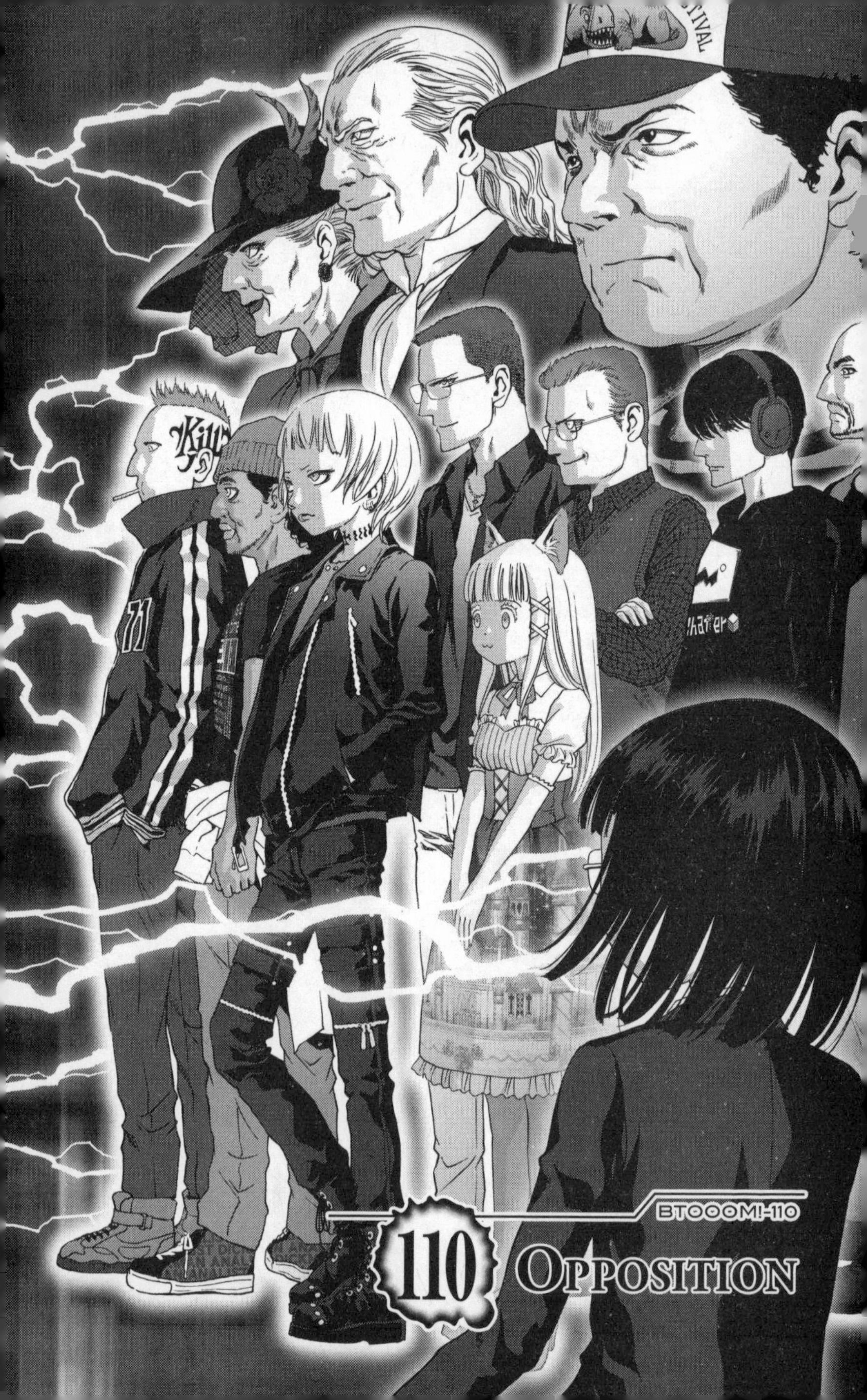
BTOOOM!-110
110
OPPOSITION

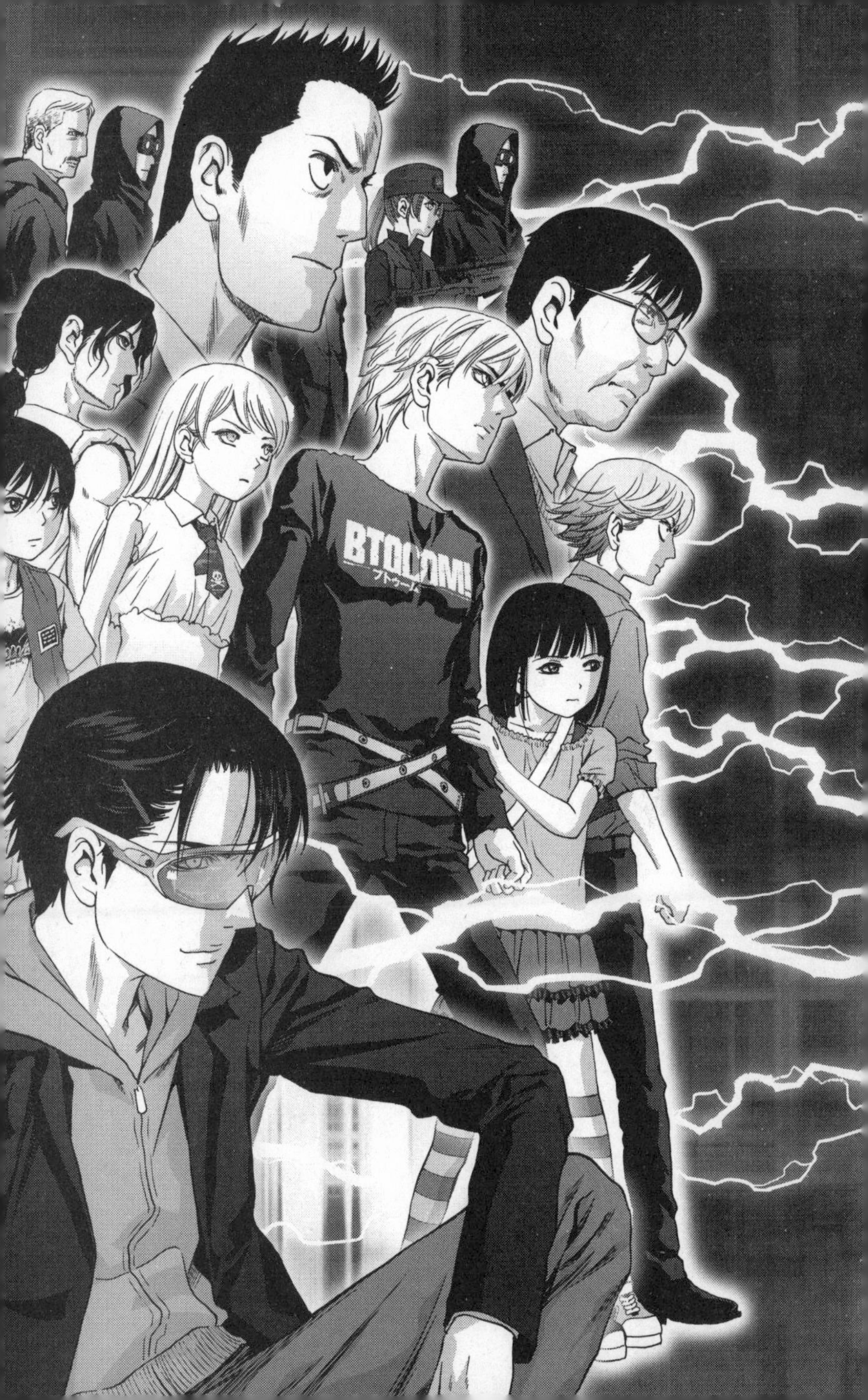
BTOOOM!
ブトゥーム

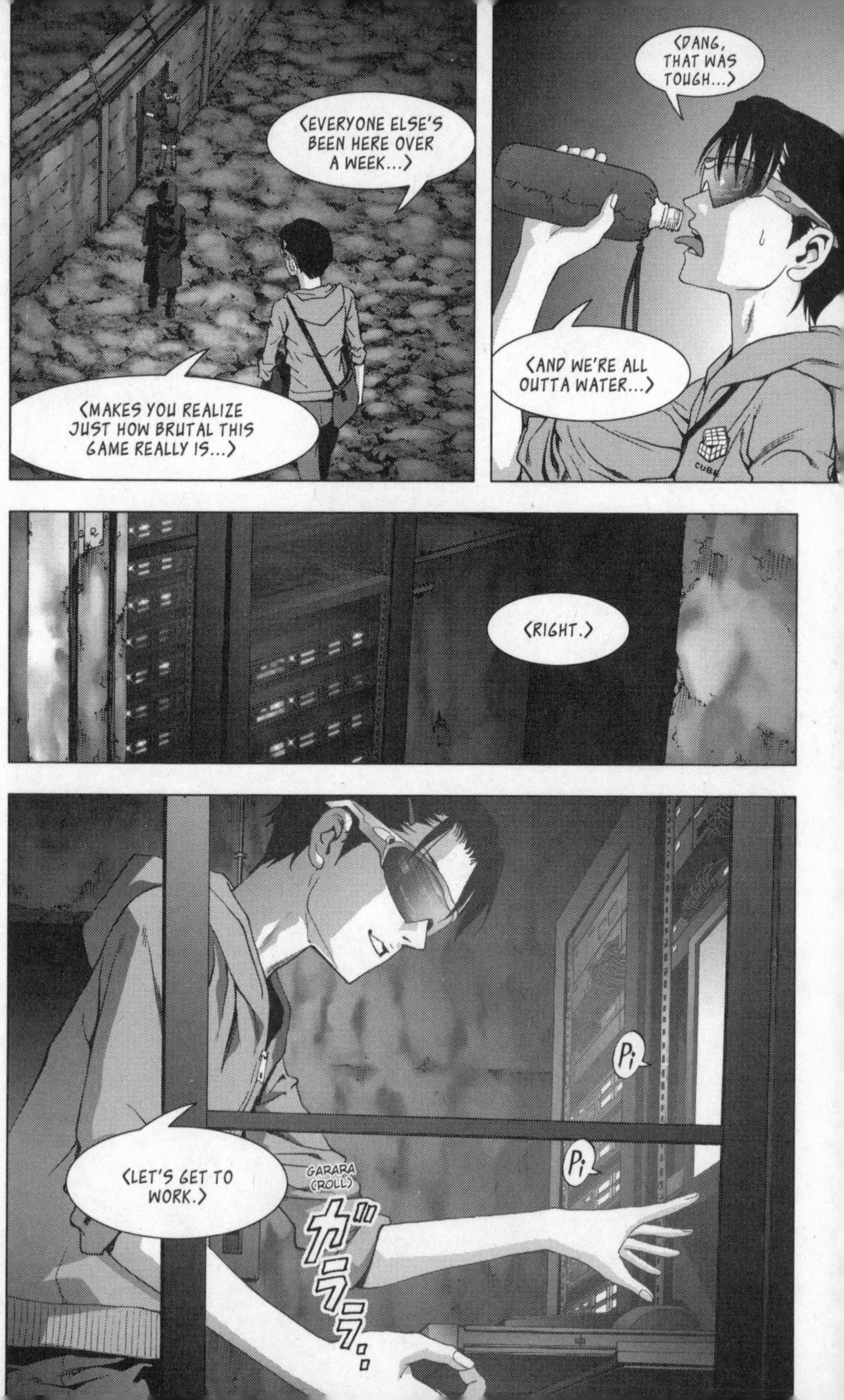
〈DANG, THAT WAS TOUGH...〉
〈AND WE'RE ALL OUTTA WATER...〉
〈EVERYONE ELSE'S BEEN HERE OVER A WEEK...〉
〈MAKES YOU REALIZE JUST HOW BRUTAL THIS GAME REALLY IS...〉
〈RIGHT.〉
Pi
Pi
GARARA (ROLL)
ガラララ
〈LET'S GET TO WORK.〉

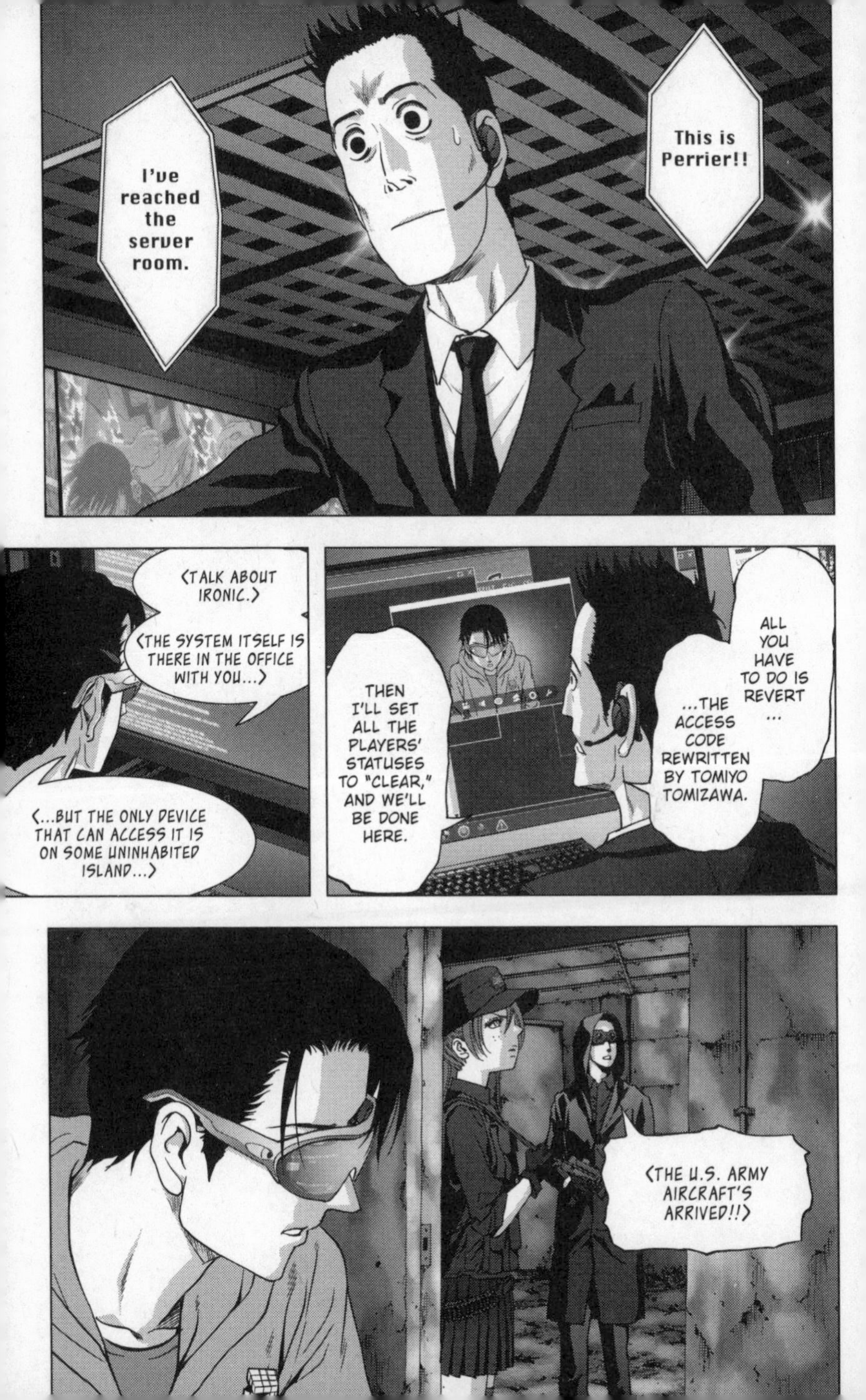
This is Perrier!!
I've reached the server room.
ALL YOU HAVE TO DO IS REVERT ...
...THE ACCESS CODE REWRITTEN BY TOMIYO TOMIZAWA.
THEN I'LL SET ALL THE PLAYERS' STATUSES TO "CLEAR," AND WE'LL BE DONE HERE.
〈TALK ABOUT IRONIC.〉
〈THE SYSTEM ITSELF IS THERE IN THE OFFICE WITH YOU...〉
〈...BUT THE ONLY DEVICE THAT CAN ACCESS IT IS ON SOME UNINHABITED ISLAND...〉
〈THE U.S. ARMY AIRCRAFT'S ARRIVED!!〉

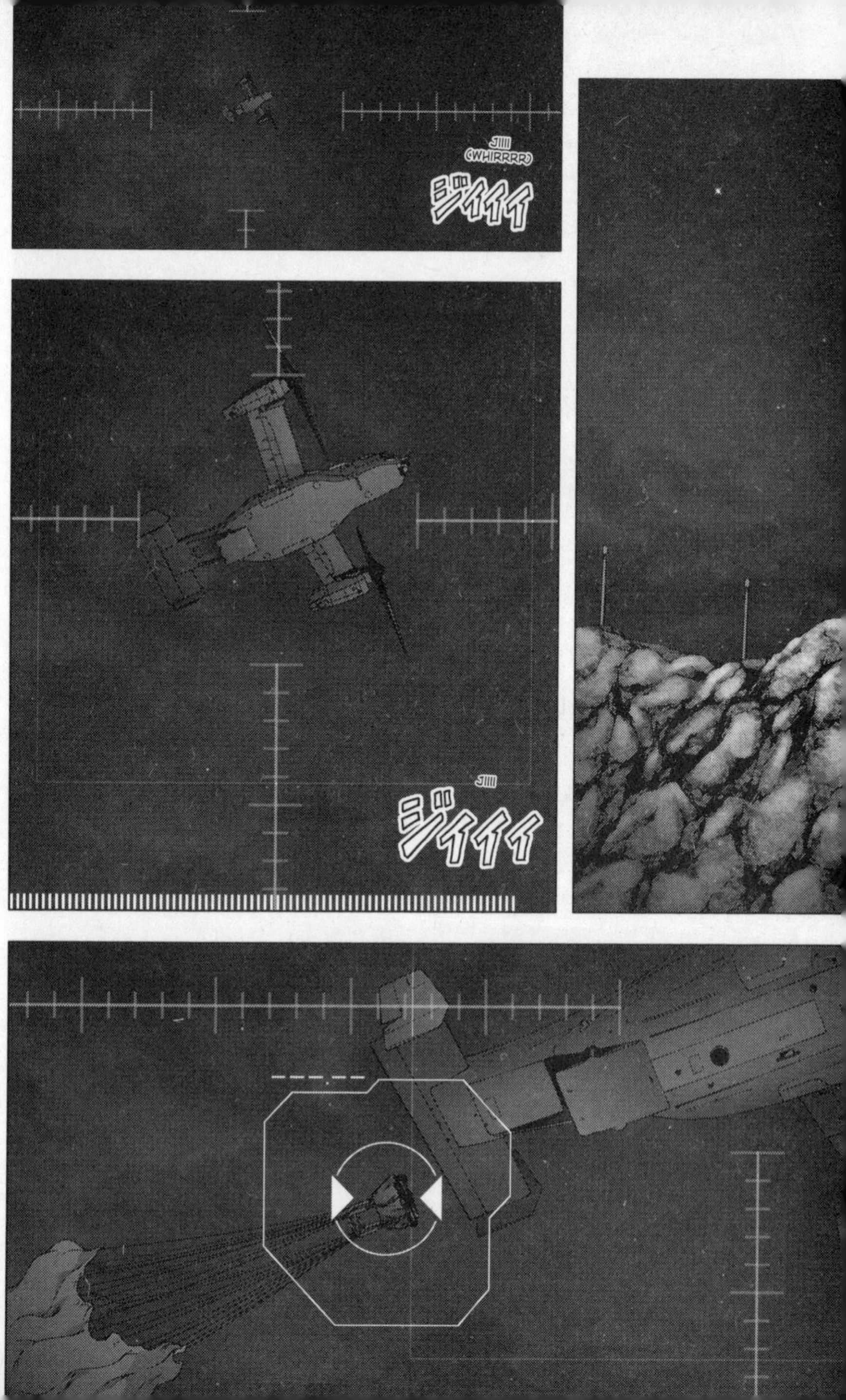
JIIII (WHIRRRR)
ジイイイ
JIIII
ジイイイ

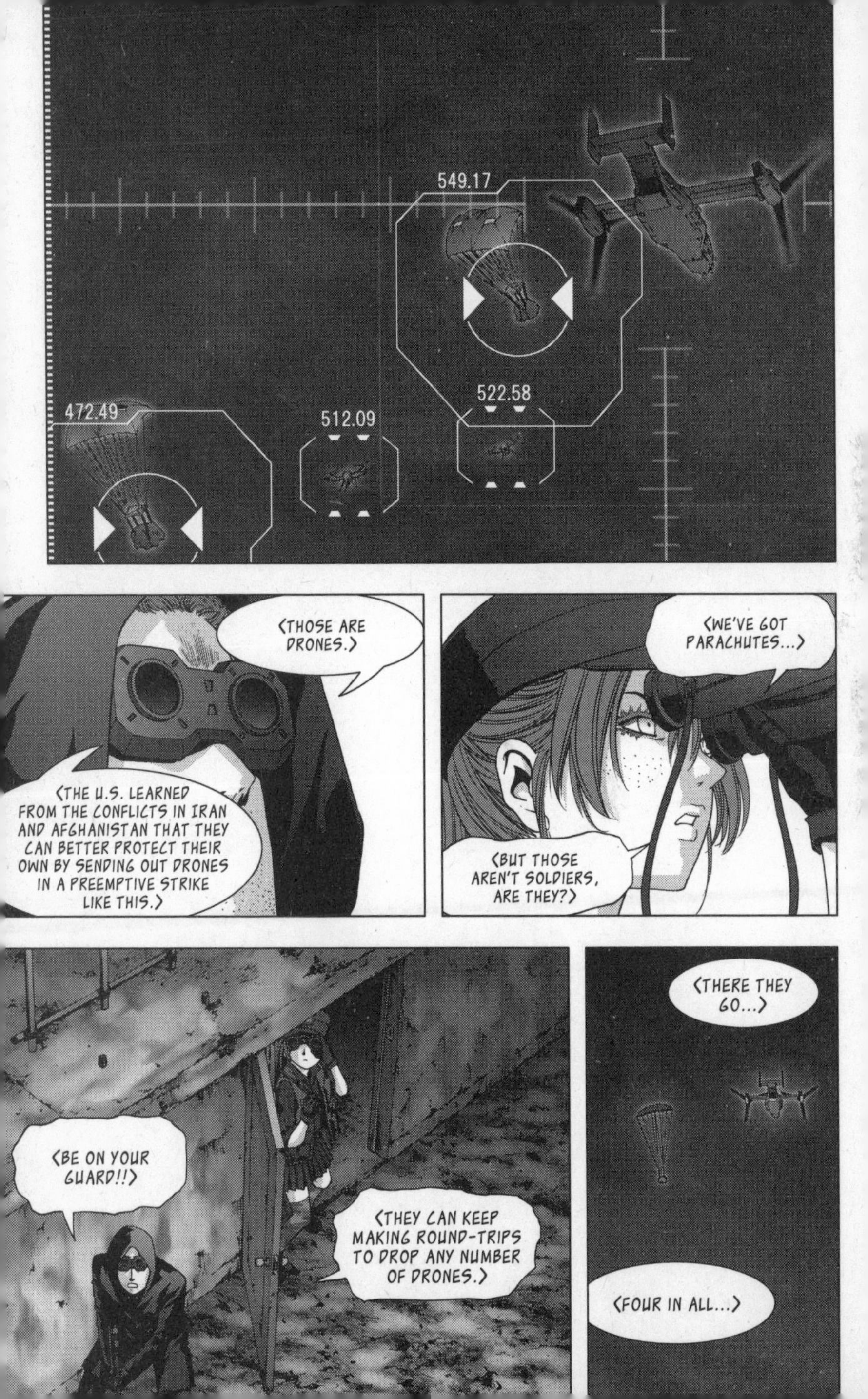
549.17
522.58
512.09
472.49
〈WE'VE GOT PARACHUTES...〉
〈BUT THOSE AREN'T SOLDIERS, ARE THEY?〉
〈THOSE ARE DRONES.〉
〈THE U.S. LEARNED FROM THE CONFLICTS IN IRAN AND AFGHANISTAN THAT THEY CAN BETTER PROTECT THEIR OWN BY SENDING OUT DRONES IN A PREEMPTIVE STRIKE LIKE THIS.〉
〈THERE THEY GO...〉
〈FOUR IN ALL...〉
〈BE ON YOUR GUARD!!〉
〈THEY CAN KEEP MAKING ROUND-TRIPS TO DROP ANY NUMBER OF DRONES.〉

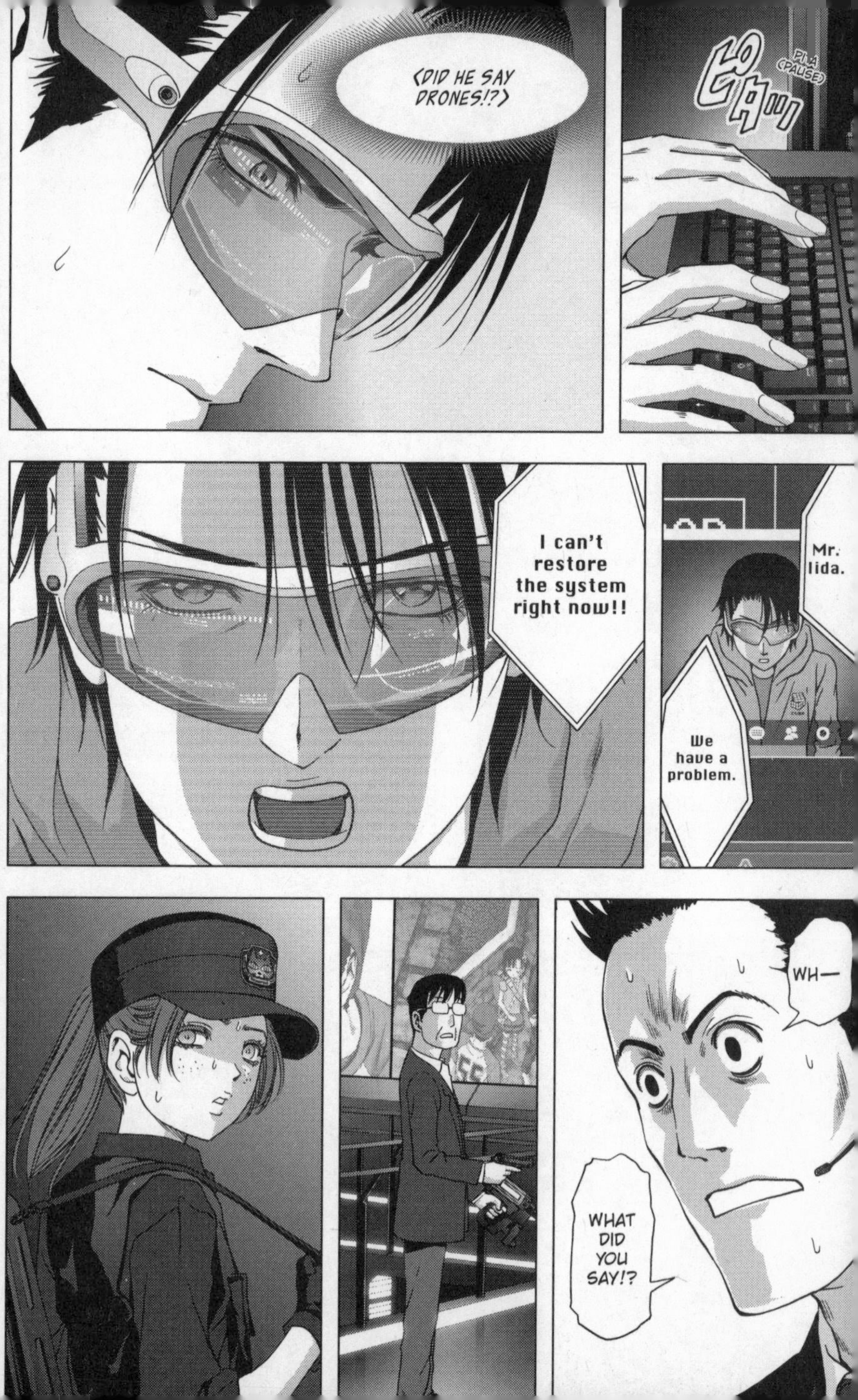
ピタッ
PITA (PAUSE)
<DID HE SAY DRONES!?>
Mr. Iida.
We have a problem.
I can't restore the system right now!!
WH—
WHAT DID YOU SAY!?

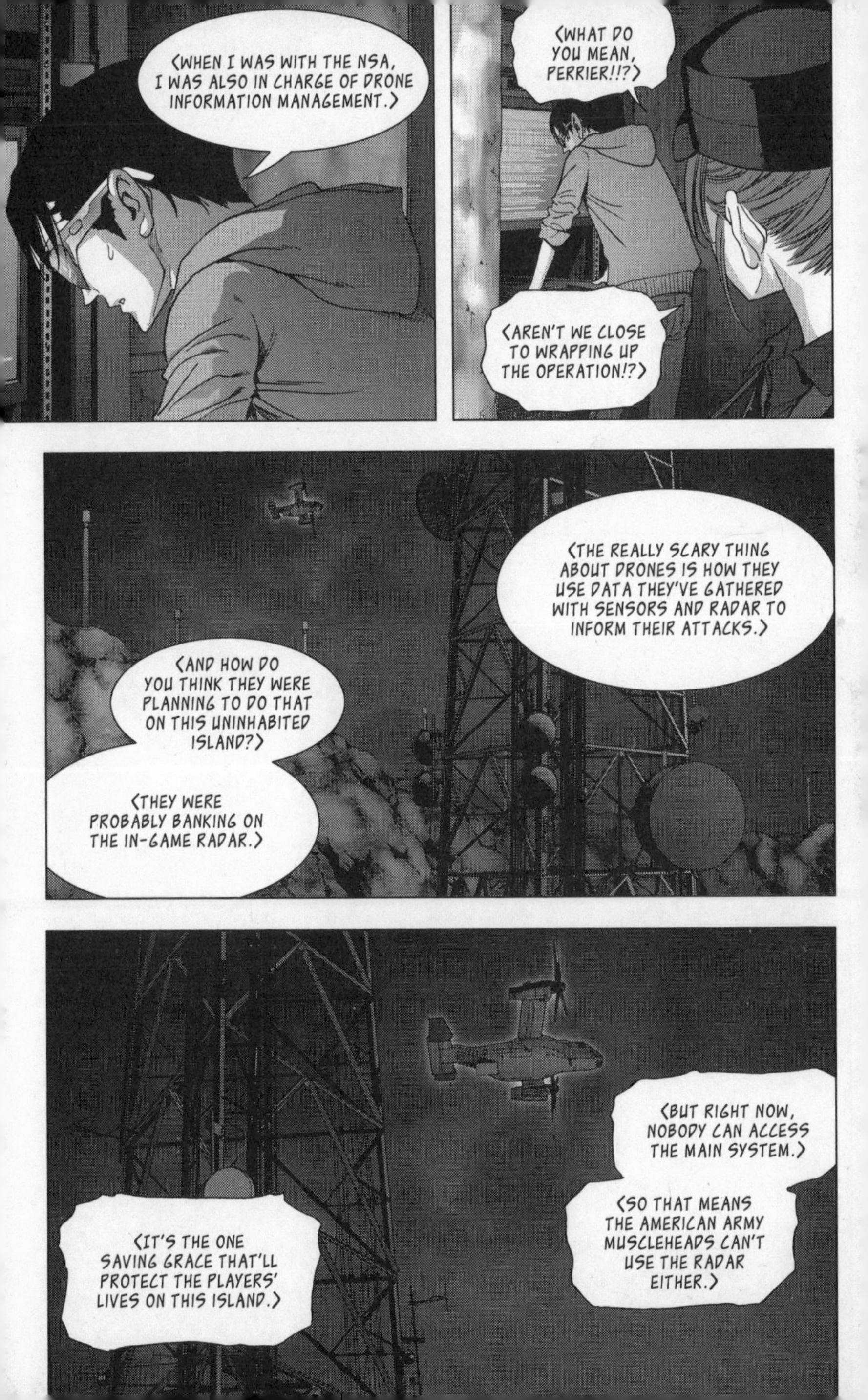
<WHAT DO YOU MEAN, PERRIER!!?>
<AREN'T WE CLOSE TO WRAPPING UP THE OPERATION!?>
<WHEN I WAS WITH THE NSA, I WAS ALSO IN CHARGE OF DRONE INFORMATION MANAGEMENT.>
<THE REALLY SCARY THING ABOUT DRONES IS HOW THEY USE DATA THEY'VE GATHERED WITH SENSORS AND RADAR TO INFORM THEIR ATTACKS.>
<AND HOW DO YOU THINK THEY WERE PLANNING TO DO THAT ON THIS UNINHABITED ISLAND?>
<THEY WERE PROBABLY BANKING ON THE IN-GAME RADAR.>
<BUT RIGHT NOW, NOBODY CAN ACCESS THE MAIN SYSTEM.>
<SO THAT MEANS THE AMERICAN ARMY MUSCLEHEADS CAN'T USE THE RADAR EITHER.>
<IT'S THE ONE SAVING GRACE THAT'LL PROTECT THE PLAYERS' LIVES ON THIS ISLAND.>

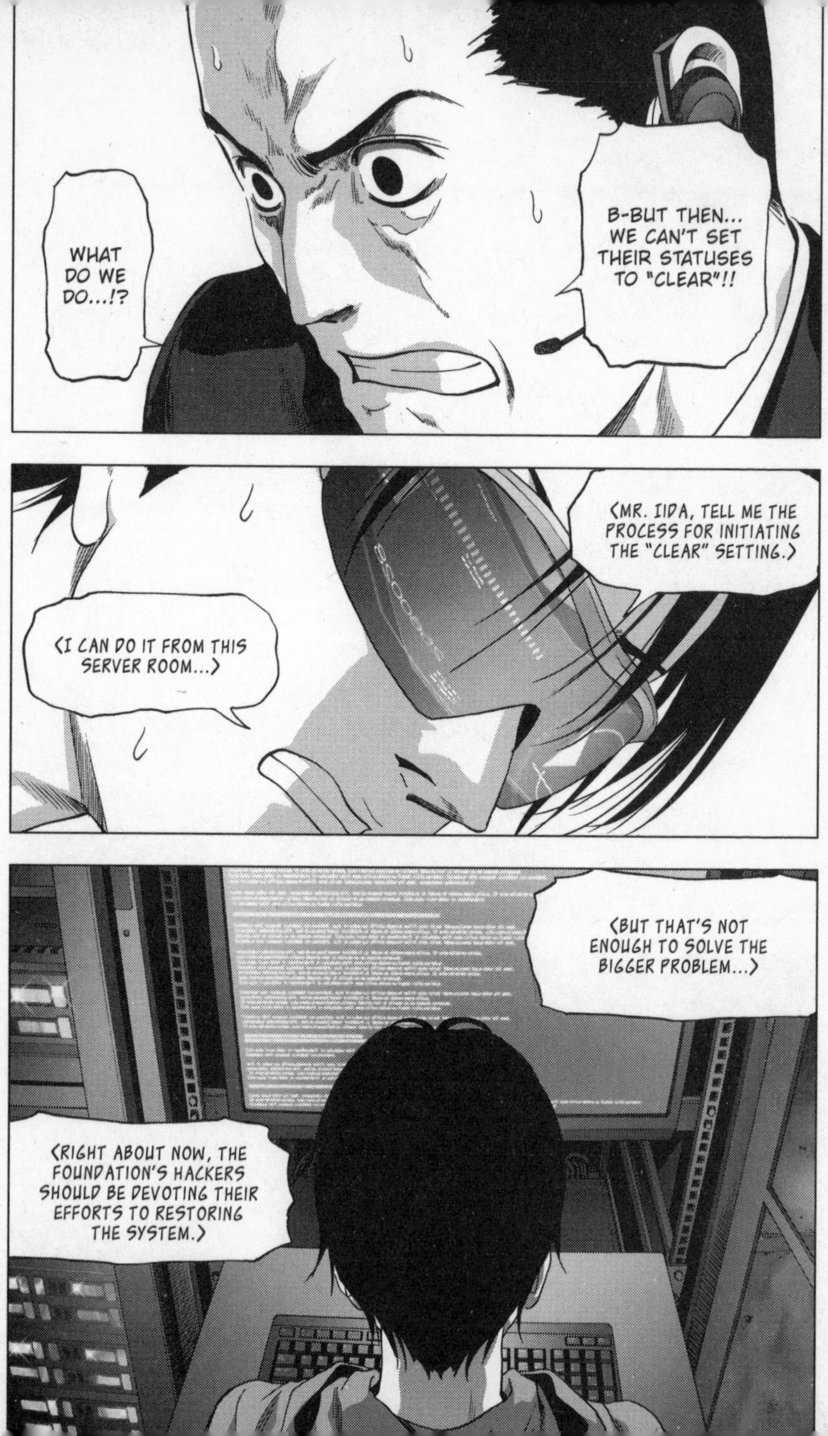
B-BUT THEN... WE CAN'T SET THEIR STATUSES TO "CLEAR"!!
WHAT DO WE DO...!?
<MR. IIDA, TELL ME THE PROCESS FOR INITIATING THE "CLEAR" SETTING.>
<I CAN DO IT FROM THIS SERVER ROOM...>
<BUT THAT'S NOT ENOUGH TO SOLVE THE BIGGER PROBLEM...>
<RIGHT ABOUT NOW, THE FOUNDATION'S HACKERS SHOULD BE DEVOTING THEIR EFFORTS TO RESTORING THE SYSTEM.>

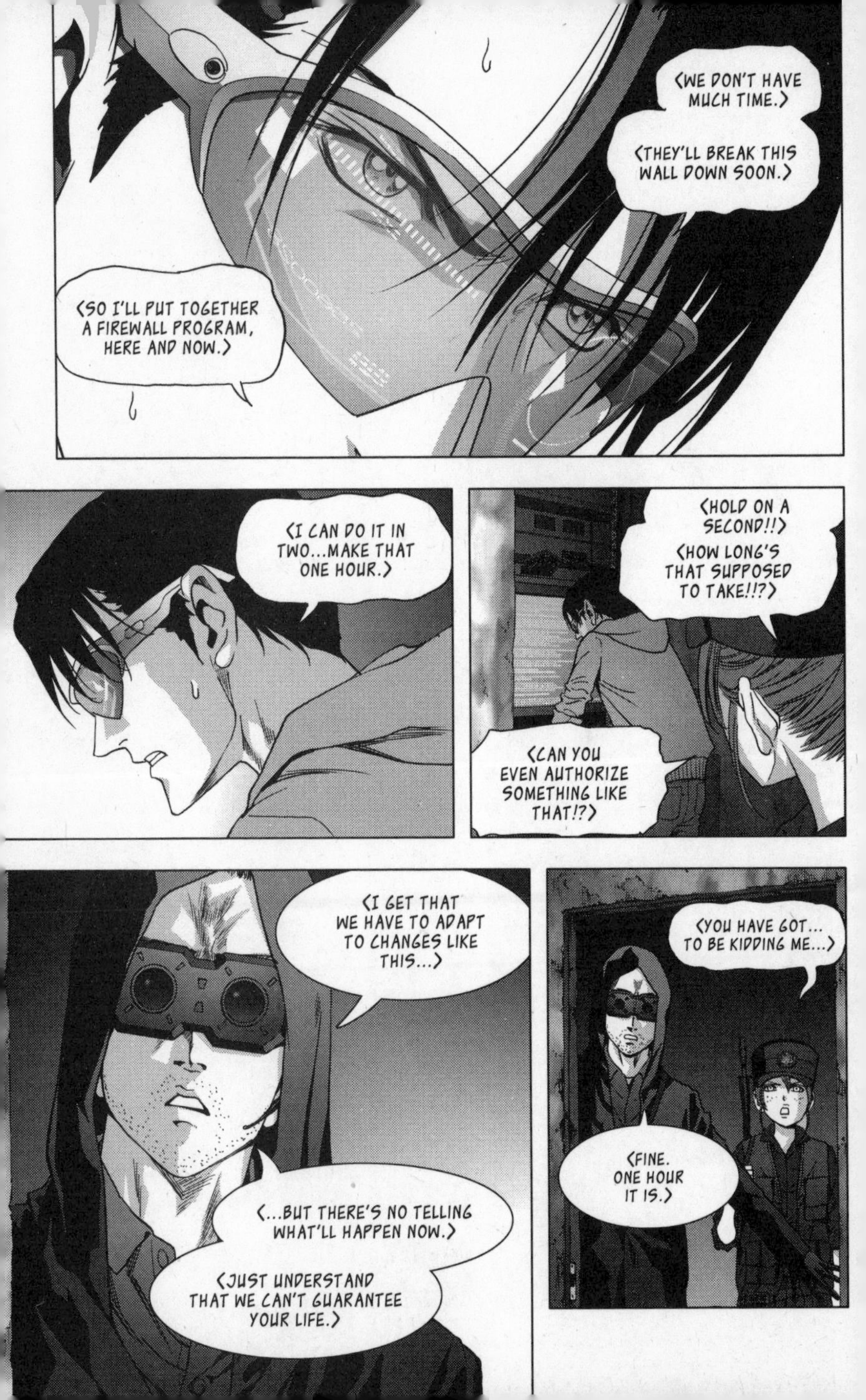
‹WE DON'T HAVE MUCH TIME.›
‹THEY'LL BREAK THIS WALL DOWN SOON.›
‹SO I'LL PUT TOGETHER A FIREWALL PROGRAM, HERE AND NOW.›
‹HOLD ON A SECOND!!›
‹HOW LONG'S THAT SUPPOSED TO TAKE!!?›
‹CAN YOU EVEN AUTHORIZE SOMETHING LIKE THAT!?›
‹I CAN DO IT IN TWO...MAKE THAT ONE HOUR.›
‹YOU HAVE GOT... TO BE KIDDING ME...›
‹FINE. ONE HOUR IT IS.›
‹I GET THAT WE HAVE TO ADAPT TO CHANGES LIKE THIS...›
‹...BUT THERE'S NO TELLING WHAT'LL HAPPEN NOW.›
‹JUST UNDERSTAND THAT WE CAN'T GUARANTEE YOUR LIFE.›

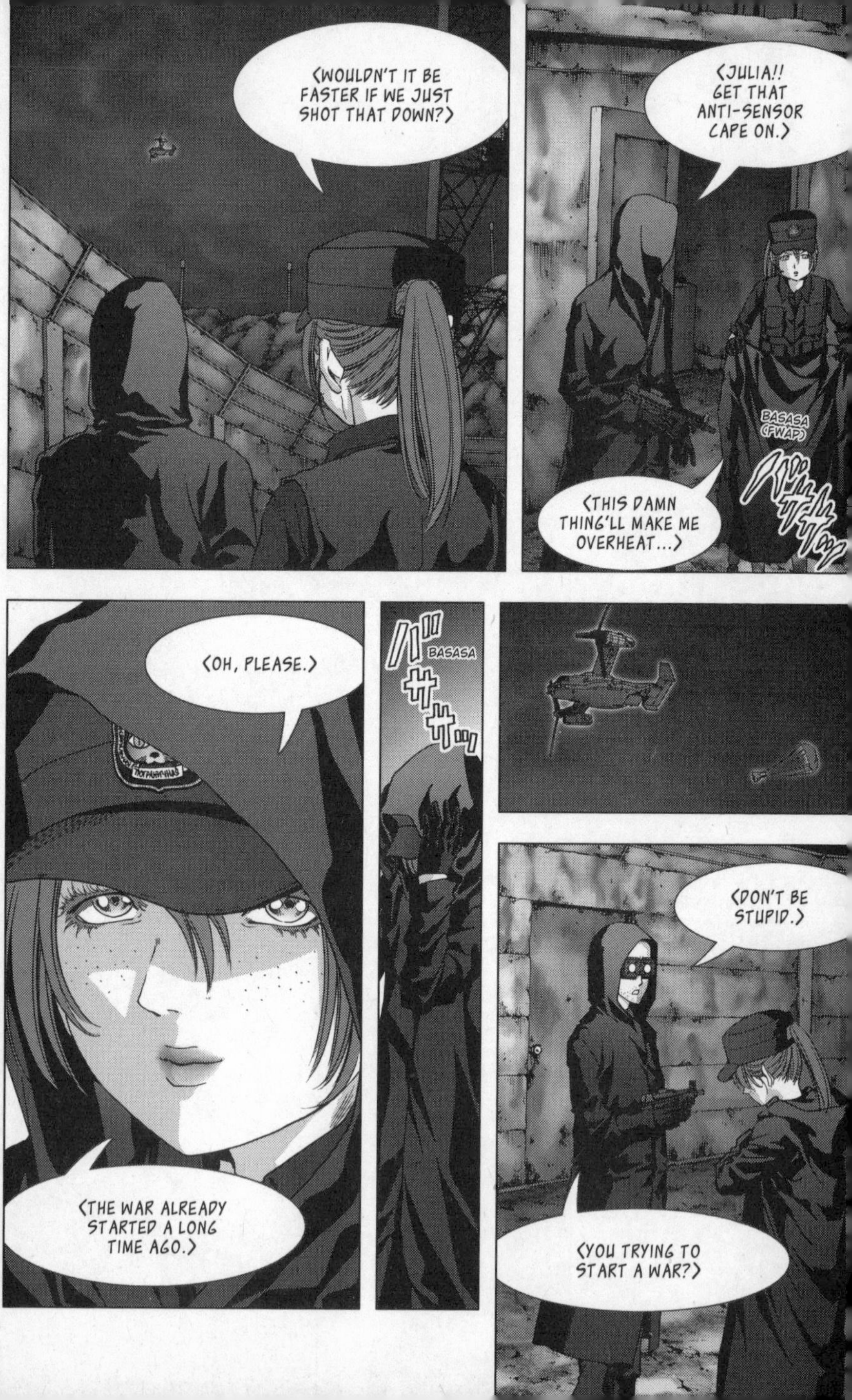
〈JULIA!! GET THAT ANTI-SENSOR CAPE ON.〉
BASASA (FWAP)
〈THIS DAMN THING'LL MAKE ME OVERHEAT...〉
〈WOULDN'T IT BE FASTER IF WE JUST SHOT THAT DOWN?〉
〈DON'T BE STUPID.〉
〈YOU TRYING TO START A WAR?〉
BASASA
〈OH, PLEASE.〉
〈THE WAR ALREADY STARTED A LONG TIME AGO.〉

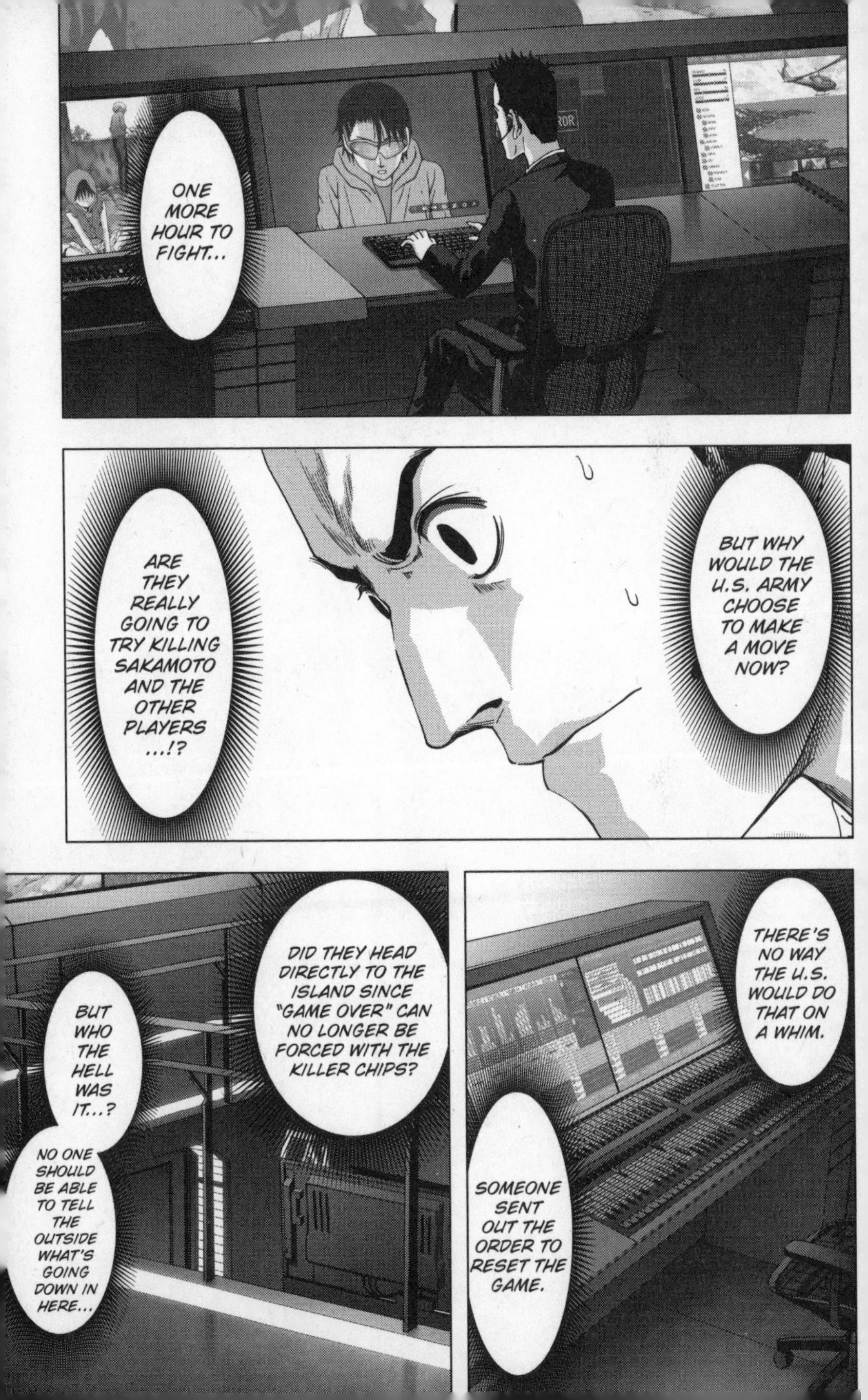
ONE MORE HOUR TO FIGHT...
BUT WHY WOULD THE U.S. ARMY CHOOSE TO MAKE A MOVE NOW?
ARE THEY REALLY GOING TO TRY KILLING SAKAMOTO AND THE OTHER PLAYERS ...!?
THERE'S NO WAY THE U.S. WOULD DO THAT ON A WHIM.
SOMEONE SENT OUT THE ORDER TO RESET THE GAME.
DID THEY HEAD DIRECTLY TO THE ISLAND SINCE "GAME OVER" CAN NO LONGER BE FORCED WITH THE KILLER CHIPS?
BUT WHO THE HELL WAS IT...?
NO ONE SHOULD BE ABLE TO TELL THE OUTSIDE WHAT'S GOING DOWN IN HERE...

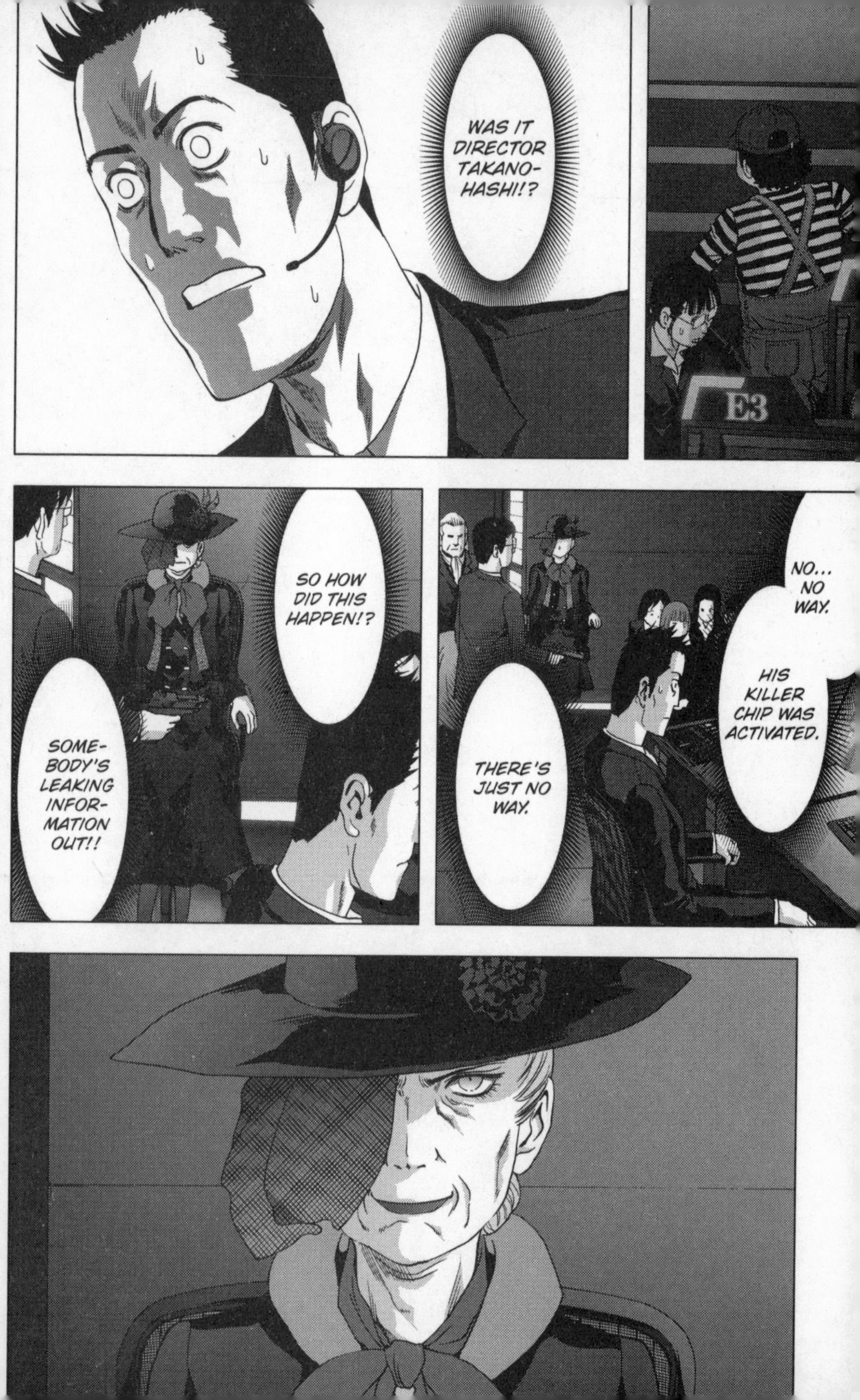
WAS IT DIRECTOR TAKANO-HASHI!?
NO... NO WAY.
HIS KILLER CHIP WAS ACTIVATED.
THERE'S JUST NO WAY.
SO HOW DID THIS HAPPEN!?
SOME-BODY'S LEAKING INFOR-MATION OUT!!

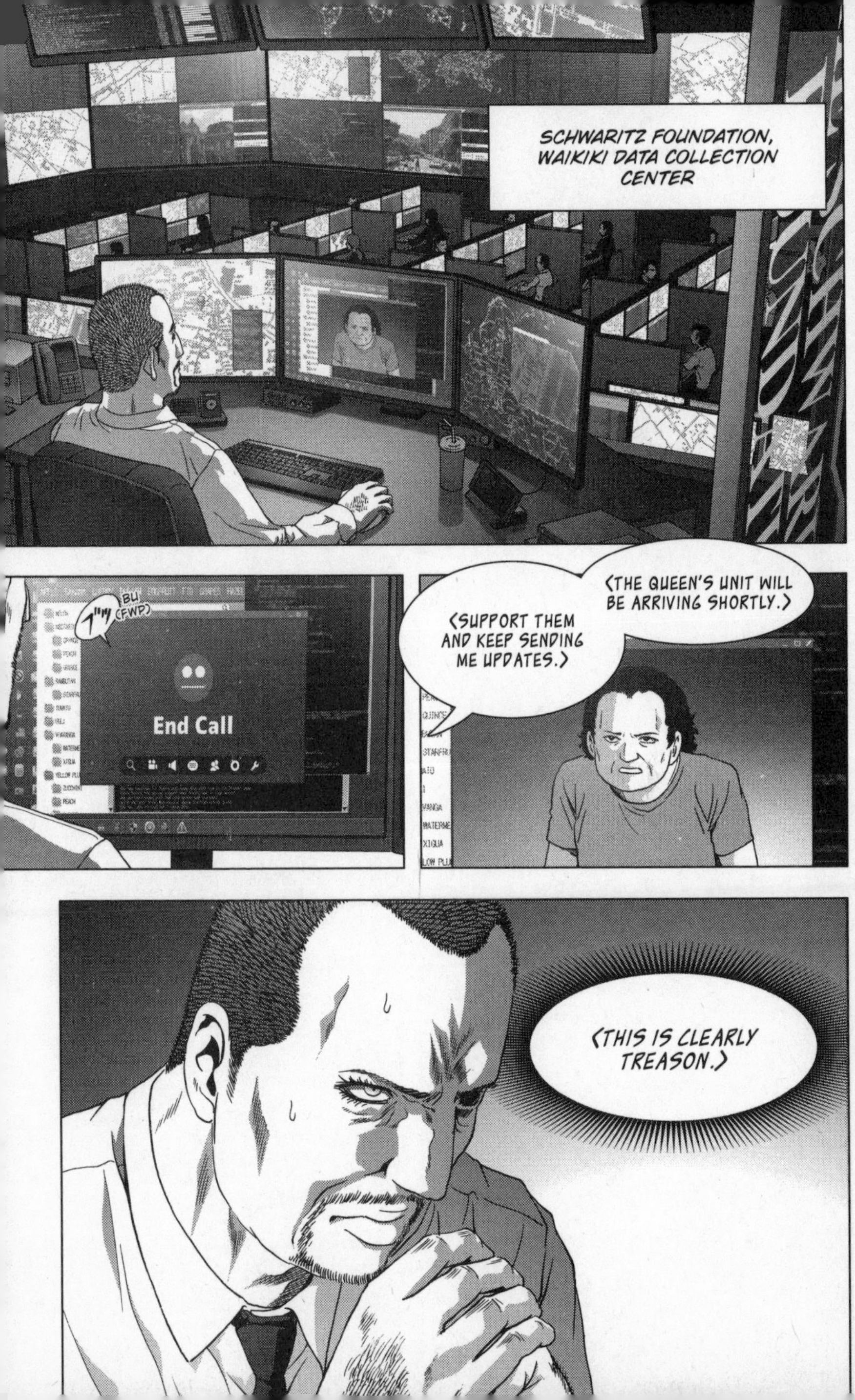
SCHWARITZ FOUNDATION, WAIKIKI DATA COLLECTION CENTER
<THE QUEEN'S UNIT WILL BE ARRIVING SHORTLY.>
<SUPPORT THEM AND KEEP SENDING ME UPDATES.>
BU (FWP)
End Call
<THIS IS CLEARLY TREASON.>

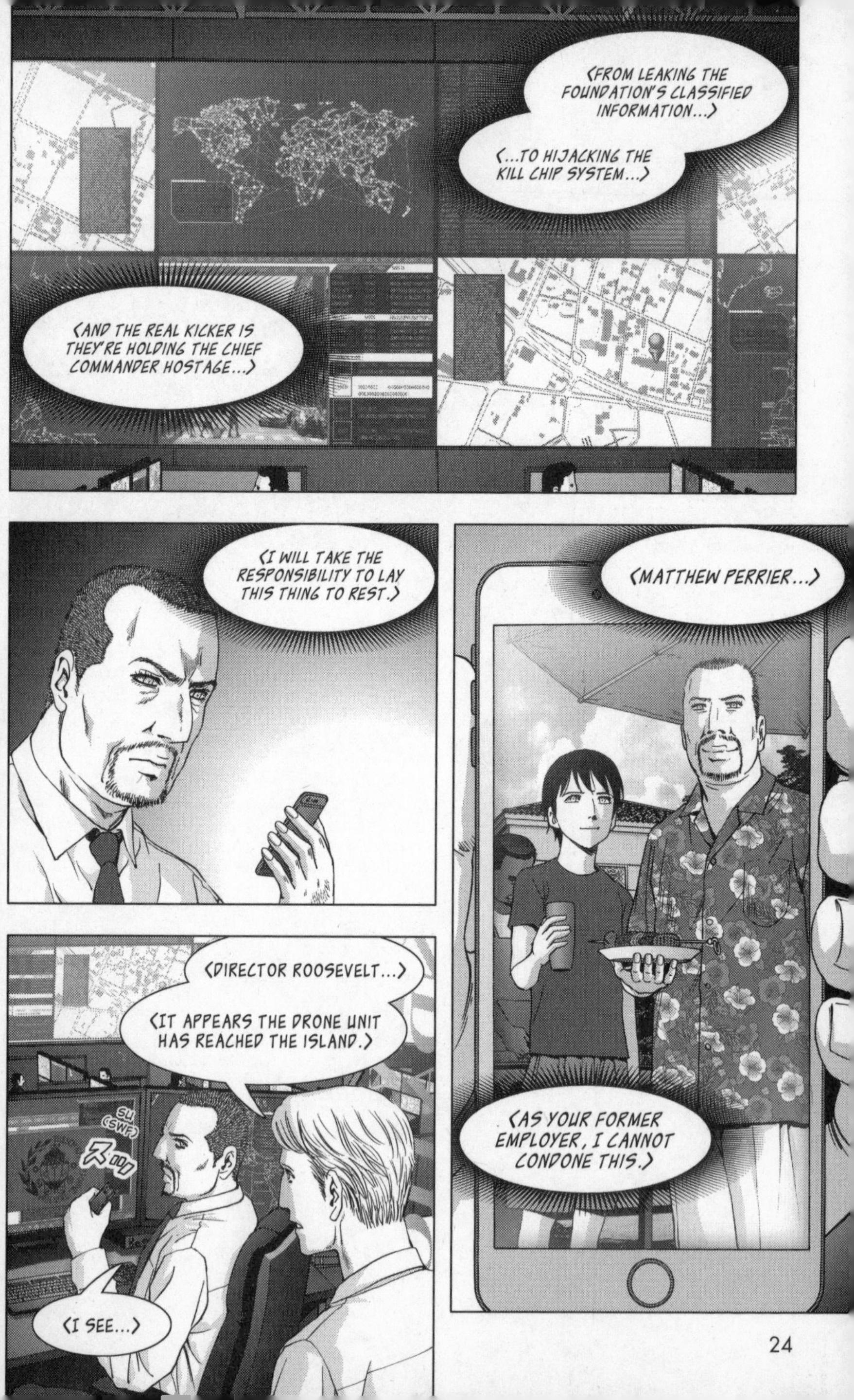
⟨FROM LEAKING THE FOUNDATION'S CLASSIFIED INFORMATION...⟩
⟨...TO HIJACKING THE KILL CHIP SYSTEM...⟩
⟨AND THE REAL KICKER IS THEY'RE HOLDING THE CHIEF COMMANDER HOSTAGE...⟩
⟨MATTHEW PERRIER...⟩
⟨AS YOUR FORMER EMPLOYER, I CANNOT CONDONE THIS.⟩
⟨I WILL TAKE THE RESPONSIBILITY TO LAY THIS THING TO REST.⟩
⟨DIRECTOR ROOSEVELT...⟩
⟨IT APPEARS THE DRONE UNIT HAS REACHED THE ISLAND.⟩
SU (SWF)
スッ
⟨I SEE...⟩

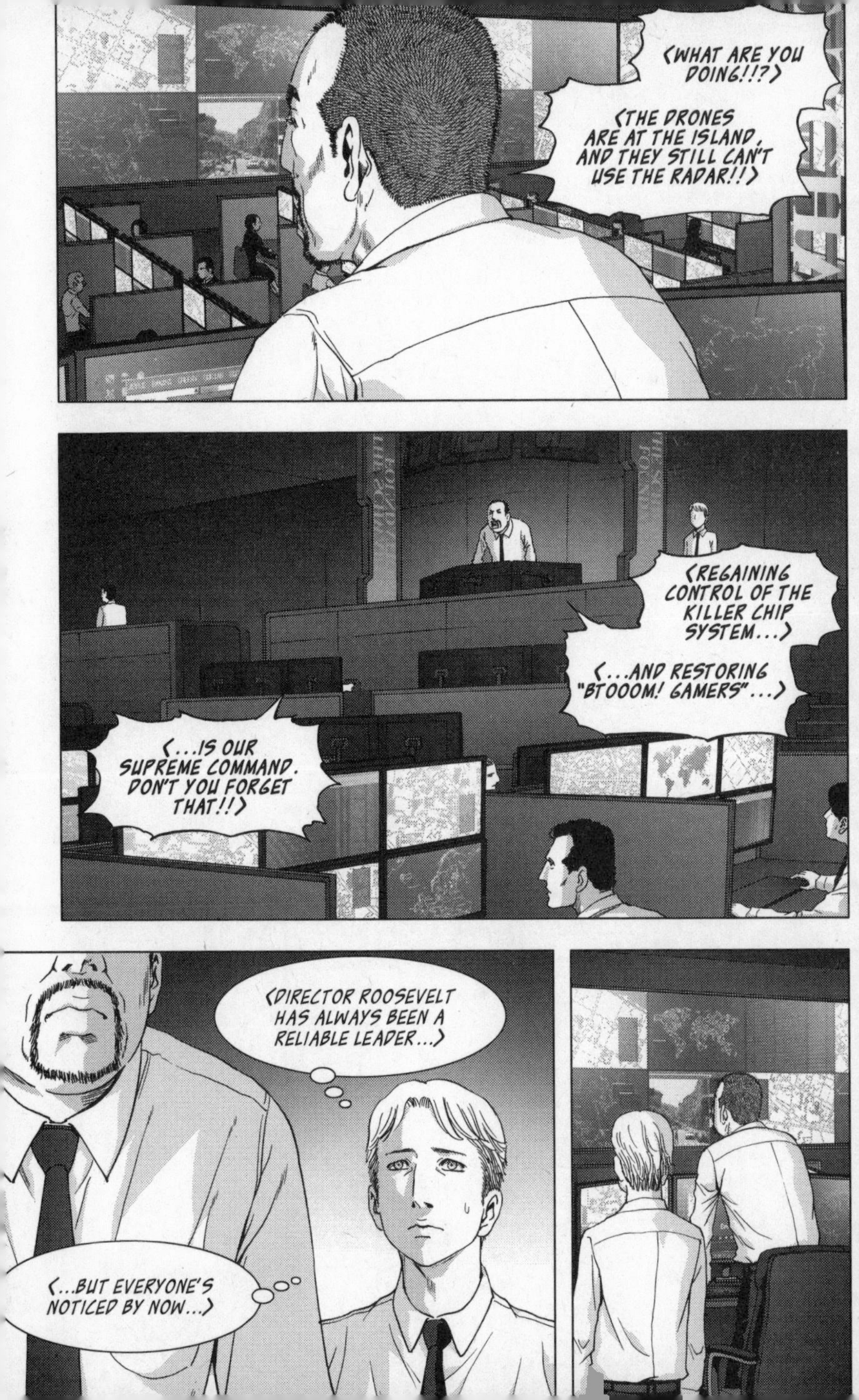

<WHAT ARE YOU DOING!!?>
<THE DRONES ARE AT THE ISLAND, AND THEY STILL CAN'T USE THE RADAR!!>
<REGAINING CONTROL OF THE KILLER CHIP SYSTEM...>
<...AND RESTORING "BTOOOM! GAMERS"...>
<...IS OUR SUPREME COMMAND. DON'T YOU FORGET THAT!!>
<DIRECTOR ROOSEVELT HAS ALWAYS BEEN A RELIABLE LEADER...>
<...BUT EVERYONE'S NOTICED BY NOW...>

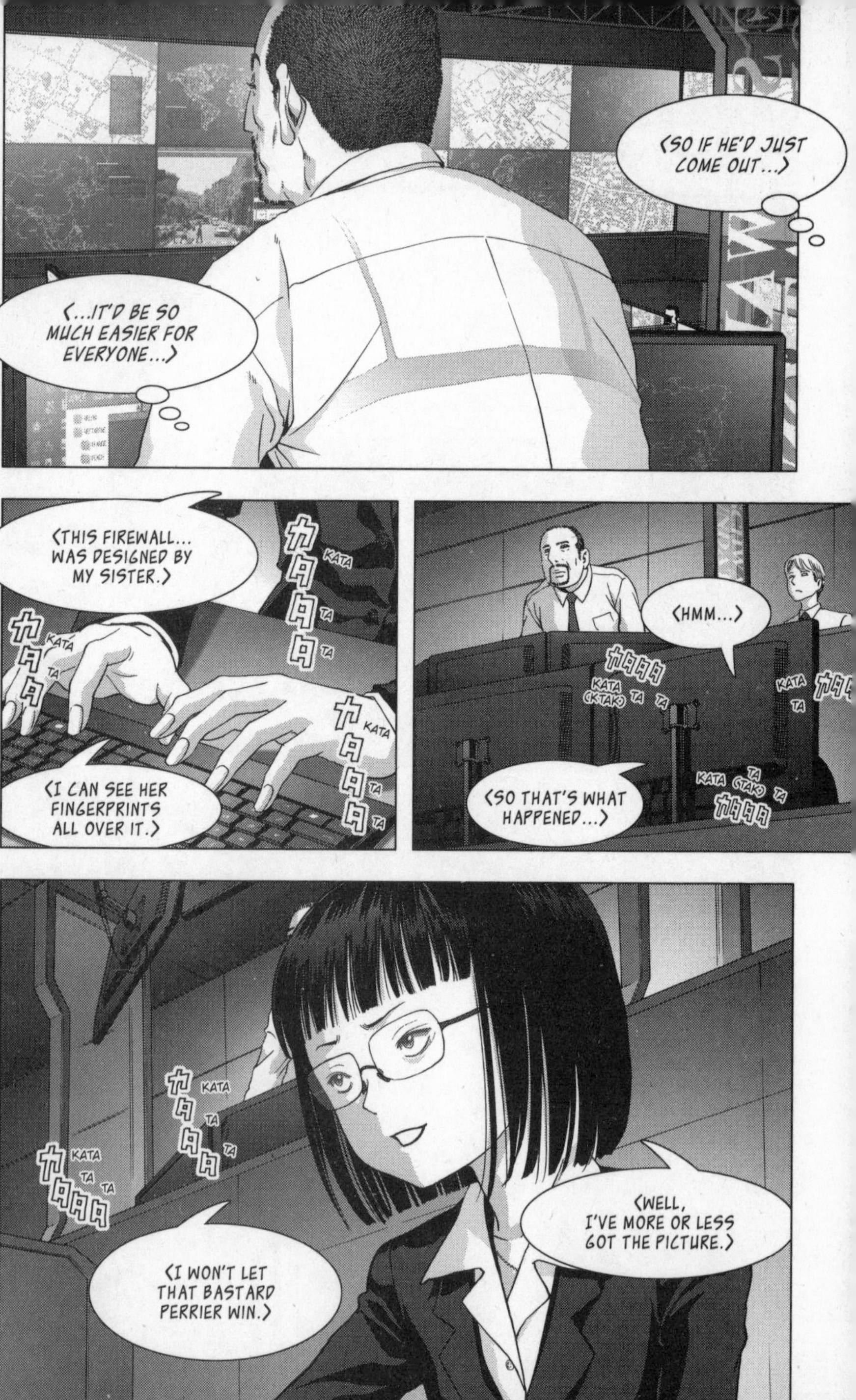

〈SO IF HE'D JUST COME OUT...〉
〈...IT'D BE SO MUCH EASIER FOR EVERYONE...〉
〈HMM...〉
KATA (KTAK) TA TA
KATA TA
〈SO THAT'S WHAT HAPPENED...〉
KATA TA (TAK) TA
〈THIS FIREWALL... WAS DESIGNED BY MY SISTER.〉
KATA TA TA
KATA TA
KATA TA TA
〈I CAN SEE HER FINGERPRINTS ALL OVER IT.〉
〈WELL, I'VE MORE OR LESS GOT THE PICTURE.〉
KATA TA TA
KATA TA TA
〈I WON'T LET THAT BASTARD PERRIER WIN.〉

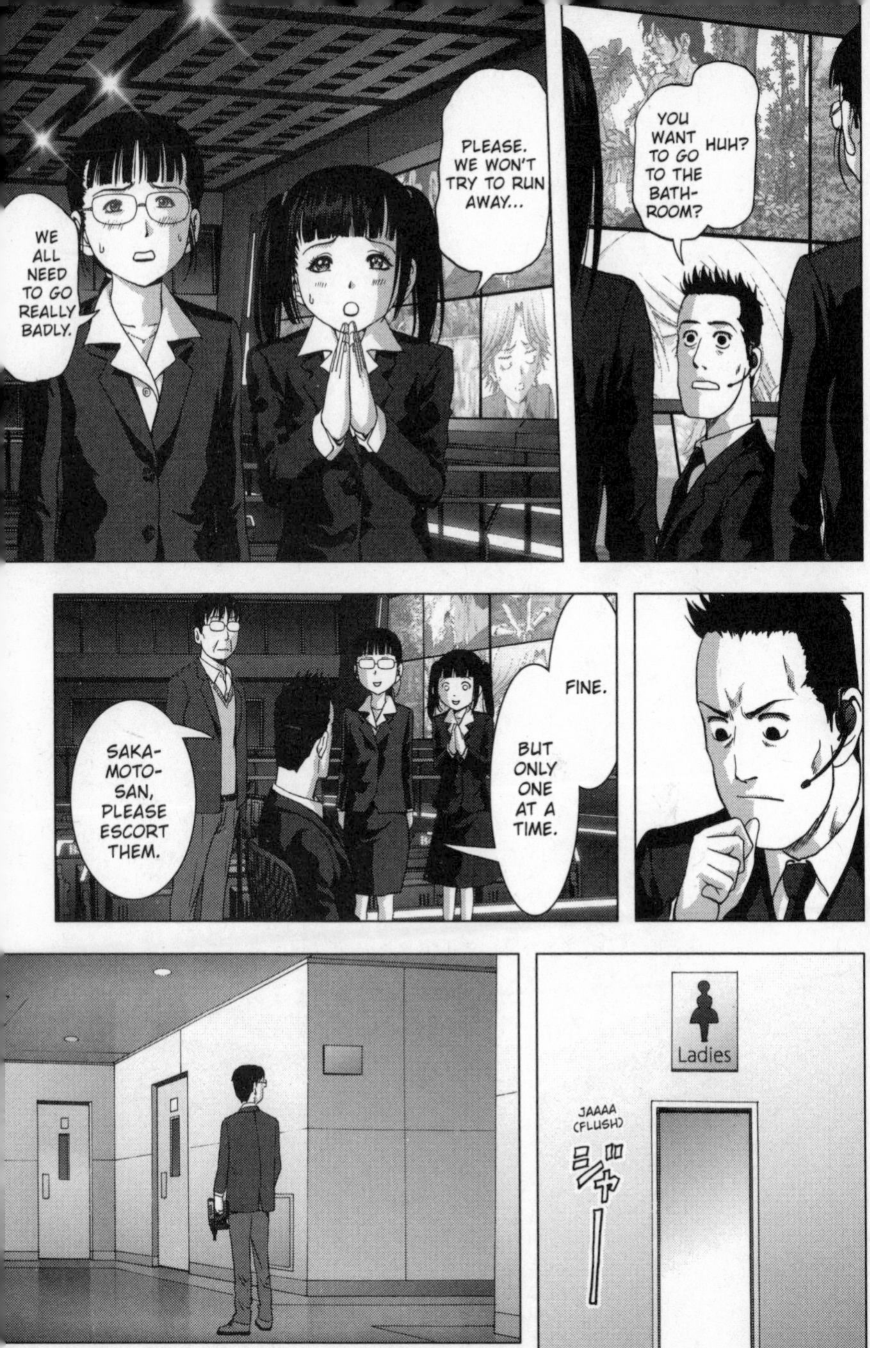
HUH?
YOU WANT TO GO TO THE BATH-ROOM?
PLEASE. WE WON'T TRY TO RUN AWAY...
WE ALL NEED TO GO REALLY BADLY.
FINE.
BUT ONLY ONE AT A TIME.
SAKA-MOTO-SAN, PLEASE ESCORT THEM.
Ladies
JAAAA (FLUSH)
ジャー

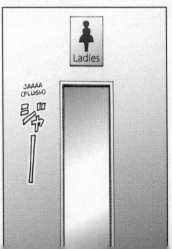

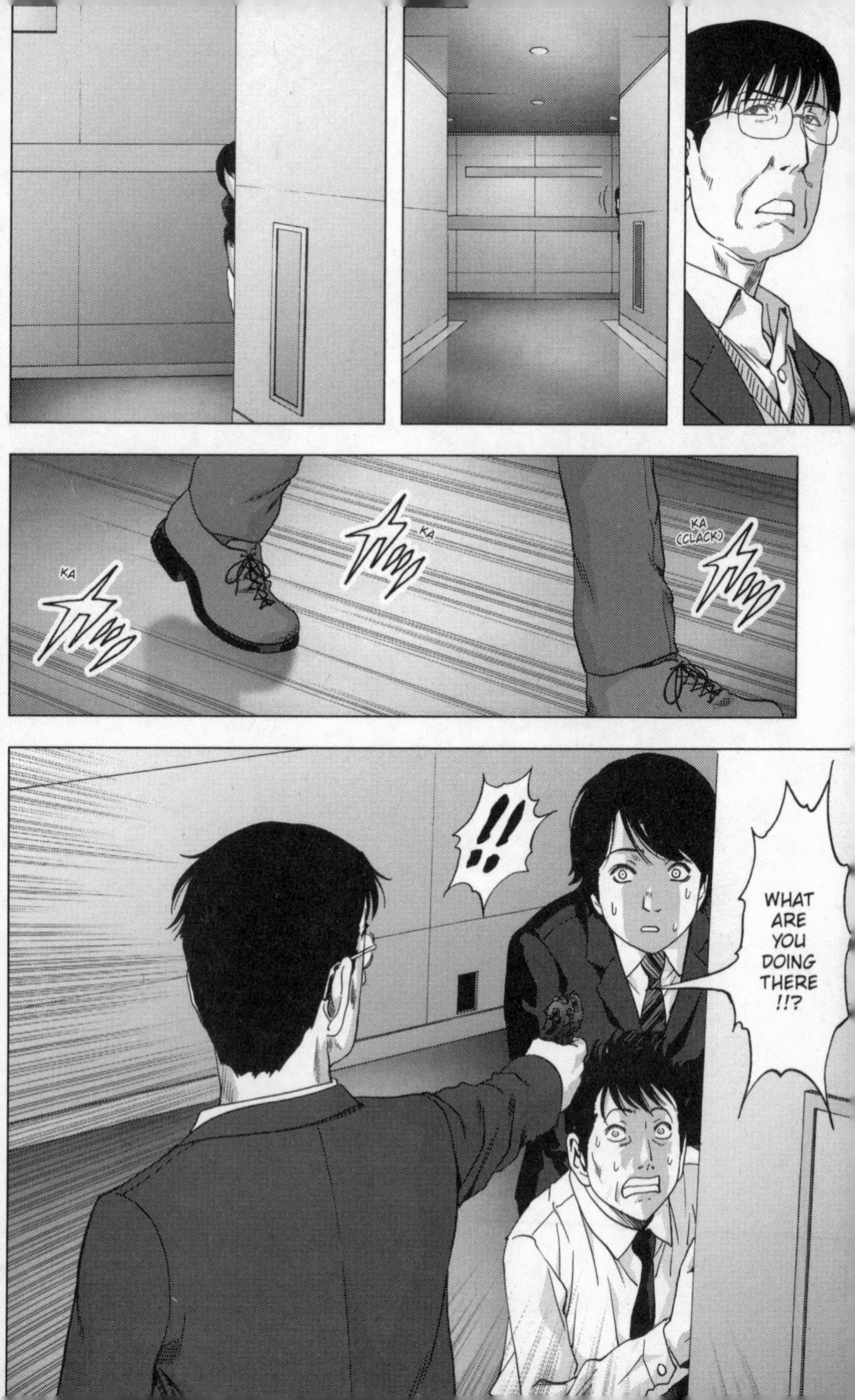
KA
(CLACK)
KA
KA
WHAT ARE YOU DOING THERE !!?
!!

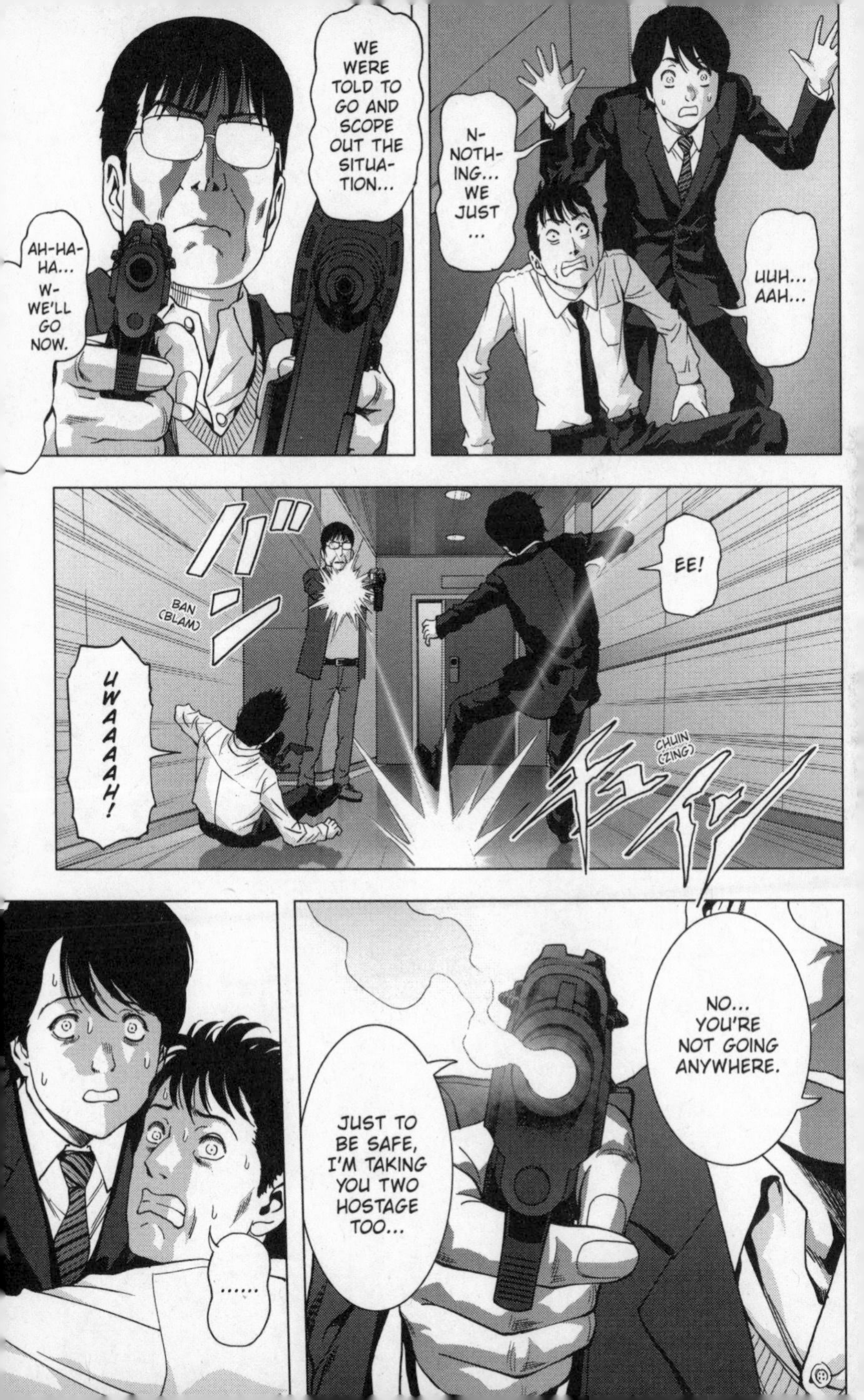

N-NOTHING... WE JUST ...
UUH... AAH...
WE WERE TOLD TO GO AND SCOPE OUT THE SITUATION...
AH-HA-HA... W-WE'LL GO NOW.
EE!
BAN (BLAM)
UWAAAAAH!
CHUIN (ZING)
NO... YOU'RE NOT GOING ANYWHERE.
JUST TO BE SAFE, I'M TAKING YOU TWO HOSTAGE TOO...
......

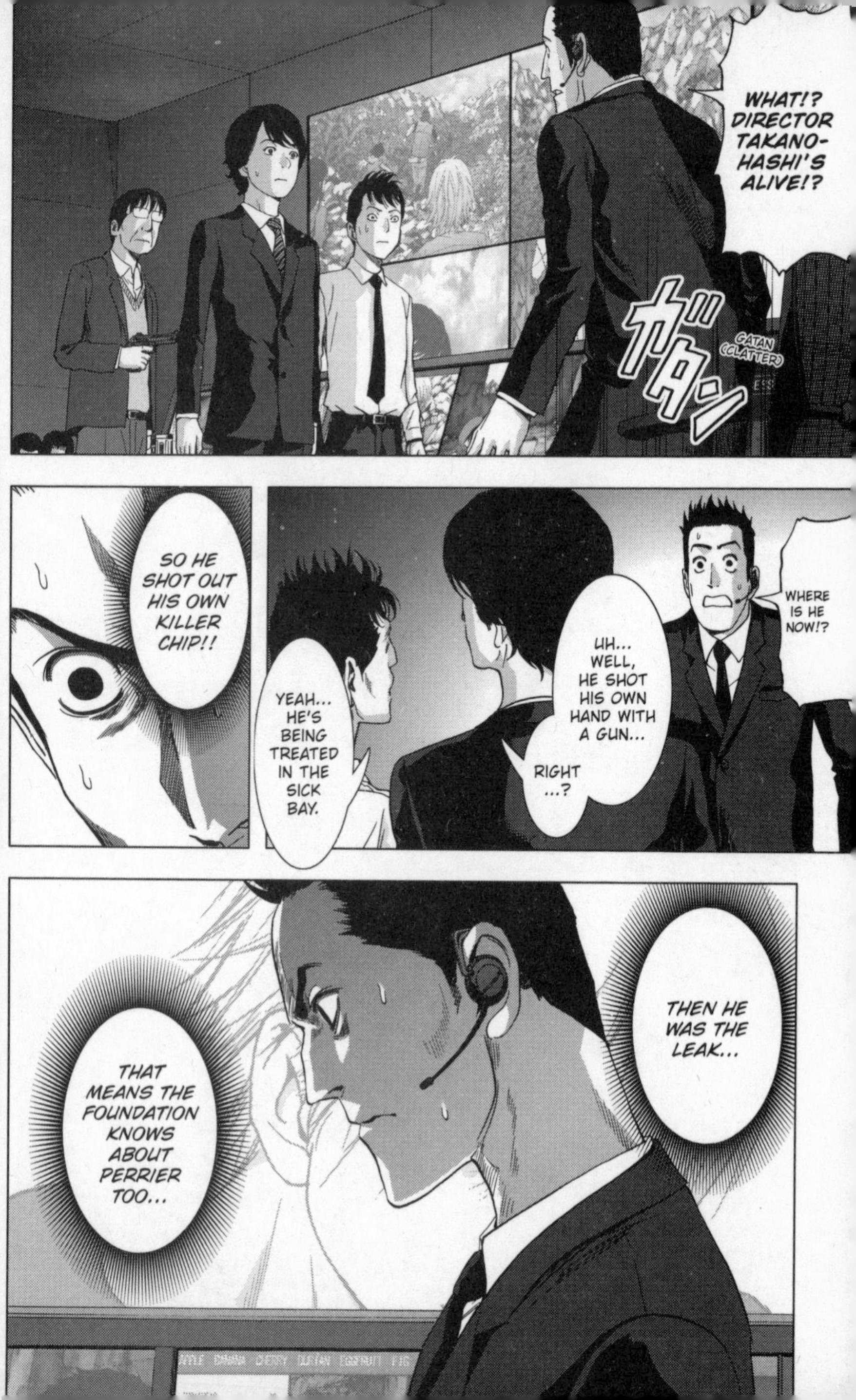
WHAT!? DIRECTOR TAKANO-HASHI'S ALIVE!?
ガタン
GATAN (CLATTER)
WHERE IS HE NOW!?
UH... WELL, HE SHOT HIS OWN HAND WITH A GUN...
RIGHT ...?
YEAH... HE'S BEING TREATED IN THE SICK BAY.
SO HE SHOT OUT HIS OWN KILLER CHIP!!
THEN HE WAS THE LEAK...
THAT MEANS THE FOUNDATION KNOWS ABOUT PERRIER TOO...

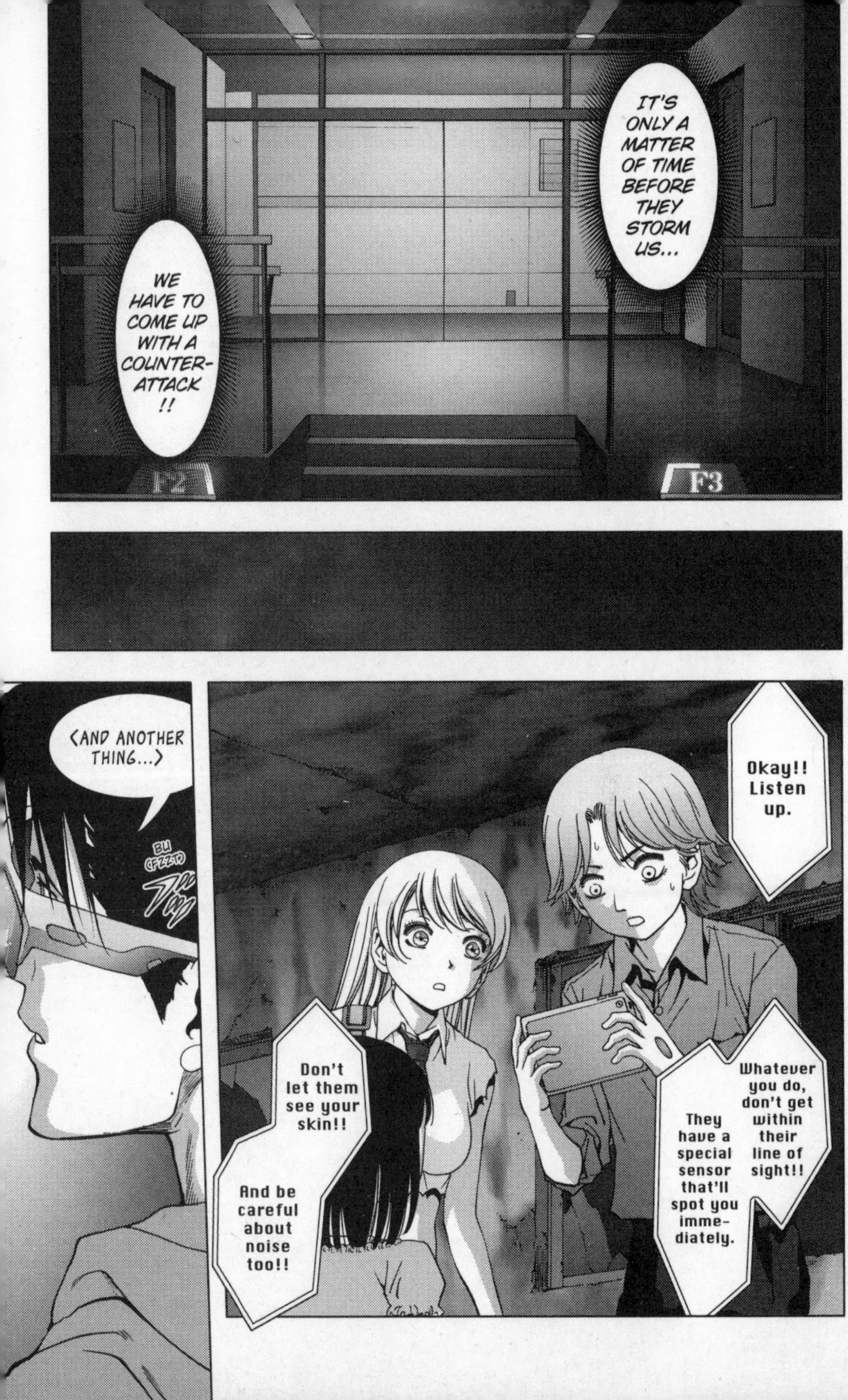
IT'S ONLY A MATTER OF TIME BEFORE THEY STORM US...
WE HAVE TO COME UP WITH A COUNTER-ATTACK!!
F3
F2
Okay!! Listen up.
Whatever you do, don't get within their line of sight!!
They have a special sensor that'll spot you immediately.
Don't let them see your skin!!
And be careful about noise too!!
<AND ANOTHER THING...>
BU (FZZT)

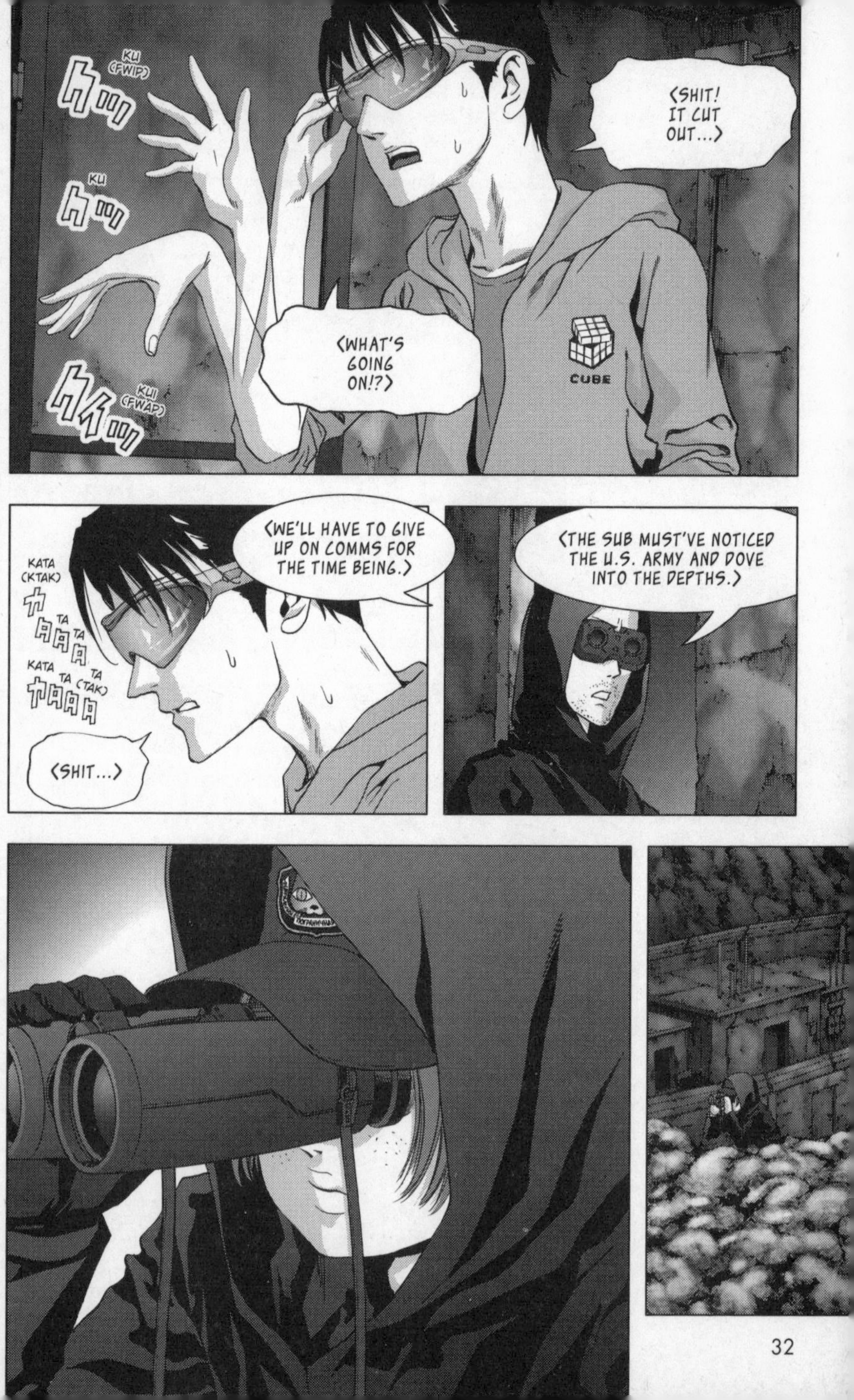
〈SHIT! IT CUT OUT...〉
KU (FWIP)
KU
〈WHAT'S GOING ON!?〉
KUI (FWAP)
〈THE SUB MUST'VE NOTICED THE U.S. ARMY AND DOVE INTO THE DEPTHS.〉
〈WE'LL HAVE TO GIVE UP ON COMMS FOR THE TIME BEING.〉
KATA (KTAK) TA TA TA
KATA TA TA (TAK)
〈SHIT...〉

〈WE'VE GOT SOME NEAR SAKAMOTO AND THE OTHERS...〉
Pi
Pi
Pi
Pi
1243.81
〈...ALSO BY ODA...〉
〈...IN THE WOODS TO THE EAST...〉
Pi
Pi
〈...AND RIGHT OVERHEAD...〉
228.25
Pi
129.71
Pi

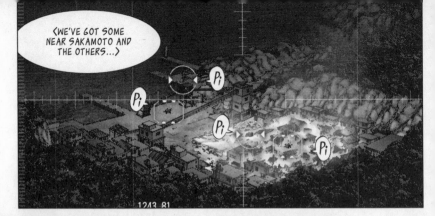

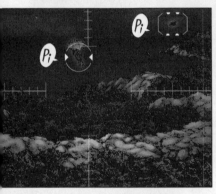

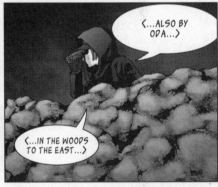

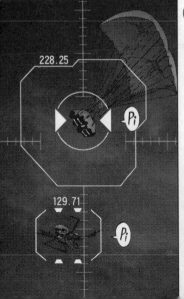

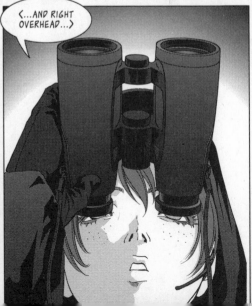

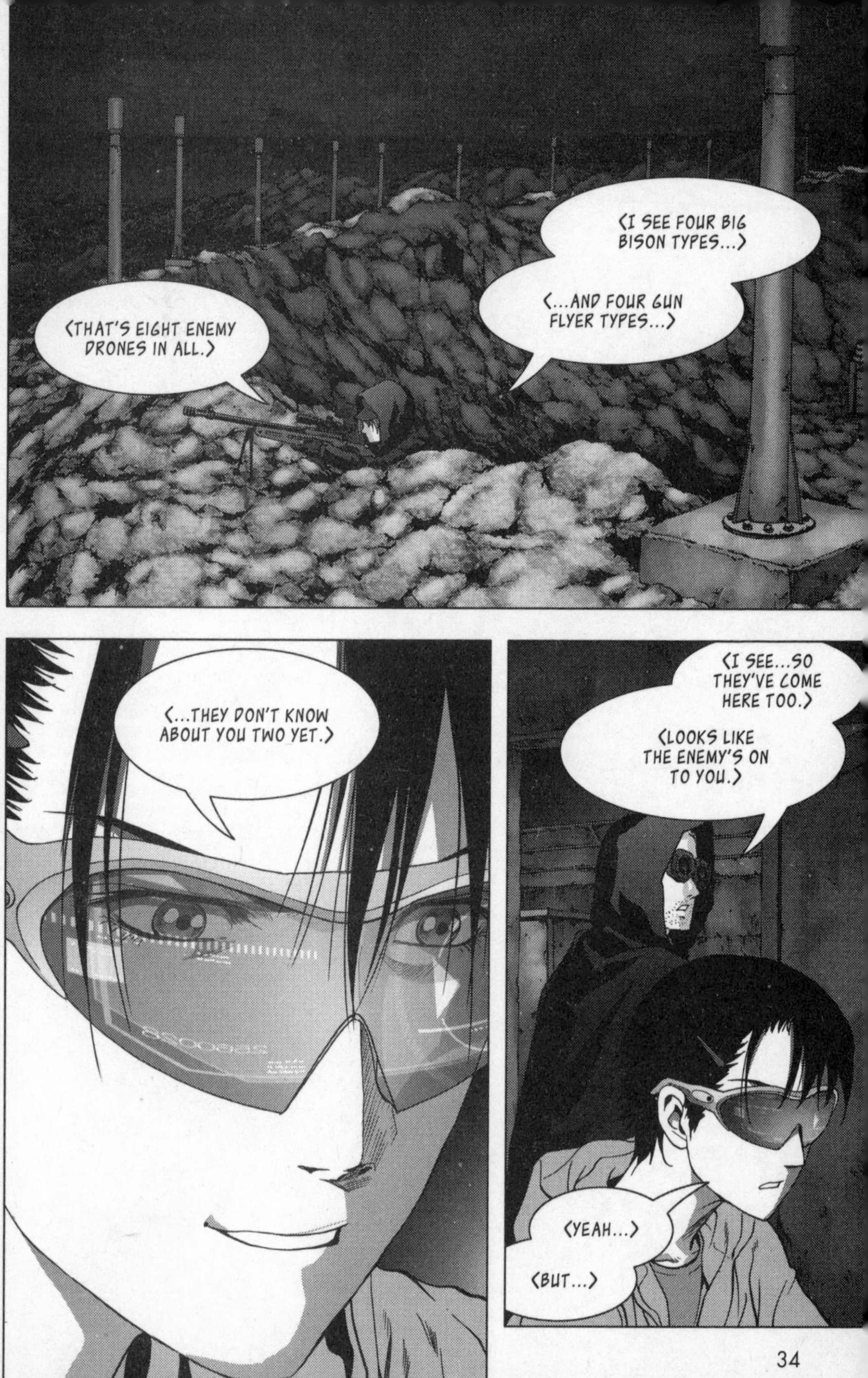
⟨I SEE FOUR BIG BISON TYPES...⟩
⟨...AND FOUR GUN FLYER TYPES...⟩
⟨THAT'S EIGHT ENEMY DRONES IN ALL.⟩
⟨I SEE...SO THEY'VE COME HERE TOO.⟩
⟨LOOKS LIKE THE ENEMY'S ON TO YOU.⟩
⟨YEAH...⟩
⟨BUT...⟩
⟨...THEY DON'T KNOW ABOUT YOU TWO YET.⟩

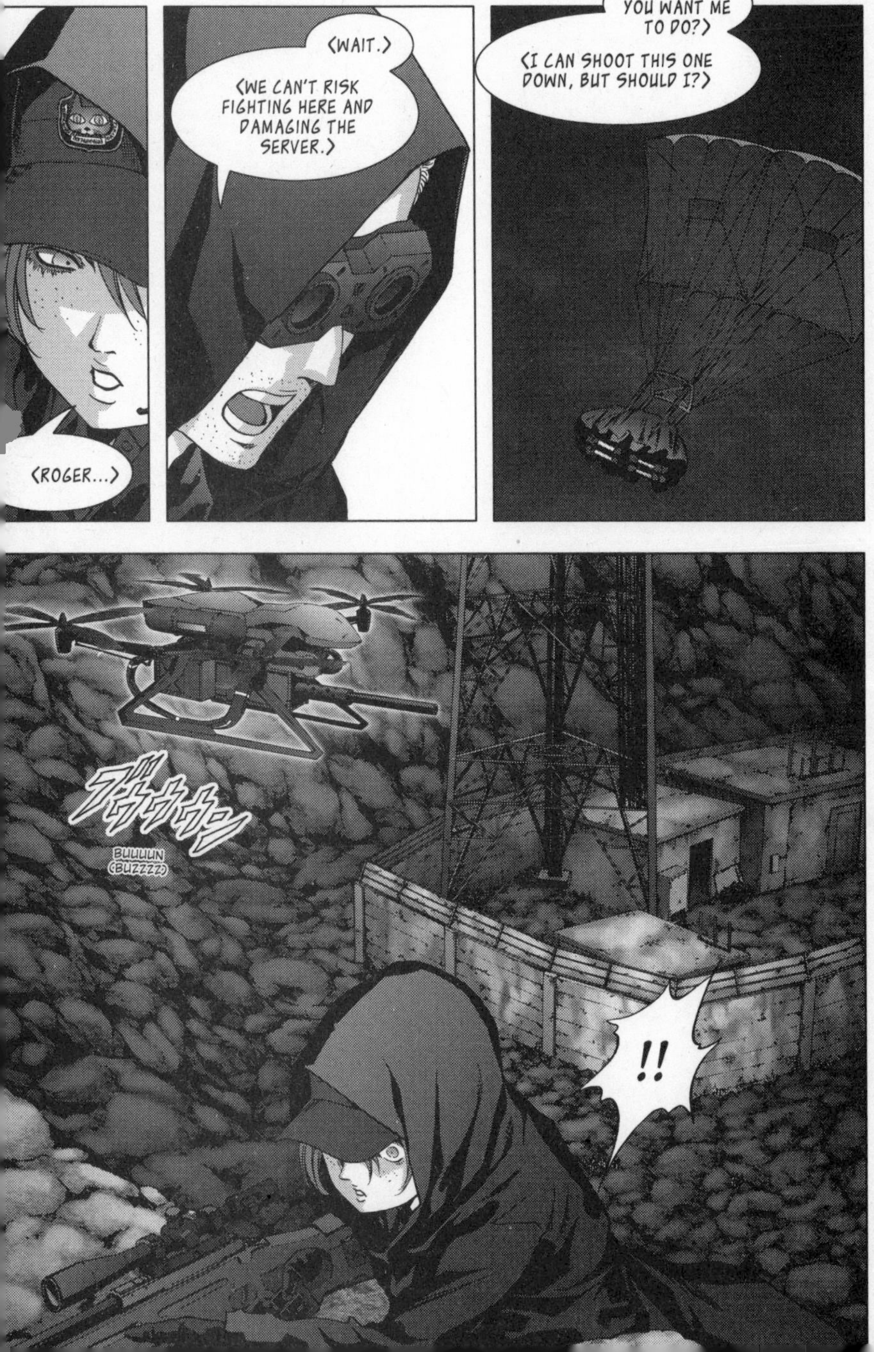
‹WHAT DO YOU WANT ME TO DO?›
‹I CAN SHOOT THIS ONE DOWN, BUT SHOULD I?›
‹WAIT.›
‹WE CAN'T RISK FIGHTING HERE AND DAMAGING THE SERVER.›
‹ROGER...›
BUUUUN (BUZZZZ)
!!

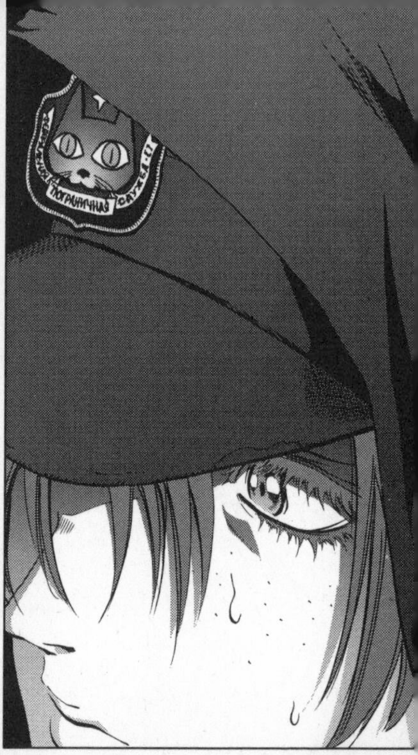

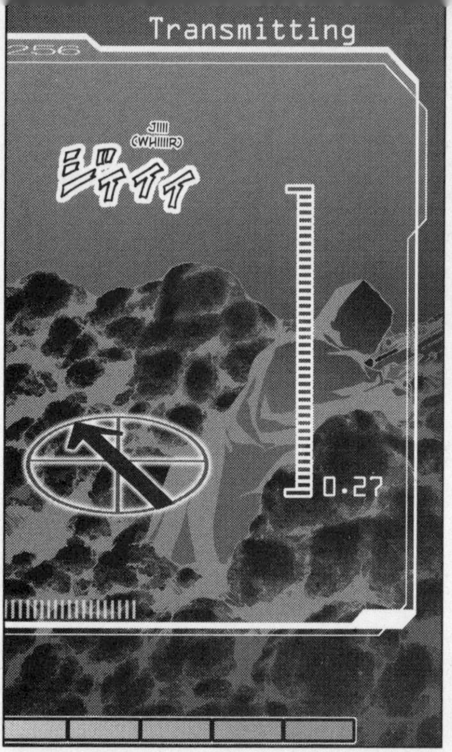
Transmitting
256
JIIII (WHIIIIR)
ジィィィ
0.27

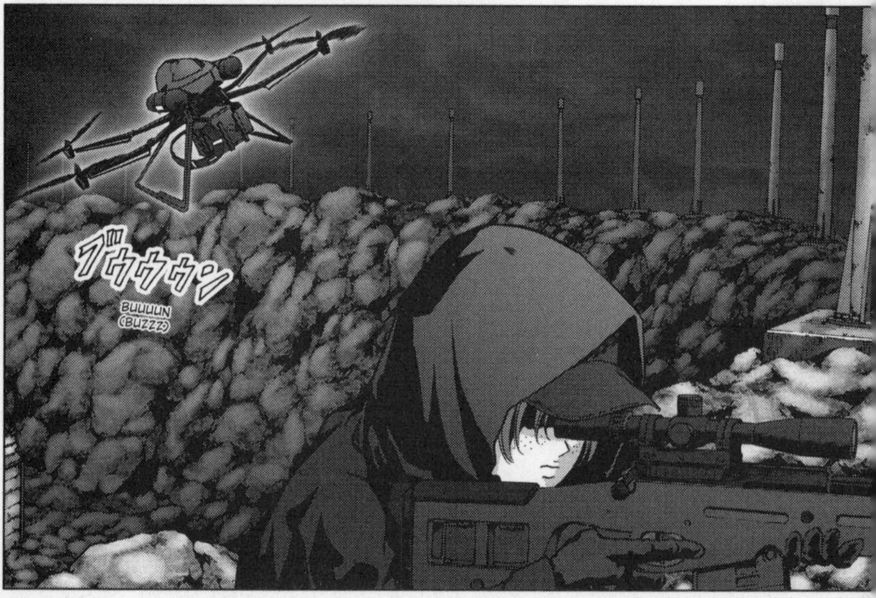
ブウウウン
BUUUUN (BUZZZ)

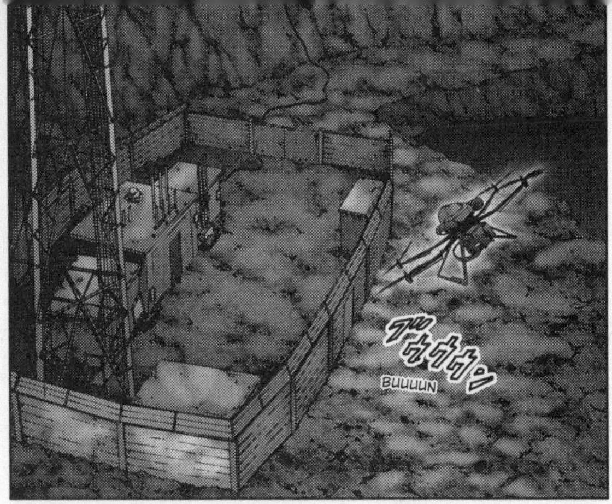
BUUUUN

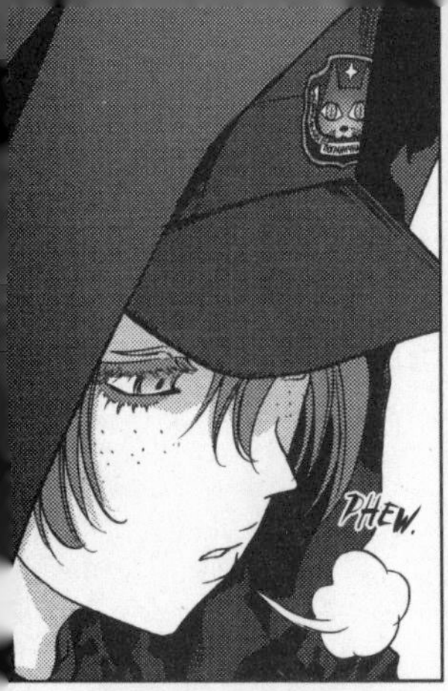
PHEW.

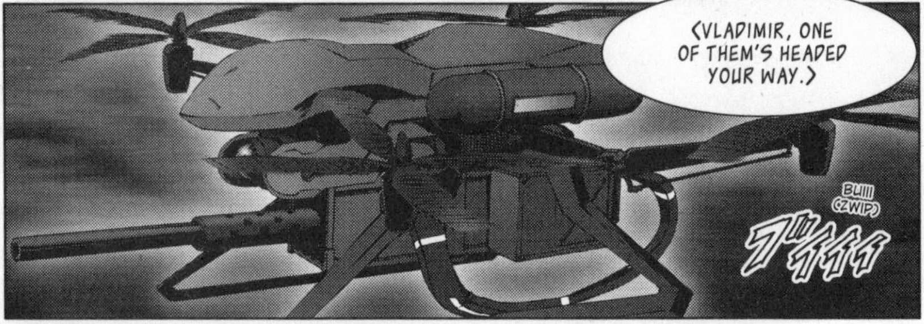
<VLADIMIR, ONE OF THEM'S HEADED YOUR WAY.>
BUIII (ZWIP)

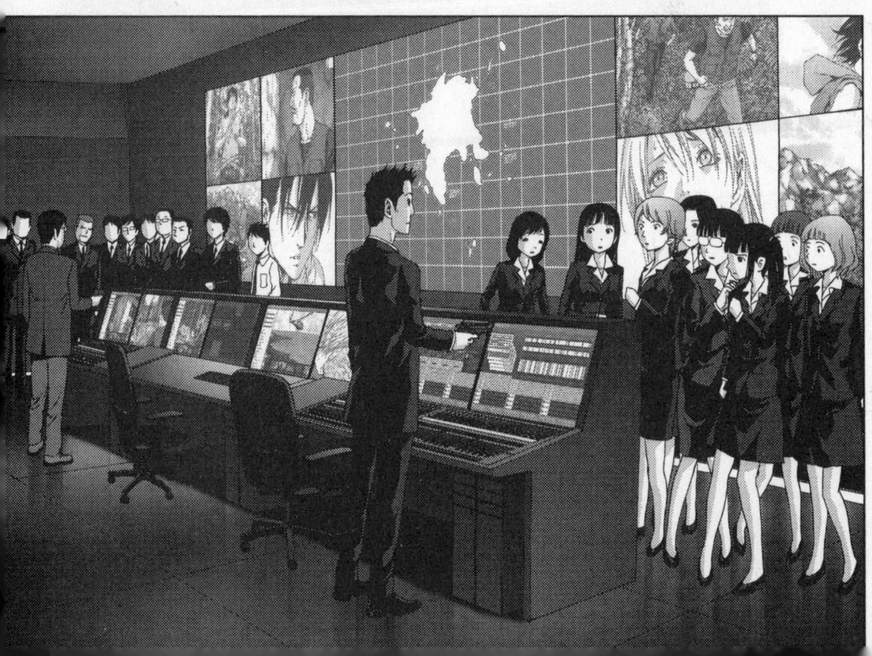

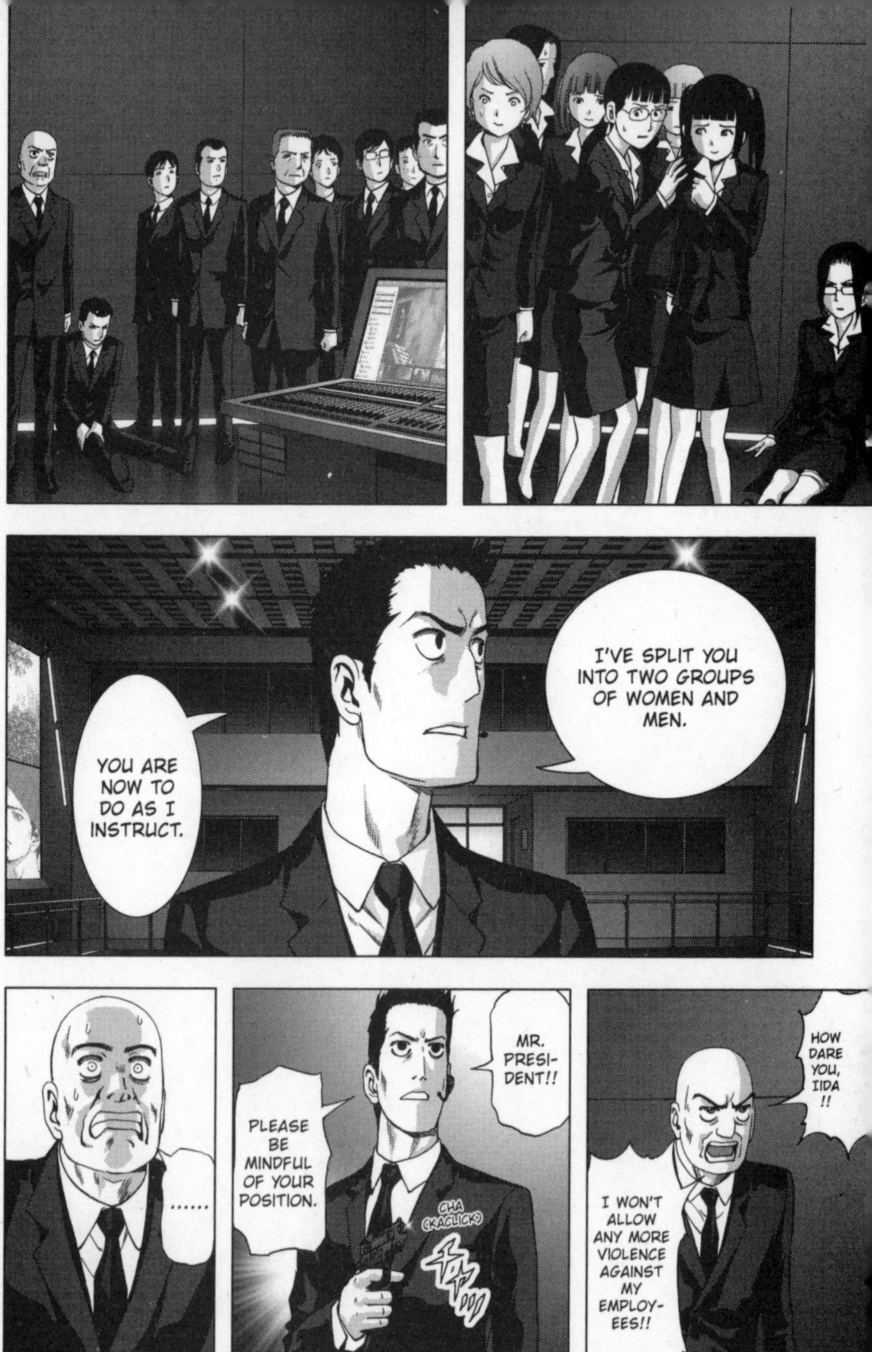
I'VE SPLIT YOU INTO TWO GROUPS OF WOMEN AND MEN.
YOU ARE NOW TO DO AS I INSTRUCT.
HOW DARE YOU, IIDA!!
I WON'T ALLOW ANY MORE VIOLENCE AGAINST MY EMPLOYEES!!
MR. PRESIDENT!!
PLEASE BE MINDFUL OF YOUR POSITION.
CHA (KACLICK)
......

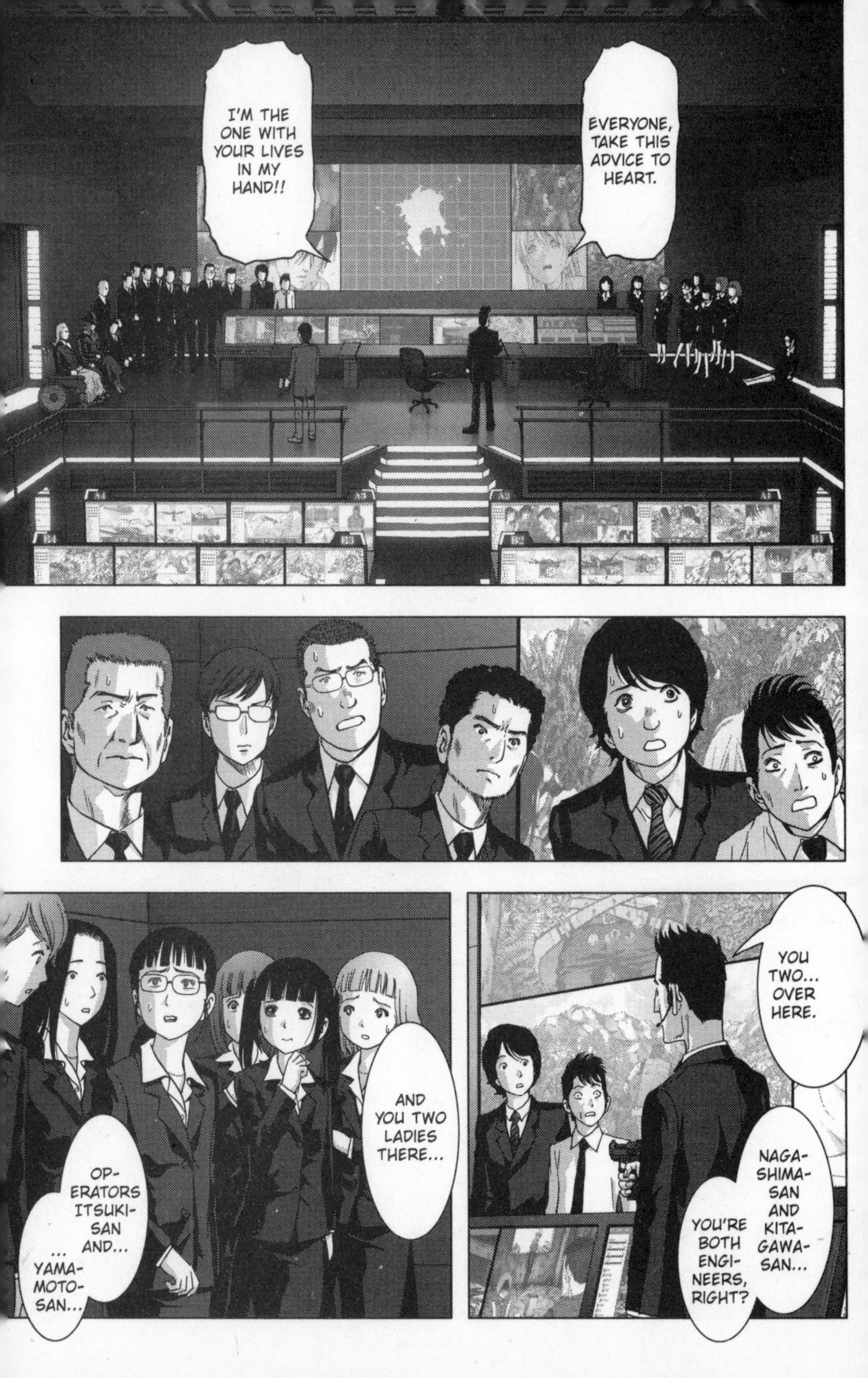
EVERYONE, TAKE THIS ADVICE TO HEART.
I'M THE ONE WITH YOUR LIVES IN MY HAND!!
YOU TWO... OVER HERE.
NAGA-SHIMA-SAN AND KITA-GAWA-SAN...
YOU'RE BOTH ENGI-NEERS, RIGHT?
AND YOU TWO LADIES THERE...
OP-ERATORS ITSUKI-SAN AND...
... YAMA-MOTO-SAN...

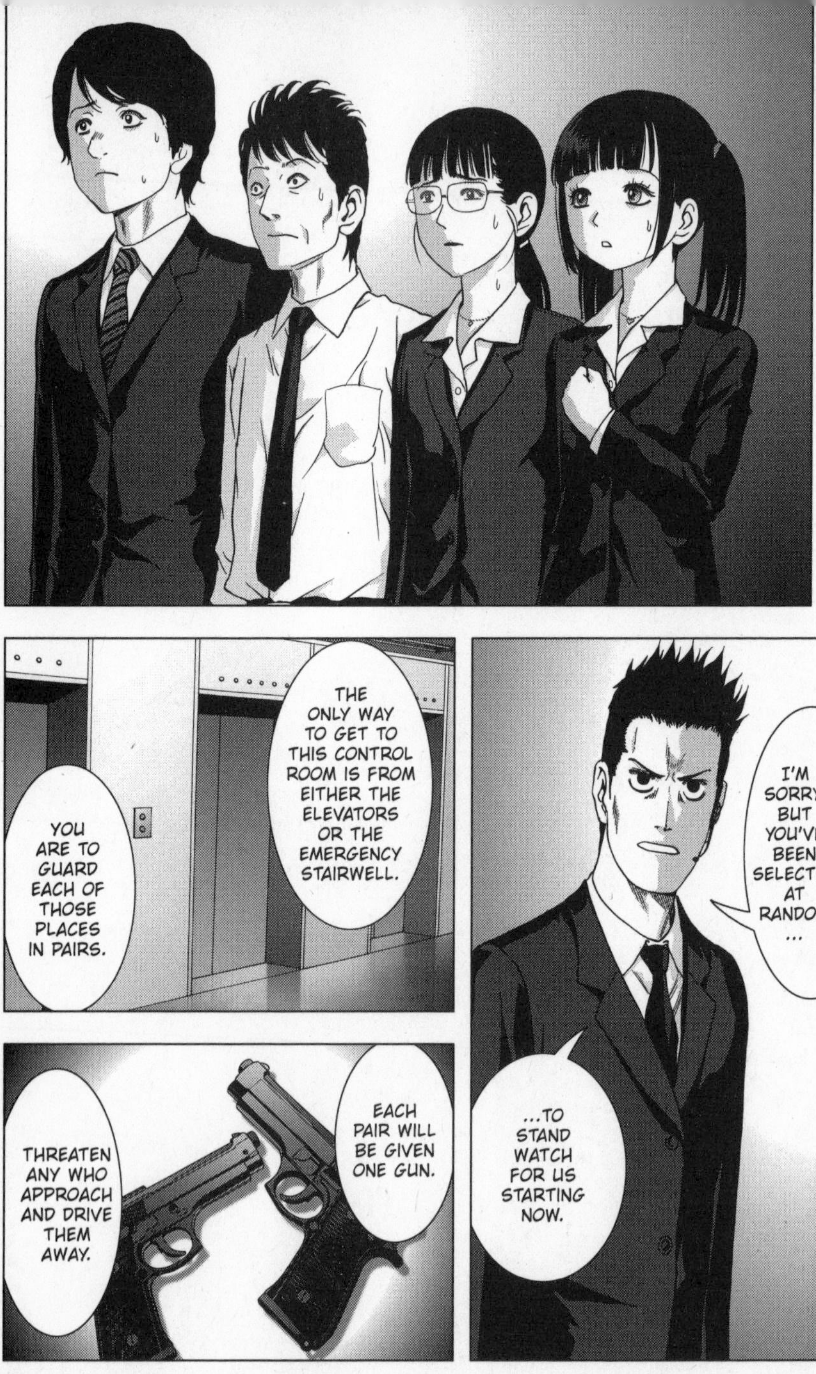
I'M SORRY, BUT YOU'VE BEEN SELECTED AT RANDOM...
...TO STAND WATCH FOR US STARTING NOW.
THE ONLY WAY TO GET TO THIS CONTROL ROOM IS FROM EITHER THE ELEVATORS OR THE EMERGENCY STAIRWELL.
YOU ARE TO GUARD EACH OF THOSE PLACES IN PAIRS.
EACH PAIR WILL BE GIVEN ONE GUN.
THREATEN ANY WHO APPROACH AND DRIVE THEM AWAY.

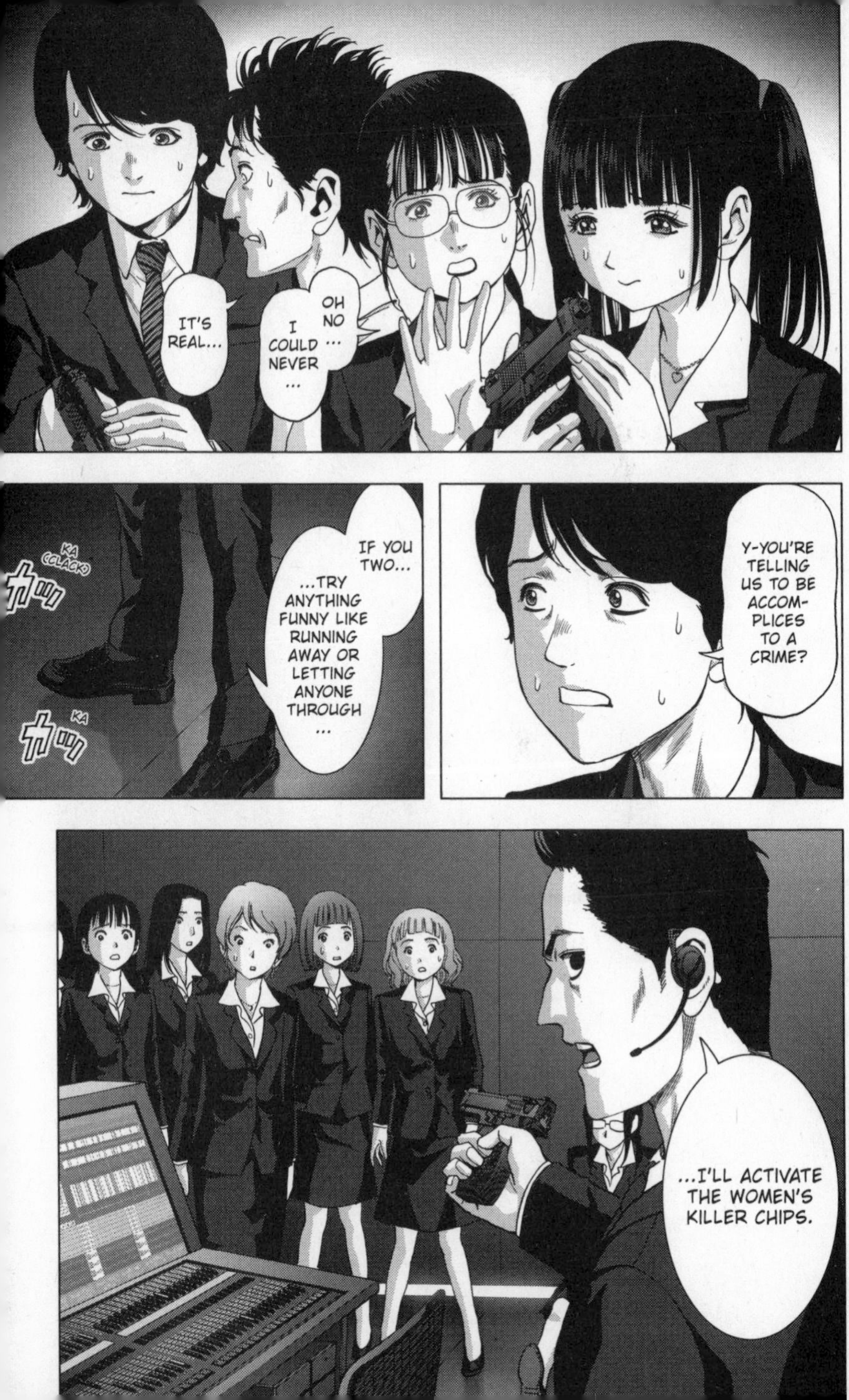
OH NO ... I COULD NEVER ...
IT'S REAL...
Y-YOU'RE TELLING US TO BE ACCOM-PLICES TO A CRIME?
IF YOU TWO...
...TRY ANYTHING FUNNY LIKE RUNNING AWAY OR LETTING ANYONE THROUGH ...
カッ KA (CLACK)
カッ KA
...I'LL ACTIVATE THE WOMEN'S KILLER CHIPS.

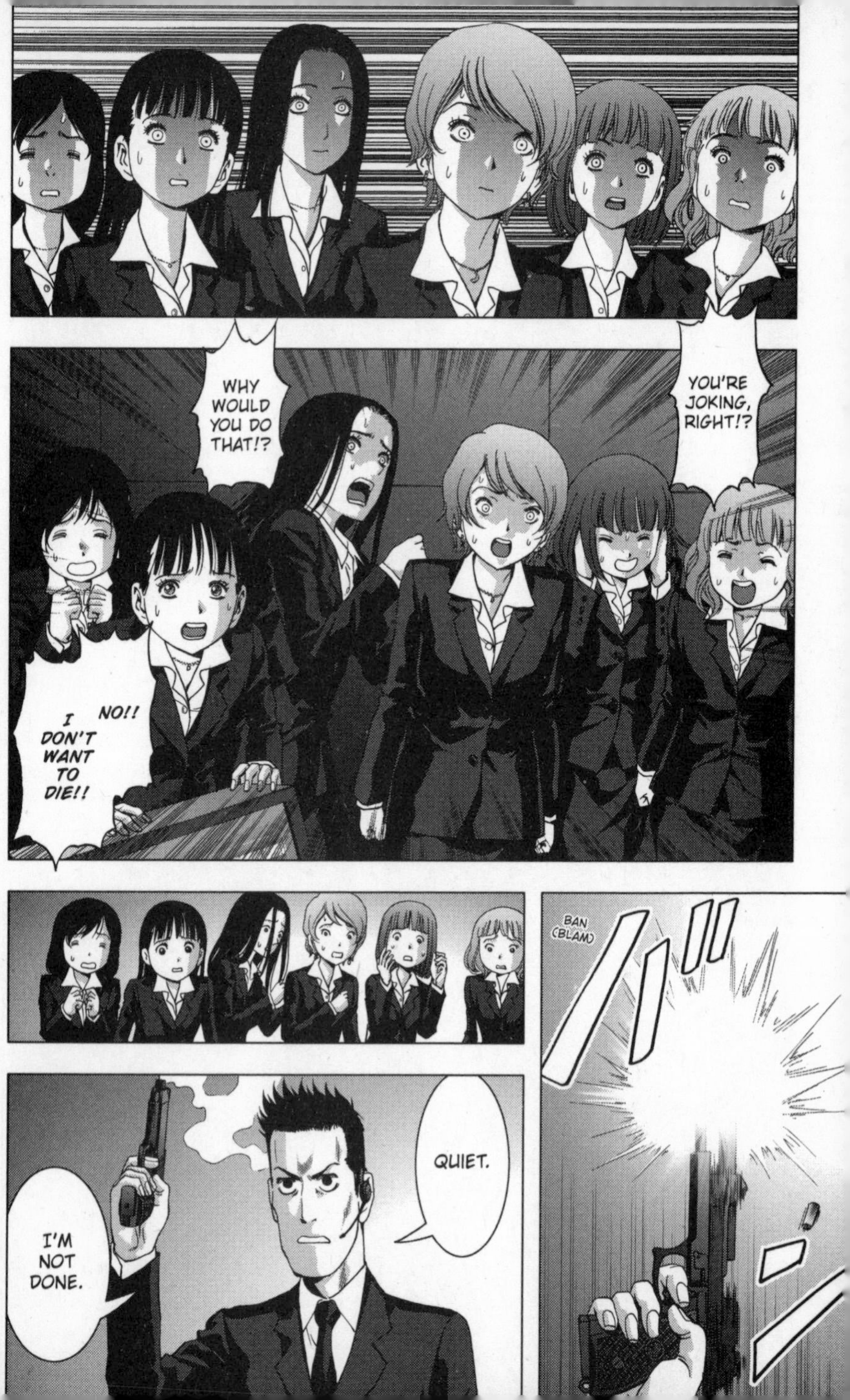
YOU'RE JOKING, RIGHT!?
WHY WOULD YOU DO THAT!?
NO!! I DON'T WANT TO DIE!!
BAN (BLAM)
QUIET.
I'M NOT DONE.

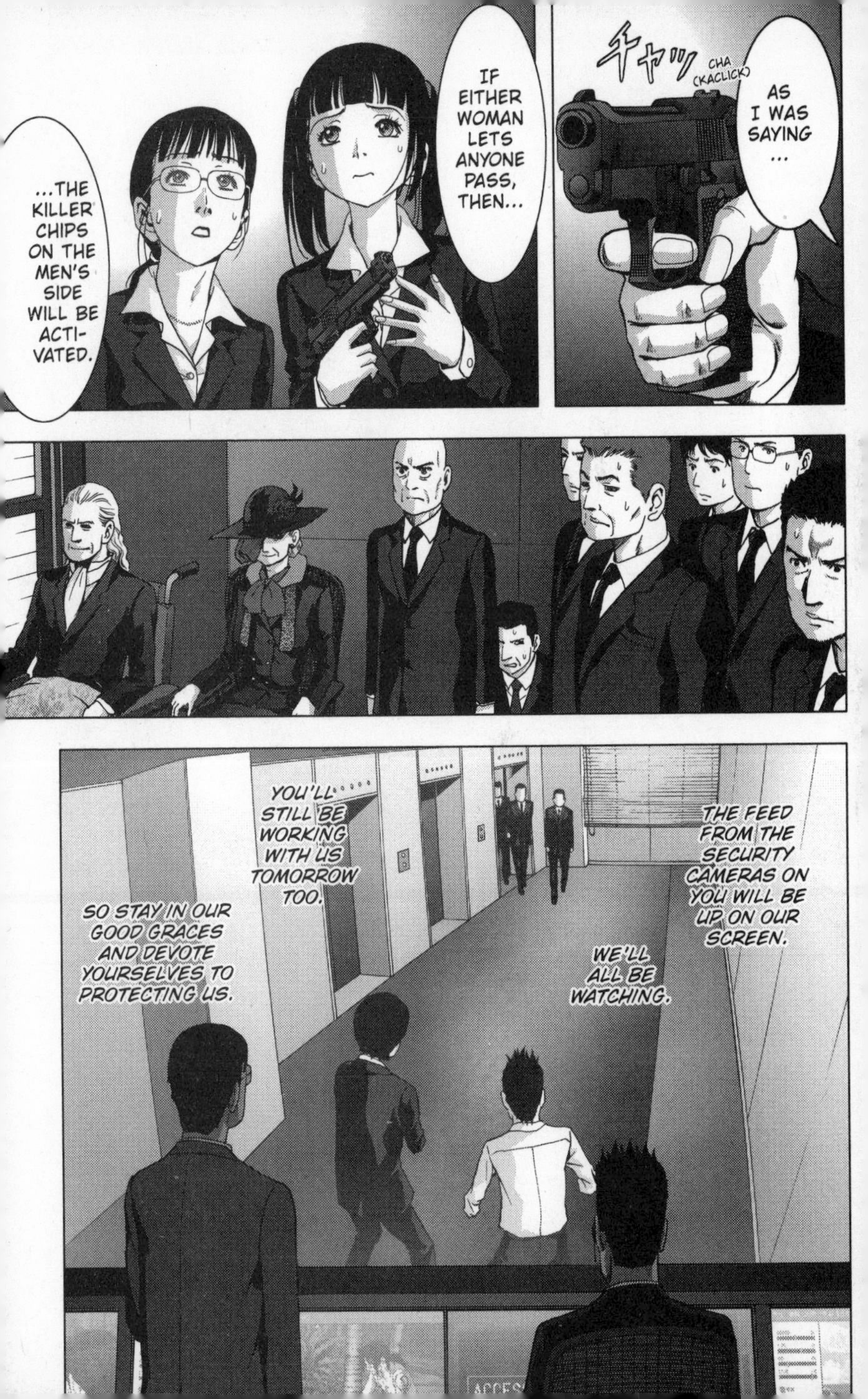
チャッ
CHA (KACLICK)
AS I WAS SAYING ...
IF EITHER WOMAN LETS ANYONE PASS, THEN...
...THE KILLER CHIPS ON THE MEN'S SIDE WILL BE ACTI-VATED.
THE FEED FROM THE SECURITY CAMERAS ON YOU WILL BE UP ON OUR SCREEN.
YOU'LL STILL BE WORKING WITH US TOMORROW TOO.
WE'LL ALL BE WATCHING.
SO STAY IN OUR GOOD GRACES AND DEVOTE YOURSELVES TO PROTECTING US.

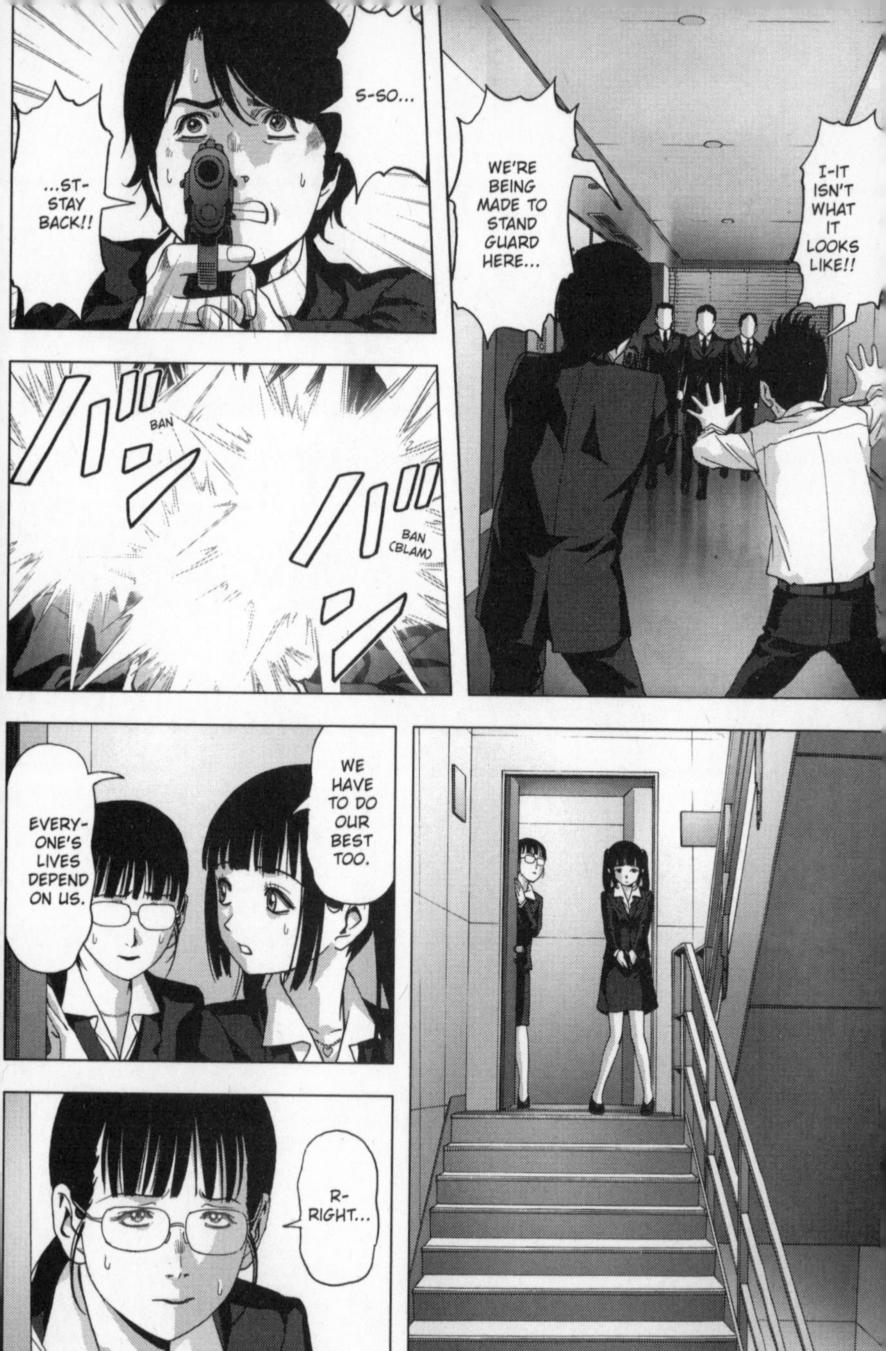
I-IT ISN'T WHAT IT LOOKS LIKE!!
WE'RE BEING MADE TO STAND GUARD HERE...
S-SO...
...ST-STAY BACK!!
BAN
BAN (BLAM)
WE HAVE TO DO OUR BEST TOO.
EVERY-ONE'S LIVES DEPEND ON US.
R-RIGHT...

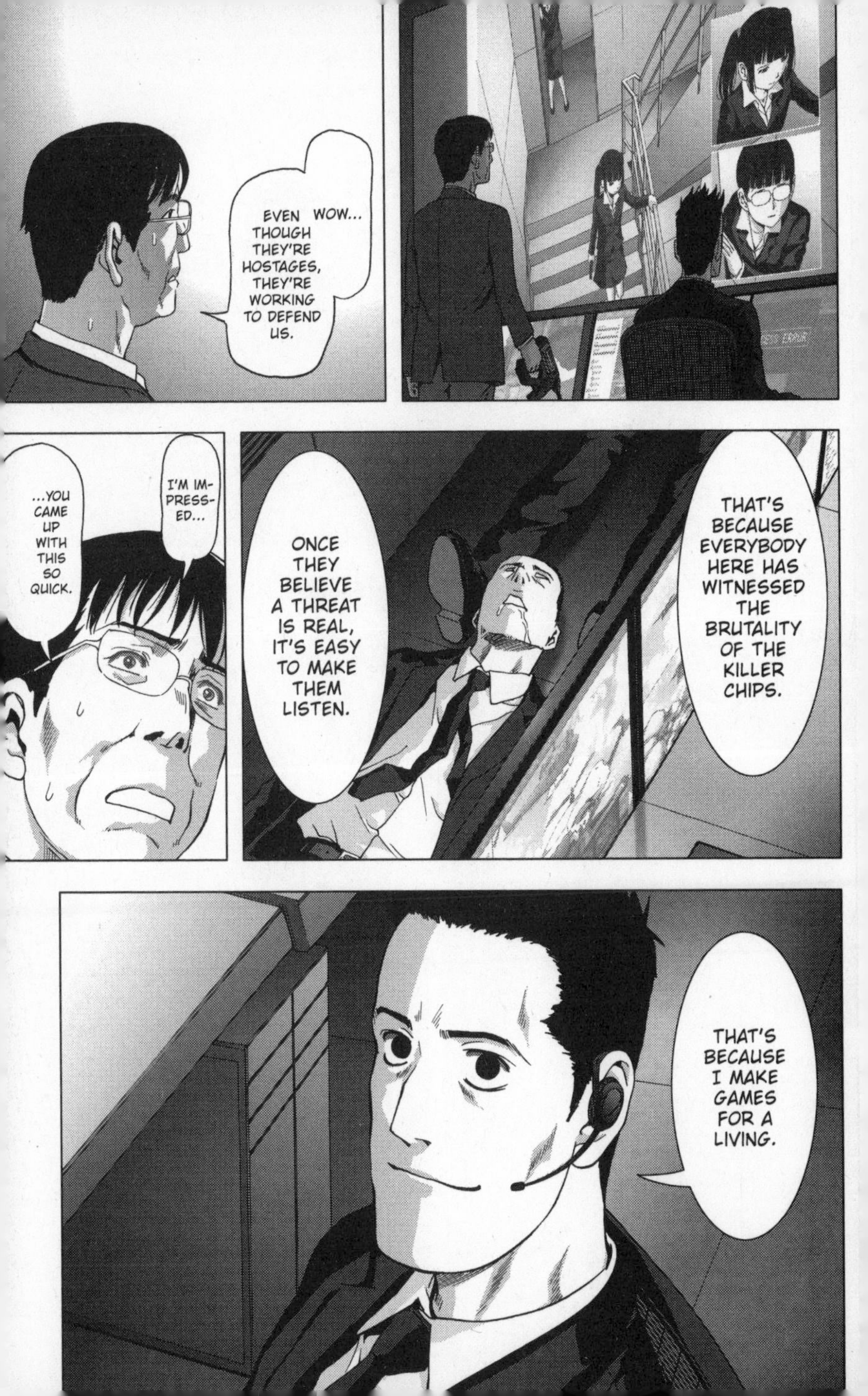
WOW... EVEN THOUGH THEY'RE HOSTAGES, THEY'RE WORKING TO DEFEND US.
THAT'S BECAUSE EVERYBODY HERE HAS WITNESSED THE BRUTALITY OF THE KILLER CHIPS.
ONCE THEY BELIEVE A THREAT IS REAL, IT'S EASY TO MAKE THEM LISTEN.
I'M IM-PRESS-ED...
...YOU CAME UP WITH THIS SO QUICK.
THAT'S BECAUSE I MAKE GAMES FOR A LIVING.

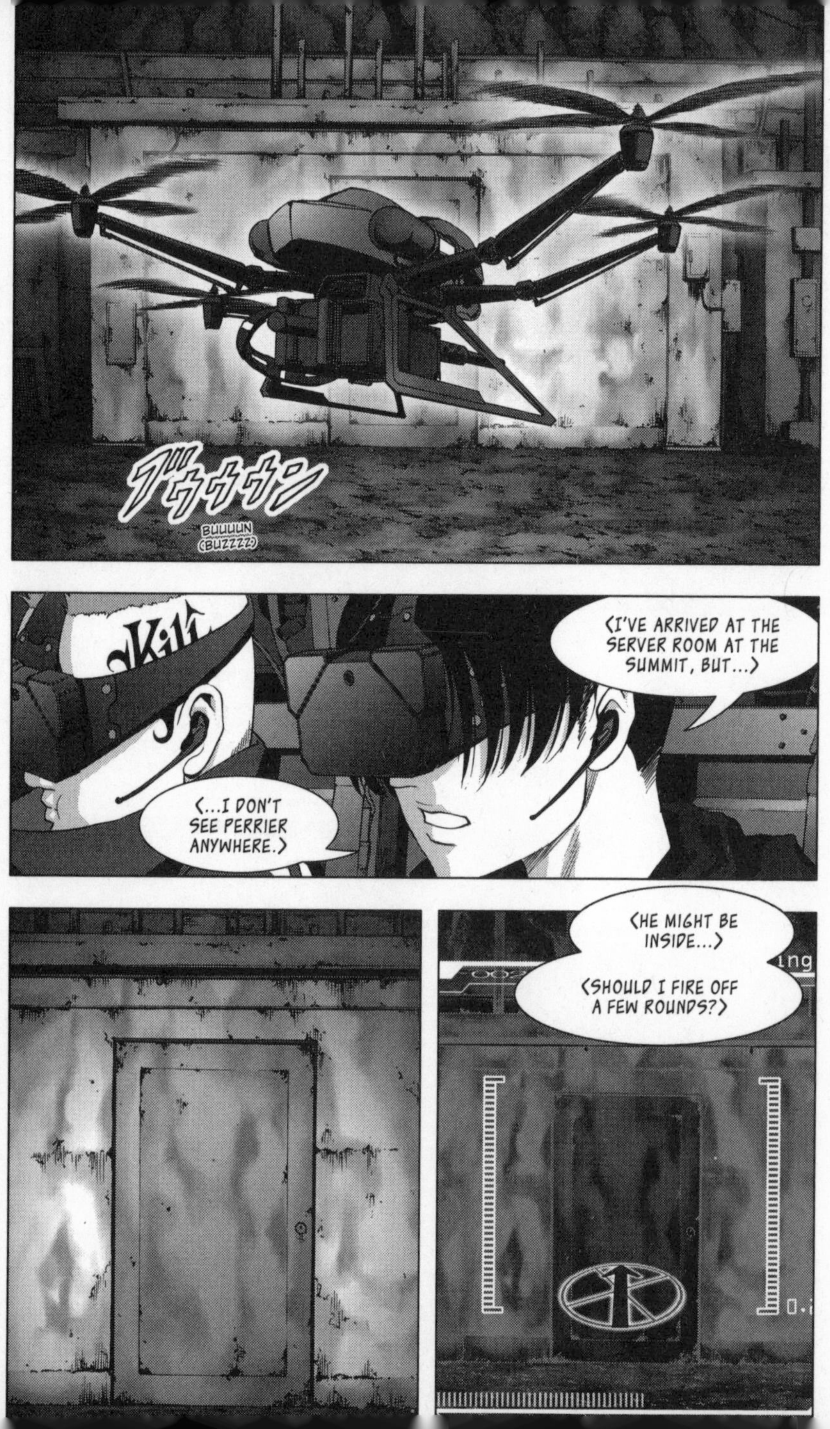
ブウウウン
BUUUUN (BUZZZZ)
〈I'VE ARRIVED AT THE SERVER ROOM AT THE SUMMIT, BUT...〉
〈...I DON'T SEE PERRIER ANYWHERE.〉
〈HE MIGHT BE INSIDE...〉
〈SHOULD I FIRE OFF A FEW ROUNDS?〉

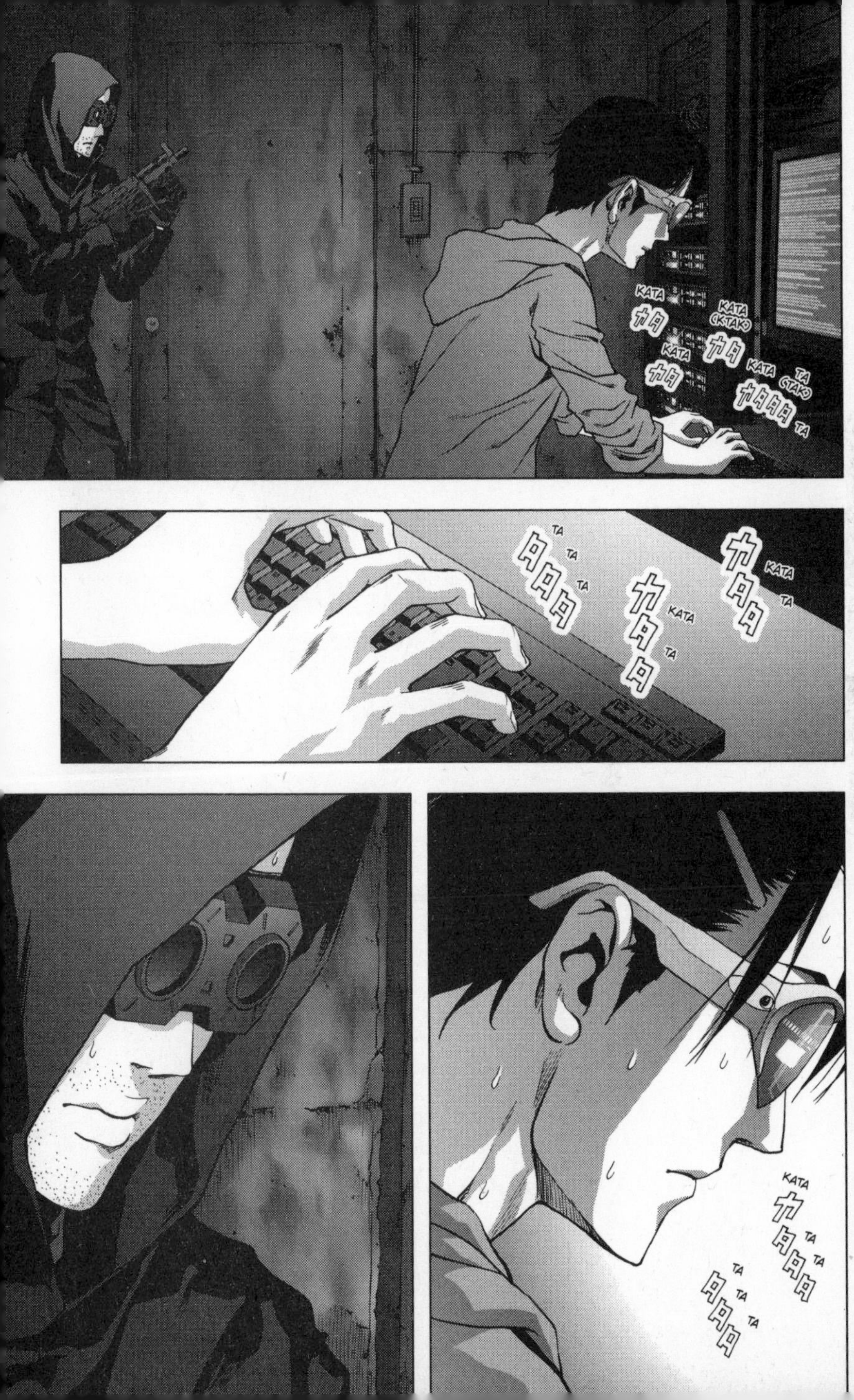
KATA
KATA (KTAK)
KATA
KATA
TA (TAK)
TA
KATA TA
KATA TA
TA TA TA
KATA TA TA
TA TA TA

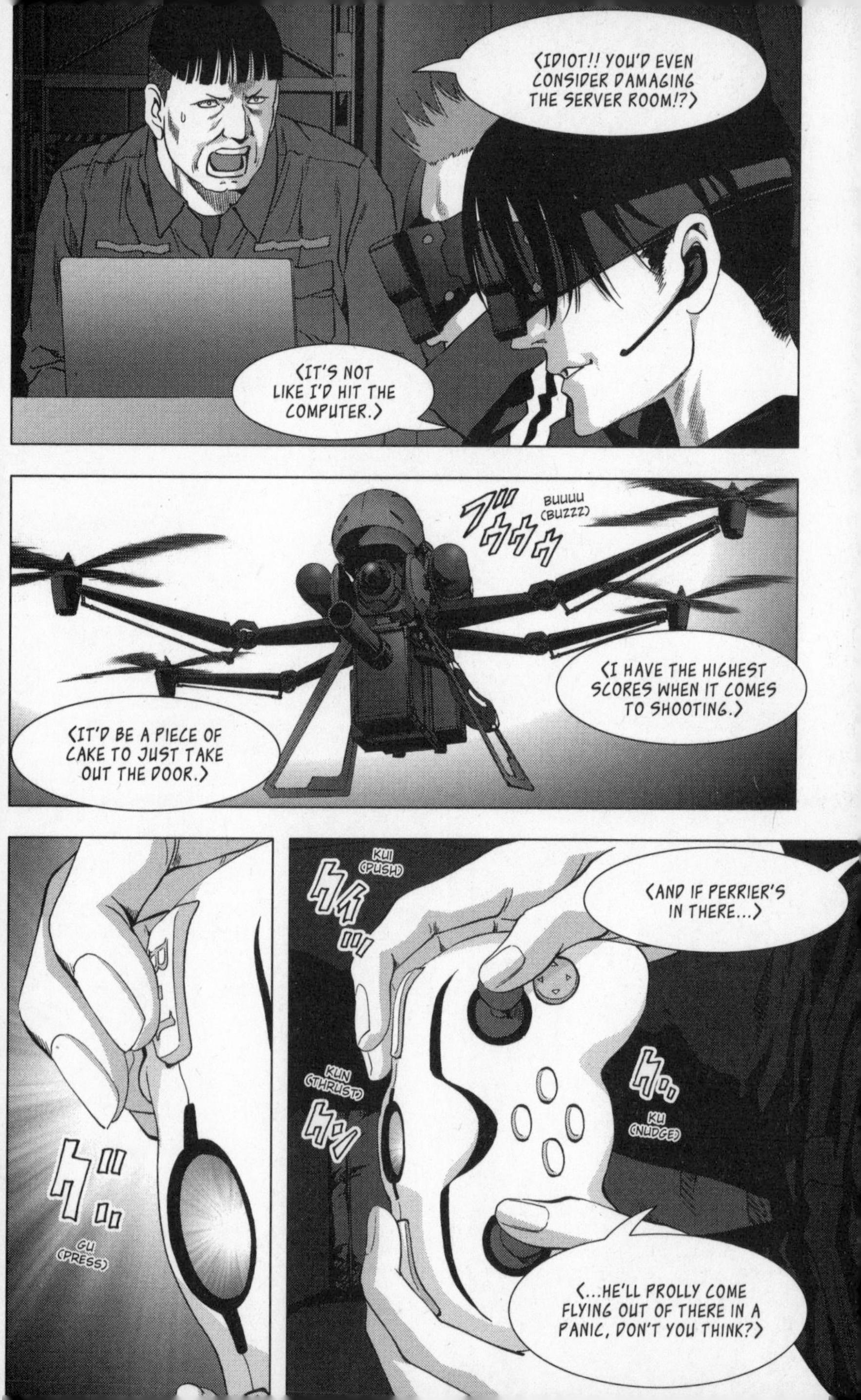
‹IDIOT!! YOU'D EVEN CONSIDER DAMAGING THE SERVER ROOM!?›
‹IT'S NOT LIKE I'D HIT THE COMPUTER.›
BUUUU (BUZZZ)
‹I HAVE THE HIGHEST SCORES WHEN IT COMES TO SHOOTING.›
‹IT'D BE A PIECE OF CAKE TO JUST TAKE OUT THE DOOR.›
KUI (PUSH)
‹AND IF PERRIER'S IN THERE...›
KUN (THRUST)
KU (NUDGE)
‹...HE'LL PROLLY COME FLYING OUT OF THERE IN A PANIC, DON'T YOU THINK?›
GU (PRESS)

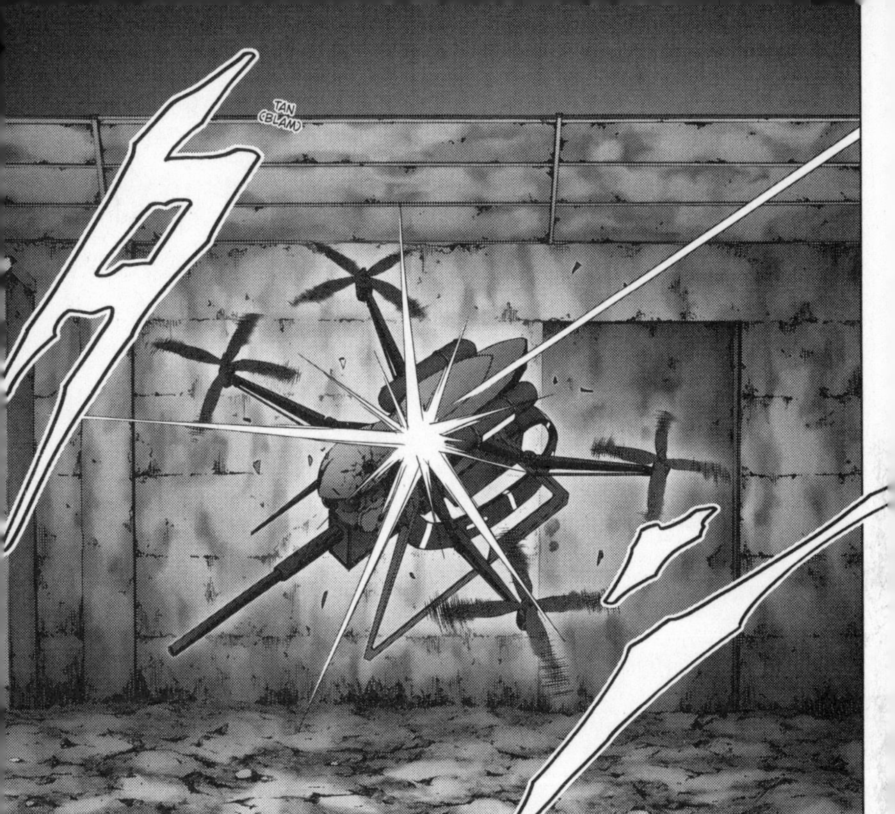
TAN
(BLAM)
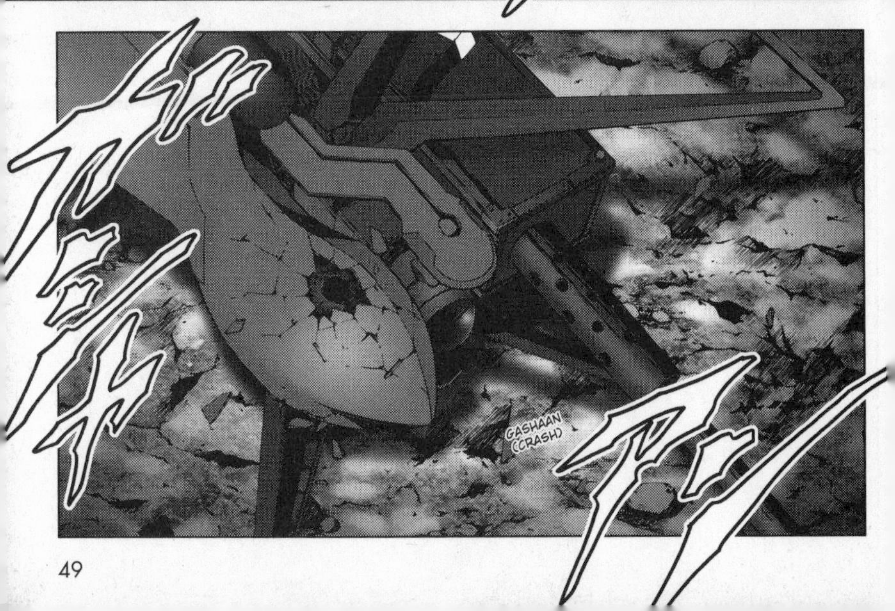
GASHAAN
(CRASH)

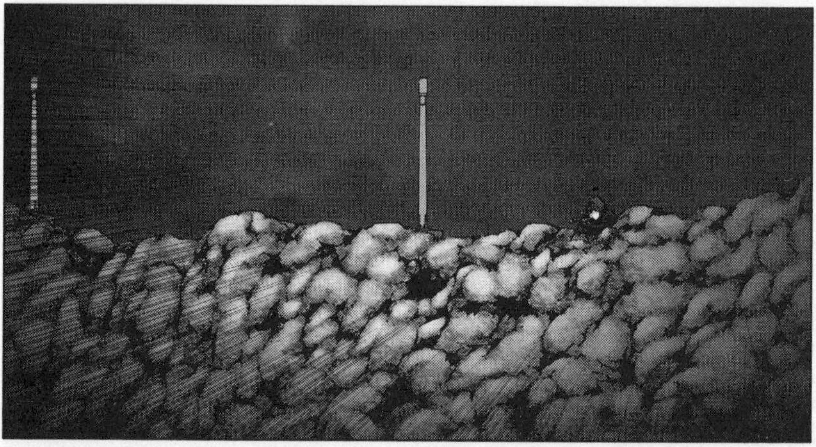

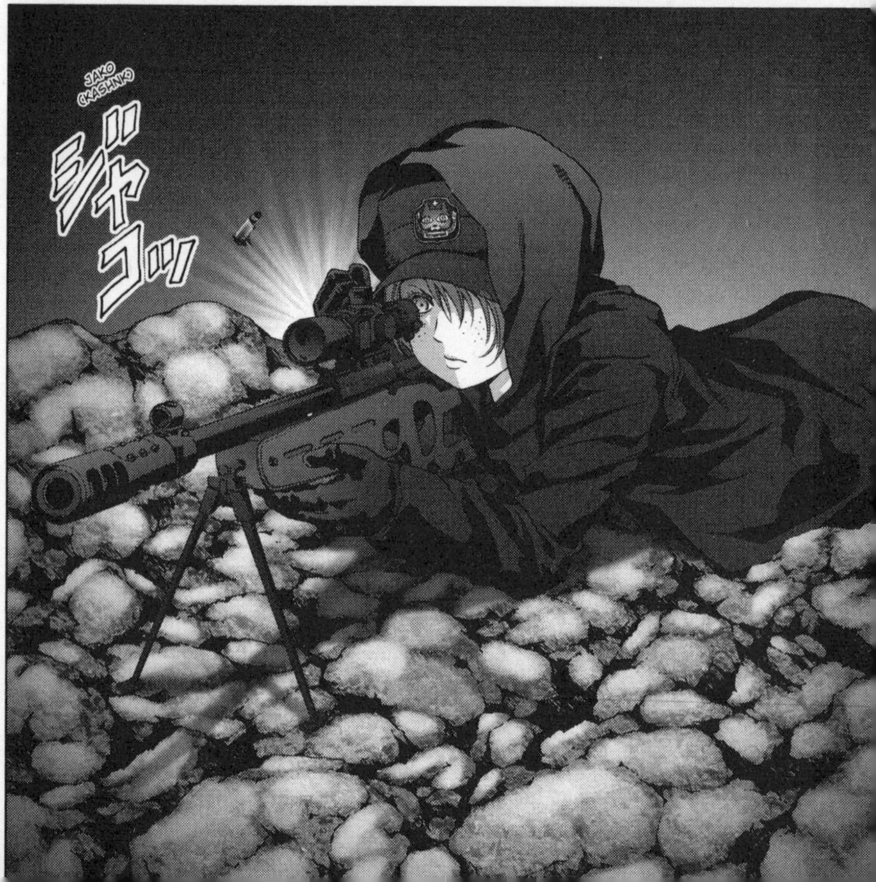
JAKO (KASHNK)
ジャコッ

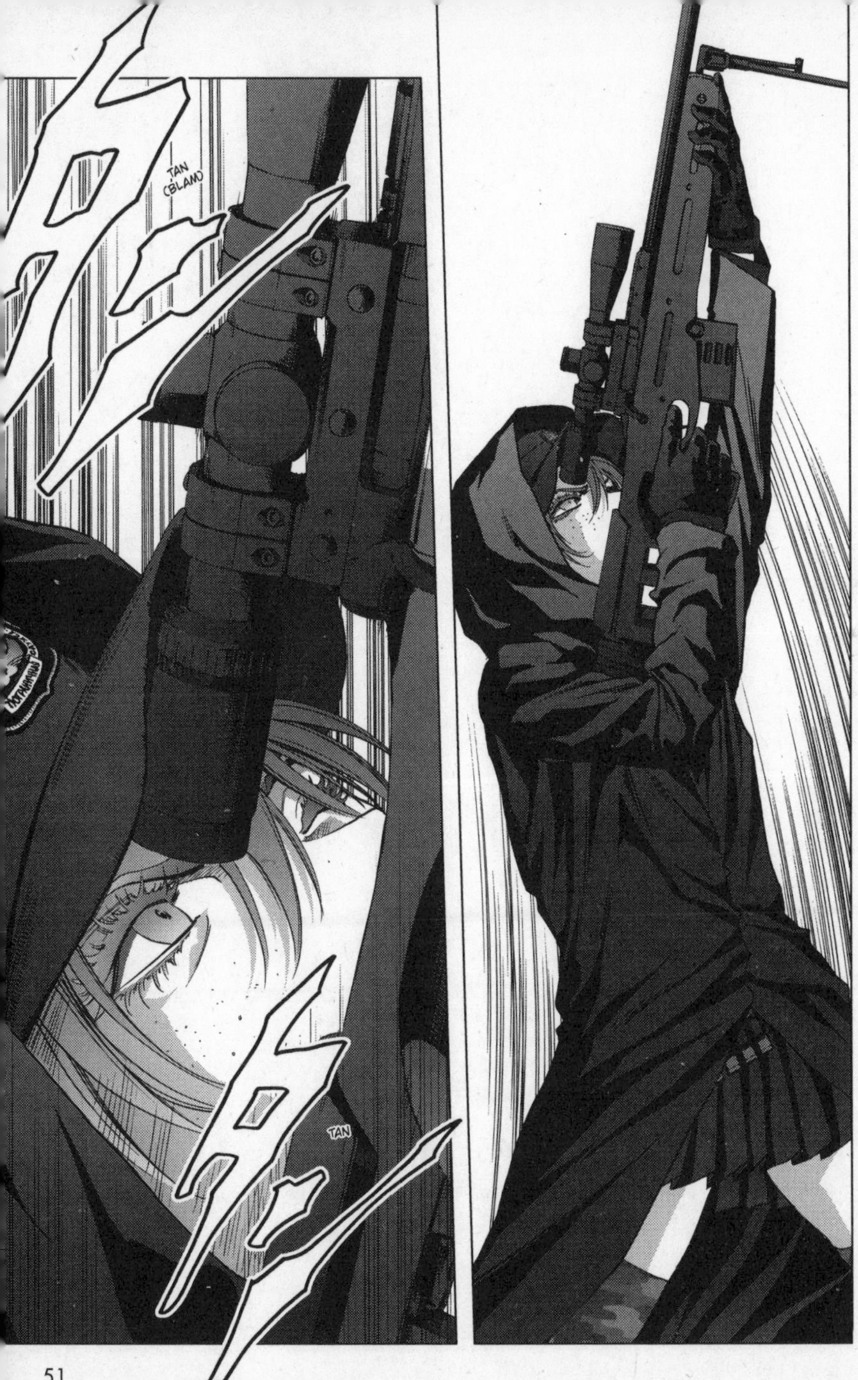
TAN
(BLAM)
TAN

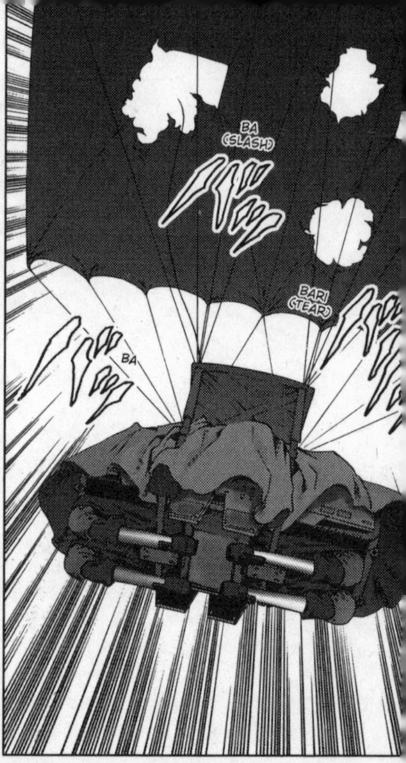
BA
(SLASH)
BARI
(TEAR)
BA
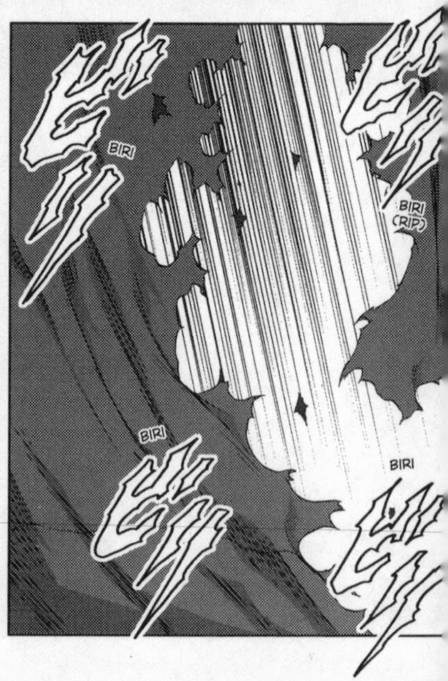
BIRI
(RIP)
BIRI
BIRI
BIRI
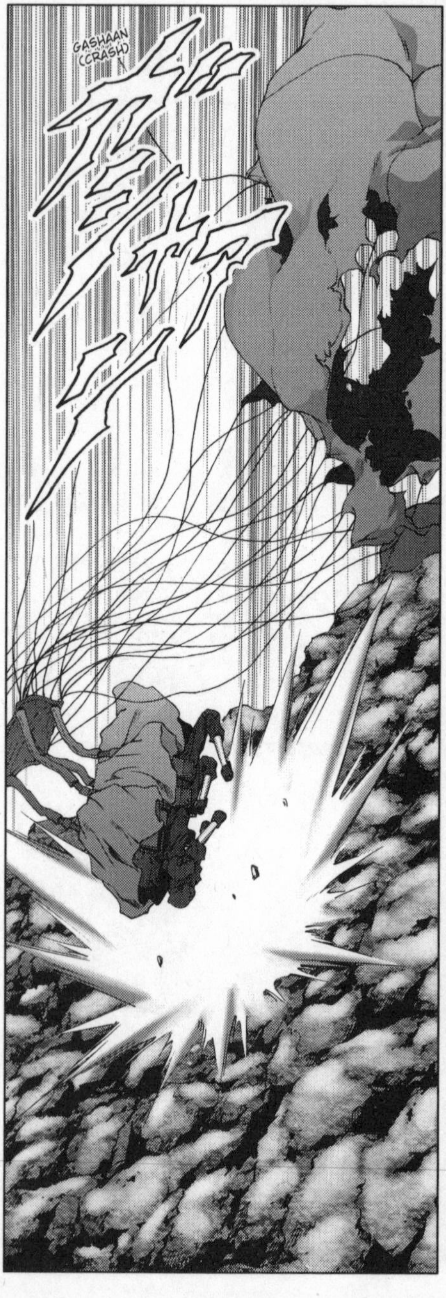
GASHAAN
(CRASH)

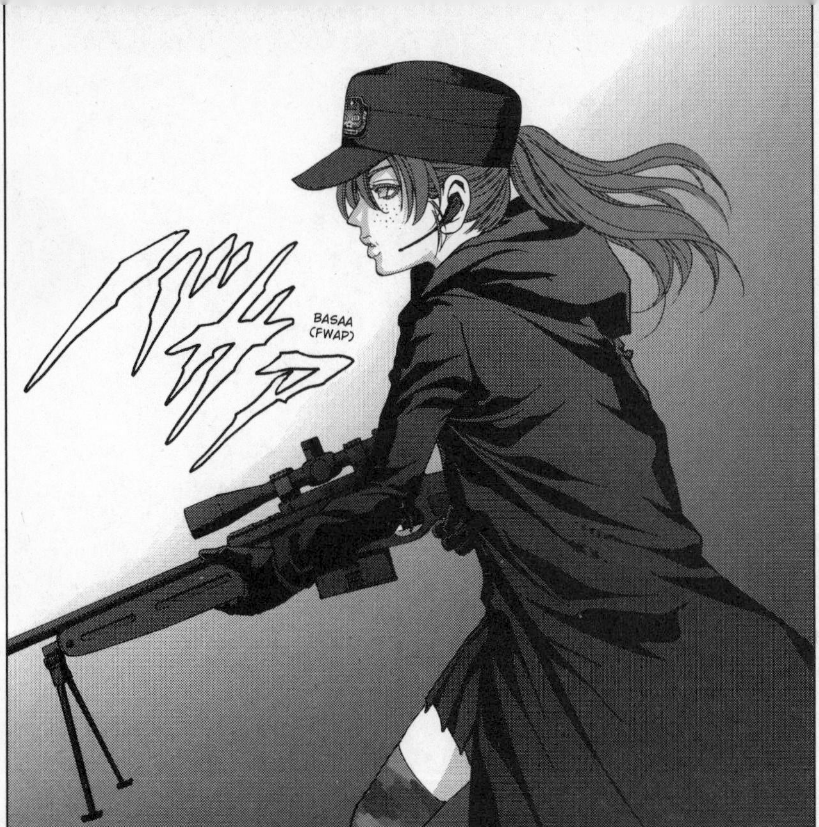
BASAA
(FWAP)

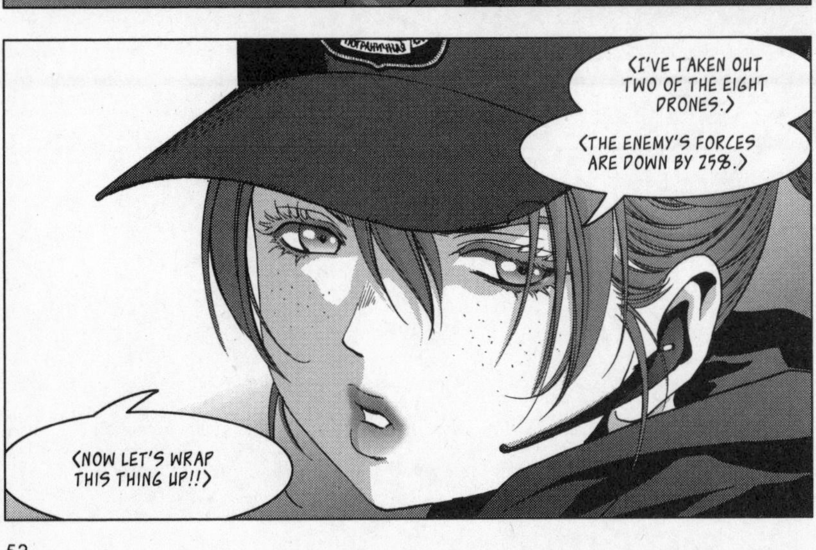
<I'VE TAKEN OUT TWO OF THE EIGHT DRONES.>
<THE ENEMY'S FORCES ARE DOWN BY 25%.>
<NOW LET'S WRAP THIS THING UP!!>

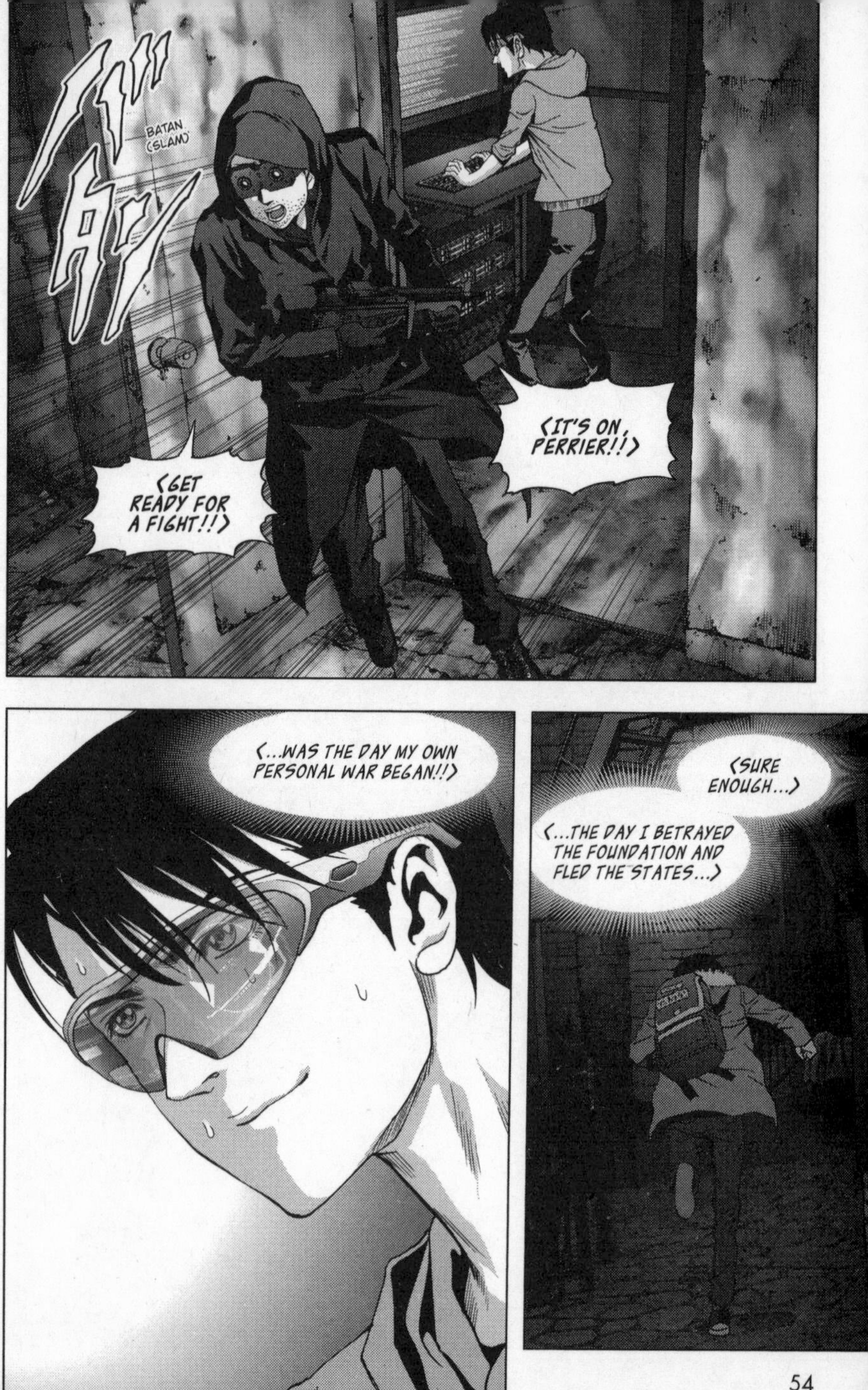
BATAN (SLAM)
<IT'S ON, PERRIER!!>
<GET READY FOR A FIGHT!!>
<SURE ENOUGH...>
<...THE DAY I BETRAYED THE FOUNDATION AND FLED THE STATES...>
<...WAS THE DAY MY OWN PERSONAL WAR BEGAN!!>

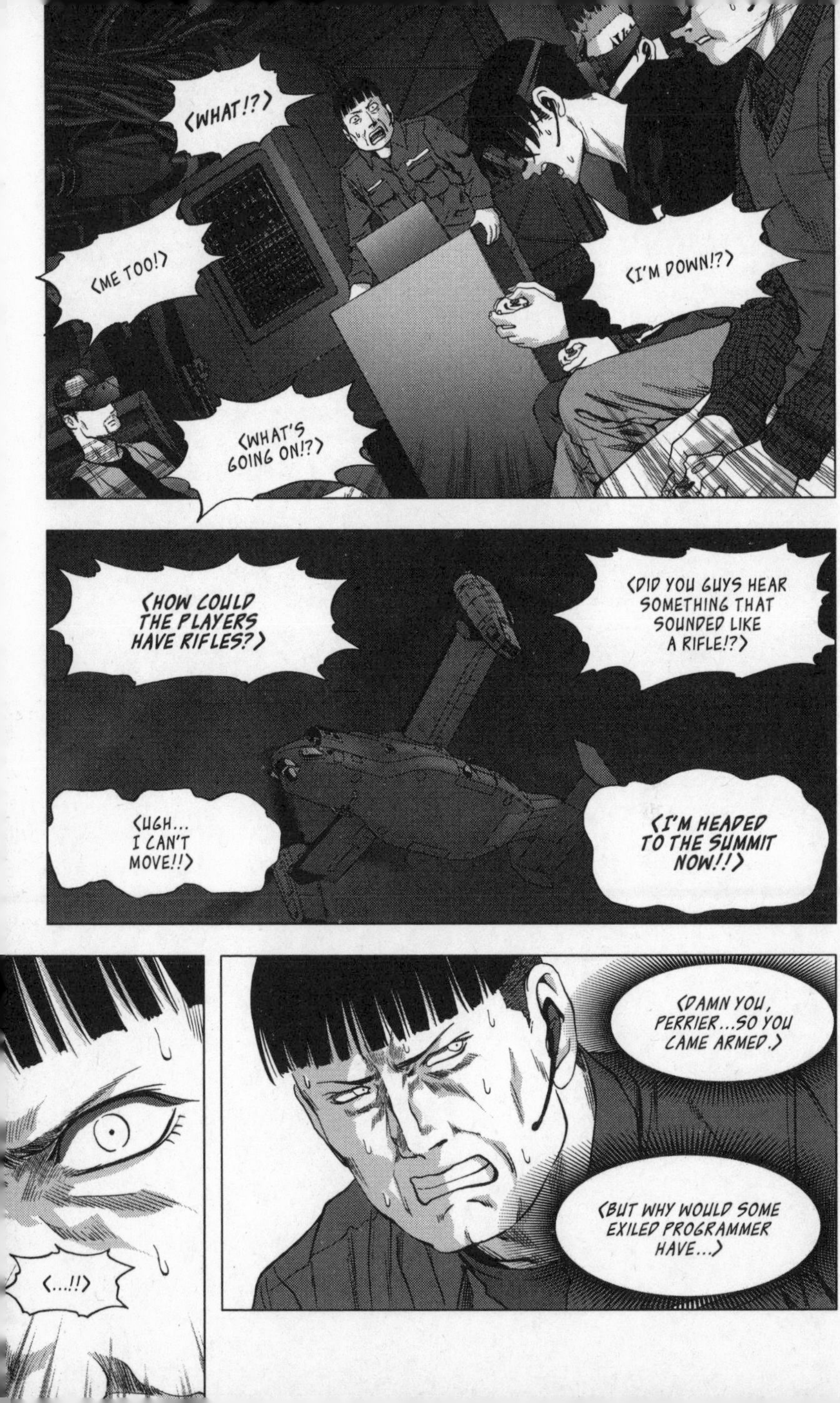
<WHAT!?>
<I'M DOWN!?>
<ME TOO!>
<WHAT'S GOING ON!?>
<DID YOU GUYS HEAR SOMETHING THAT SOUNDED LIKE A RIFLE!?>
<HOW COULD THE PLAYERS HAVE RIFLES?>
<I'M HEADED TO THE SUMMIT NOW!!>
<UGH... I CAN'T MOVE!!>
<DAMN YOU, PERRIER...SO YOU CAME ARMED.>
<BUT WHY WOULD SOME EXILED PROGRAMMER HAVE...>
<...!!>

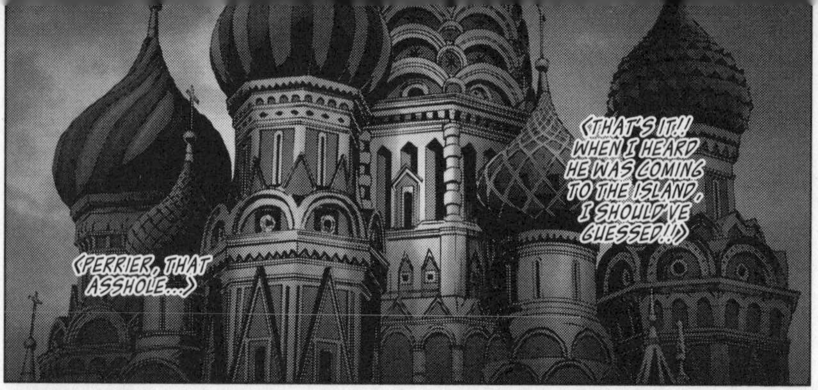
‹THAT'S IT!! WHEN I HEARD HE WAS COMING TO THE ISLAND, I SHOULD'VE GUESSED!!›
‹PERRIER, THAT ASSHOLE...›
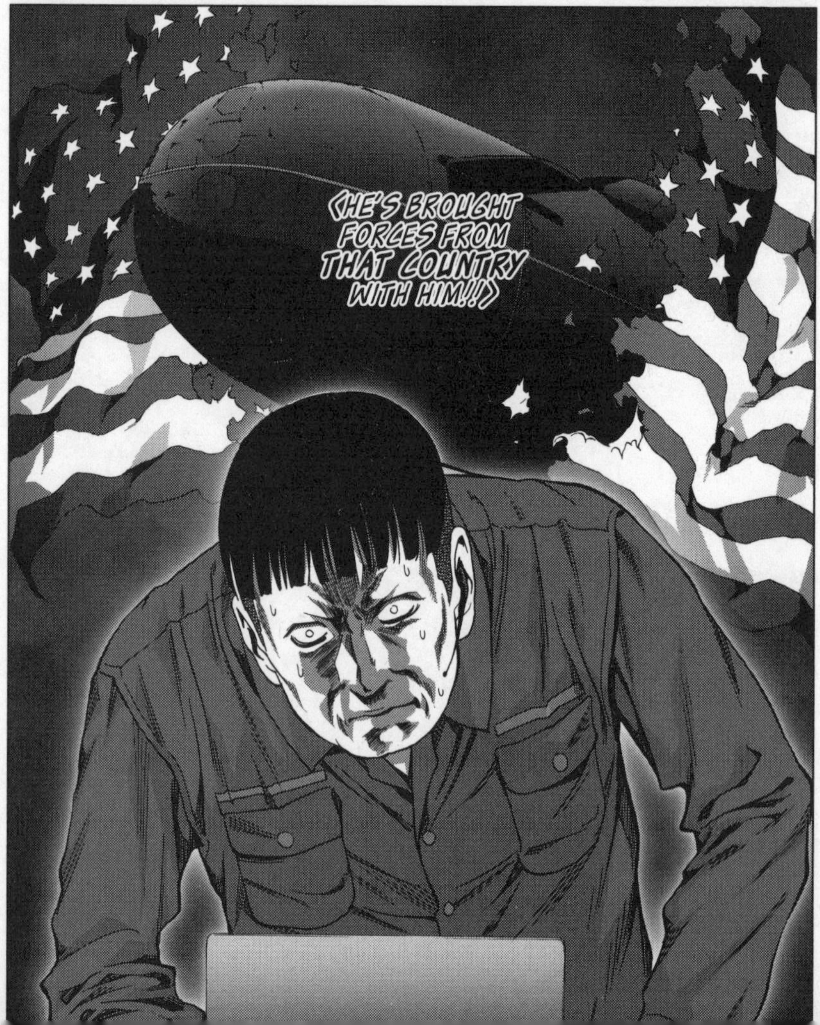
‹HE'S BROUGHT FORCES FROM THAT COUNTRY WITH HIM!!›

111 Sakamoto Countering

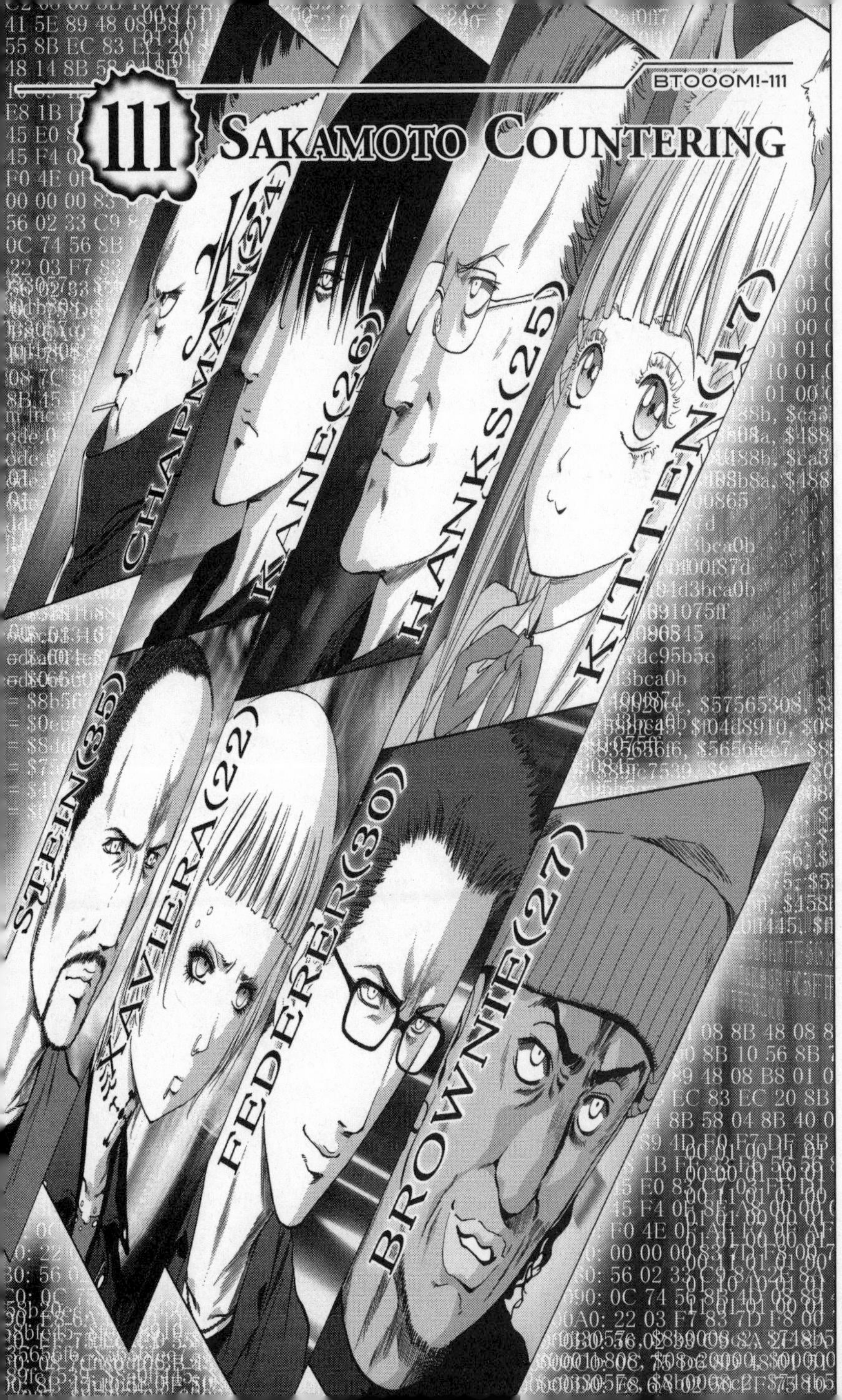
KITTEN(17)
HANKS(25)
KANE(26)
CHAPMAN(24)
BROWNIE(27)
FEDERER(30)
XAVIERA(22)
STEIN(35)

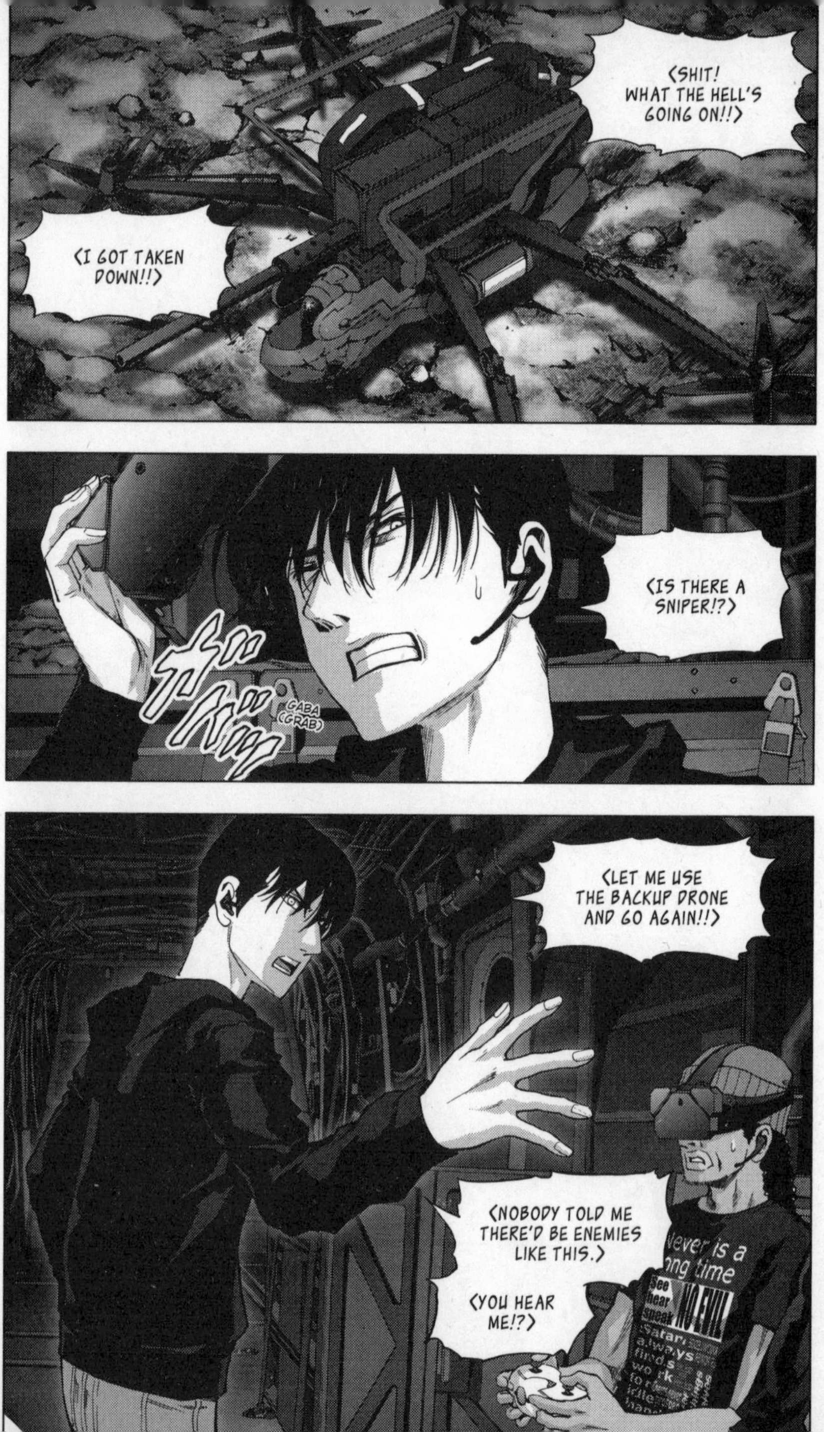
〈SHIT! WHAT THE HELL'S GOING ON!!〉
〈I GOT TAKEN DOWN!!〉
〈IS THERE A SNIPER!?〉
GABA (GRAB)
〈LET ME USE THE BACKUP DRONE AND GO AGAIN!!〉
〈NOBODY TOLD ME THERE'D BE ENEMIES LIKE THIS.〉
〈YOU HEAR ME!?〉

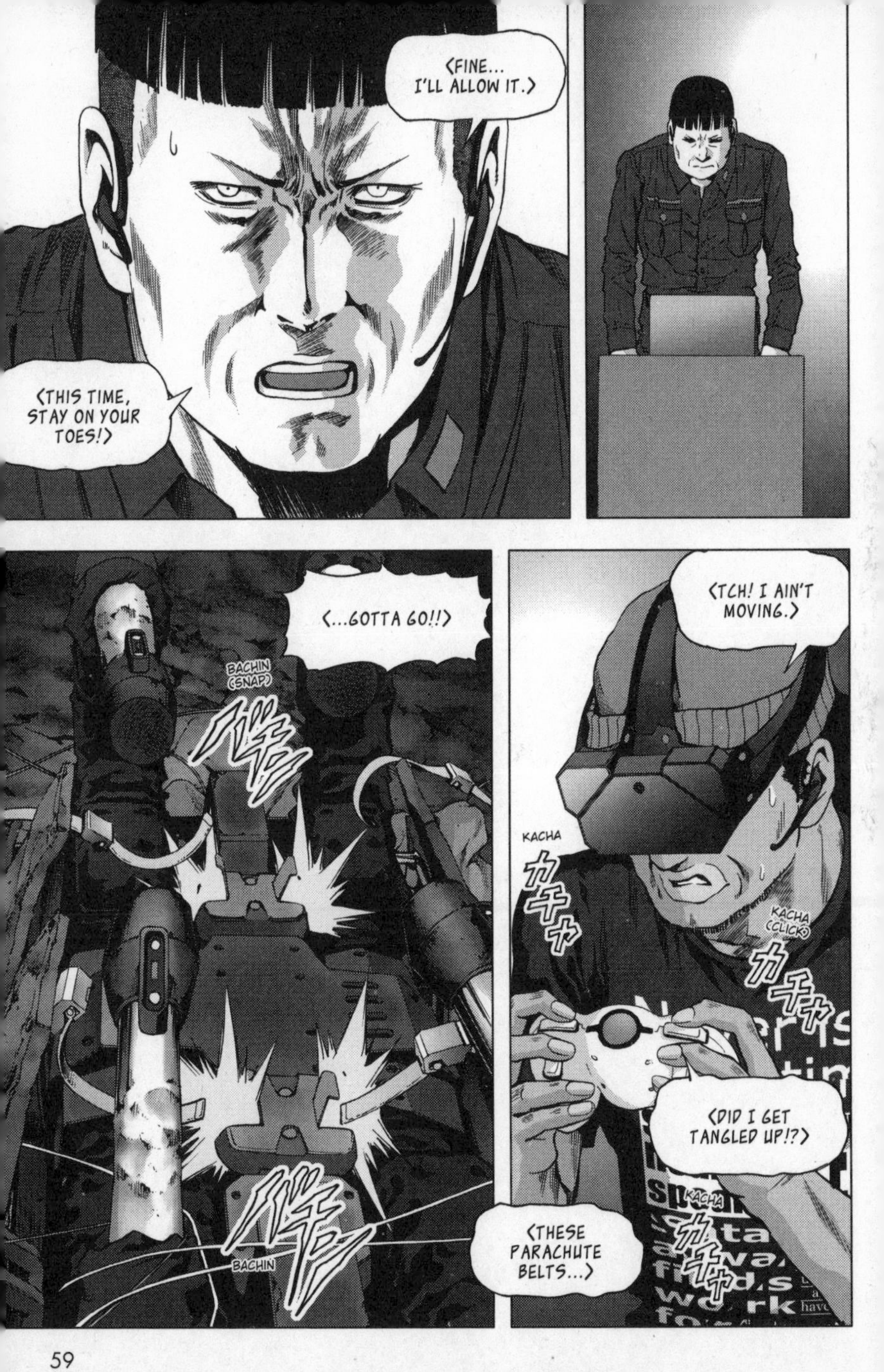

‹FINE... I'LL ALLOW IT.›
‹THIS TIME, STAY ON YOUR TOES!›
‹TCH! I AIN'T MOVING.›
KACHA
KACHA (CLICK)
‹DID I GET TANGLED UP!?›
KACHA
‹THESE PARACHUTE BELTS...›
‹...GOTTA GO!!›
BACHIN (SNAP)
BACHIN

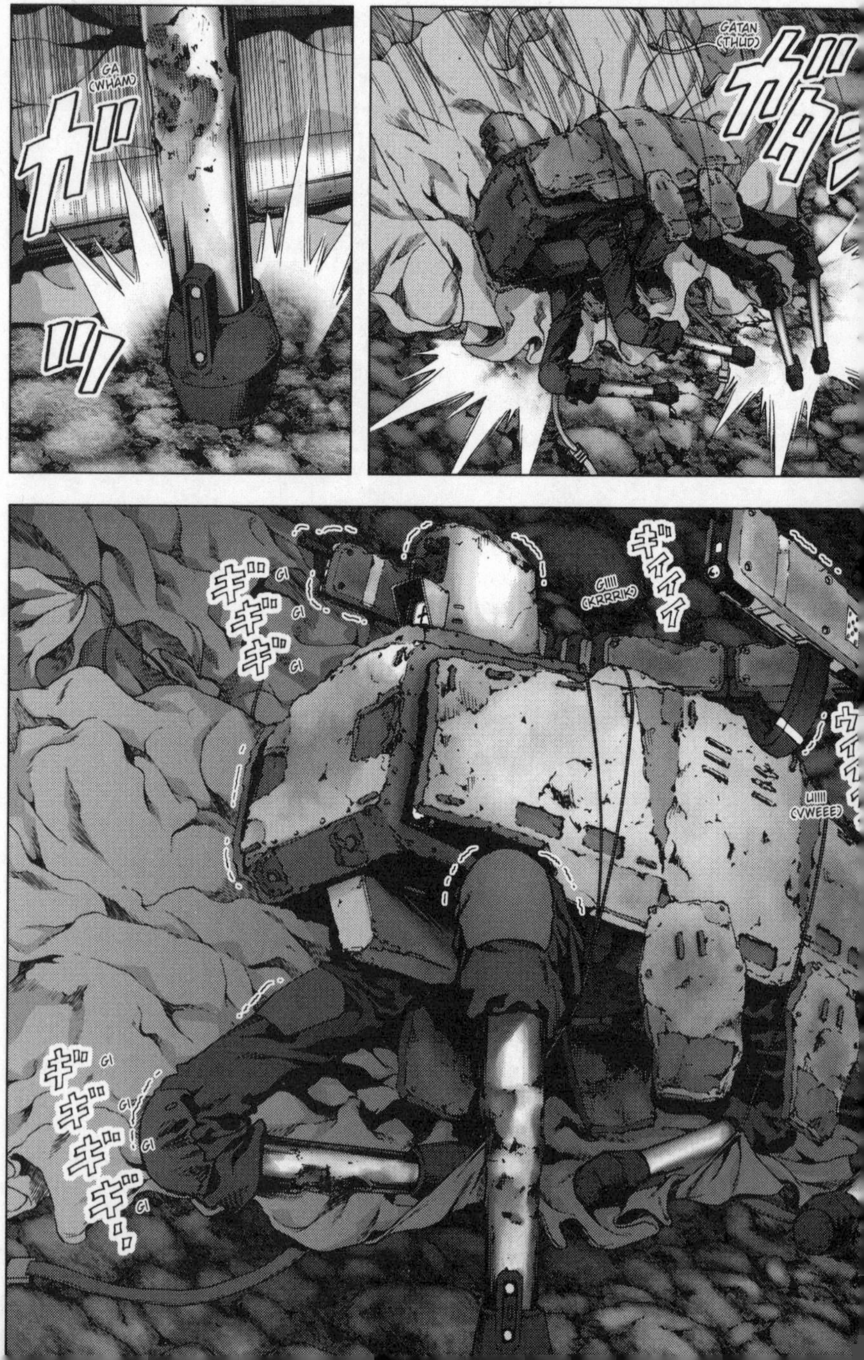
GATAN (THUD)
GA (WHAM)
UIII (VWEEE)
GIIII (KRRRIK)
GI GI GI
GI GI GI GI

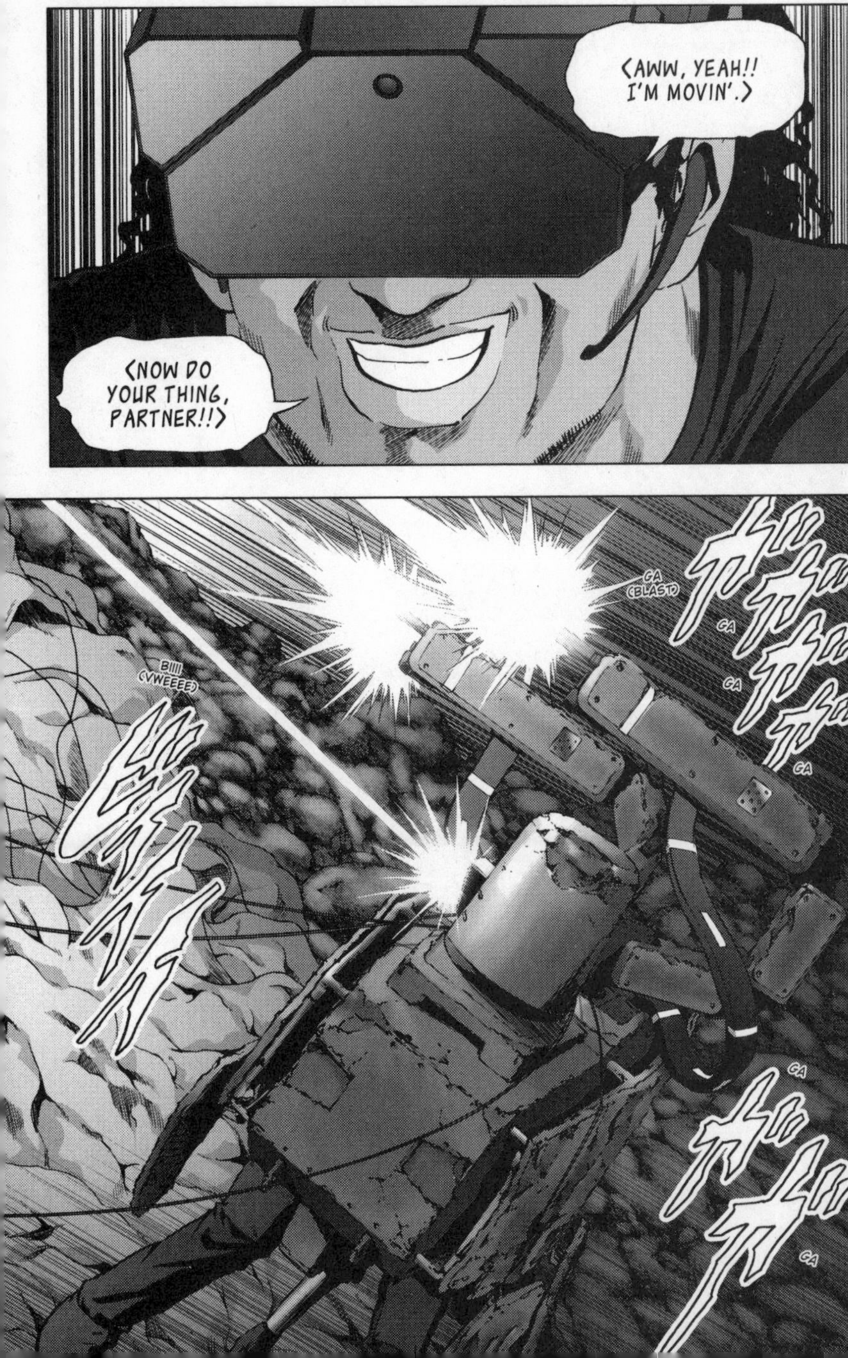
<AWW, YEAH!! I'M MOVIN'.>
<NOW DO YOUR THING, PARTNER!!>
GA (BLAST)
GA
GA
GA
BIIII (VWEEEE)
GA
GA

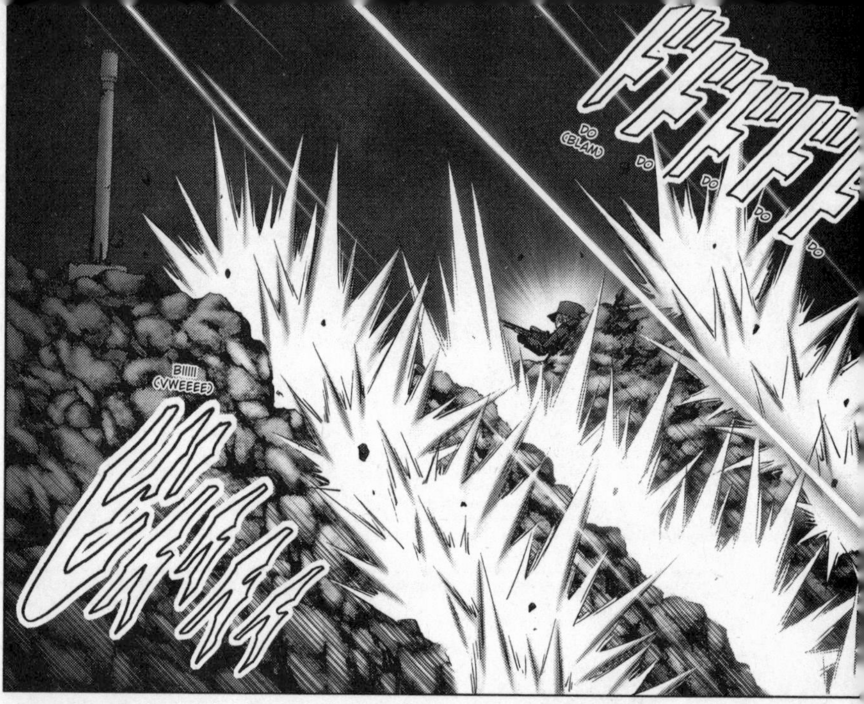
DO (BLAM)
DO
DO
DO
DO
BIIIII (VWEEEE)

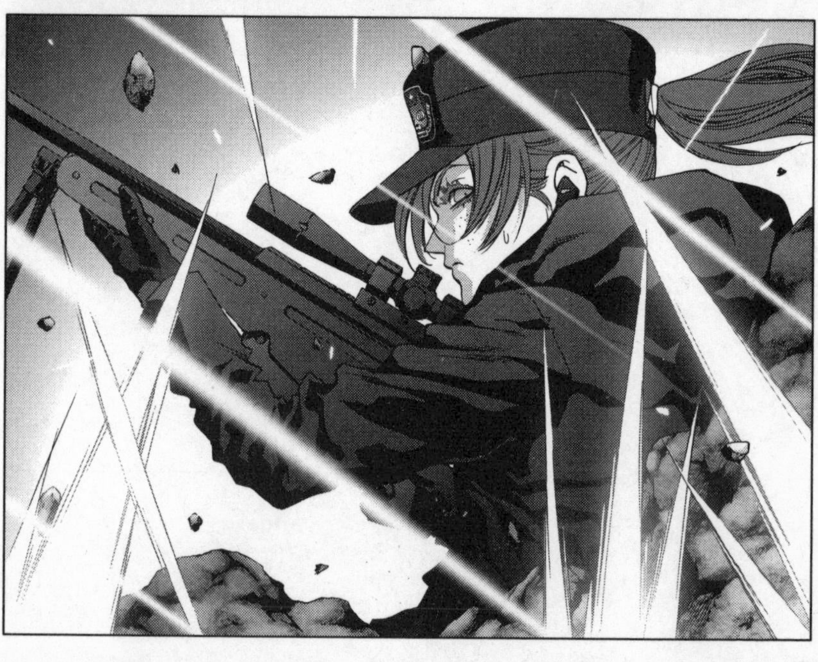

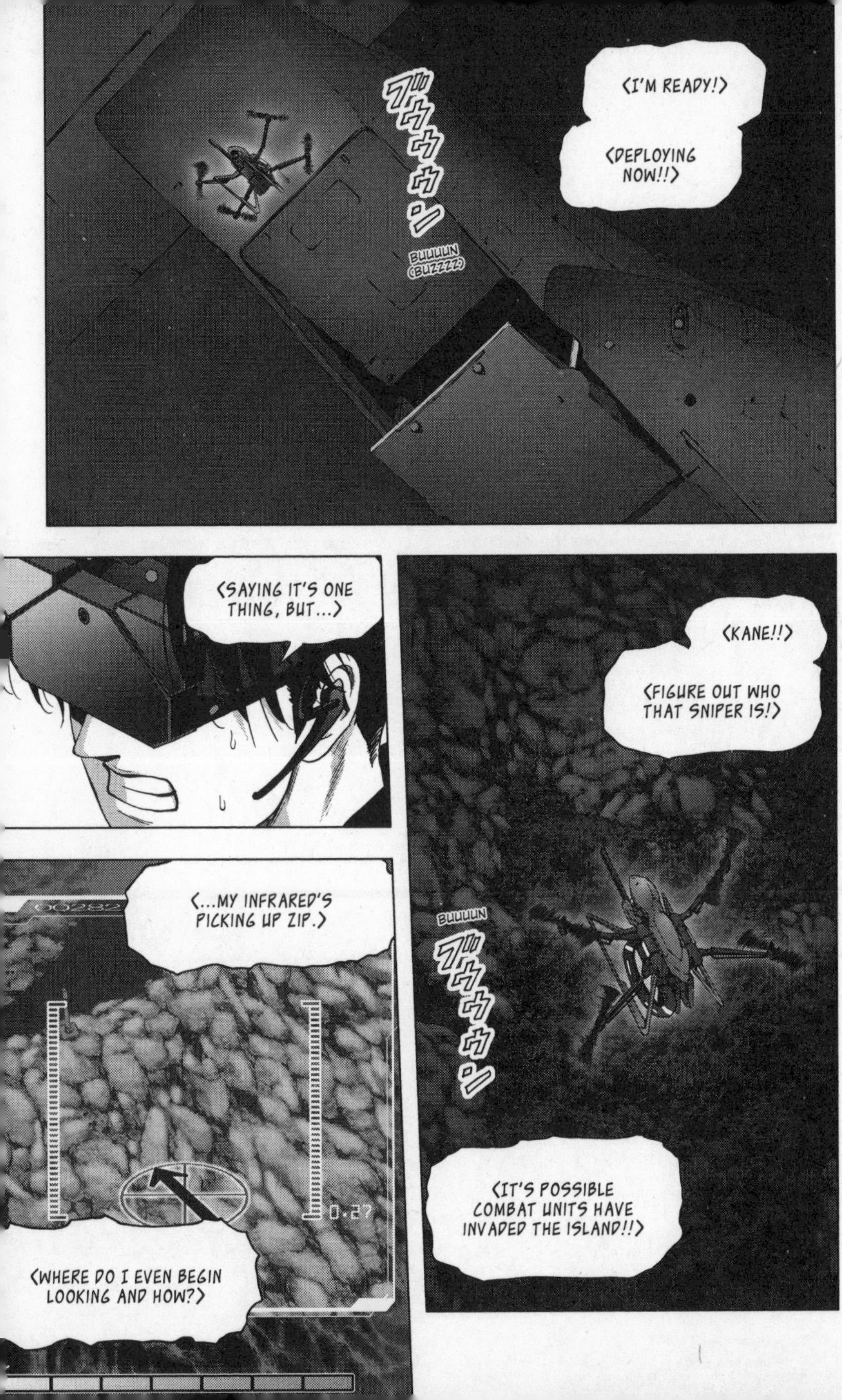

〈I'M READY!〉
〈DEPLOYING NOW!!〉
ブゥゥゥン
BUUUUN (BUZZZZ)
〈KANE!!〉
〈FIGURE OUT WHO THAT SNIPER IS!〉
BUUUUN
ブゥゥゥン
〈IT'S POSSIBLE COMBAT UNITS HAVE INVADED THE ISLAND!!〉
〈SAYING IT'S ONE THING, BUT...〉
〈...MY INFRARED'S PICKING UP ZIP.〉
0:27
〈WHERE DO I EVEN BEGIN LOOKING AND HOW?〉

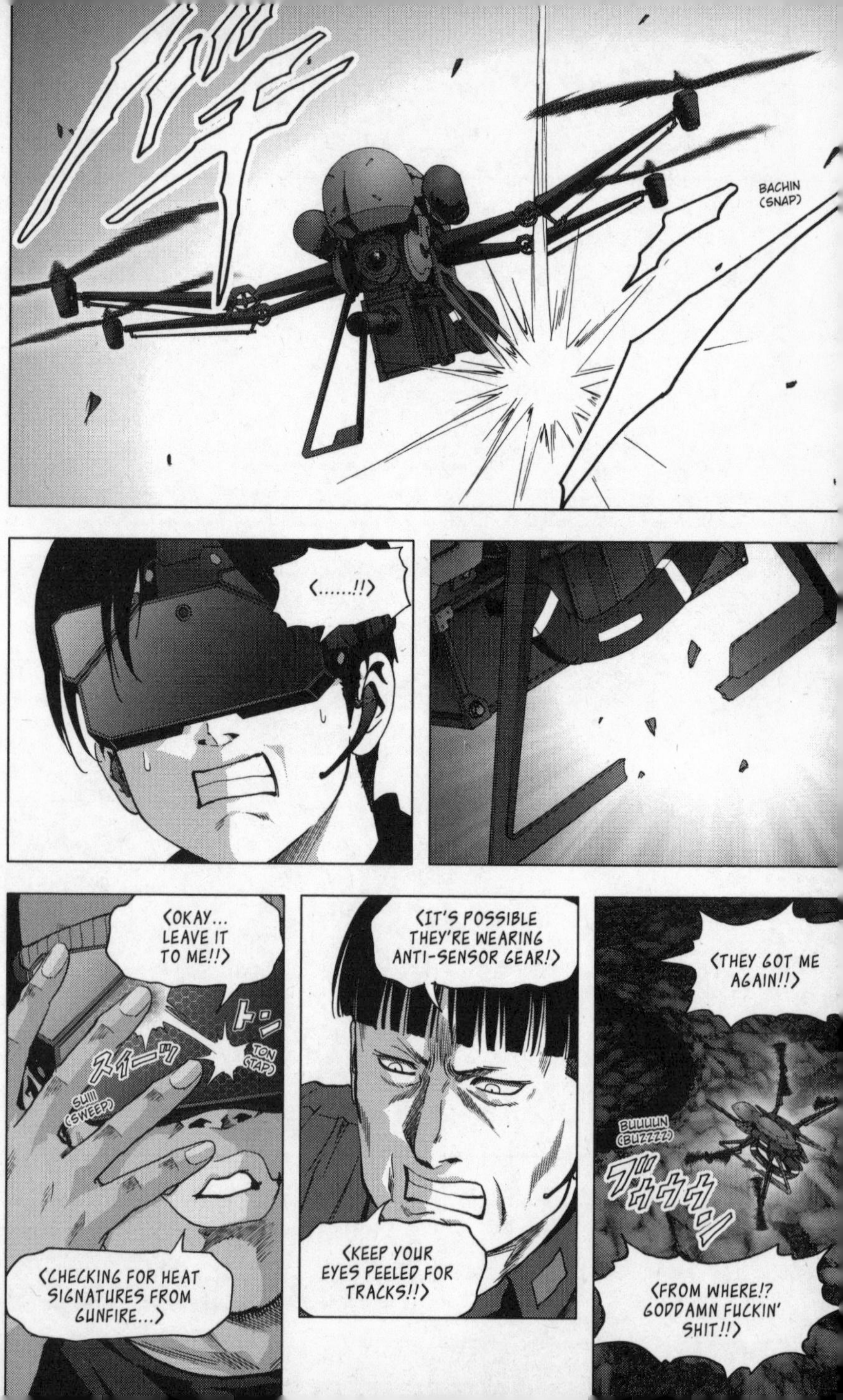
BACHIN (SNAP)
〈......!!〉
〈THEY GOT ME AGAIN!!〉
BUUUUN (BUZZZZ)
〈FROM WHERE!? GODDAMN FUCKIN' SHIT!!〉
〈IT'S POSSIBLE THEY'RE WEARING ANTI-SENSOR GEAR!〉
〈KEEP YOUR EYES PEELED FOR TRACKS!!〉
〈OKAY... LEAVE IT TO ME!!〉
TON (TAP)
SUIII (SWEEP)
〈CHECKING FOR HEAT SIGNATURES FROM GUNFIRE...〉

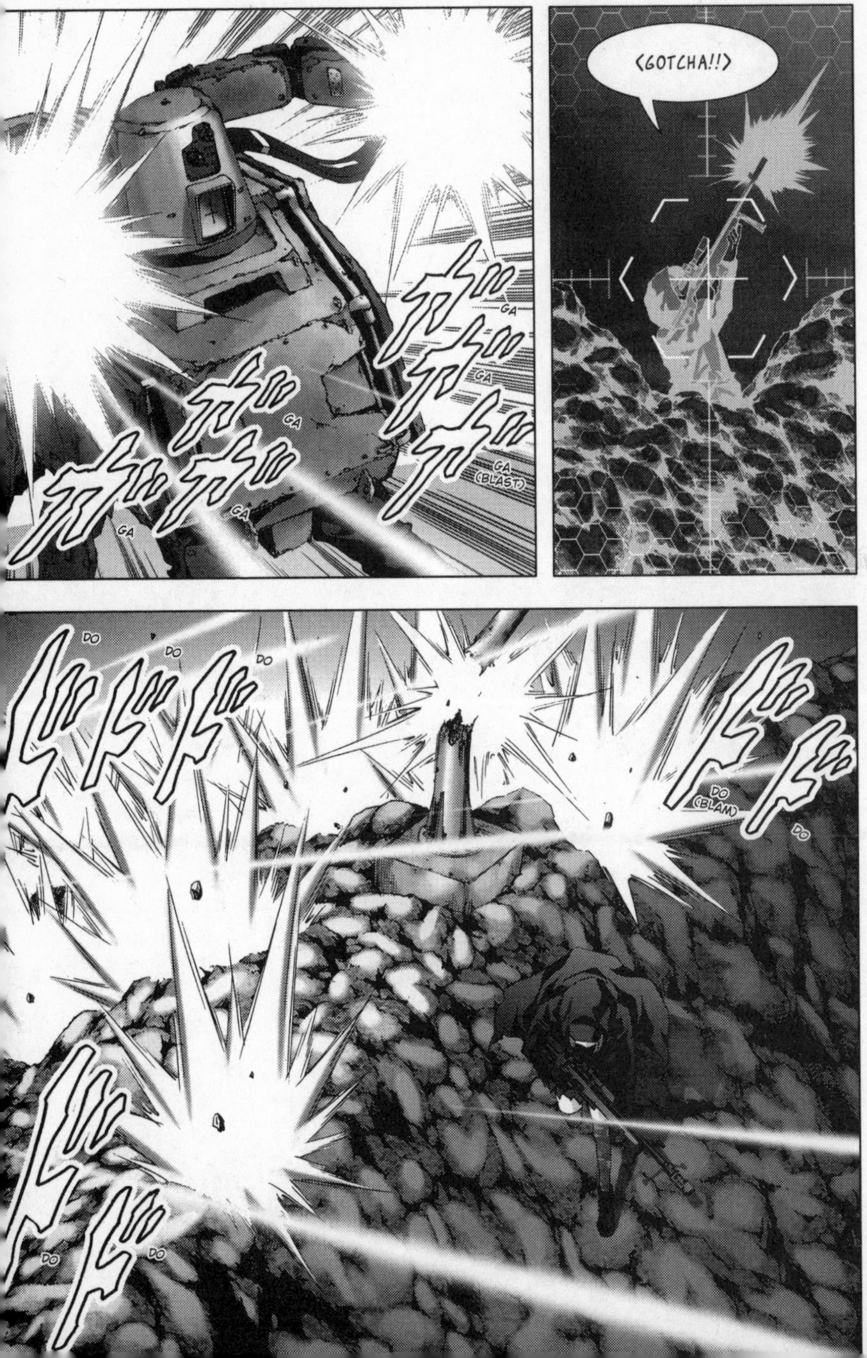
〈GOTCHA!!〉
GA
GA
GA
GA
(BLAST)
GA
GA
DO
(BLAM)
DO
DO
DO
DO
DO
DO

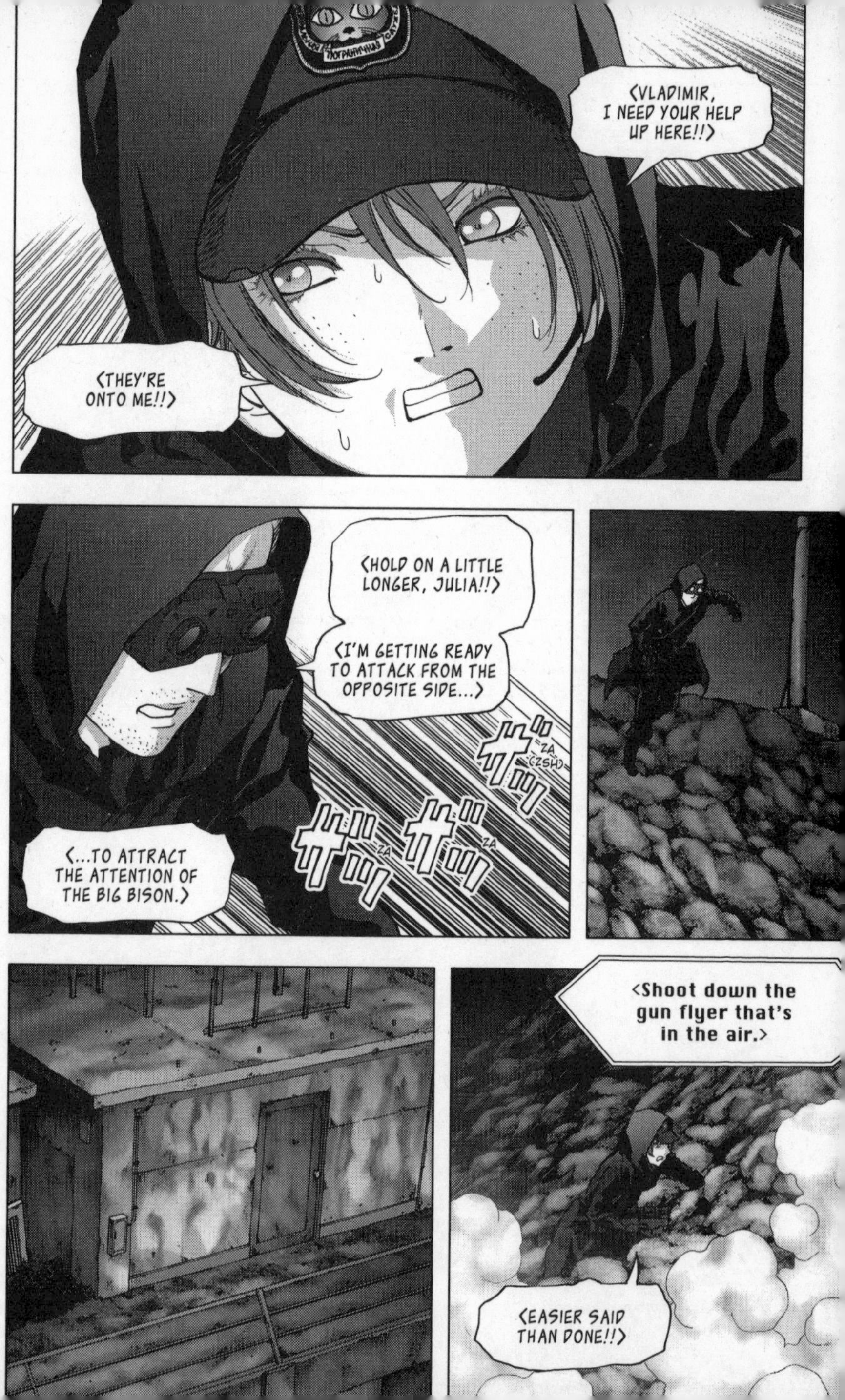
<VLADIMIR, I NEED YOUR HELP UP HERE!!>
<THEY'RE ONTO ME!!>
<HOLD ON A LITTLE LONGER, JULIA!!>
<I'M GETTING READY TO ATTACK FROM THE OPPOSITE SIDE...>
ZA (ZSH)
ZA
ZA
<...TO ATTRACT THE ATTENTION OF THE BIG BISON.>
<Shoot down the gun flyer that's in the air.>
<EASIER SAID THAN DONE!!>

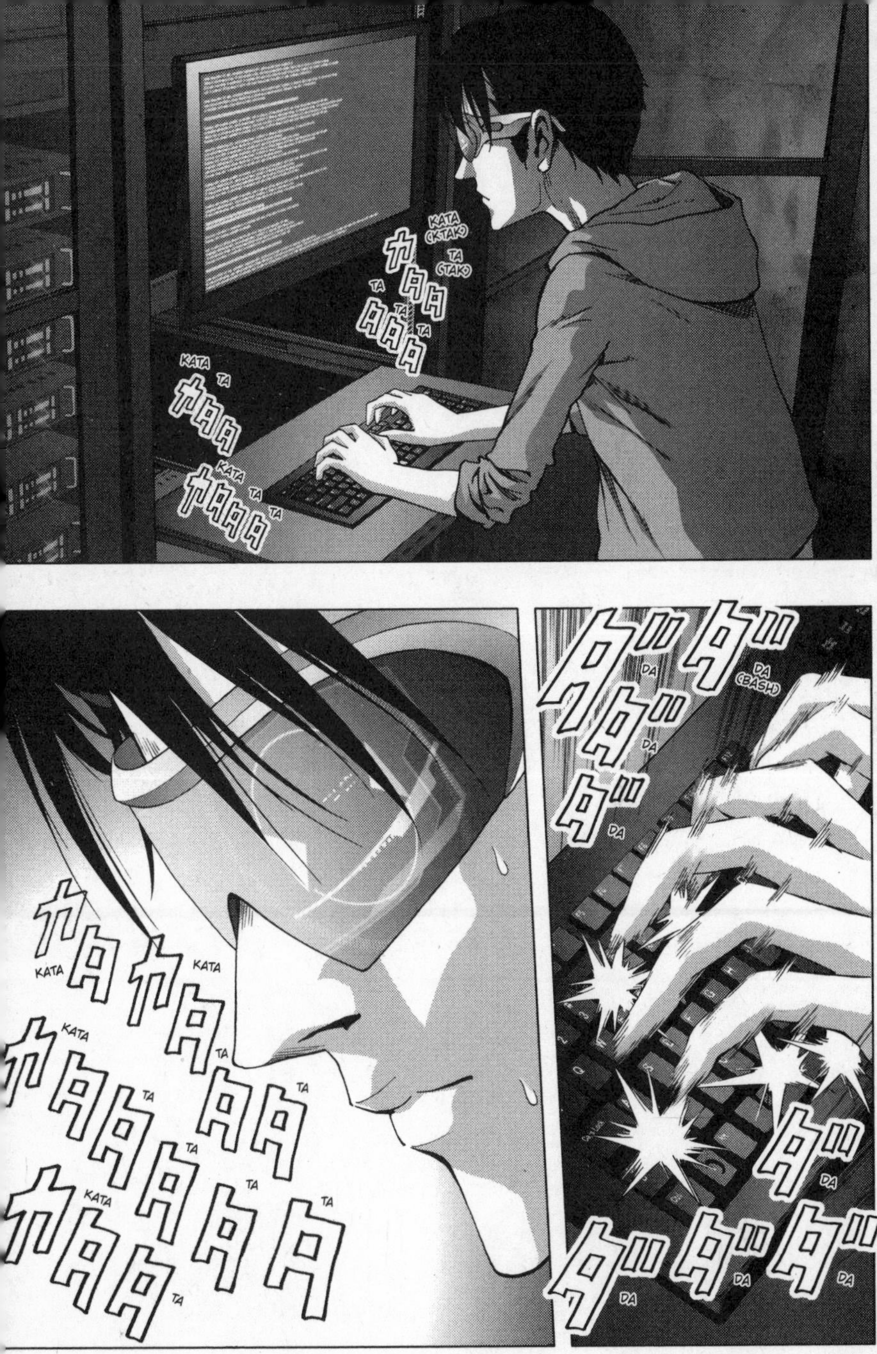
KATA (KTAK)
TA (TAK)
TA
TA
TA
KATA TA
KATA TA TA
DA (BASH)
DA
DA
DA
DA
DA
DA
DA
KATA
KATA
KATA
TA
TA
TA
TA
TA
KATA
TA
TA

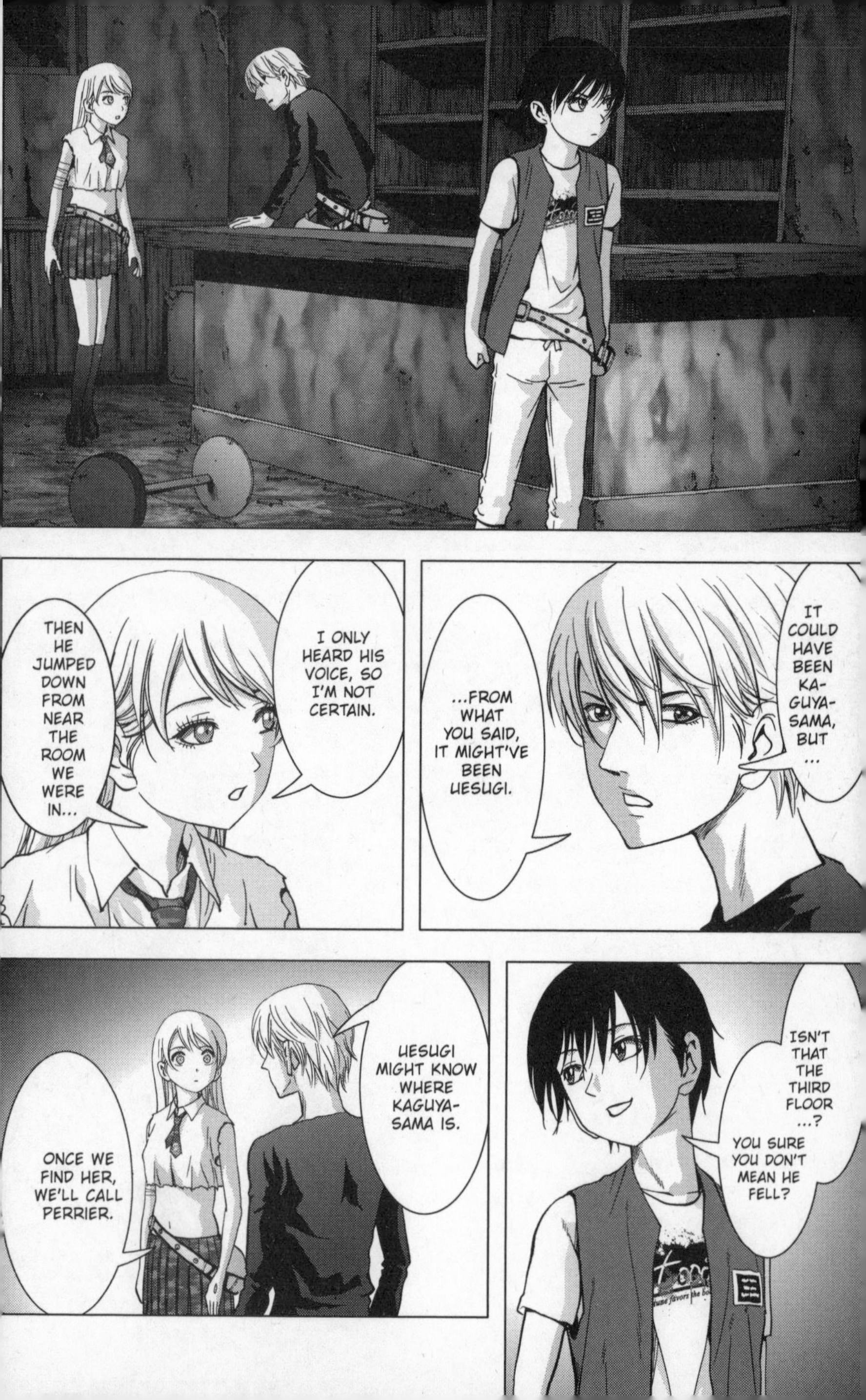
IT COULD HAVE BEEN KAGUYA-SAMA, BUT...
...FROM WHAT YOU SAID, IT MIGHT'VE BEEN UESUGI.
I ONLY HEARD HIS VOICE, SO I'M NOT CERTAIN.
THEN HE JUMPED DOWN FROM NEAR THE ROOM WE WERE IN...
ISN'T THAT THE THIRD FLOOR...?
YOU SURE YOU DON'T MEAN HE FELL?
UESUGI MIGHT KNOW WHERE KAGUYA-SAMA IS.
ONCE WE FIND HER, WE'LL CALL PERRIER.

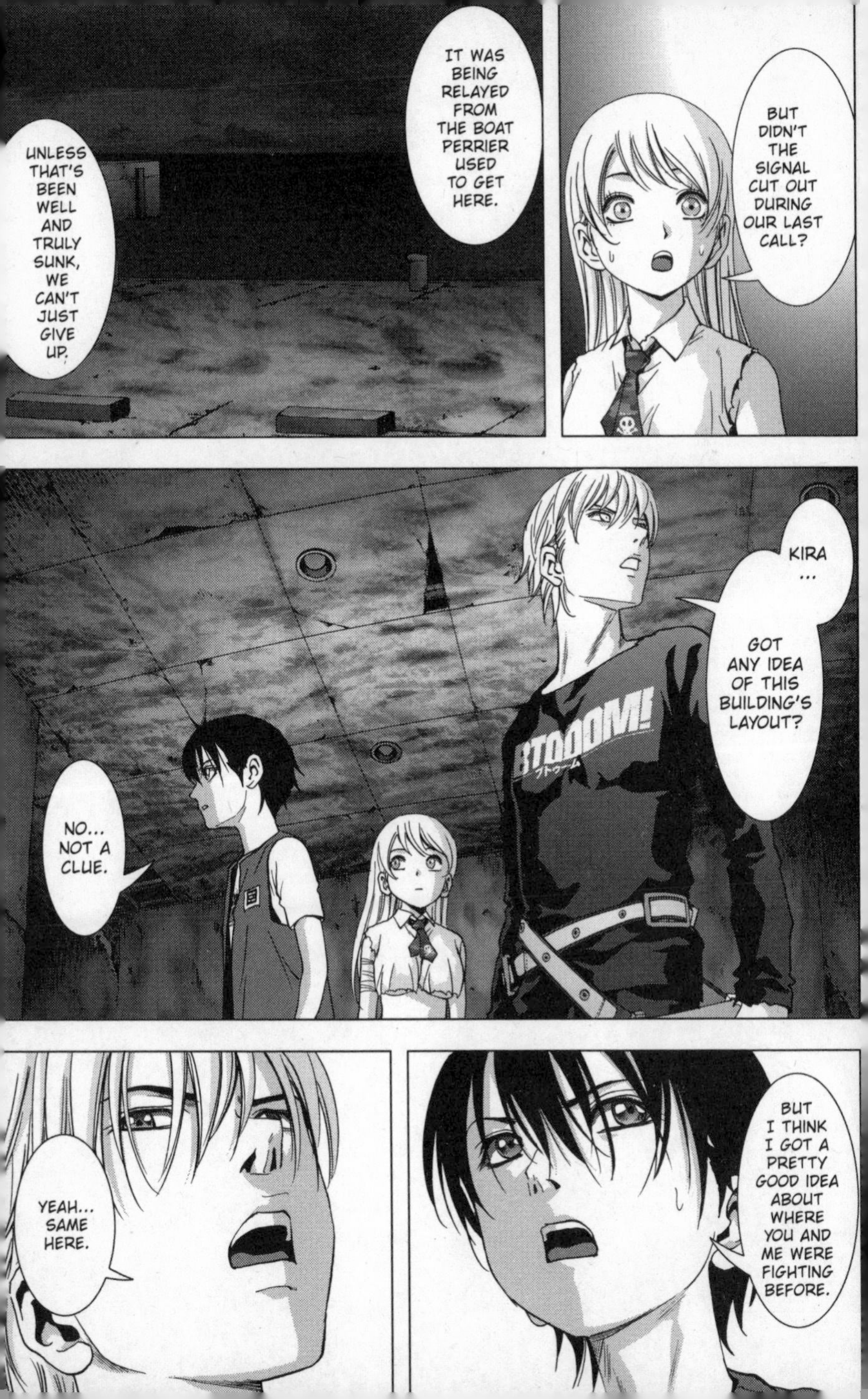
BUT DIDN'T THE SIGNAL CUT OUT DURING OUR LAST CALL?
IT WAS BEING RELAYED FROM THE BOAT PERRIER USED TO GET HERE.
UNLESS THAT'S BEEN WELL AND TRULY SUNK, WE CAN'T JUST GIVE UP.
KIRA...
GOT ANY IDEA OF THIS BUILDING'S LAYOUT?
BTOOOM!
NO... NOT A CLUE.
BUT I THINK I GOT A PRETTY GOOD IDEA ABOUT WHERE YOU AND ME WERE FIGHTING BEFORE.
YEAH... SAME HERE.

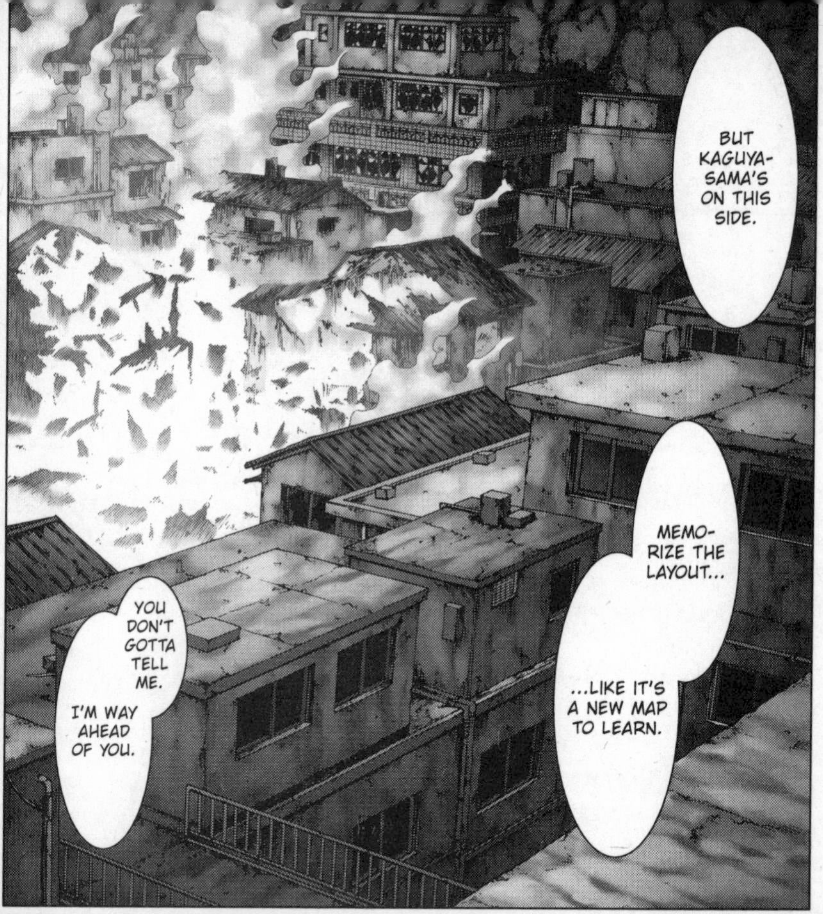
BUT KAGUYA-SAMA'S ON THIS SIDE.
MEMORIZE THE LAYOUT...
...LIKE IT'S A NEW MAP TO LEARN.
YOU DON'T GOTTA TELL ME.
I'M WAY AHEAD OF YOU.

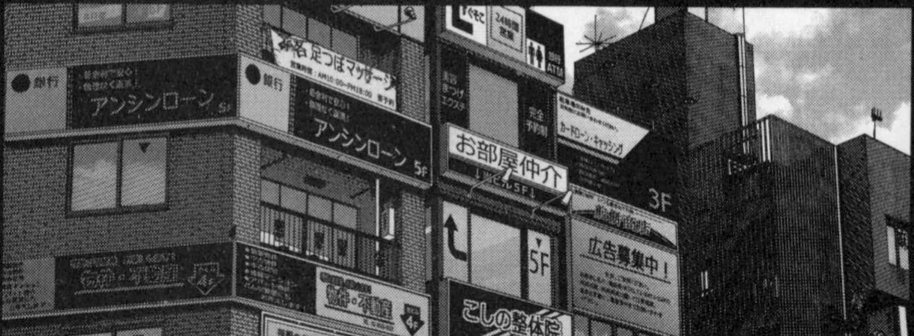
お部屋仲介
広告募集中！
アンシンローン
こしの整体院
賃貸
5F
3F
4F

SIGNS: BANK / TWENTY-FOUR HOUR SERVICE / SUPER-CLOSE! / RESERVATIONS ONLY / BEAUTY / EYEBROWS / SKIN CARE / ROOM FIND / 5TH FLOOR / KOSHINO CHIROPRACTIC CLINIC / WE'LL CURE YOUR ACHES AND PAINS! / HOURS OF OPERATION: 10:00 AM-19:00 PM / PARKING COVERED! / CARD LOAN CASHING / CRACKERS SHOP / YOUR AD HERE! / REFLEXOLOGY [illegible] 10:00 AM-18:00 PM / BY APPOINTMENT / [illegible]

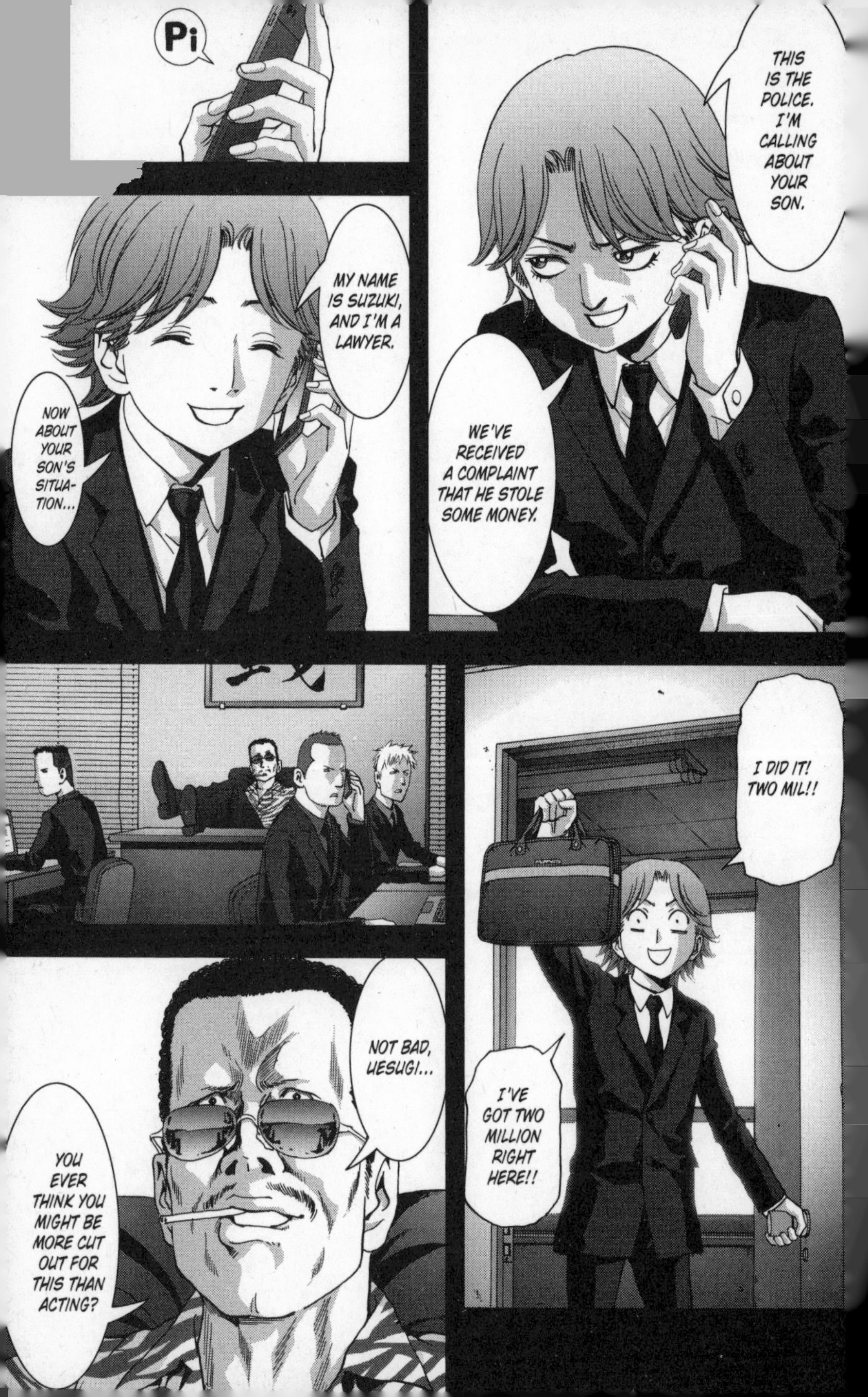
THIS IS THE POLICE. I'M CALLING ABOUT YOUR SON.
WE'VE RECEIVED A COMPLAINT THAT HE STOLE SOME MONEY.
Pi
MY NAME IS SUZUKI, AND I'M A LAWYER.
NOW ABOUT YOUR SON'S SITUA-TION...
I DID IT! TWO MIL!!
I'VE GOT TWO MILLION RIGHT HERE!!
NOT BAD, UESUGI...
YOU EVER THINK YOU MIGHT BE MORE CUT OUT FOR THIS THAN ACTING?

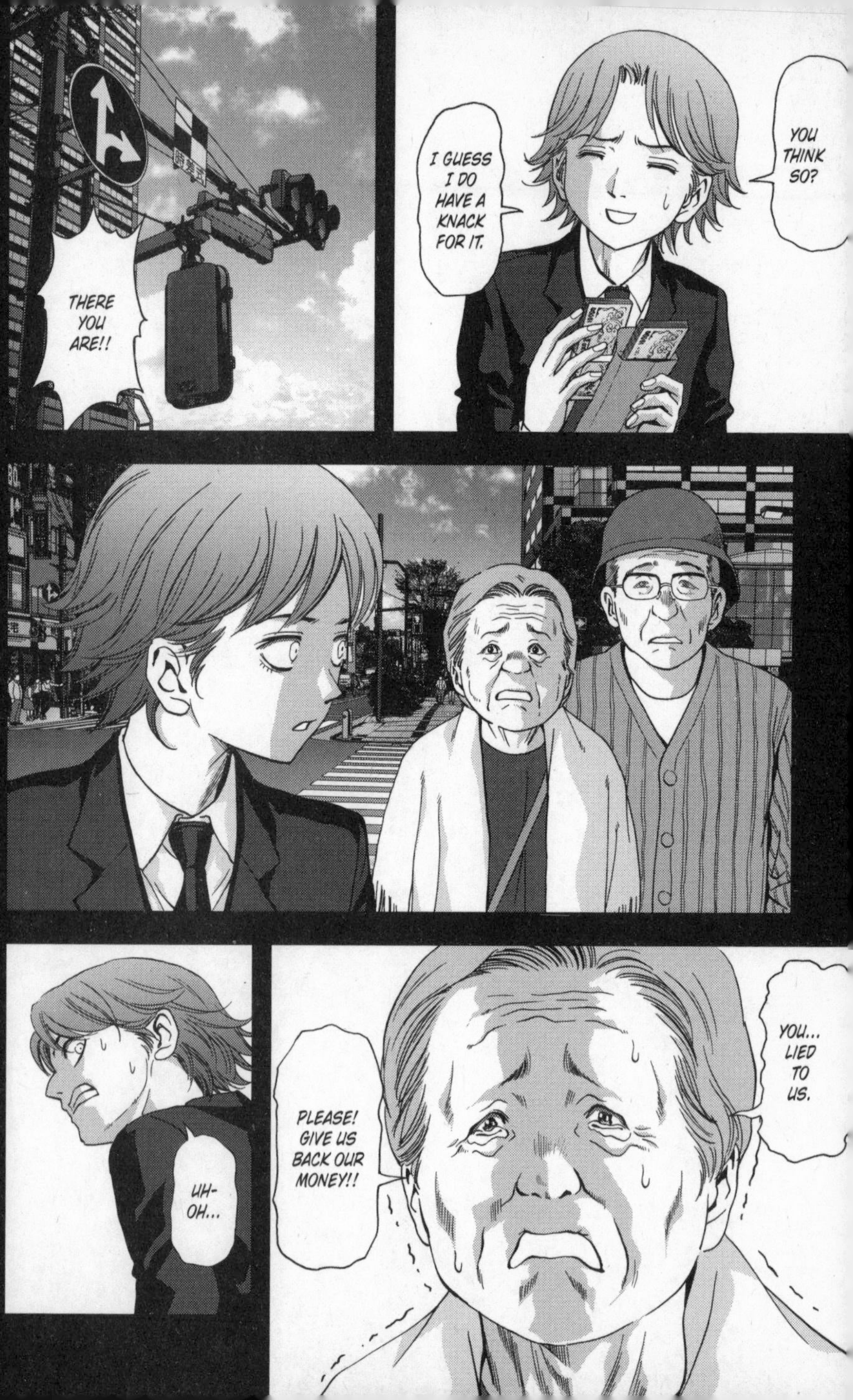
YOU THINK SO?
I GUESS I DO HAVE A KNACK FOR IT.
THERE YOU ARE!!
YOU... LIED TO US.
PLEASE! GIVE US BACK OUR MONEY!!
UH-OH...

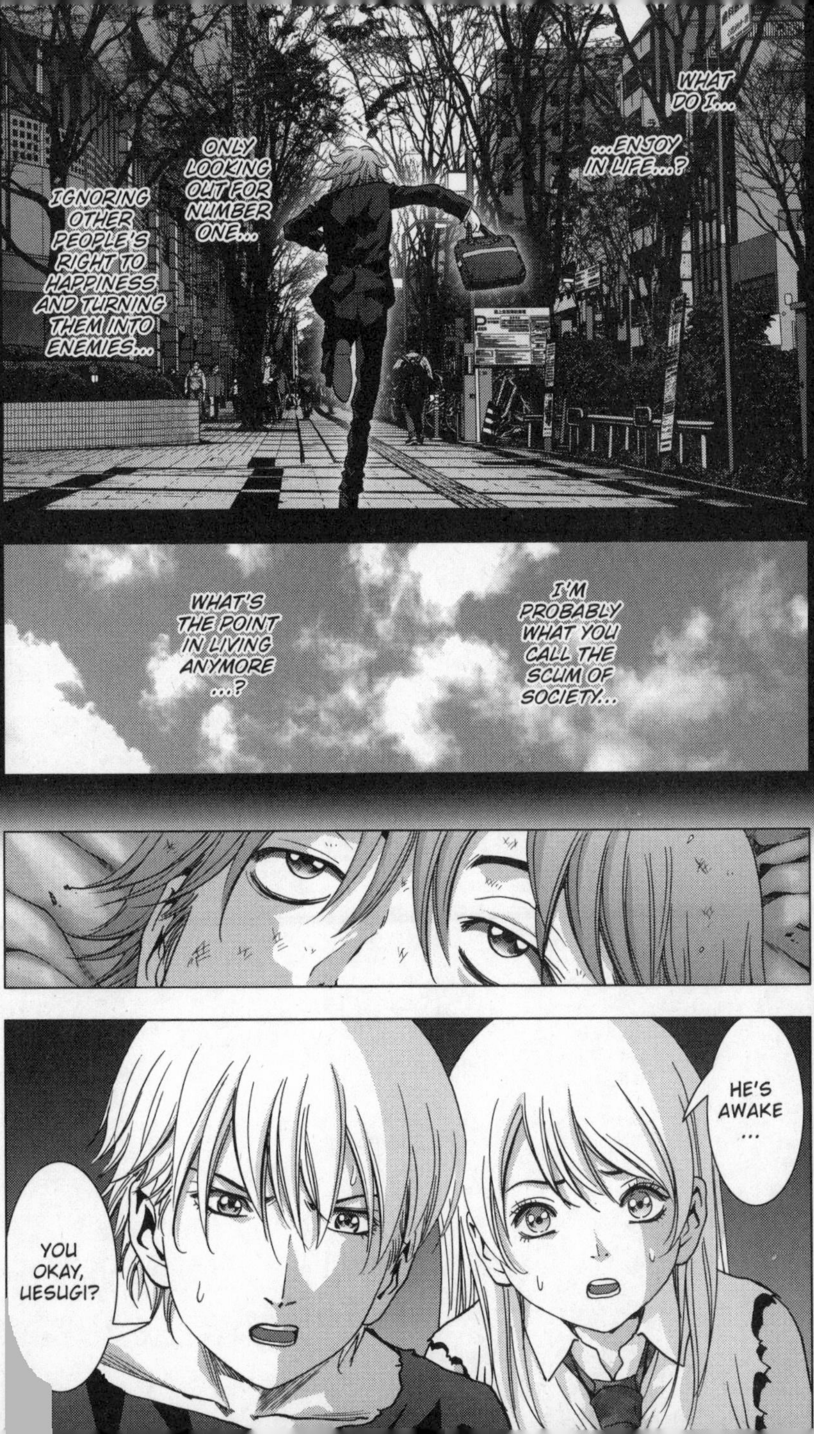
WHAT DO I...
...ENJOY IN LIFE...?
ONLY LOOKING OUT FOR NUMBER ONE...
IGNORING OTHER PEOPLE'S RIGHT TO HAPPINESS AND TURNING THEM INTO ENEMIES...
I'M PROBABLY WHAT YOU CALL THE SCUM OF SOCIETY...
WHAT'S THE POINT IN LIVING ANYMORE...?
HE'S AWAKE...
YOU OKAY, UESUGI?

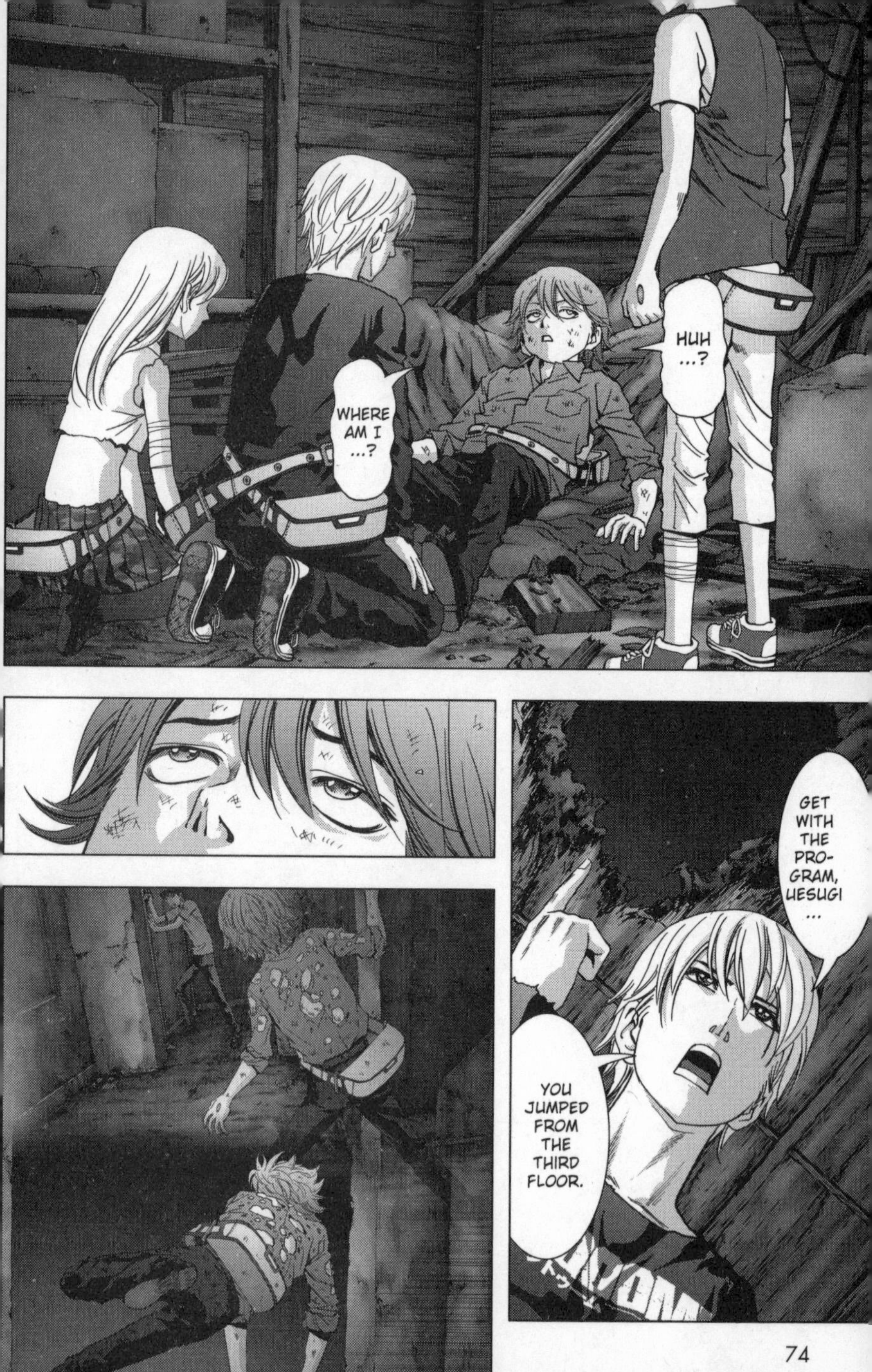
HUH ...?
WHERE AM I ...?
GET WITH THE PRO-GRAM, UESUGI ...
YOU JUMPED FROM THE THIRD FLOOR.

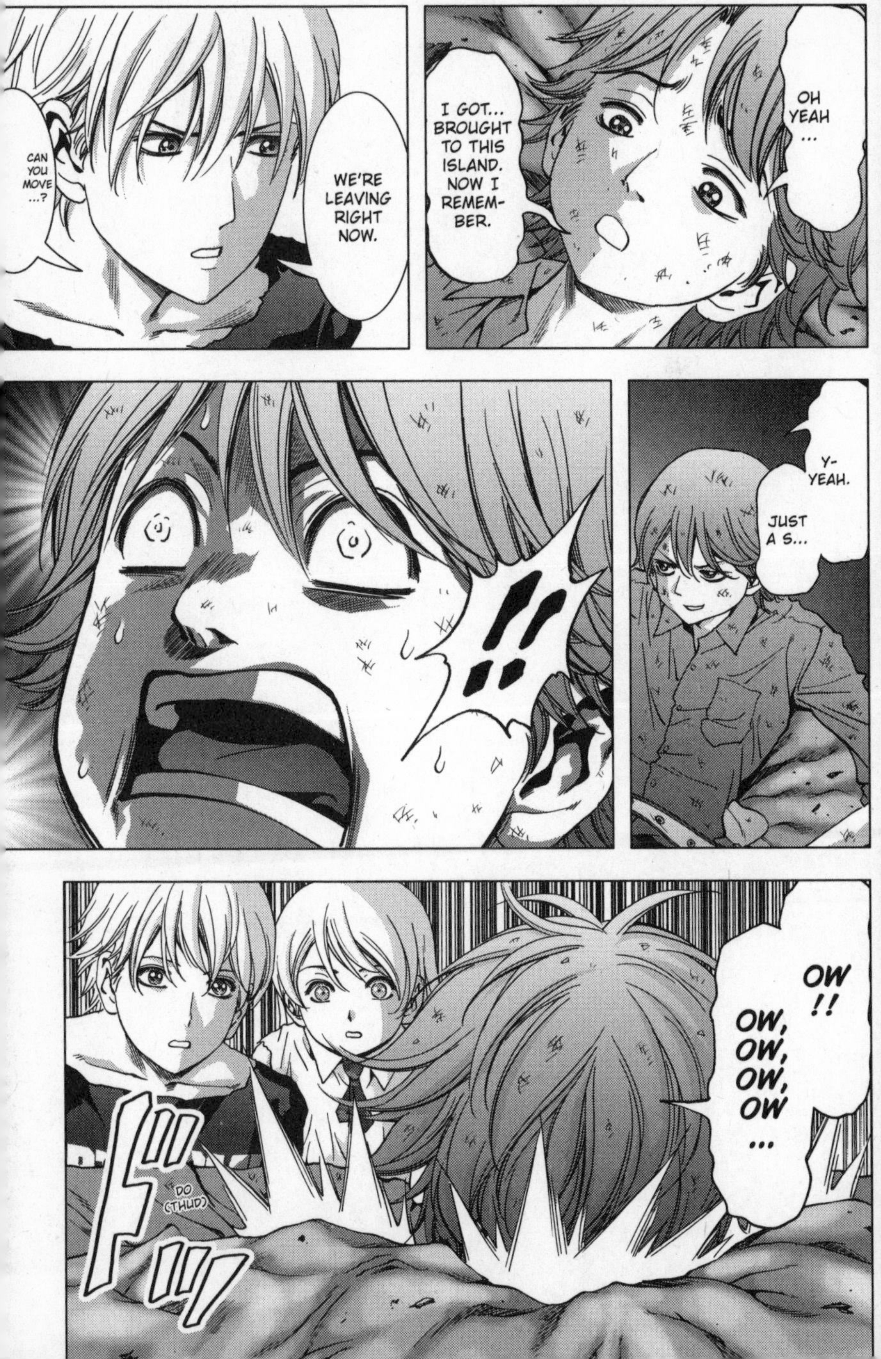
OH YEAH ...
I GOT... BROUGHT TO THIS ISLAND. NOW I REMEMBER.
WE'RE LEAVING RIGHT NOW.
CAN YOU MOVE ...?
Y-YEAH.
JUST A S...
!!
OW!! OW, OW, OW, OW ...
DO (THUD)

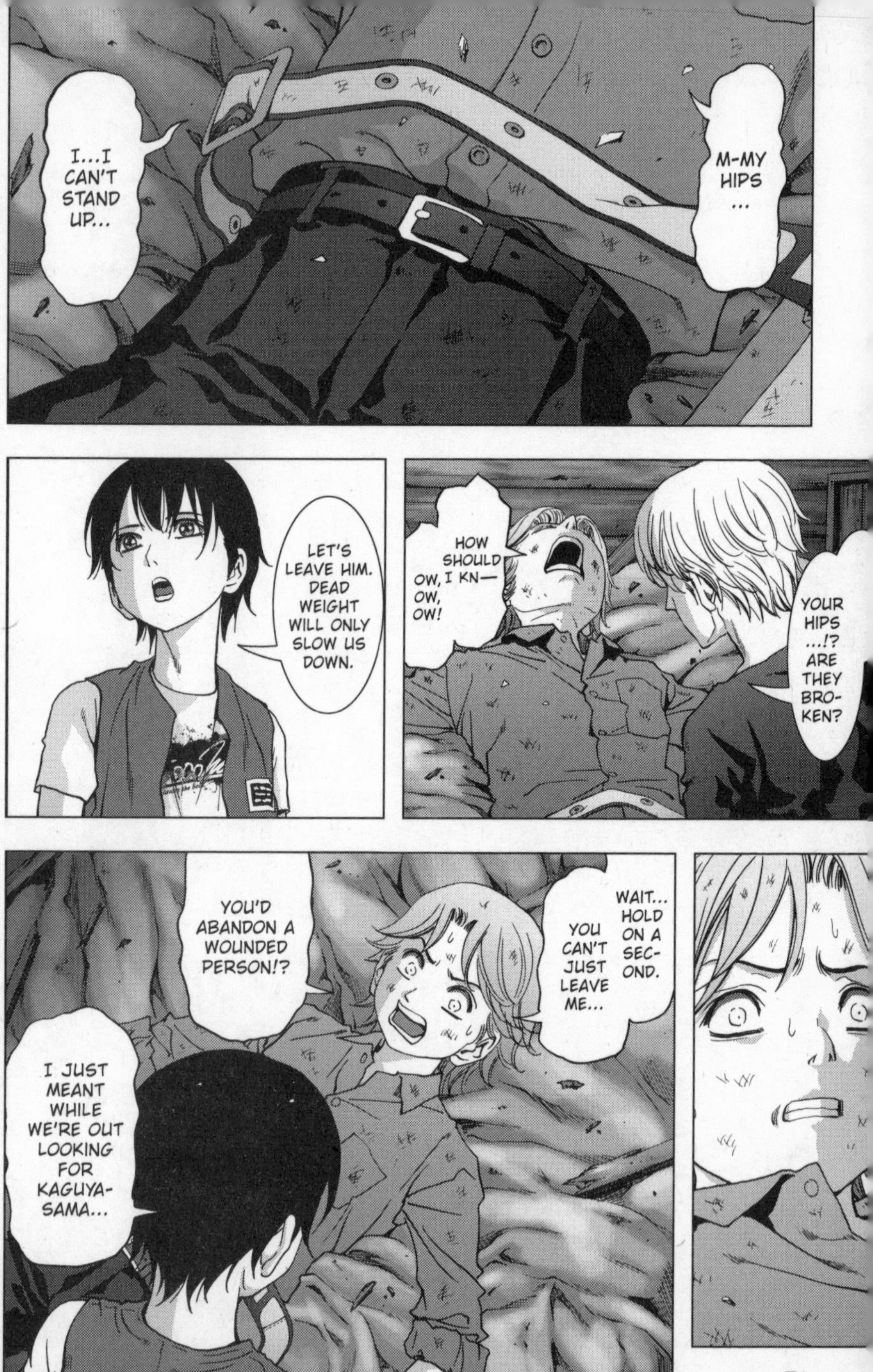
M-MY HIPS ...
I...I CAN'T STAND UP...
YOUR HIPS ...!? ARE THEY BRO-KEN?
HOW SHOULD I KN— OW, OW, OW!
LET'S LEAVE HIM. DEAD WEIGHT WILL ONLY SLOW US DOWN.
WAIT... HOLD ON A SEC-OND.
YOU CAN'T JUST LEAVE ME...
YOU'D ABANDON A WOUNDED PERSON!?
I JUST MEANT WHILE WE'RE OUT LOOKING FOR KAGUYA-SAMA...

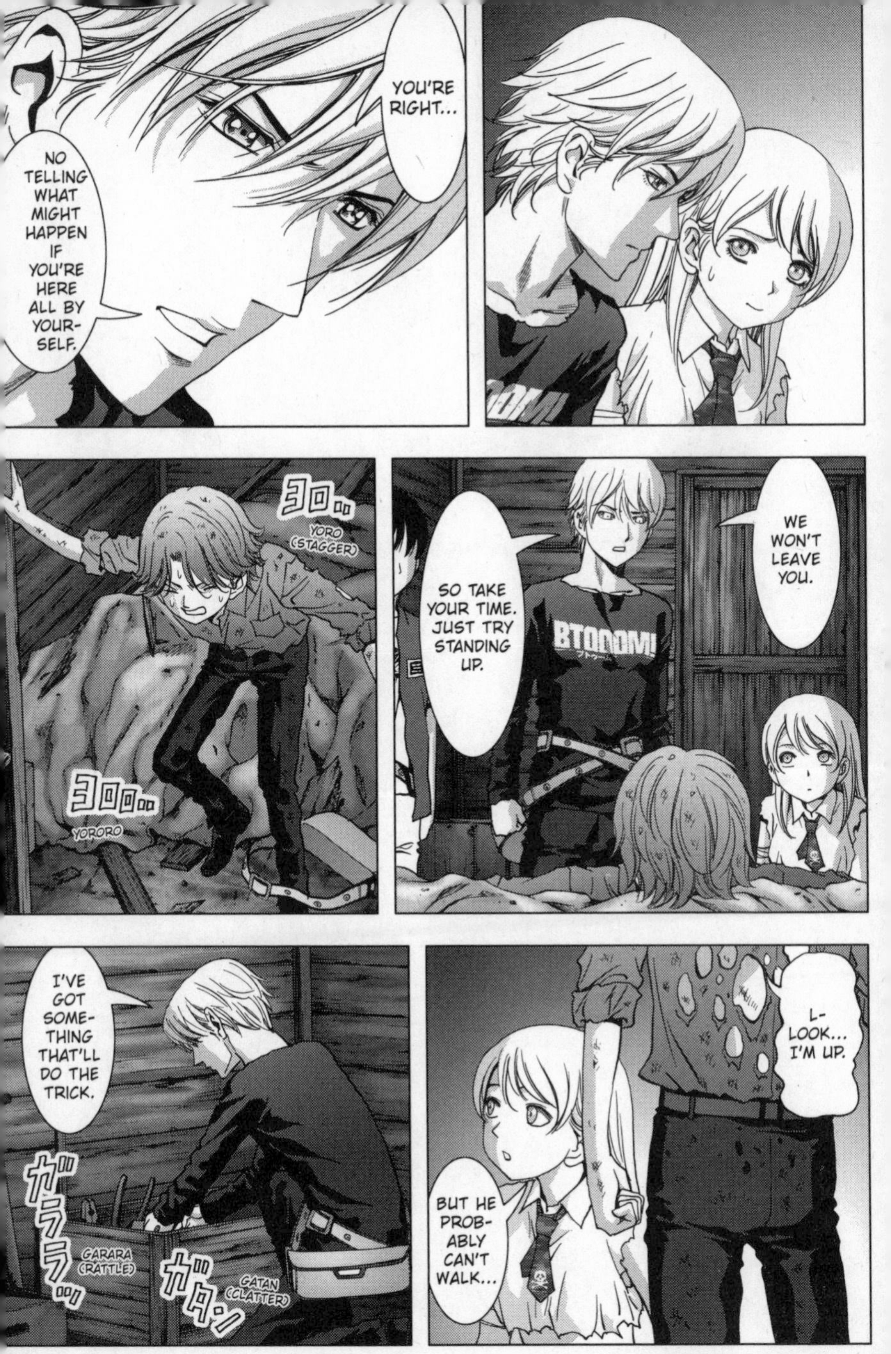

YOU'RE RIGHT...
NO TELLING WHAT MIGHT HAPPEN IF YOU'RE HERE ALL BY YOURSELF.
WE WON'T LEAVE YOU.
SO TAKE YOUR TIME. JUST TRY STANDING UP.
ヨロ..
YORO (STAGGER)
ヨロロ...
YORORO
L-LOOK... I'M UP.
BUT HE PROBABLY CAN'T WALK...
I'VE GOT SOMETHING THAT'LL DO THE TRICK.
ガララ...
GARARA (RATTLE)
ガタン
GATAN (CLATTER)

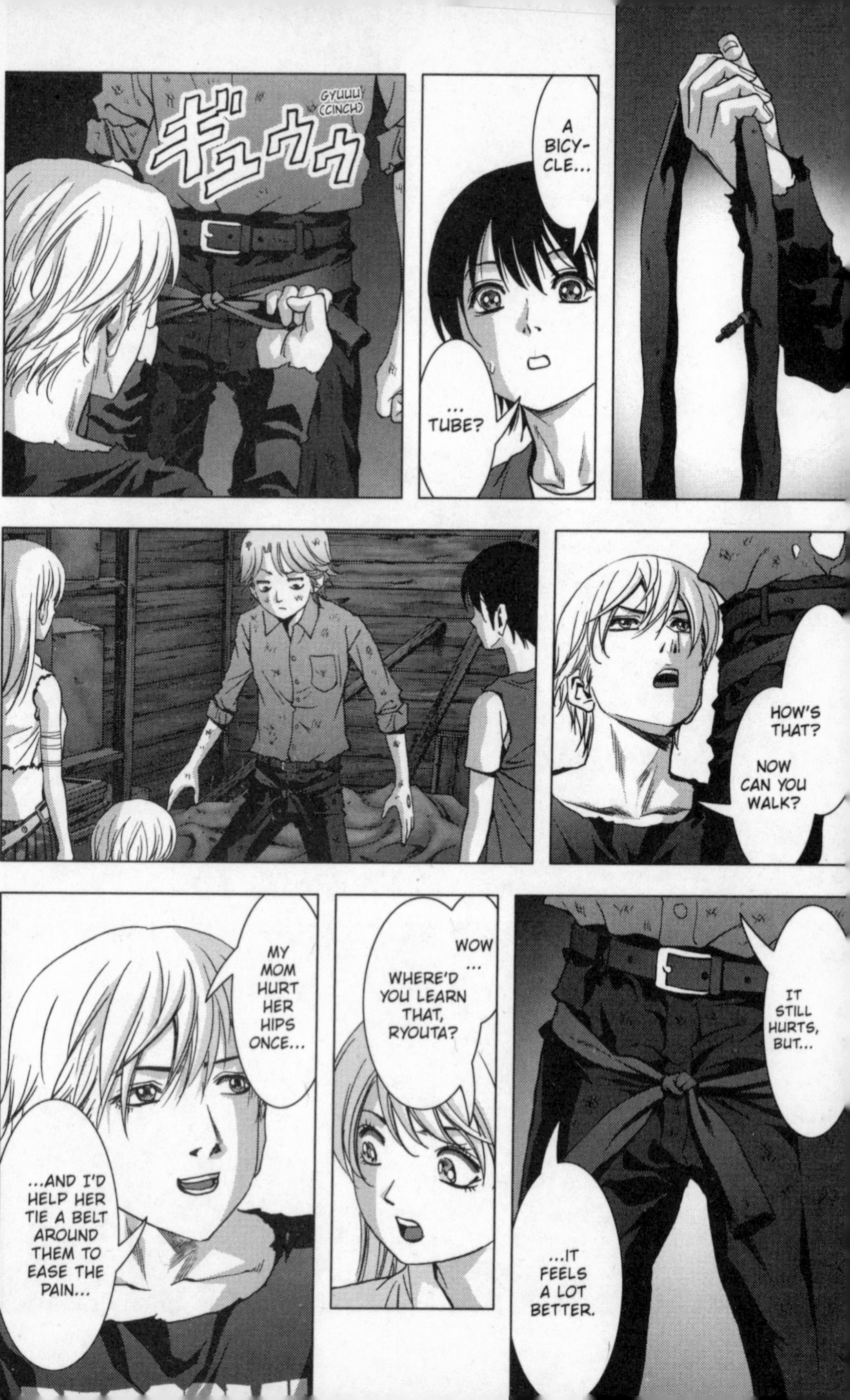
A BICYCLE...
...TUBE?
ギュウウ
GYUUU (CINCH)
HOW'S THAT?
NOW CAN YOU WALK?
IT STILL HURTS, BUT...
...IT FEELS A LOT BETTER.
WOW...
WHERE'D YOU LEARN THAT, RYOUTA?
MY MOM HURT HER HIPS ONCE...
...AND I'D HELP HER TIE A BELT AROUND THEM TO EASE THE PAIN...

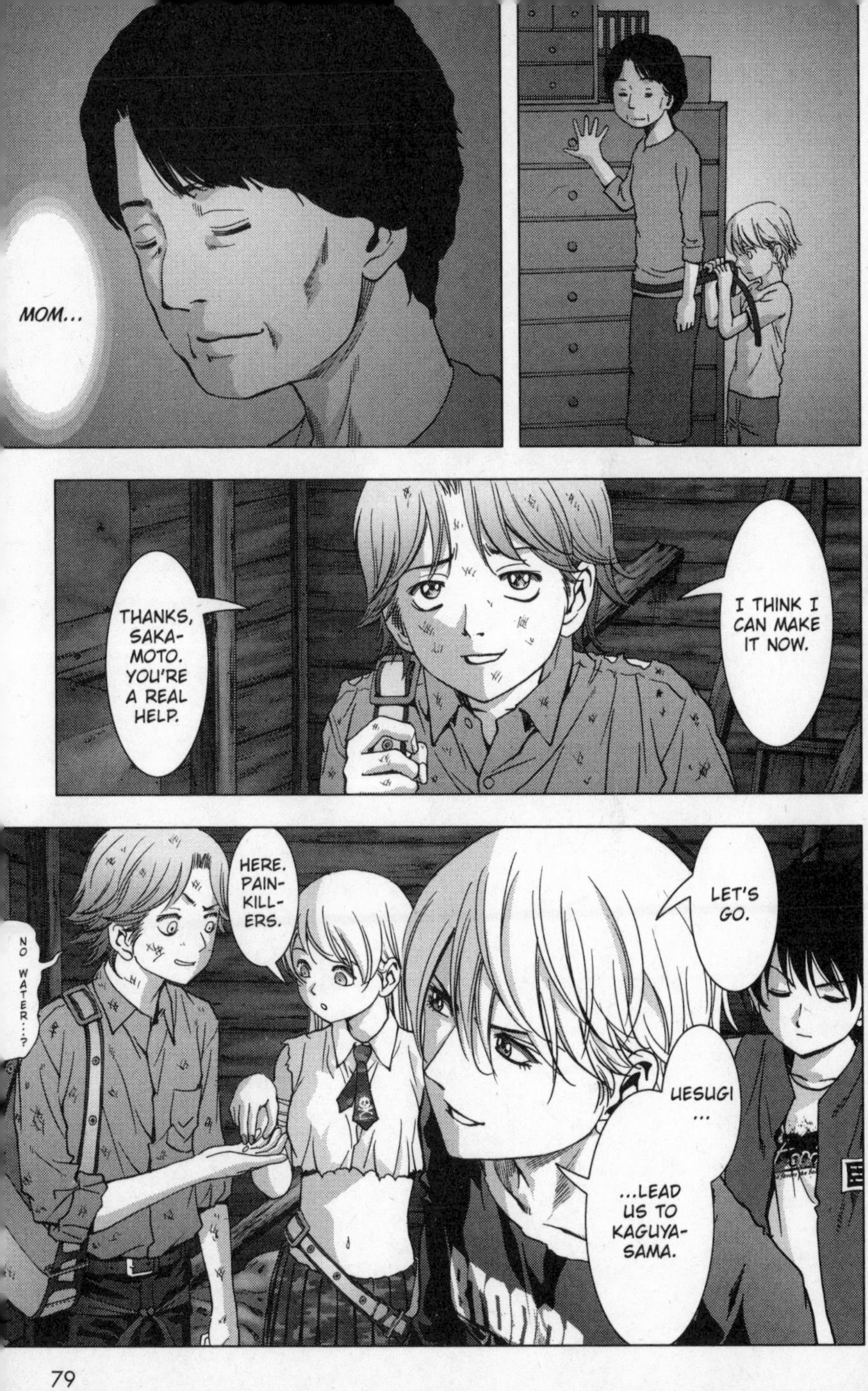
MOM...
I THINK I CAN MAKE IT NOW.
THANKS, SAKAMOTO. YOU'RE A REAL HELP.
LET'S GO.
UESUGI...
...LEAD US TO KAGUYA-SAMA.
HERE. PAINKILLERS.
NO WATER...?

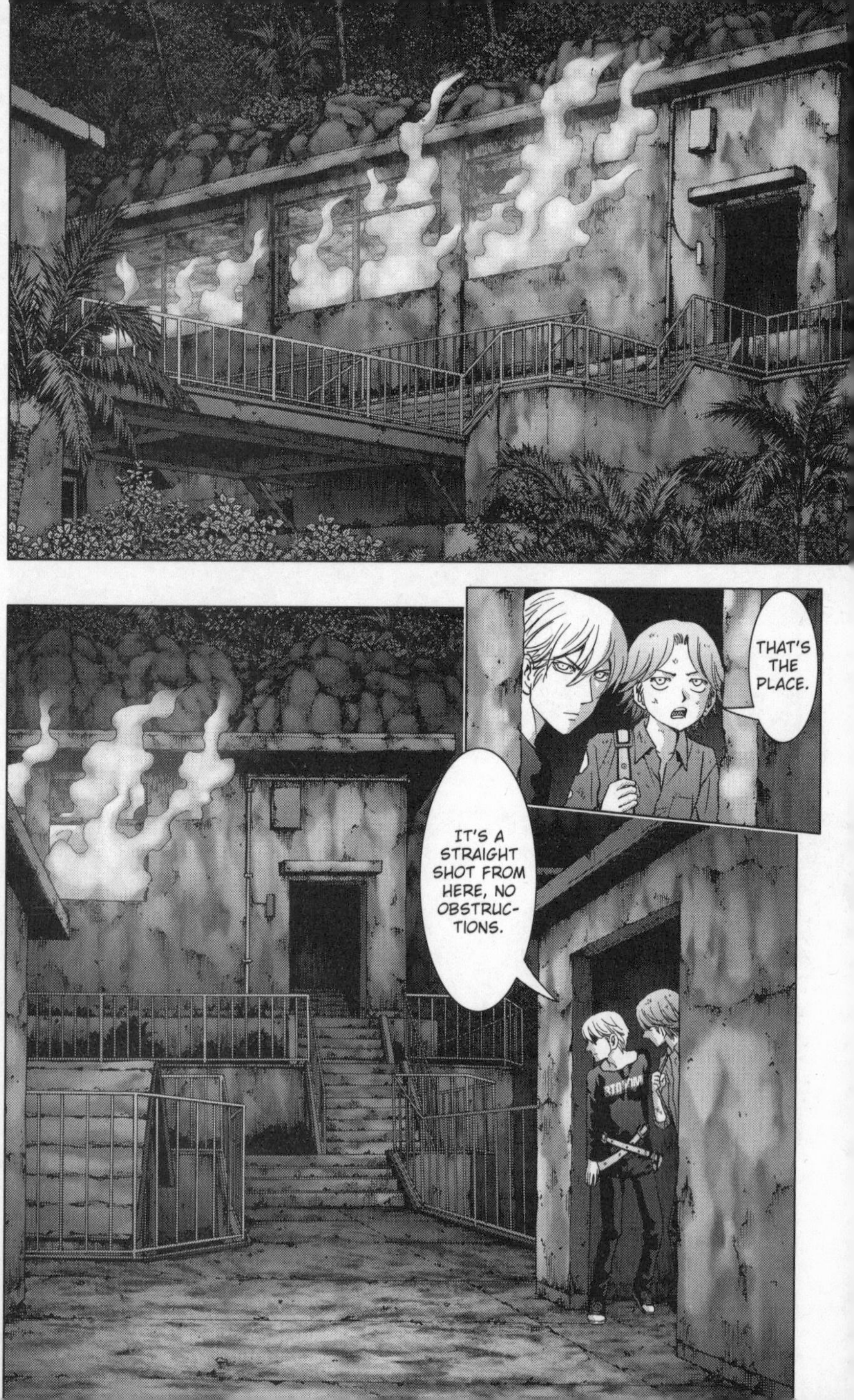
THAT'S THE PLACE.
IT'S A STRAIGHT SHOT FROM HERE, NO OBSTRUC-TIONS.

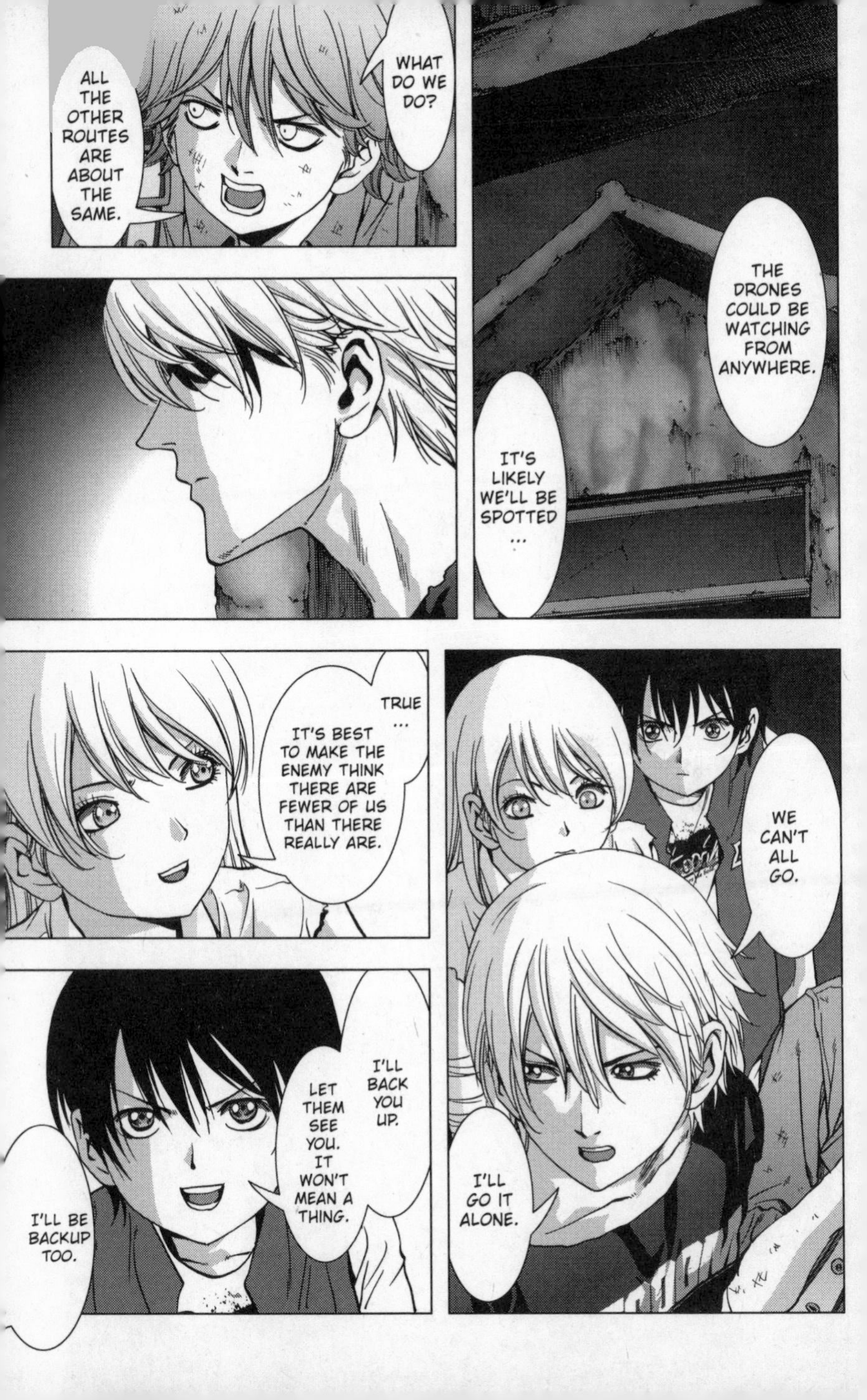
THE DRONES COULD BE WATCHING FROM ANYWHERE.
IT'S LIKELY WE'LL BE SPOTTED ...
WHAT DO WE DO?
ALL THE OTHER ROUTES ARE ABOUT THE SAME.
WE CAN'T ALL GO.
I'LL GO IT ALONE.
TRUE ...
IT'S BEST TO MAKE THE ENEMY THINK THERE ARE FEWER OF US THAN THERE REALLY ARE.
I'LL BACK YOU UP.
LET THEM SEE YOU. IT WON'T MEAN A THING.
I'LL BE BACKUP TOO.

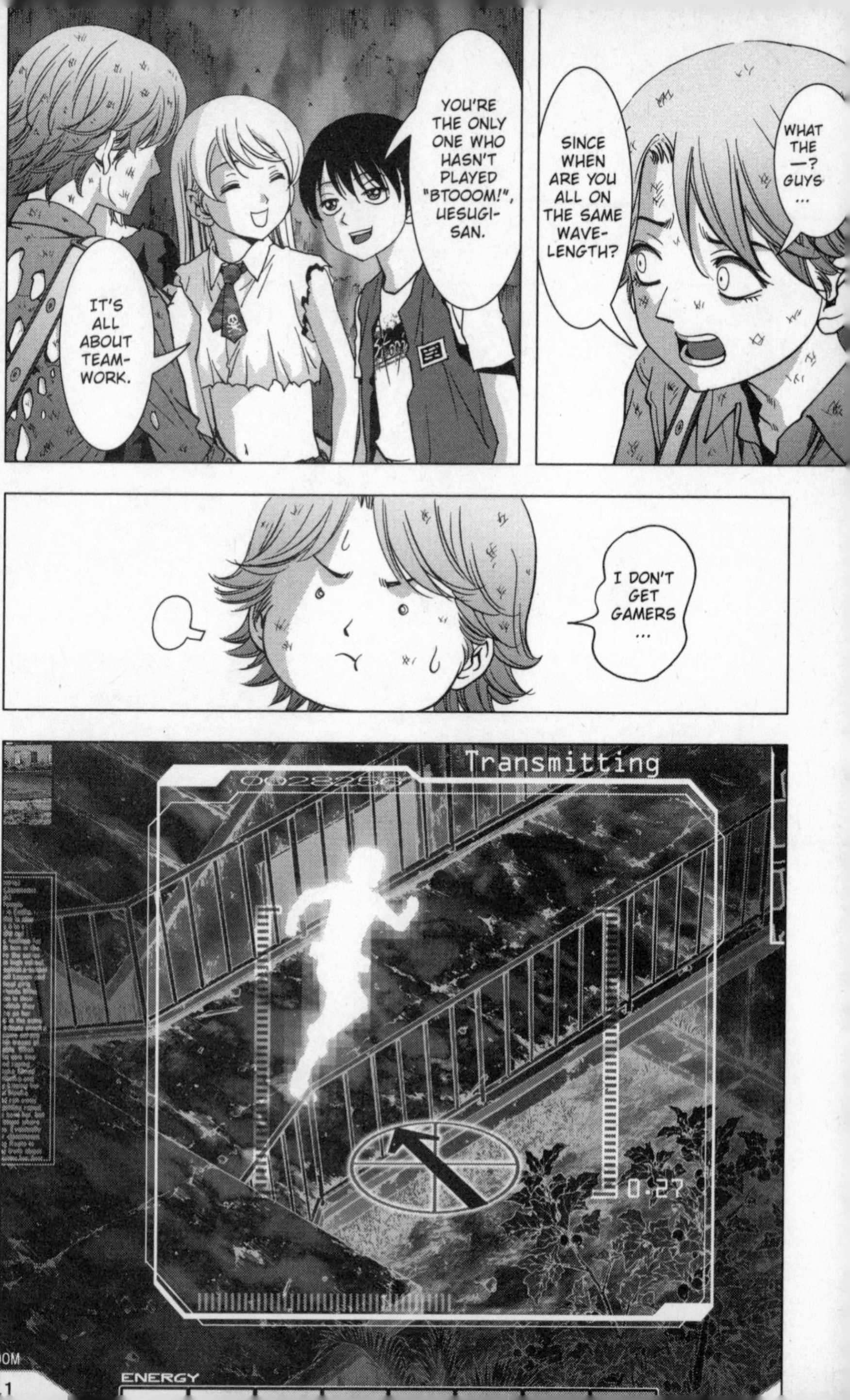
WHAT THE —? GUYS ...
SINCE WHEN ARE YOU ALL ON THE SAME WAVE-LENGTH?
YOU'RE THE ONLY ONE WHO HASN'T PLAYED "BTOOOM!", UESUGI-SAN.
IT'S ALL ABOUT TEAM-WORK.
I DON'T GET GAMERS ...
Transmitting
0.27
ENERGY

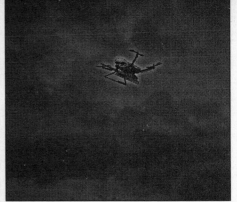

ブウウウ BUuuu (BUZZZZ)

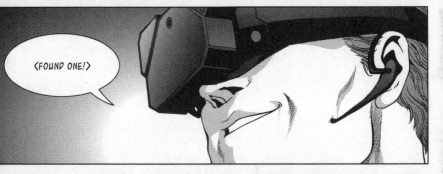

〈FOUND ONE!〉

スイーッ SUiiii (SWIPE)

スック SUi (SWISH)

スイッ SUi

〈WHERE!?〉

〈TRACE MY SEARCH COORDINATES!!〉

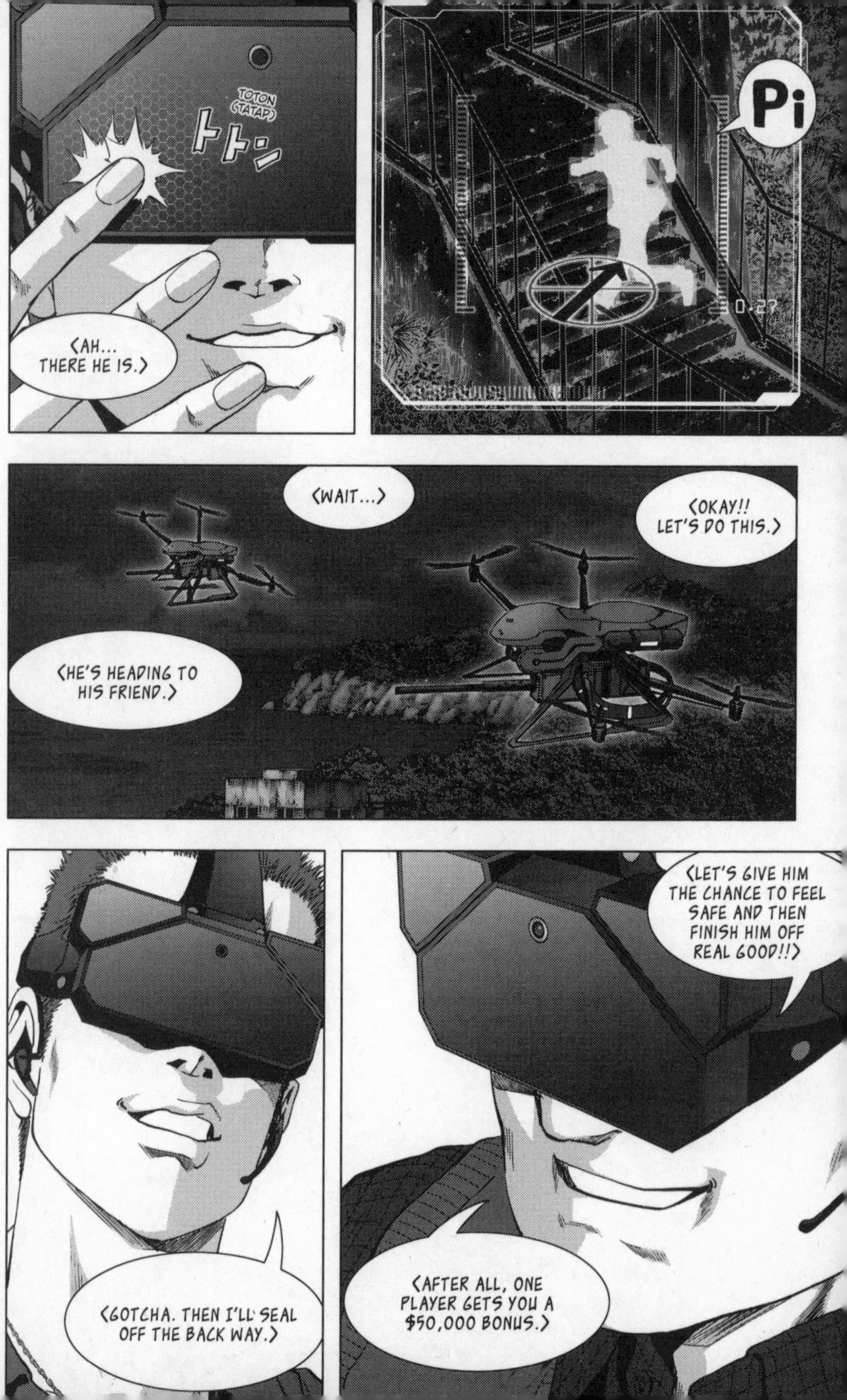
Pi
TOTON (TATAP)
トトン
〈AH... THERE HE IS.〉
〈OKAY!! LET'S DO THIS.〉
〈WAIT...〉
〈HE'S HEADING TO HIS FRIEND.〉
〈LET'S GIVE HIM THE CHANCE TO FEEL SAFE AND THEN FINISH HIM OFF REAL GOOD!!〉
〈AFTER ALL, ONE PLAYER GETS YOU A $50,000 BONUS.〉
〈GOTCHA. THEN I'LL SEAL OFF THE BACK WAY.〉

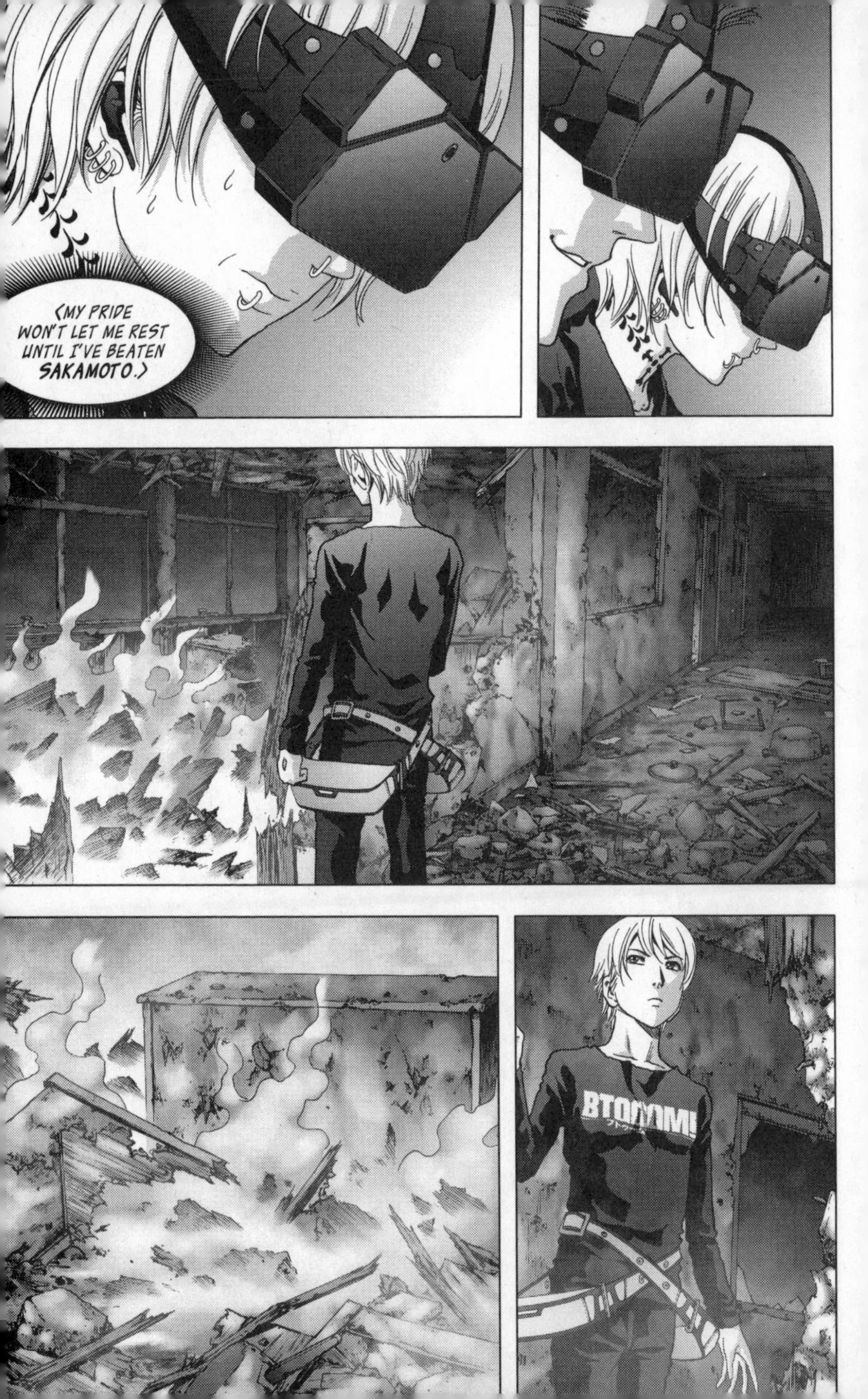

<MY PRIDE WON'T LET ME REST UNTIL I'VE BEATEN SAKAMOTO.>
BTOOOM!

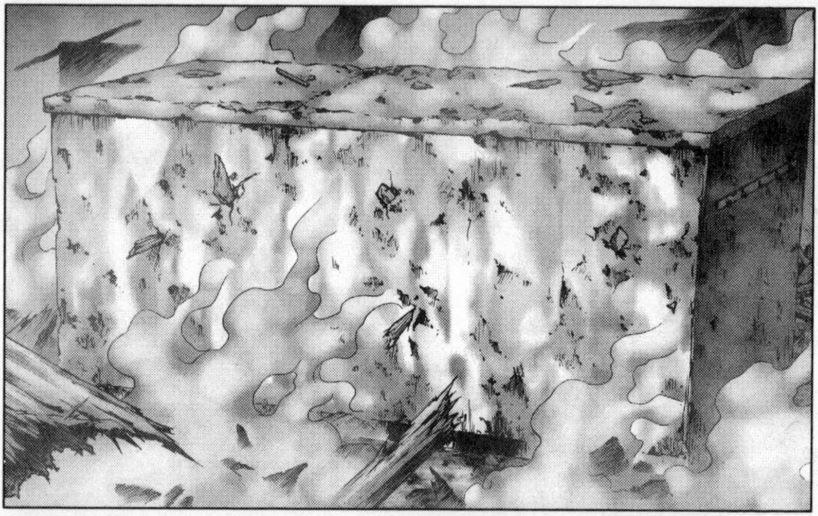

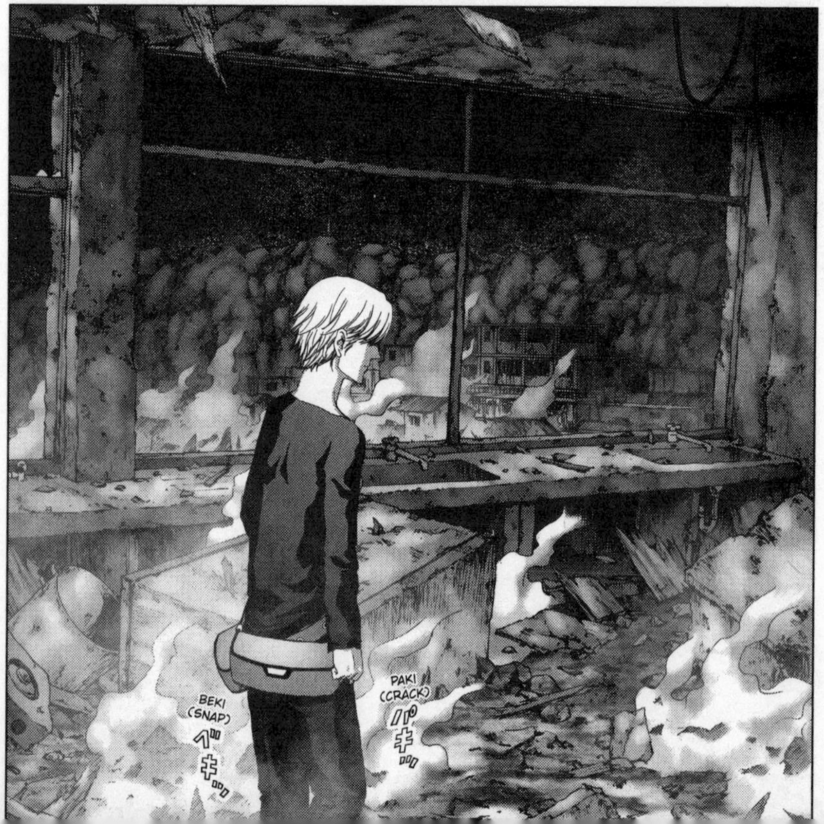
PAKI (CRACK)
BEKI (SNAP)

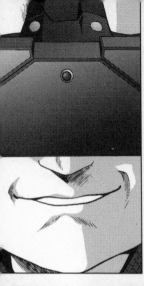

ブイイイイ BUIII
(BUZZZZ)

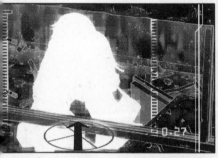

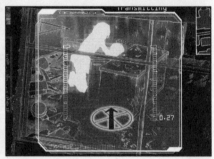

Transmitting

0.27

0.27

〈I KNEW THERE WAS A SECOND ONE!!〉

〈I DID IT!! WITH THIS...〉

GU
(PRESS)

GU

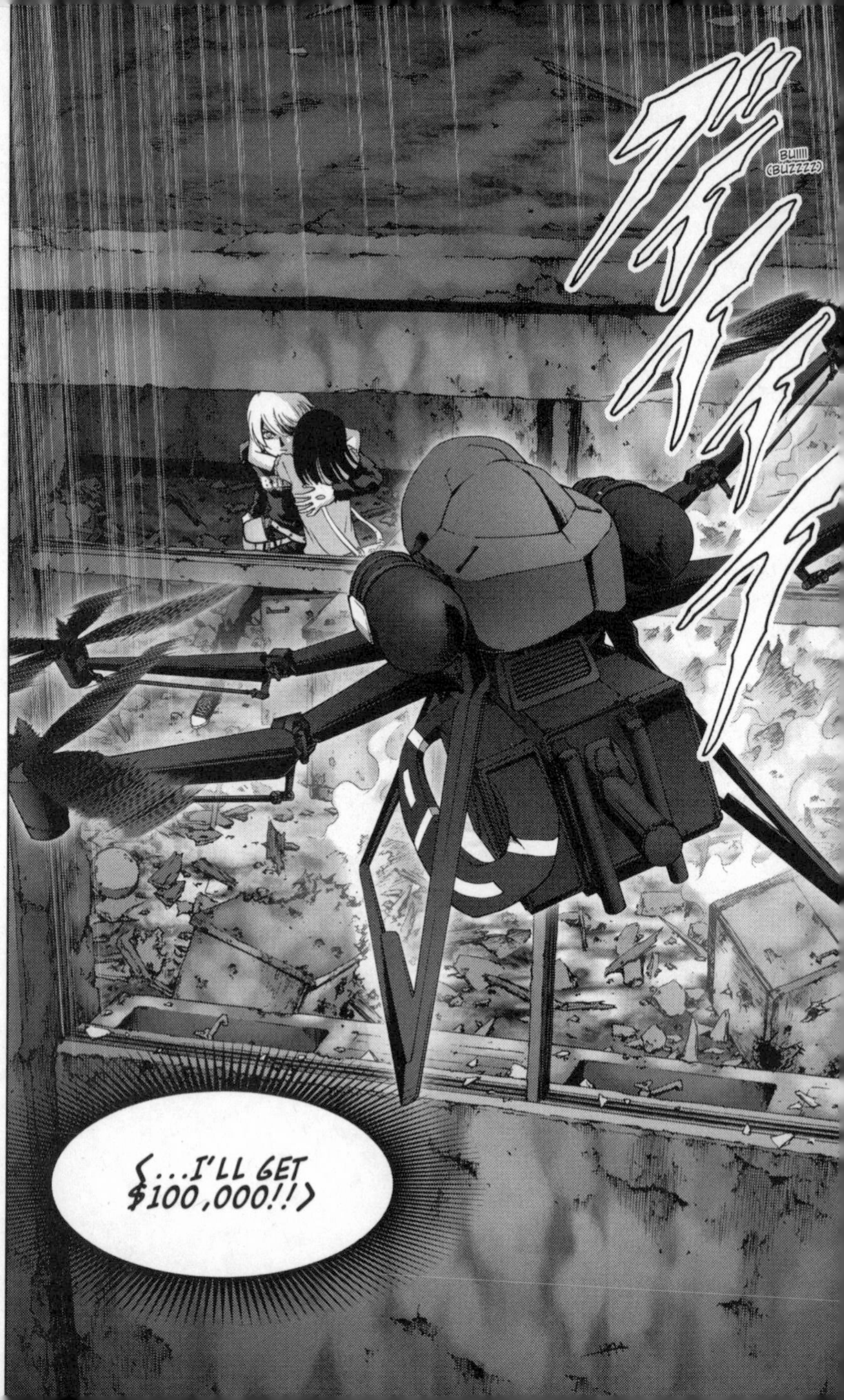
BUIIIII
(BUZZZZZ)
〈...I'LL GET $100,000!!〉

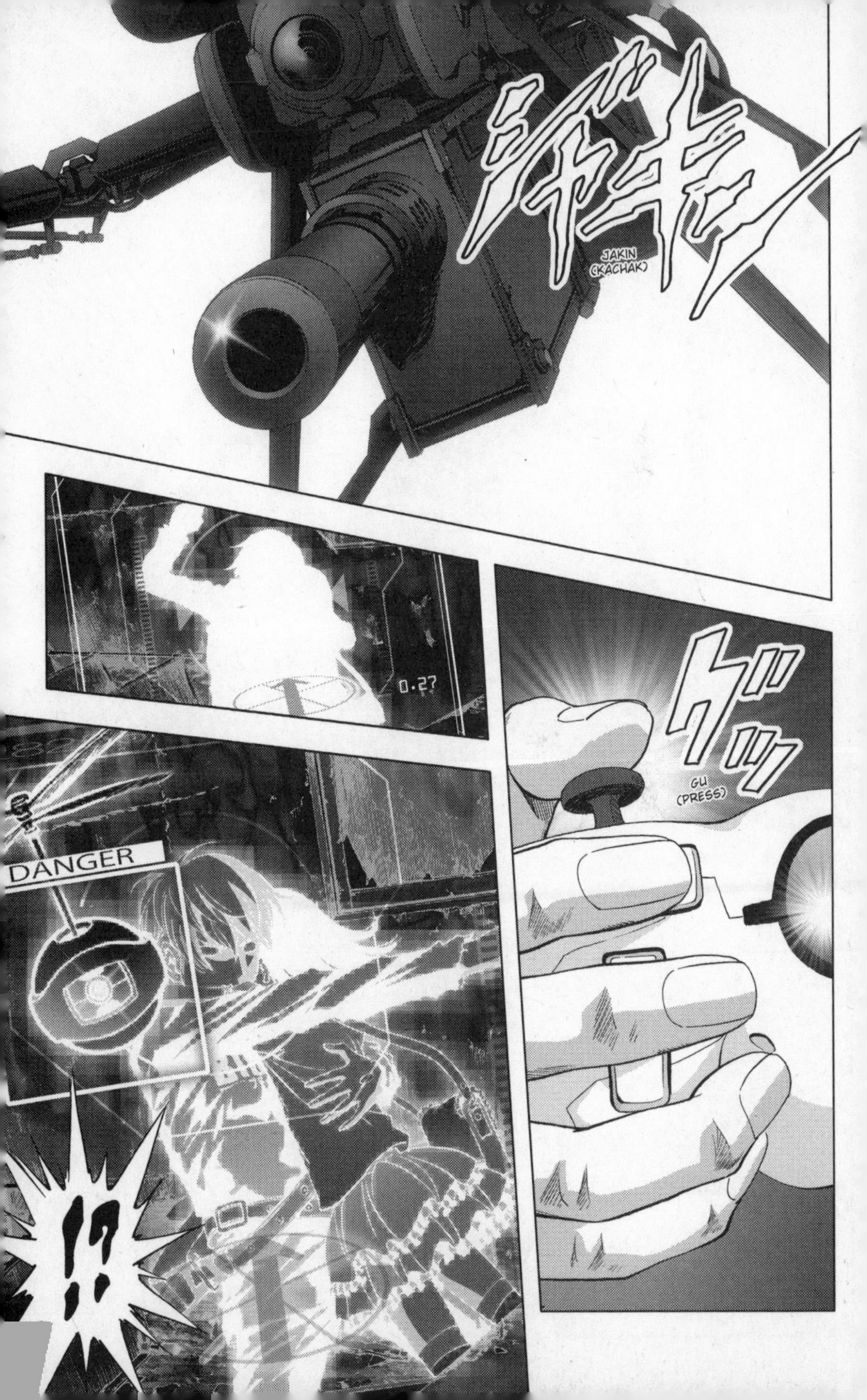
JAKIN
(KACHAK)
GU
(PRESS)
0.27
DANGER
!?

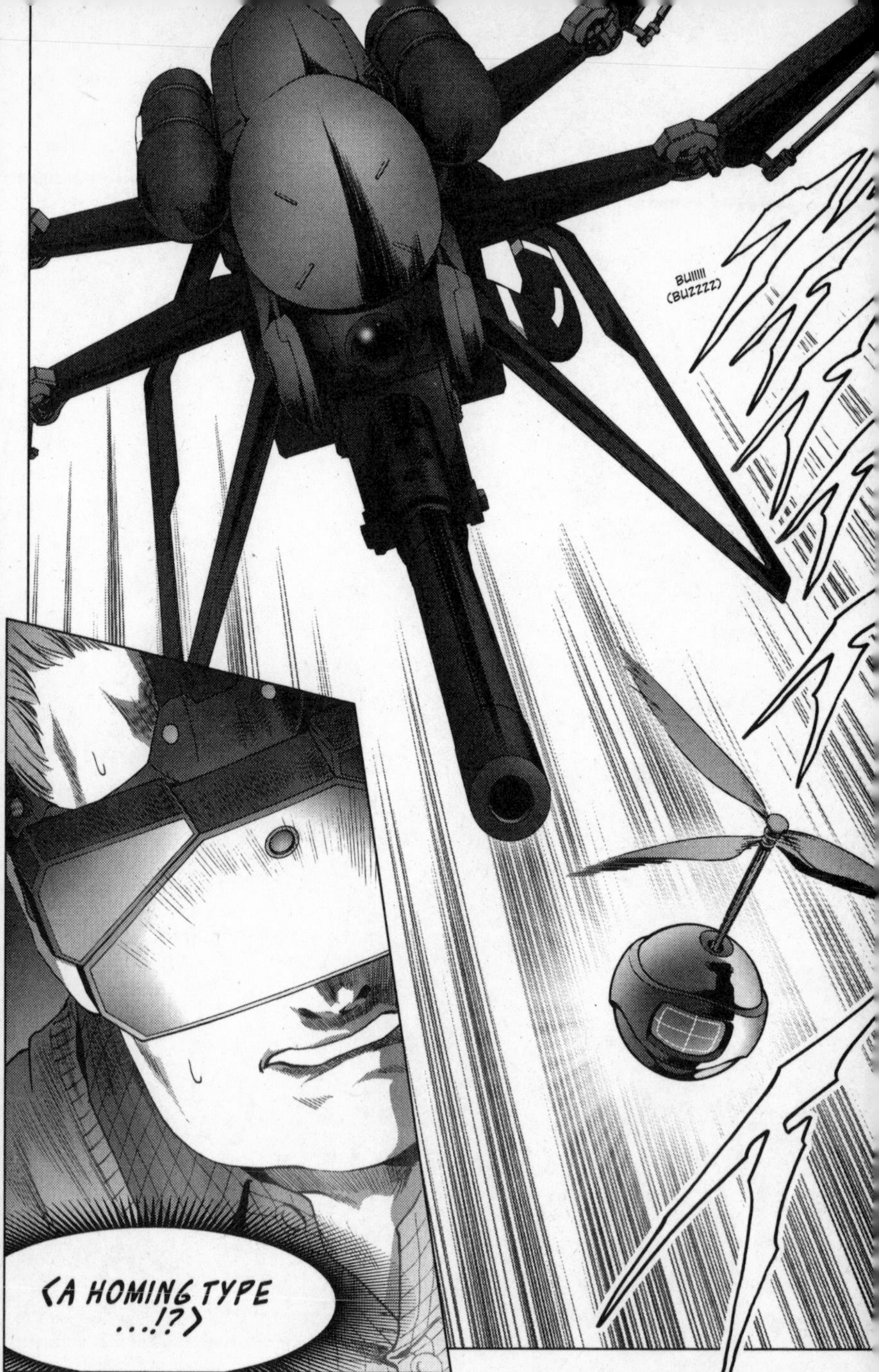
BUIIII
(BUZZZZ)
<A HOMING TYPE ...!?>

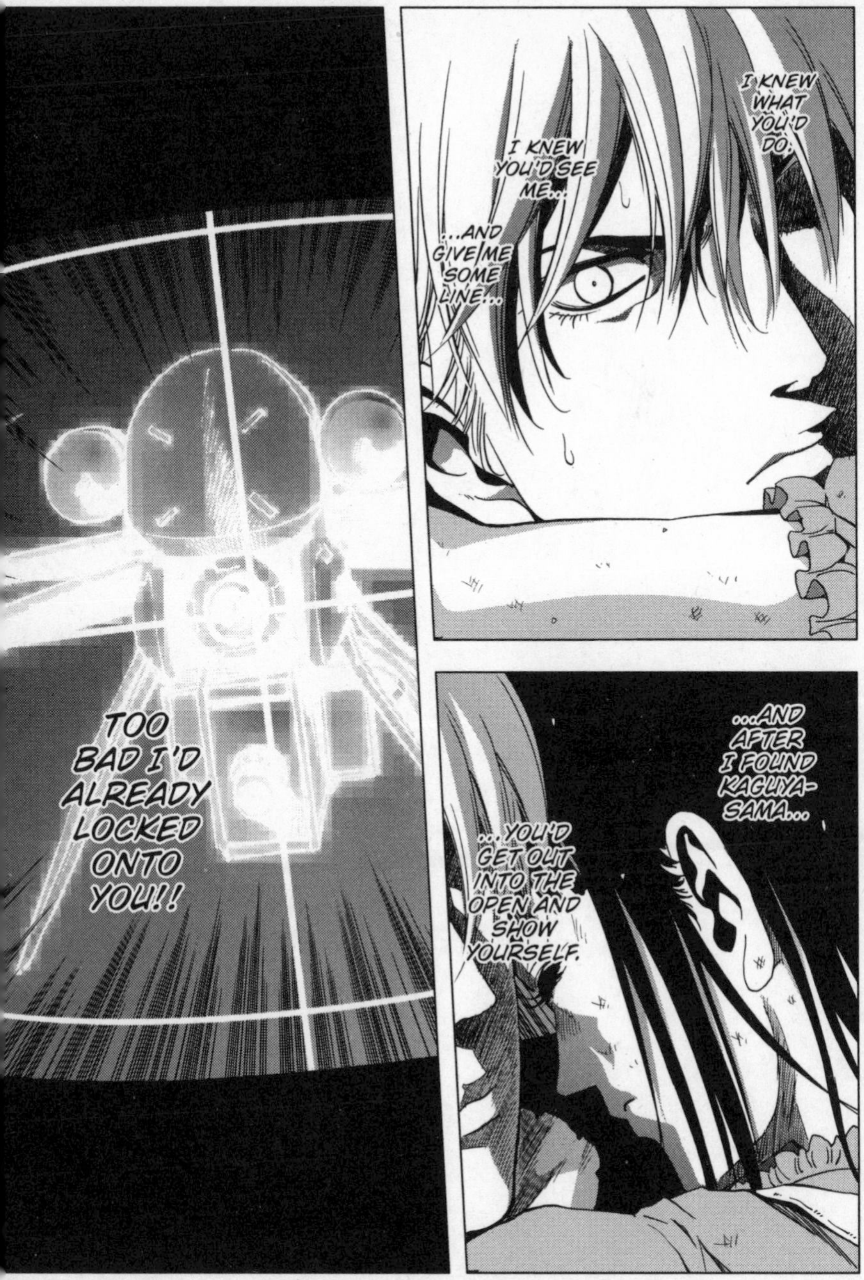
I KNEW WHAT YOU'D DO.
I KNEW YOU'D SEE ME...
...AND GIVE ME SOME LINE...
...AND AFTER I FOUND KAGUYA-SAMA...
...YOU'D GET OUT INTO THE OPEN AND SHOW YOURSELF.
TOO BAD I'D ALREADY LOCKED ONTO YOU!!

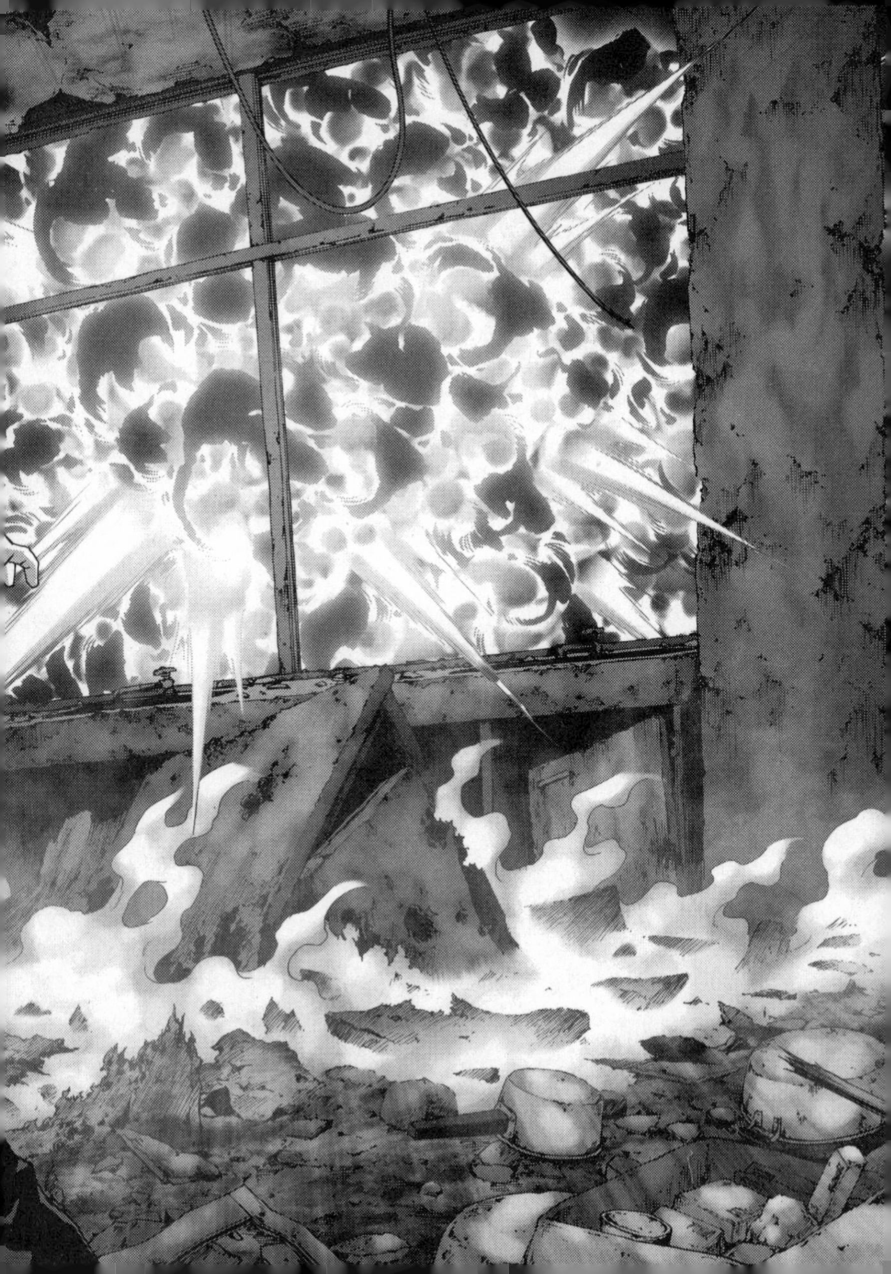

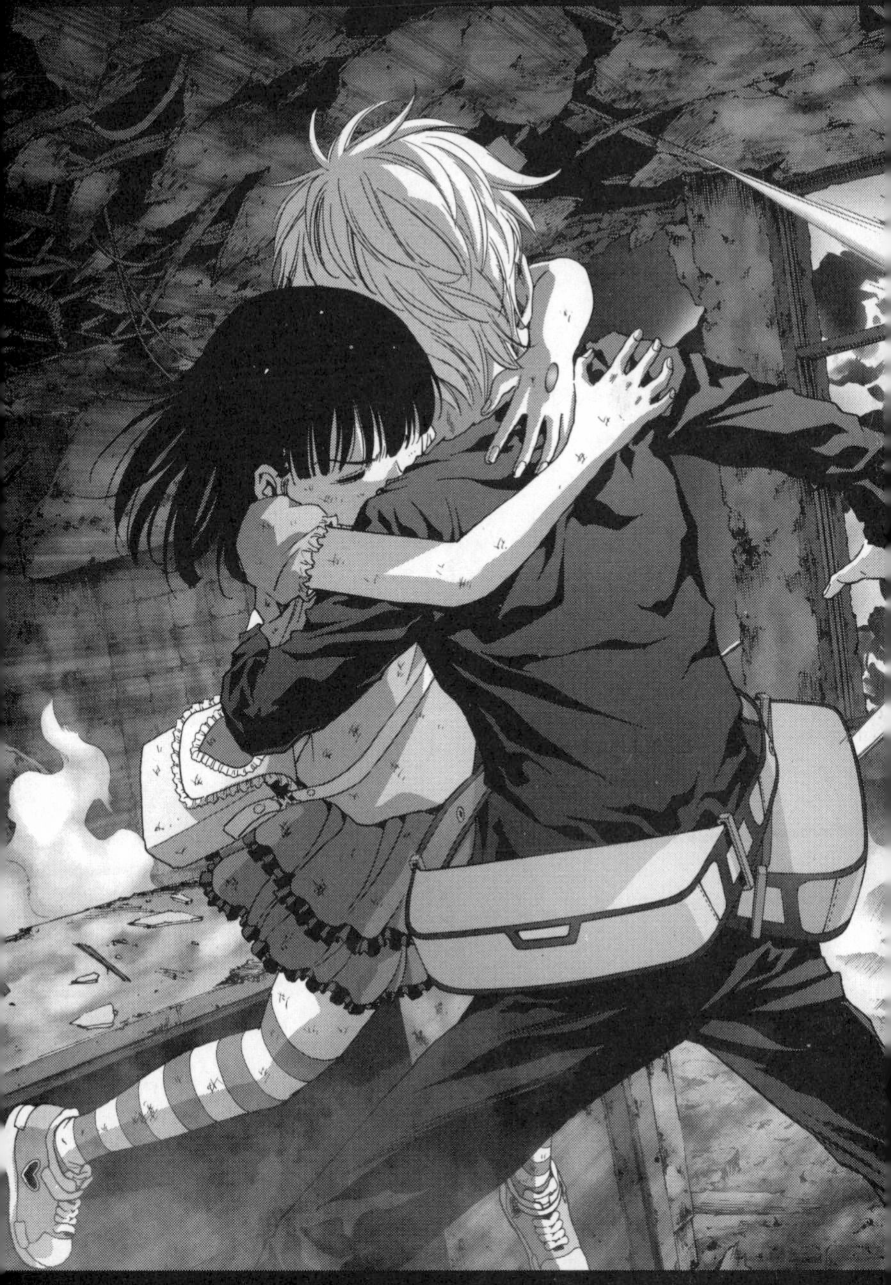

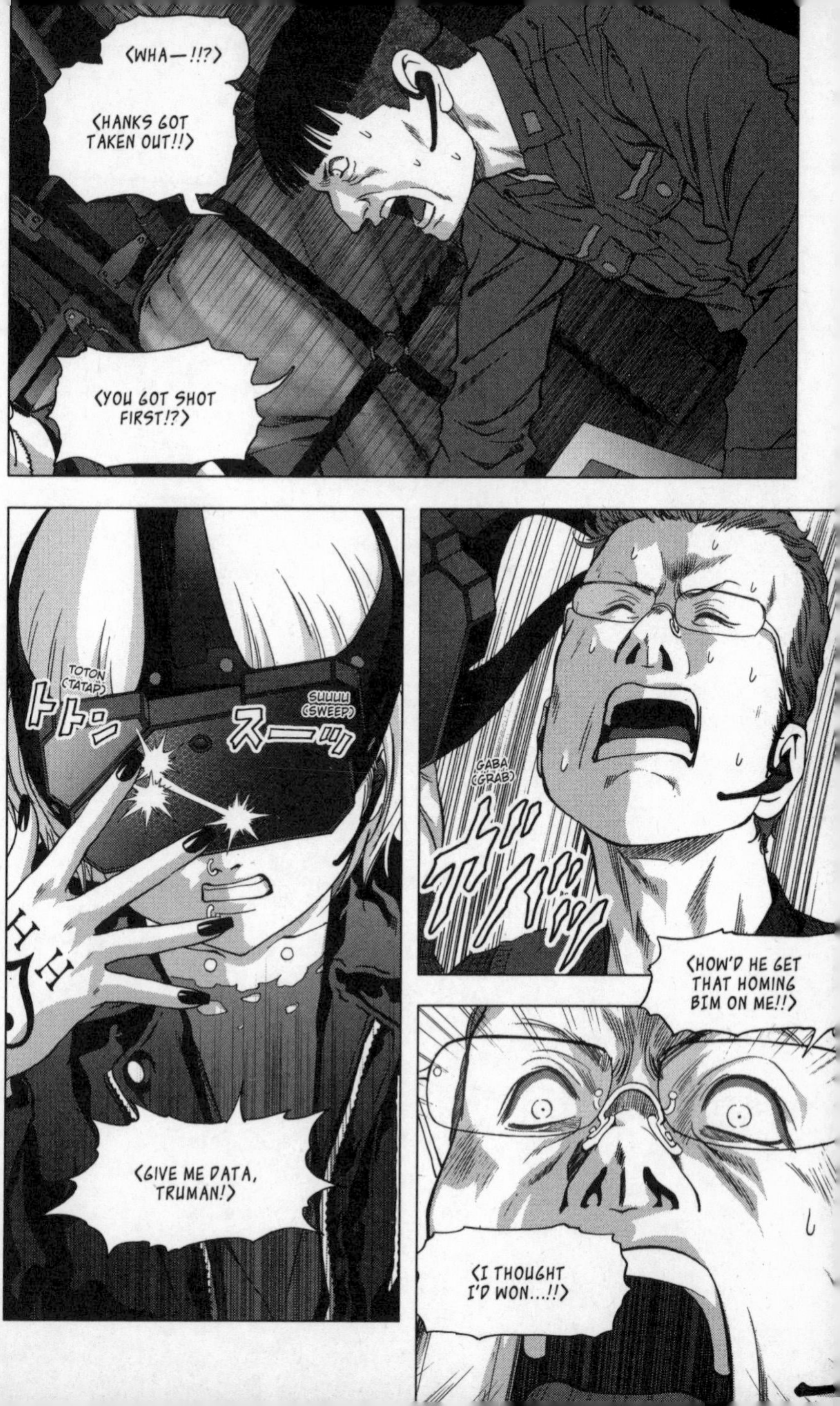

⟨WHA—!!?⟩
⟨HANKS GOT TAKEN OUT!!⟩
⟨YOU GOT SHOT FIRST!?⟩
ガバッ
GABA (GRAB)
⟨HOW'D HE GET THAT HOMING BIM ON ME!!⟩
⟨I THOUGHT I'D WON...!!⟩
トトン
TOTON (TATAP)
スーッ
SUUUU (SWEEP)
⟨GIVE ME DATA, TRUMAN!⟩

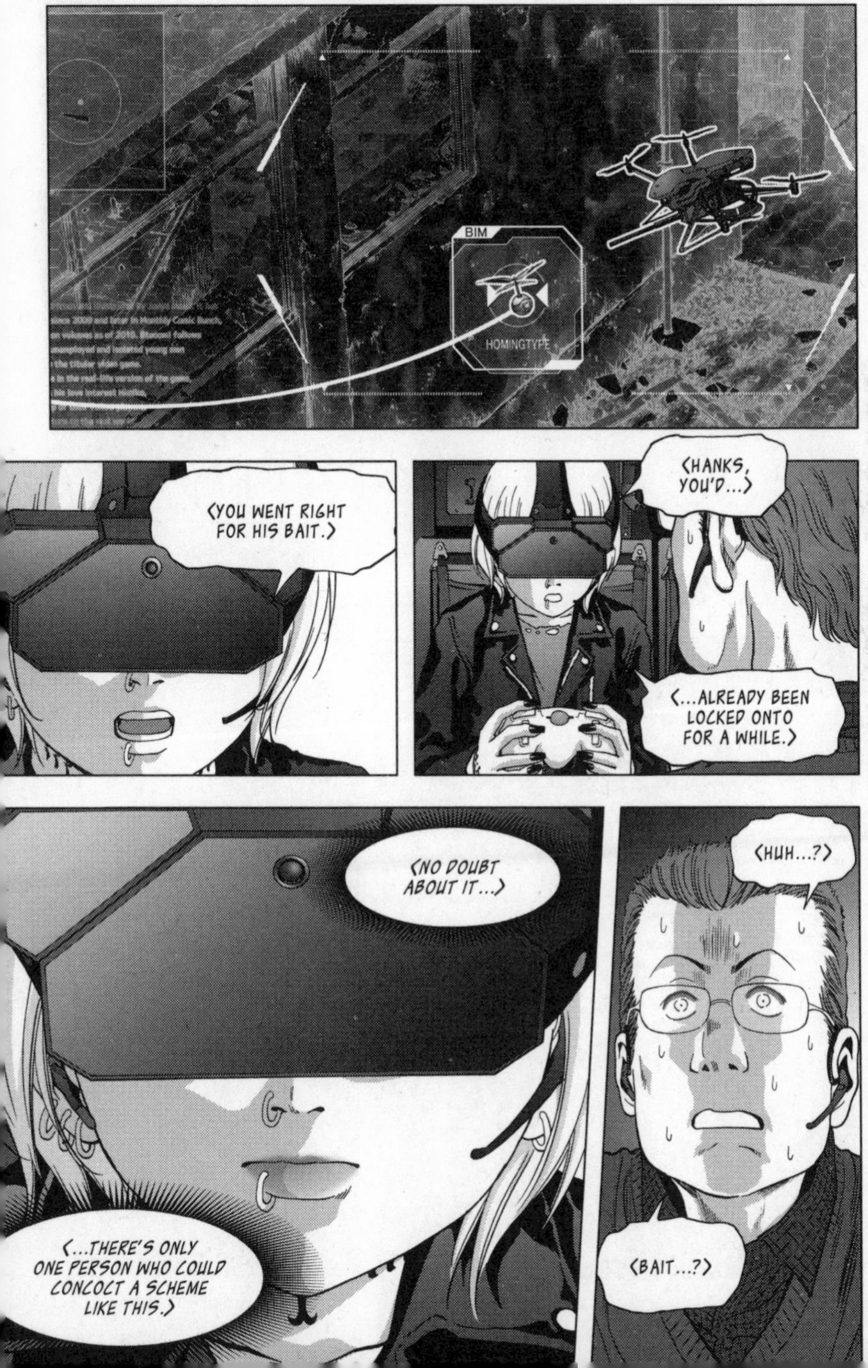
BIM
HOMINGTYPE
〈HANKS, YOU'D...〉
〈...ALREADY BEEN LOCKED ONTO FOR A WHILE.〉
〈YOU WENT RIGHT FOR HIS BAIT.〉
〈HUH...?〉
〈BAIT...?〉
〈NO DOUBT ABOUT IT...〉
〈...THERE'S ONLY ONE PERSON WHO COULD CONCOCT A SCHEME LIKE THIS.〉

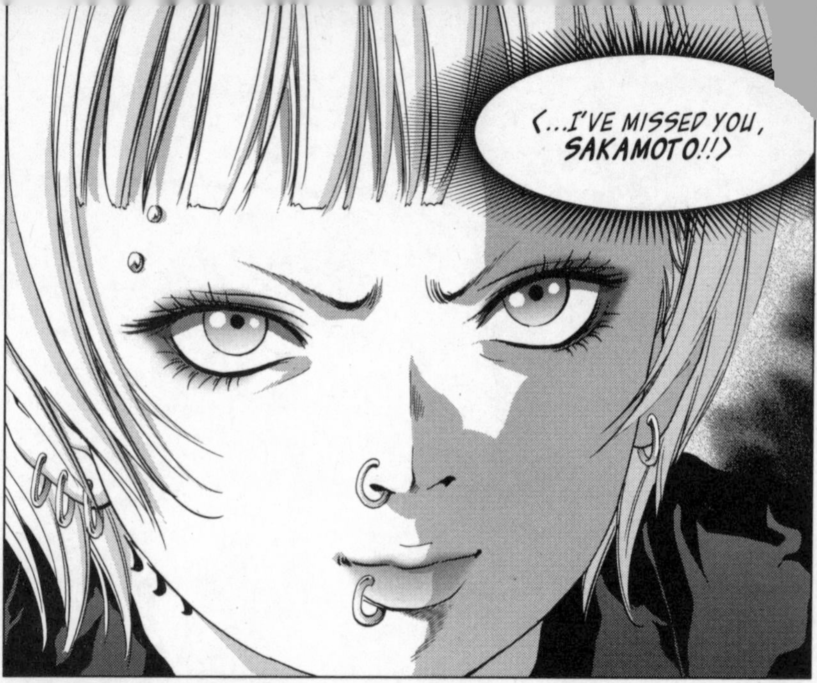

〈...I'VE MISSED YOU, SAKAMOTO!!〉

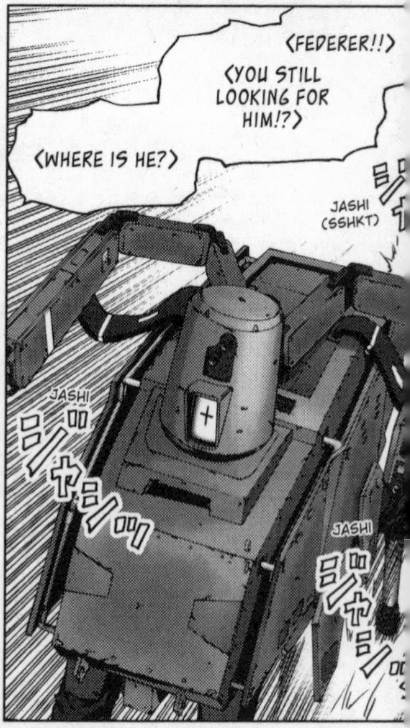

〈FEDERER!!〉
〈YOU STILL LOOKING FOR HIM!?〉
〈WHERE IS HE?〉
JASHI (SSHKT)
JASHI
JASHI

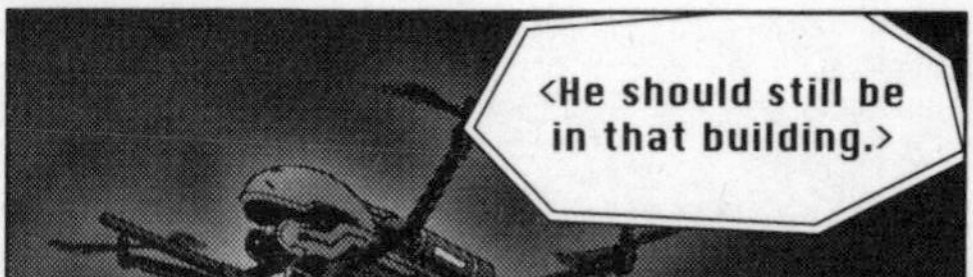

〈He should still be in that building.〉

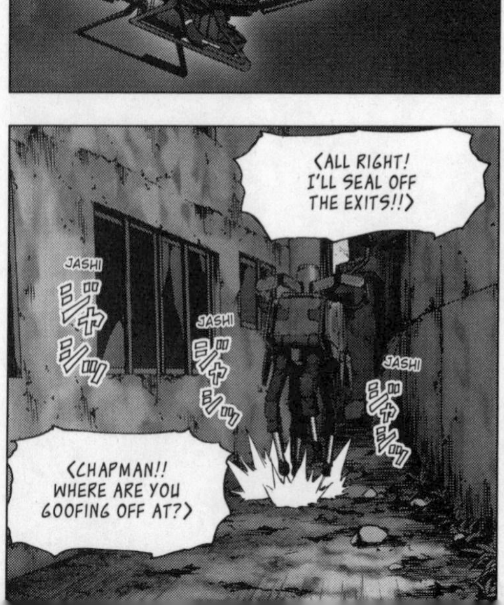

〈ALL RIGHT! I'LL SEAL OFF THE EXITS!!〉
JASHI
JASHI
JASHI
〈CHAPMAN!! WHERE ARE YOU GOOFING OFF AT?〉

A DOUBLE ECHO!

RYOUTA FOUND KAGUYA-CHAN.

...WAIT.

DID HE USE A HOMING TYPE!?

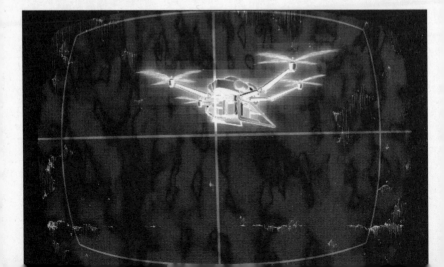

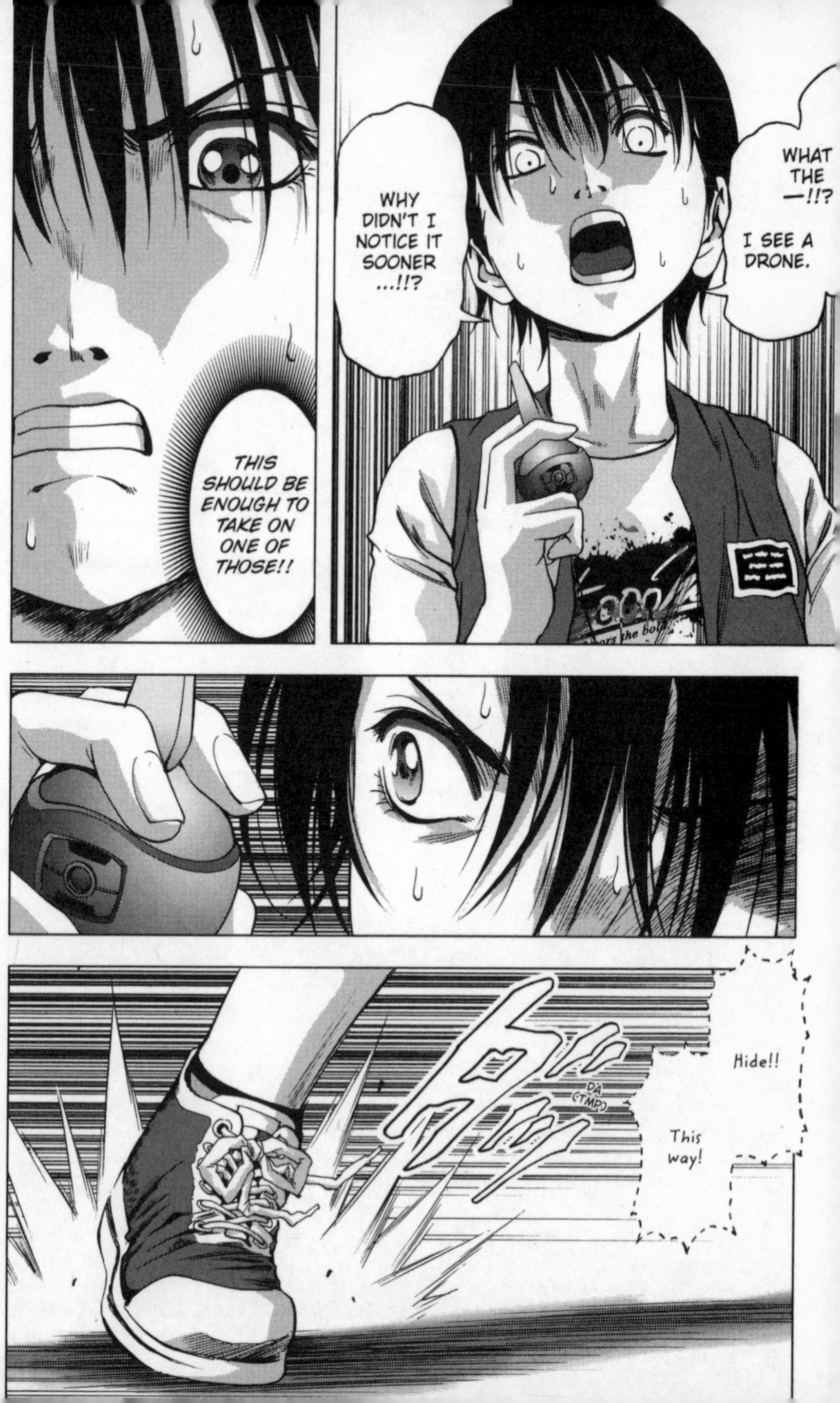
WHAT THE—!!? I SEE A DRONE.
WHY DIDN'T I NOTICE IT SOONER ...!!?
THIS SHOULD BE ENOUGH TO TAKE ON ONE OF THOSE!!
Hide!! This way!
DA (TMP)

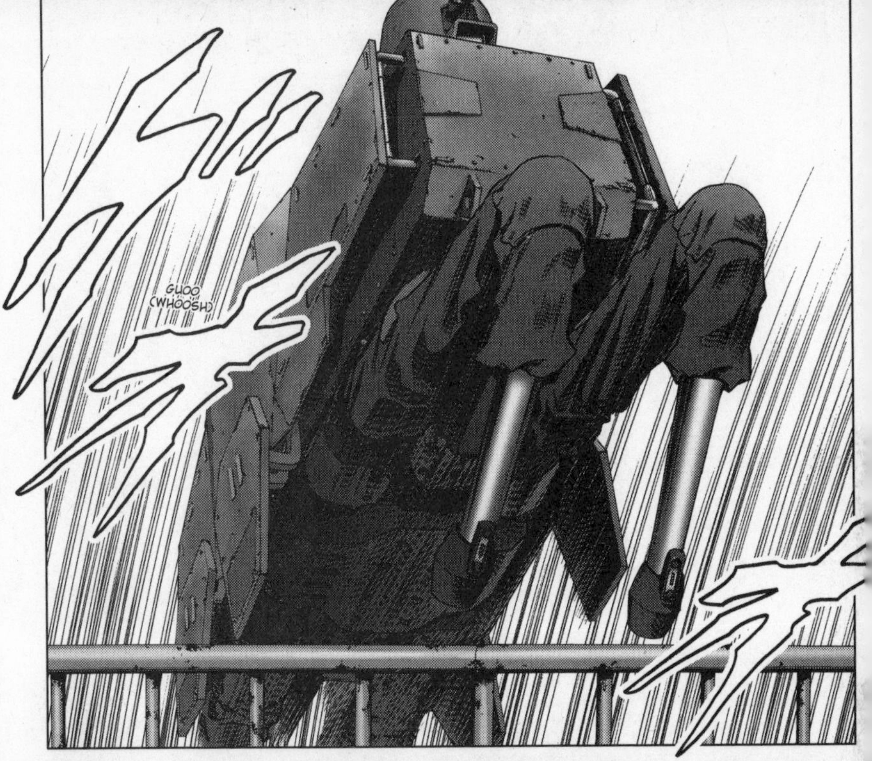
GUOO
(WHOOSH)
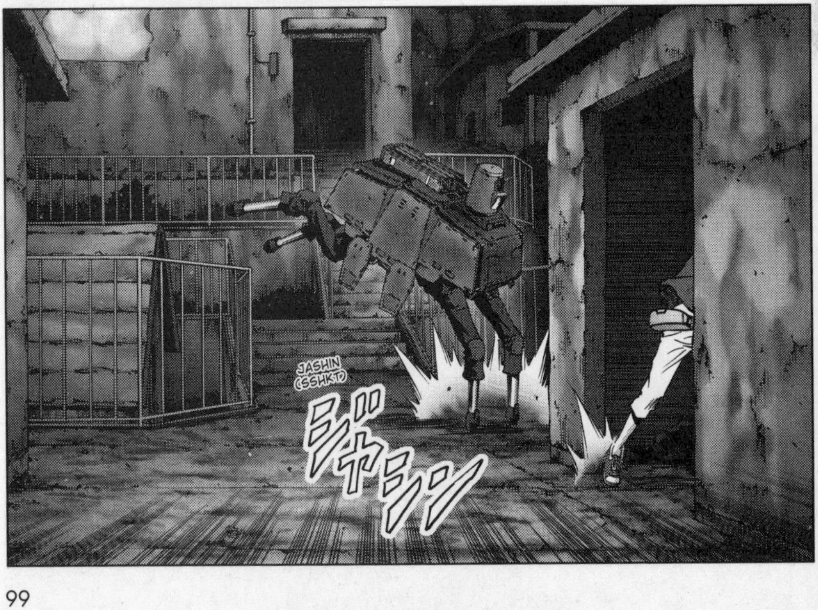
JASHIN
(SSHKT)

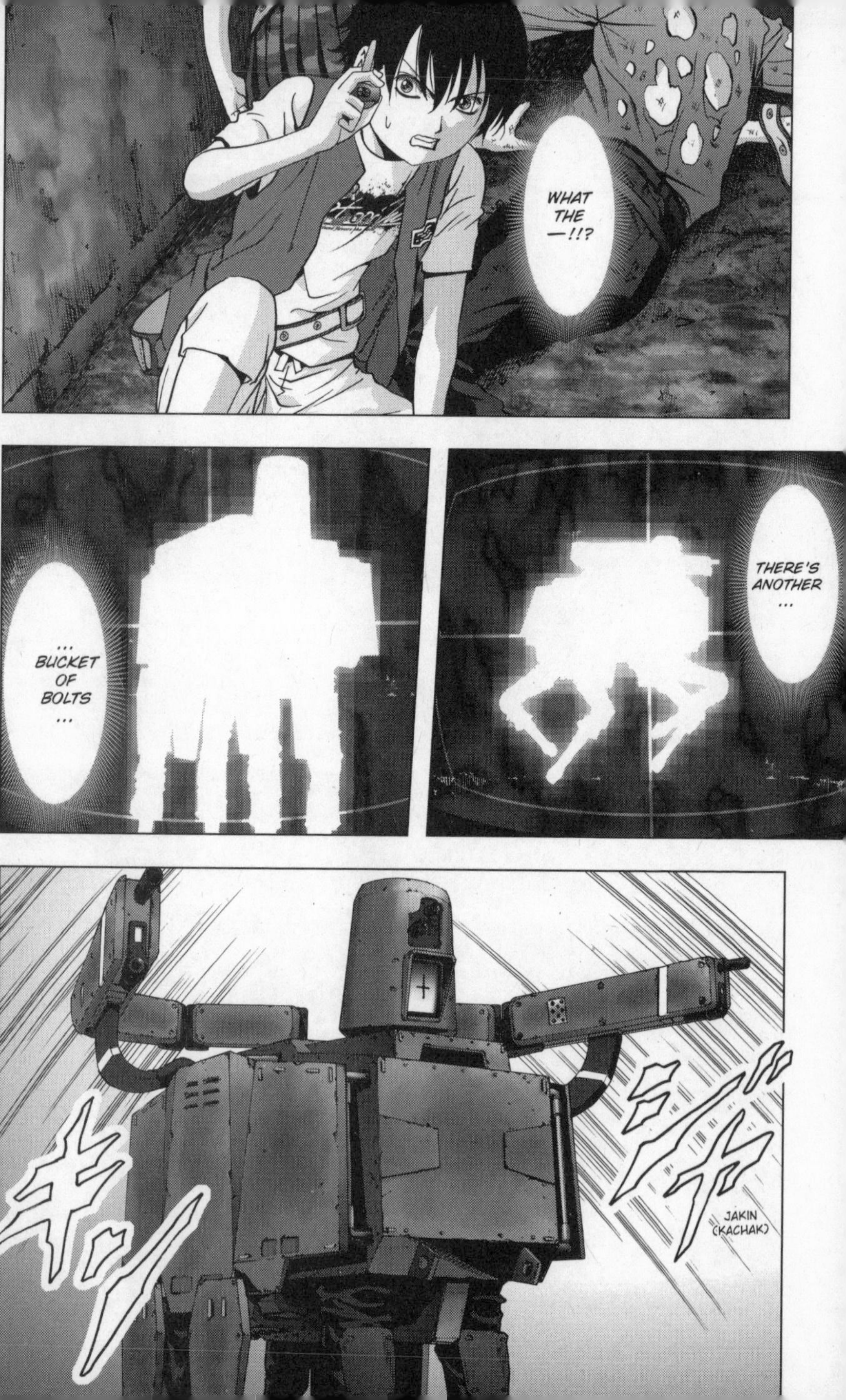
WHAT THE—!!?
THERE'S ANOTHER ...
... BUCKET OF BOLTS ...
JAKIN (KACHAK)

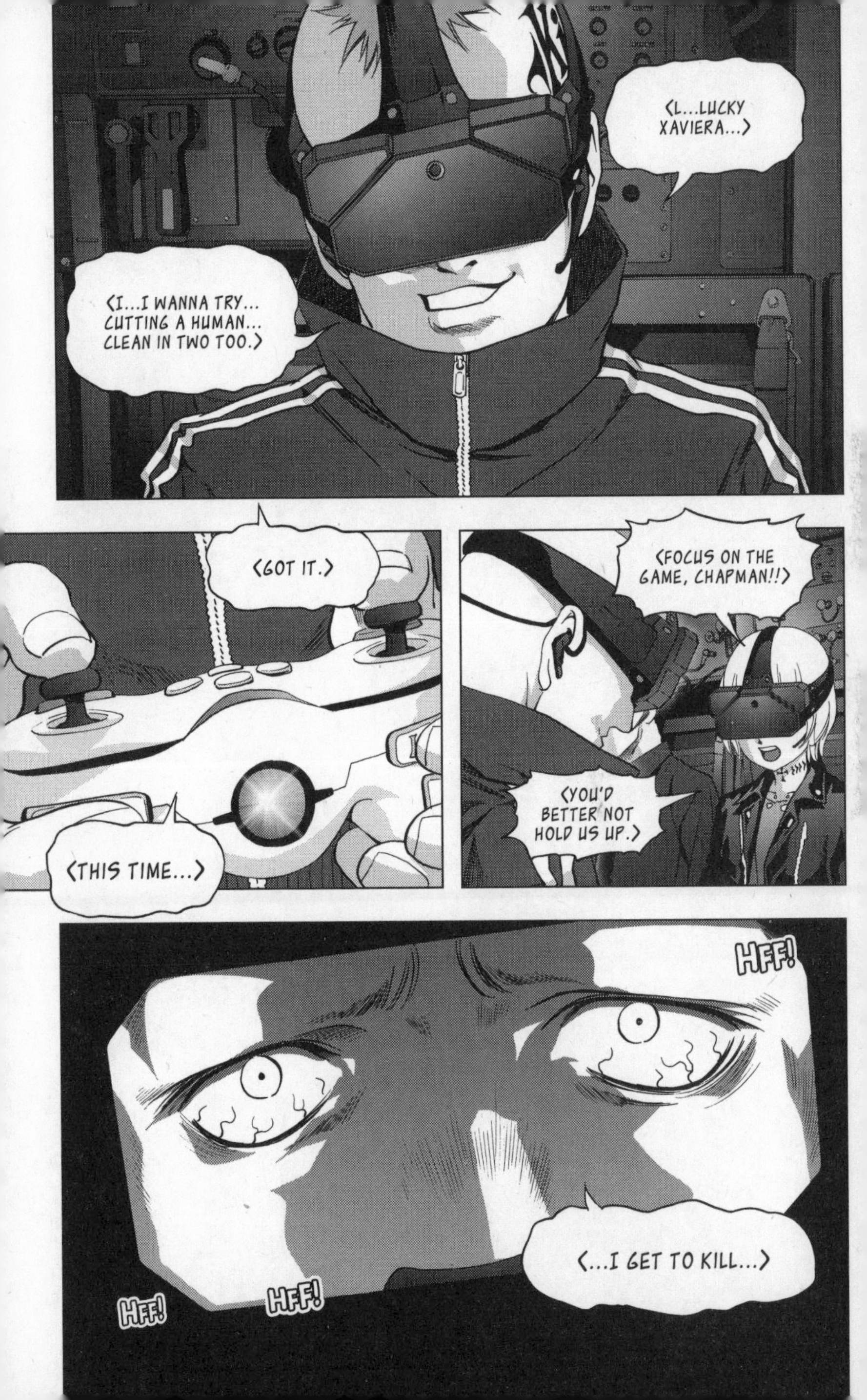
<L...LUCKY XAVIERA...>
<I...I WANNA TRY... CUTTING A HUMAN... CLEAN IN TWO TOO.>
<FOCUS ON THE GAME, CHAPMAN!!>
<YOU'D BETTER NOT HOLD US UP.>
<GOT IT.>
<THIS TIME...>
HFF!
<...I GET TO KILL...>
HFF!
HFF!

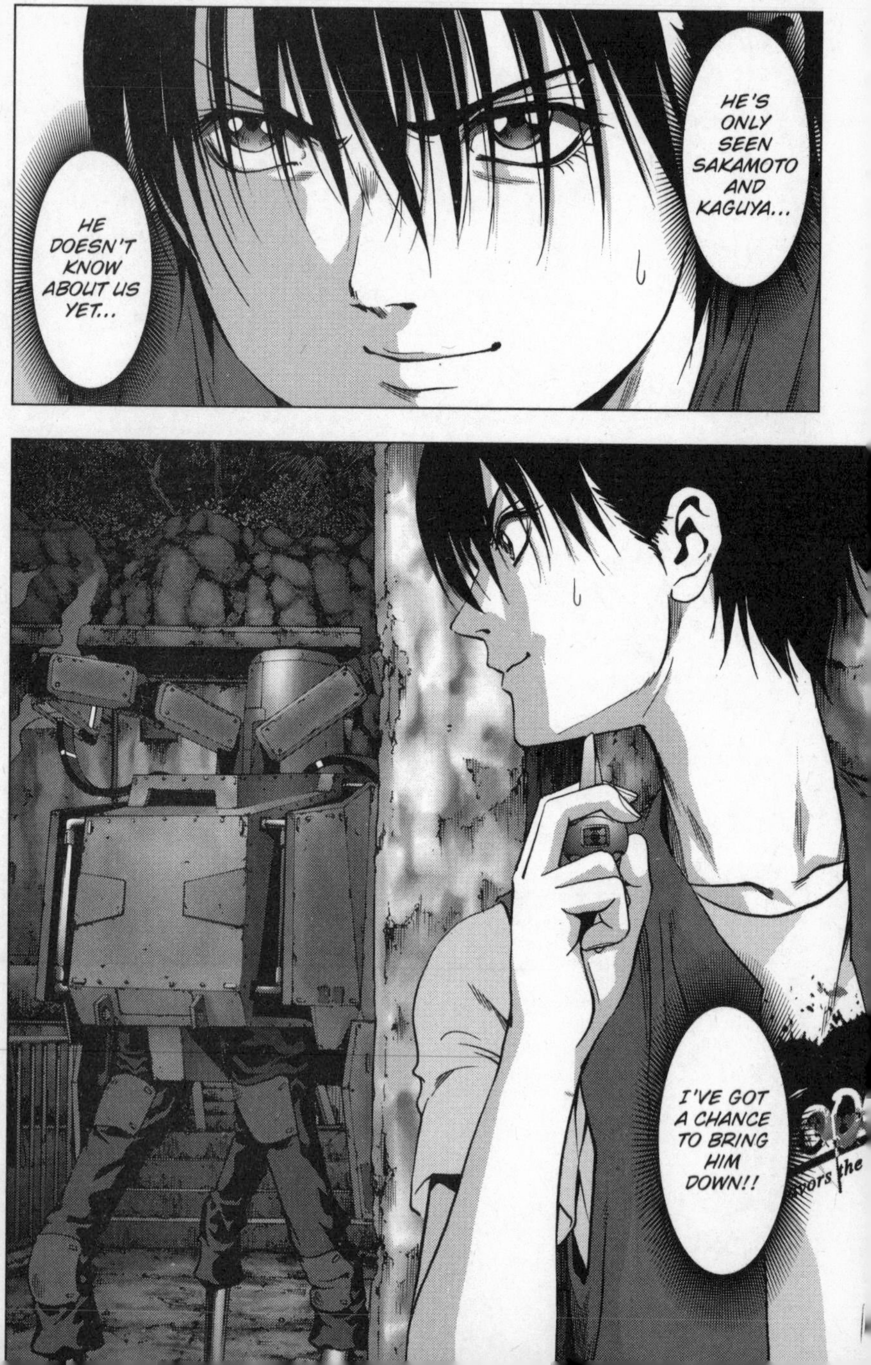
HE'S ONLY SEEN SAKAMOTO AND KAGUYA...
HE DOESN'T KNOW ABOUT US YET...
I'VE GOT A CHANCE TO BRING HIM DOWN!!

BTOOOM!

REFERENCE MATERIAL TRIP LOG

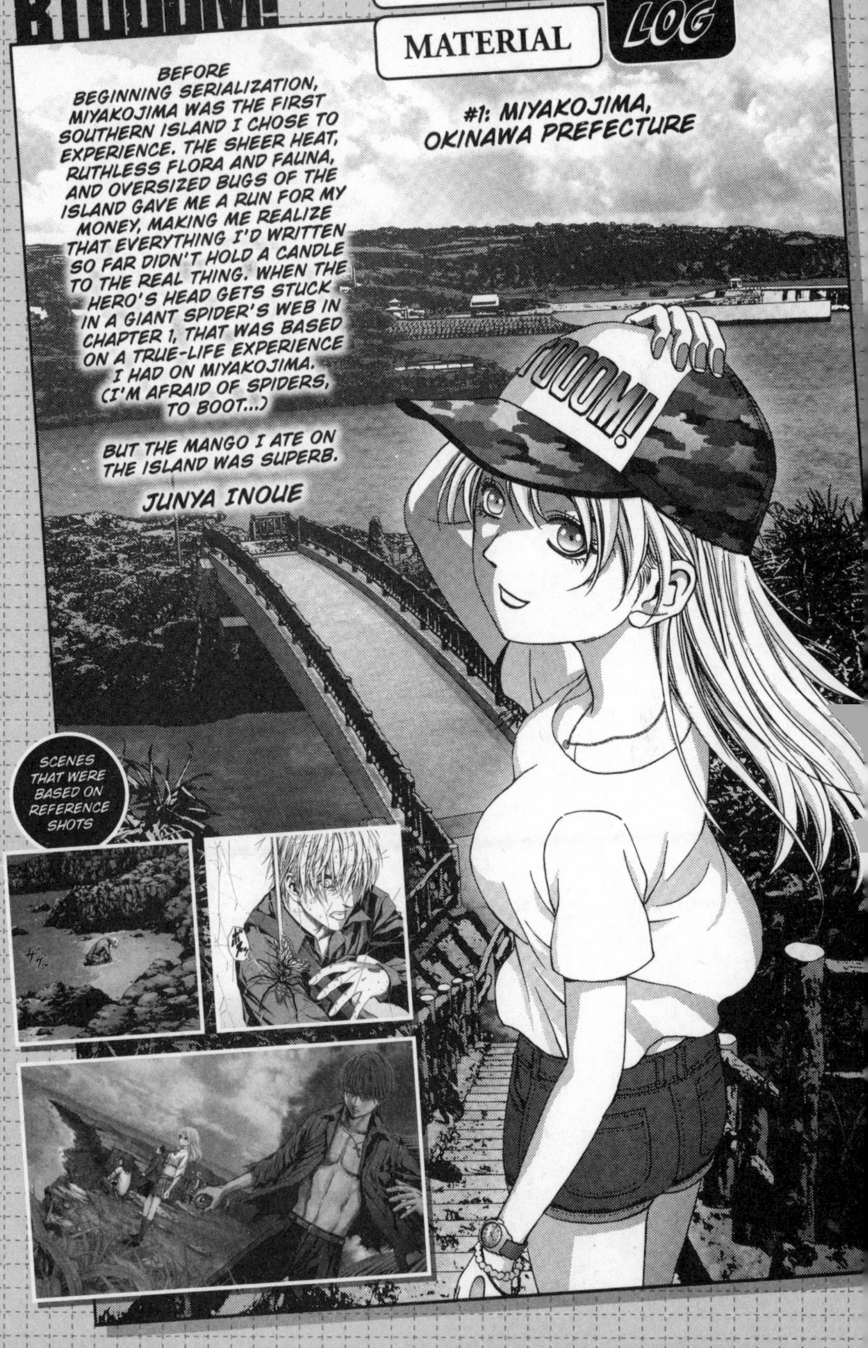
#1: MIYAKOJIMA, OKINAWA PREFECTURE
BEFORE BEGINNING SERIALIZATION, MIYAKOJIMA WAS THE FIRST SOUTHERN ISLAND I CHOSE TO EXPERIENCE. THE SHEER HEAT, RUTHLESS FLORA AND FAUNA, AND OVERSIZED BUGS OF THE ISLAND GAVE ME A RUN FOR MY MONEY, MAKING ME REALIZE THAT EVERYTHING I'D WRITTEN SO FAR DIDN'T HOLD A CANDLE TO THE REAL THING. WHEN THE HERO'S HEAD GETS STUCK IN A GIANT SPIDER'S WEB IN CHAPTER 1, THAT WAS BASED ON A TRUE-LIFE EXPERIENCE I HAD ON MIYAKOJIMA. (I'M AFRAID OF SPIDERS, TO BOOT...)
BUT THE MANGO I ATE ON THE ISLAND WAS SUPERB.
JUNYA INOUE
BTOOOM!
SCENES THAT WERE BASED ON REFERENCE SHOTS

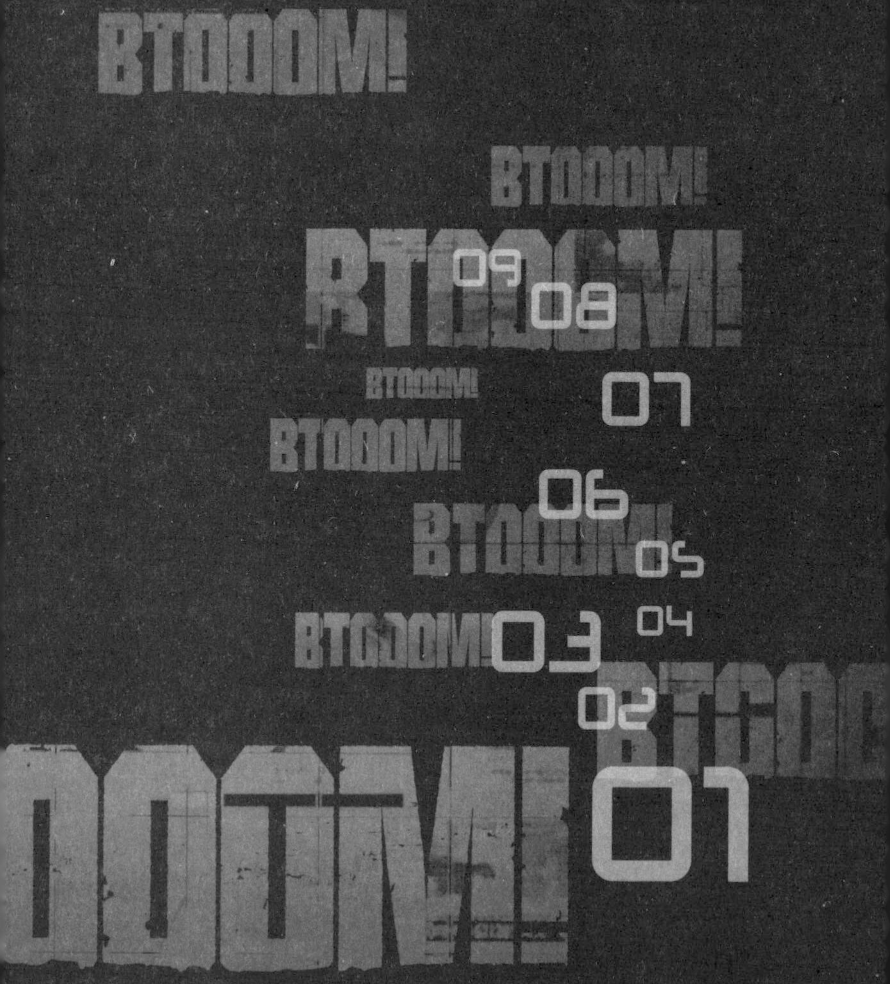
BTOOOM!
BTOOOM!
BTOOOM!
09
08
BTOOOM!
07
BTOOOM!
06
BTOOOM!
05
BTOOOM!
03
04
02
BTOOOM!
01

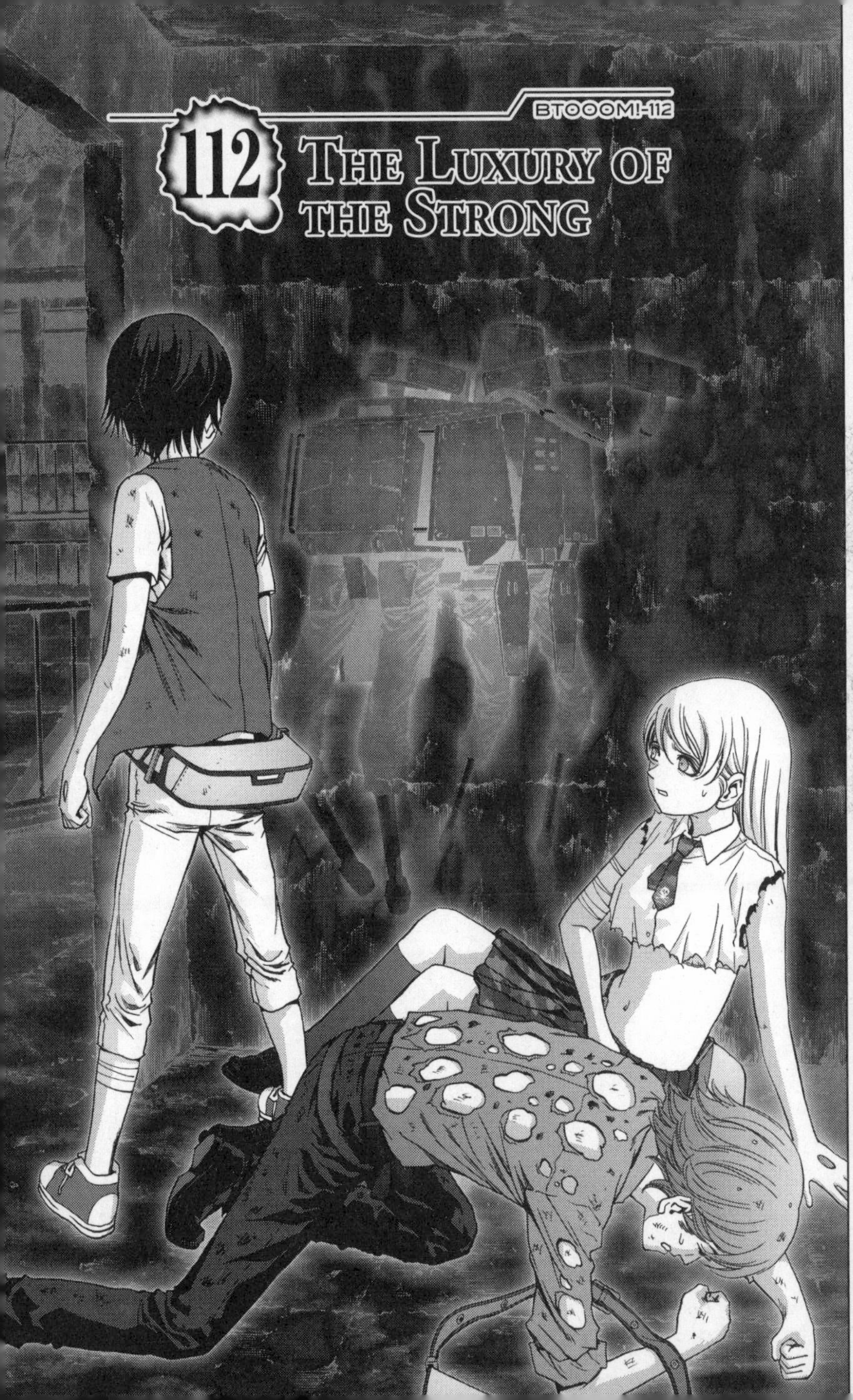
BTOOOM!-112
112
THE LUXURY OF THE STRONG

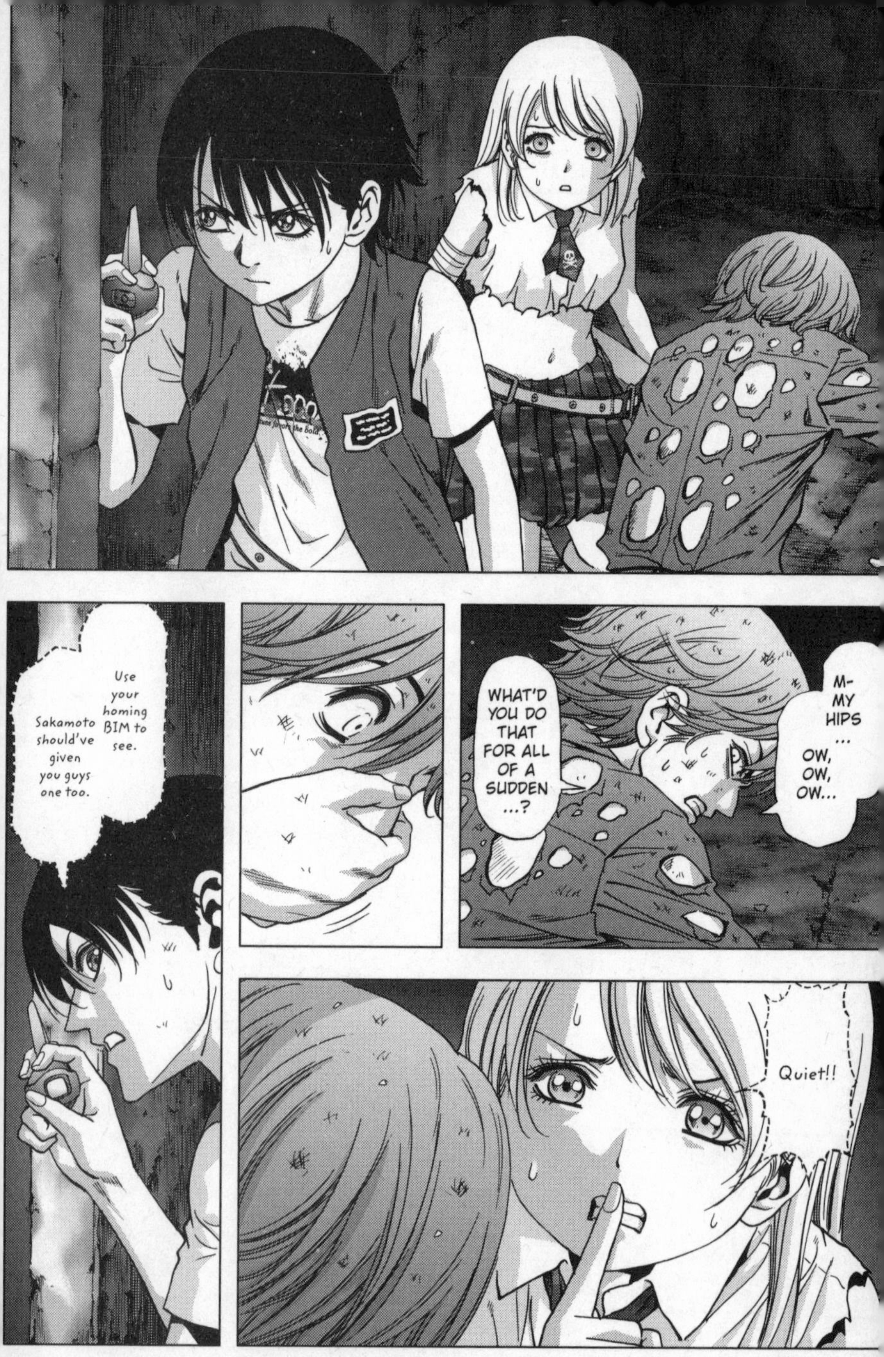
M-MY HIPS ... OW, OW, OW...
WHAT'D YOU DO THAT FOR ALL OF A SUDDEN ...?
Quiet!!
Use your homing BIM to see.
Sakamoto should've given you guys one too.

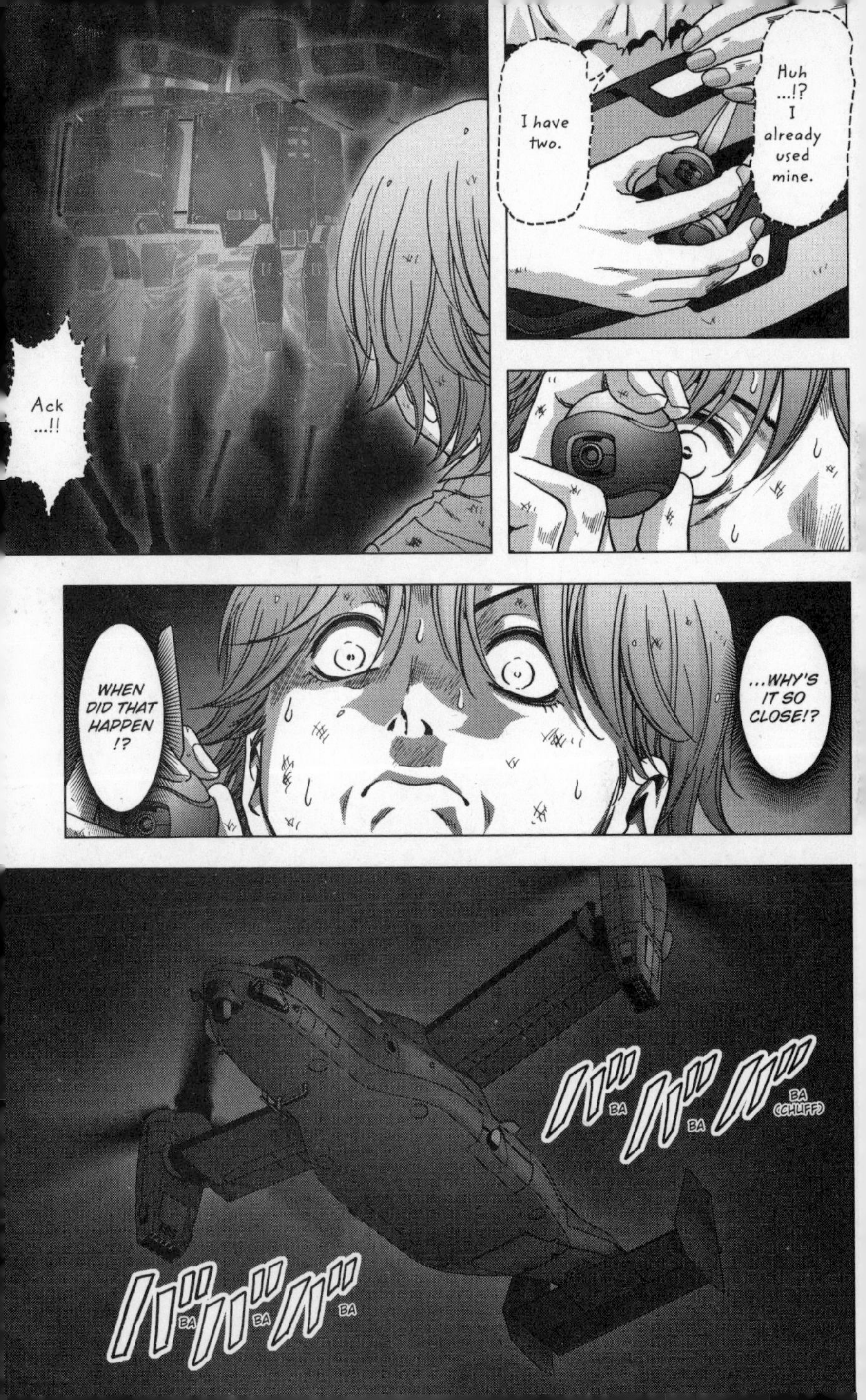
Huh ...!? I already used mine.
I have two.
Ack ...!!
...WHY'S IT SO CLOSE!?
WHEN DID THAT HAPPEN!?
BA BA BA (CHUFF)
BA BA BA

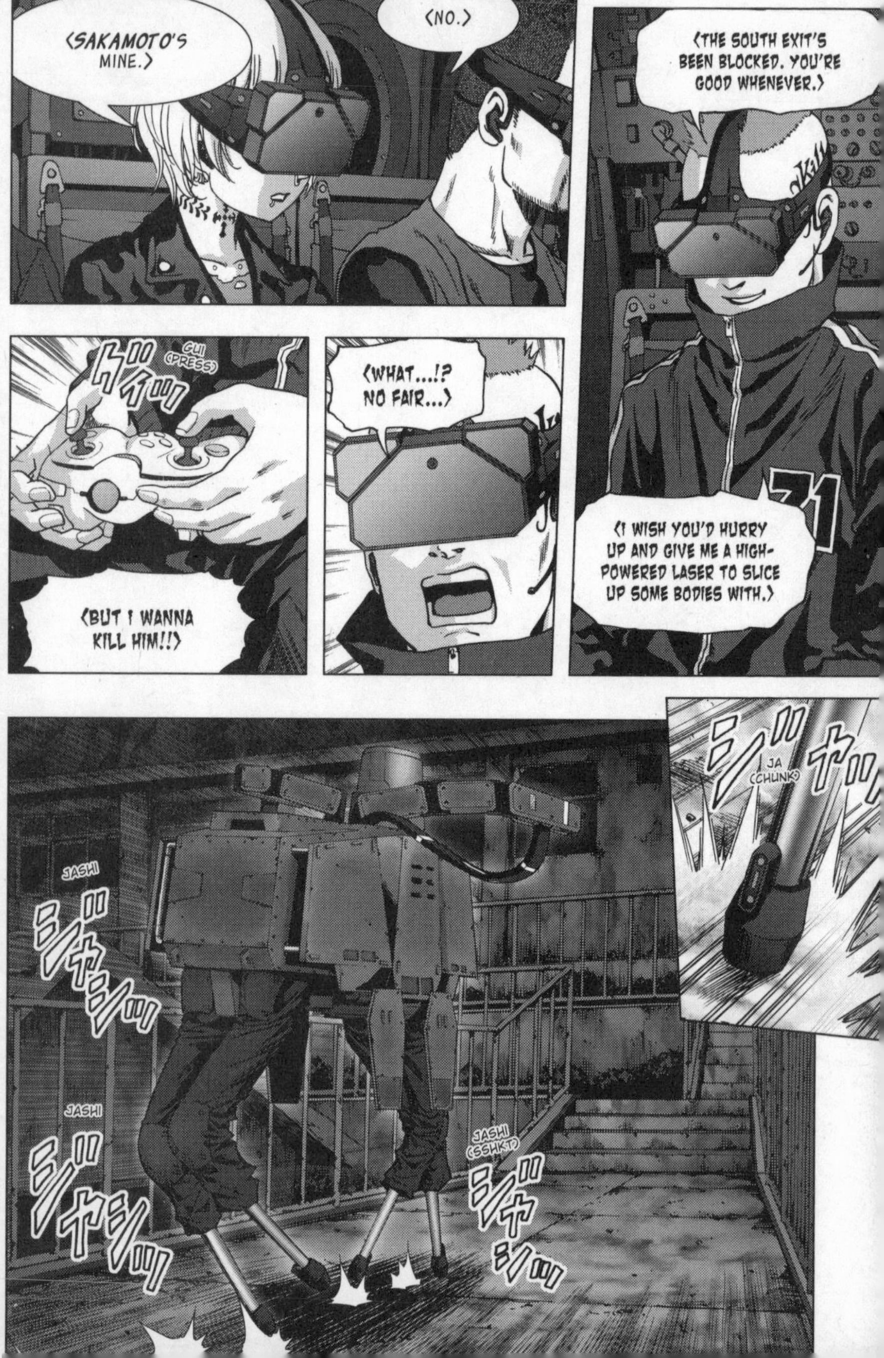
⟨THE SOUTH EXIT'S BEEN BLOCKED. YOU'RE GOOD WHENEVER.⟩
⟨I WISH YOU'D HURRY UP AND GIVE ME A HIGH-POWERED LASER TO SLICE UP SOME BODIES WITH.⟩
⟨SAKAMOTO'S MINE.⟩
⟨NO.⟩
⟨WHAT...!? NO FAIR...⟩
GUI (PRESS)
⟨BUT I WANNA KILL HIM!!⟩
JA (CHUNK)
JASHI
JASHI
JASHI (SSHKT)

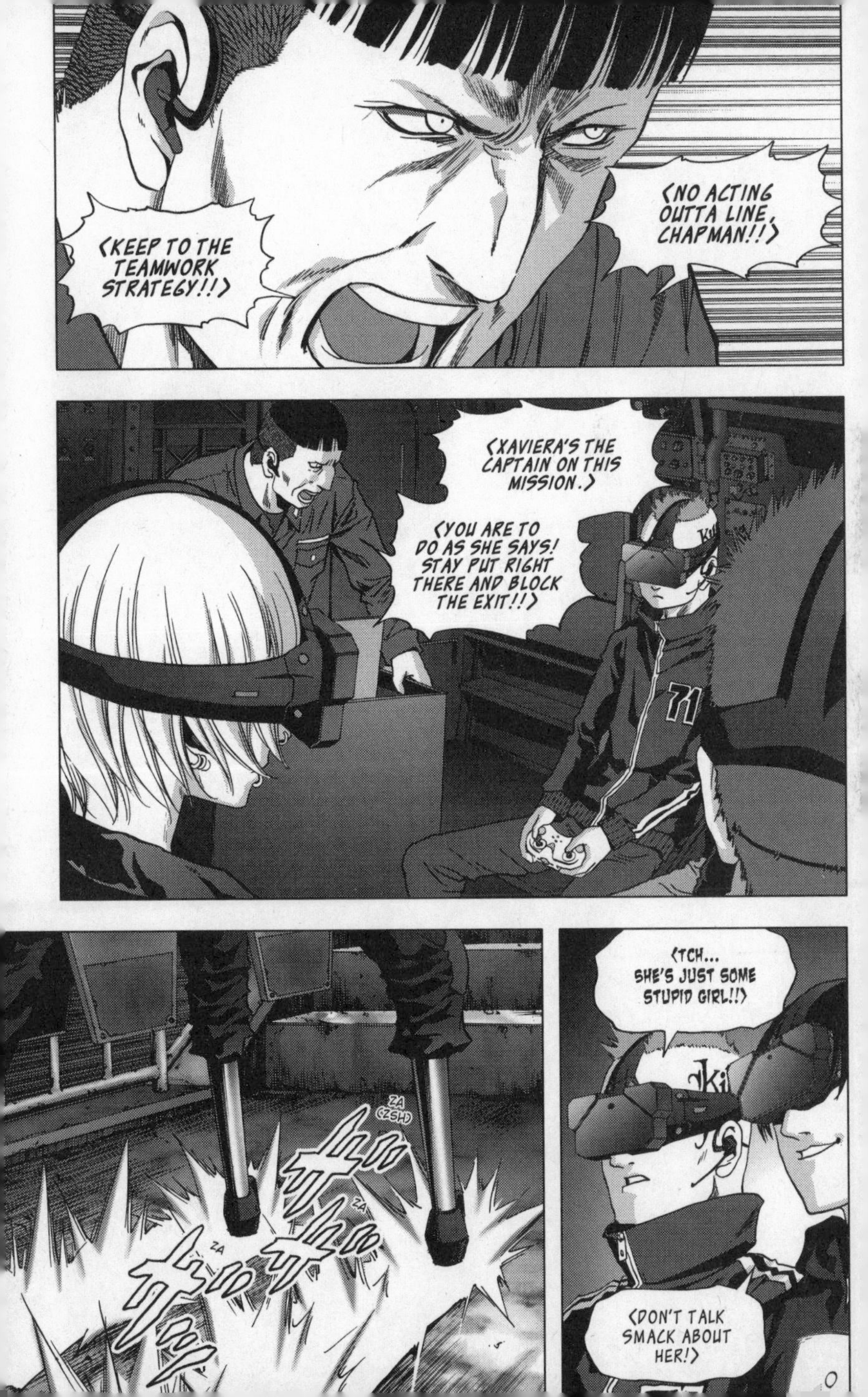
‹NO ACTING OUTTA LINE, CHAPMAN!!›
‹KEEP TO THE TEAMWORK STRATEGY!!›
‹XAVIERA'S THE CAPTAIN ON THIS MISSION.›
‹YOU ARE TO DO AS SHE SAYS! STAY PUT RIGHT THERE AND BLOCK THE EXIT!!›
‹TCH... SHE'S JUST SOME STUPID GIRL!!›
‹DON'T TALK SMACK ABOUT HER!›
ZA (ZSHD)
ZA
ZA

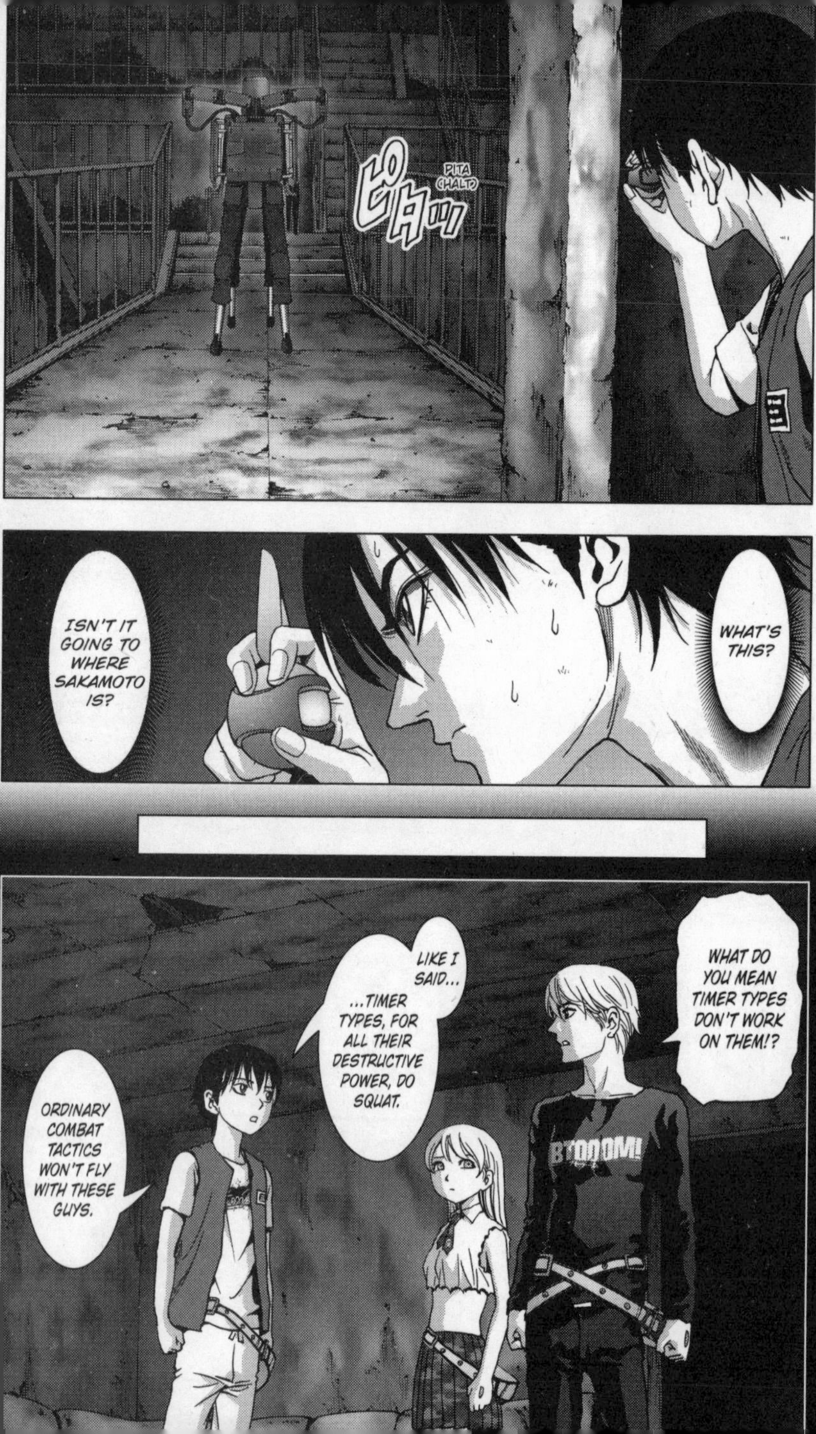
ピタッ!!
PITA (HALT)
WHAT'S THIS?
ISN'T IT GOING TO WHERE SAKAMOTO IS?
WHAT DO YOU MEAN TIMER TYPES DON'T WORK ON THEM!?
LIKE I SAID...
...TIMER TYPES, FOR ALL THEIR DESTRUCTIVE POWER, DO SQUAT.
ORDINARY COMBAT TACTICS WON'T FLY WITH THESE GUYS.

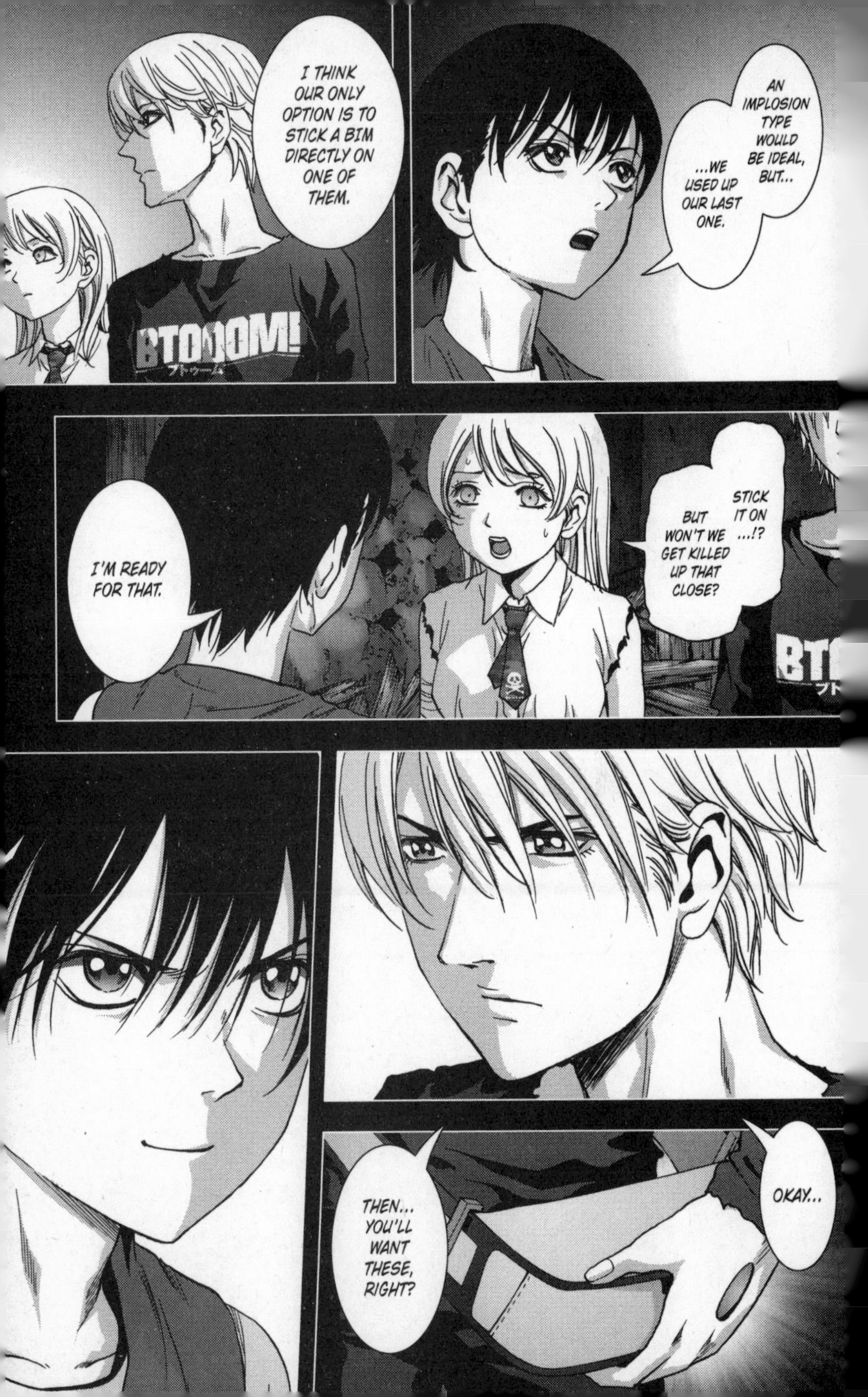
AN IMPLOSION TYPE WOULD BE IDEAL, BUT...
...WE USED UP OUR LAST ONE.
I THINK OUR ONLY OPTION IS TO STICK A BIM DIRECTLY ON ONE OF THEM.
STICK IT ON ...!?
BUT WON'T WE GET KILLED UP THAT CLOSE?
I'M READY FOR THAT.
OKAY...
THEN... YOU'LL WANT THESE, RIGHT?

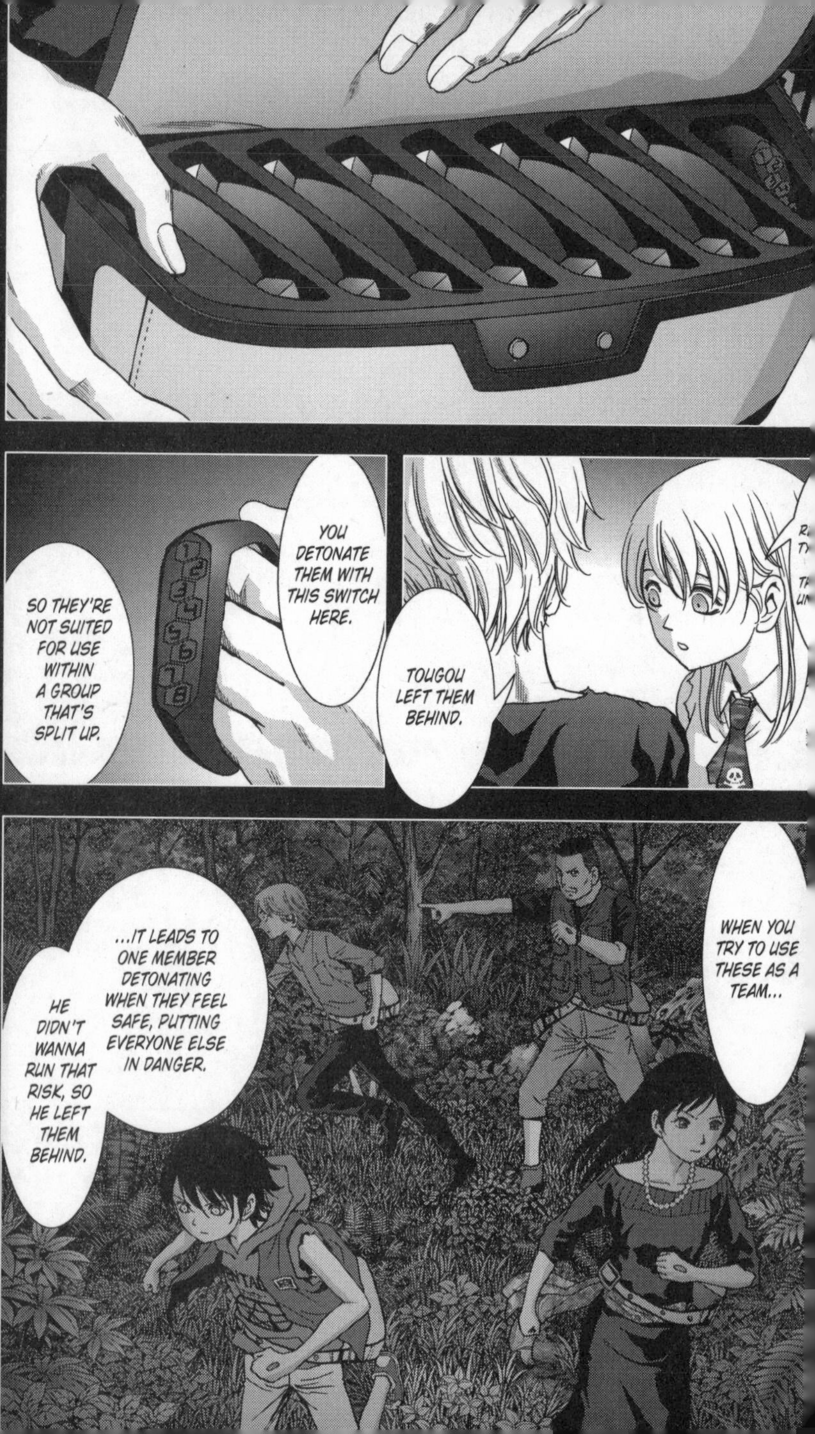
TOUGOU LEFT THEM BEHIND.
YOU DETONATE THEM WITH THIS SWITCH HERE.
SO THEY'RE NOT SUITED FOR USE WITHIN A GROUP THAT'S SPLIT UP.
WHEN YOU TRY TO USE THESE AS A TEAM...
...IT LEADS TO ONE MEMBER DETONATING WHEN THEY FEEL SAFE, PUTTING EVERYONE ELSE IN DANGER.
HE DIDN'T WANNA RUN THAT RISK, SO HE LEFT THEM BEHIND.

LISTEN, KIRA...

BUT NOW THE SITUATION'S CHANGED.

THE RISK'S A GIVEN.

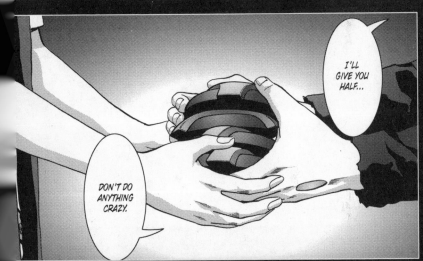

I'LL GIVE YOU HALF...

DON'T DO ANYTHING CRAZY.

WHEN I'VE PLANTED ONE, I'LL SIGNAL YOU WITH A TRIPLE ECHO.

THAT WAY, WE CAN BLOW 'EM UP POINT-BLANK.

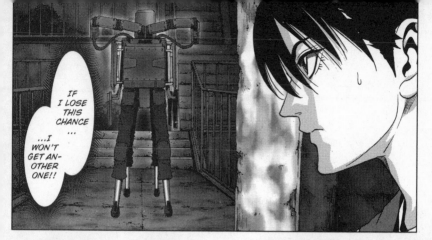

IF I LOSE THIS CHANCE... ...I WON'T GET ANOTHER ONE!!

Kira-kun...

You can't mean...

Pi

ダッ
DA
(DASH)

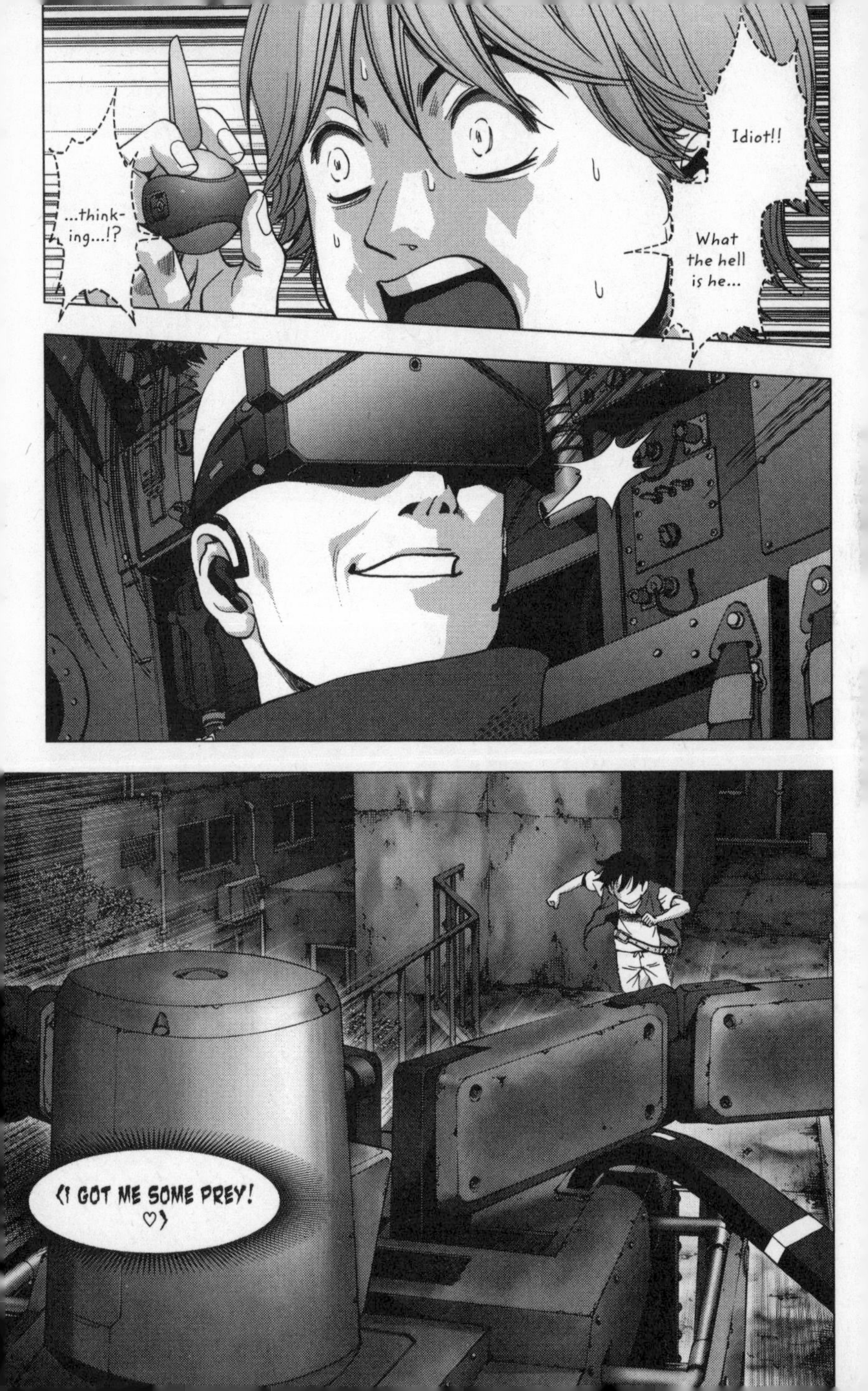
Idiot!!
What the hell is he...
...think-ing...!?
‹I GOT ME SOME PREY! ♡›

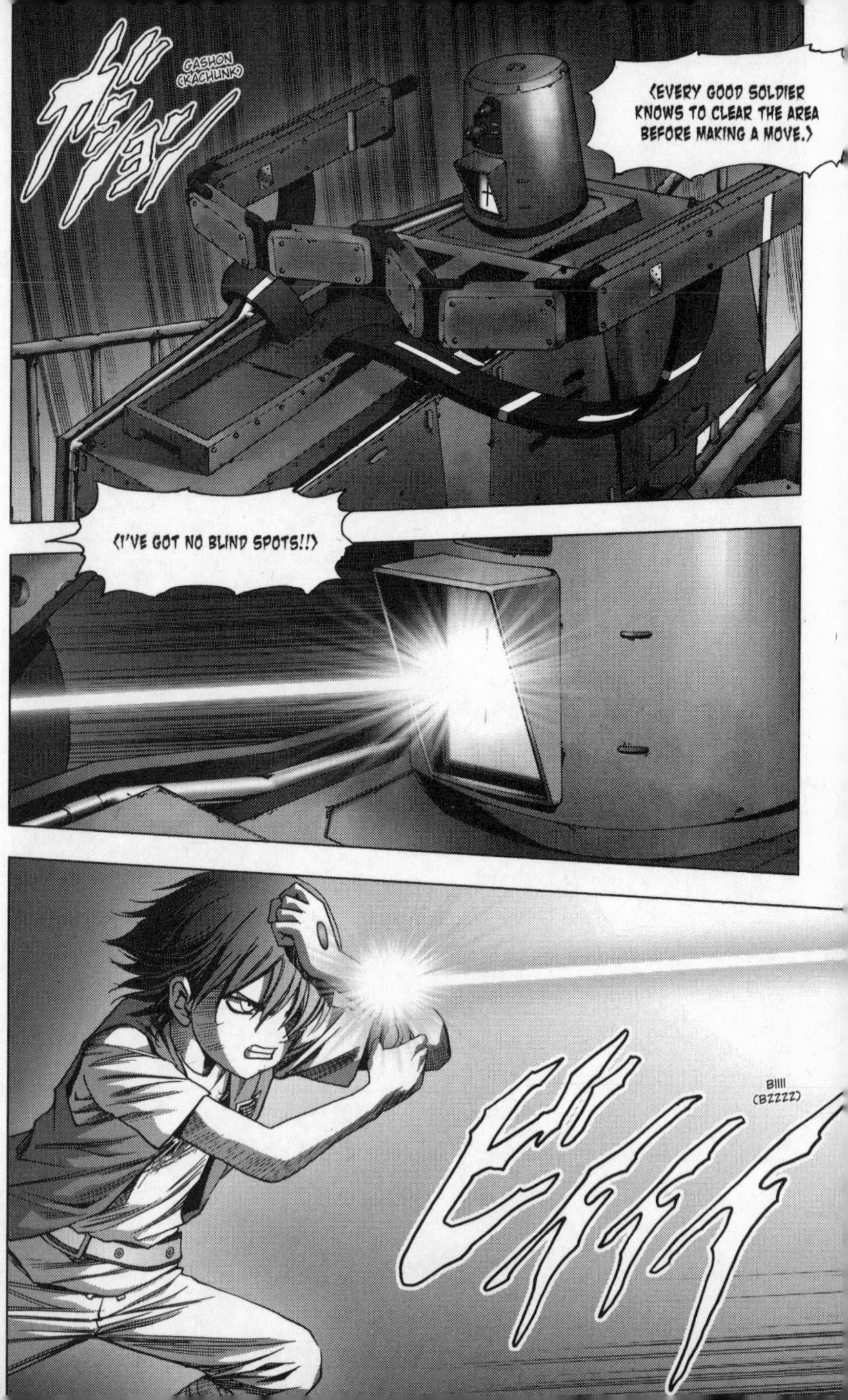
GASHON
(KACHUNK)
<EVERY GOOD SOLDIER KNOWS TO CLEAR THE AREA BEFORE MAKING A MOVE.>
<I'VE GOT NO BLIND SPOTS!!>
BIIII
(BZZZZ)

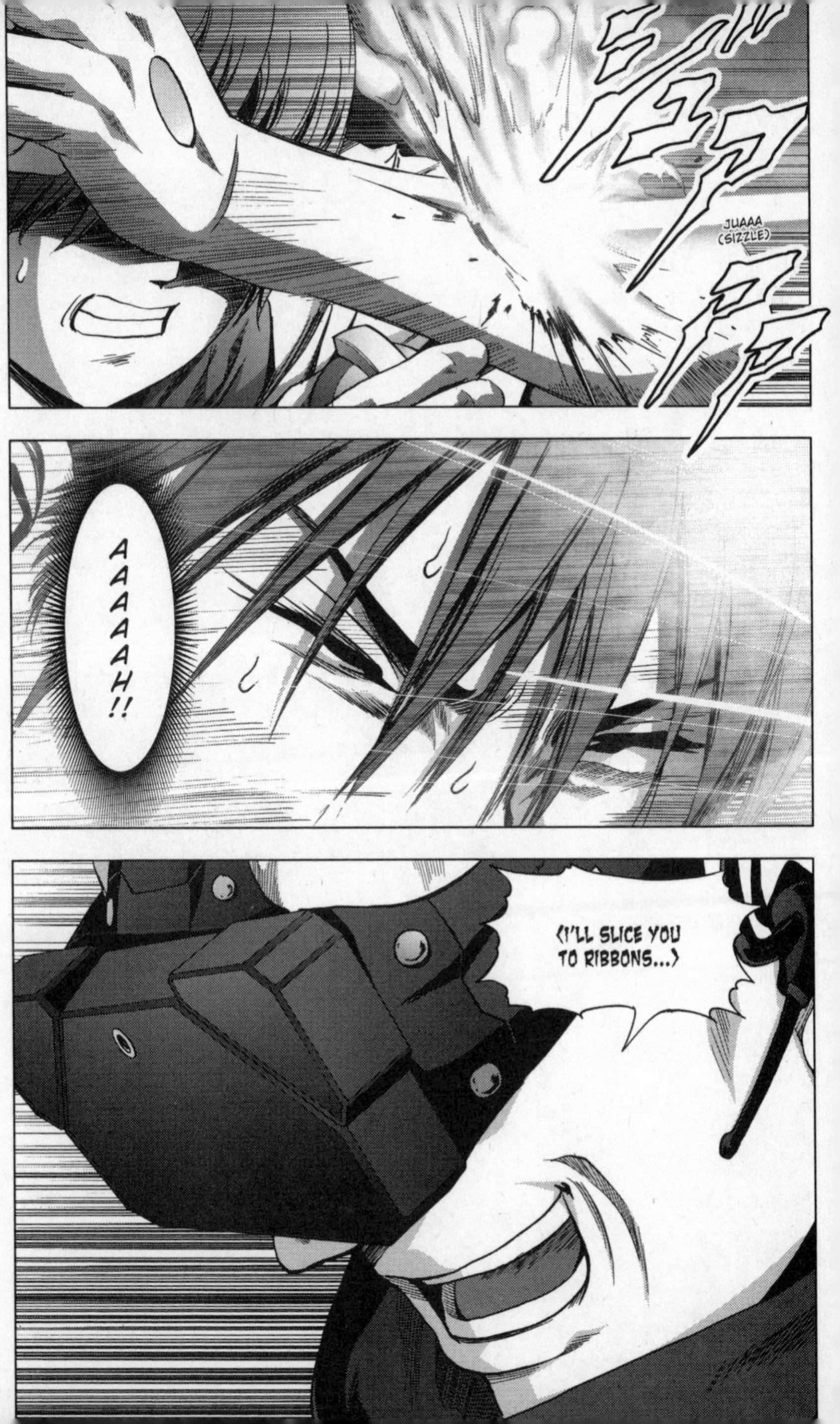
JUAAA (SIZZLE)
AAAAAAH!!
‹I'LL SLICE YOU TO RIBBONS...›

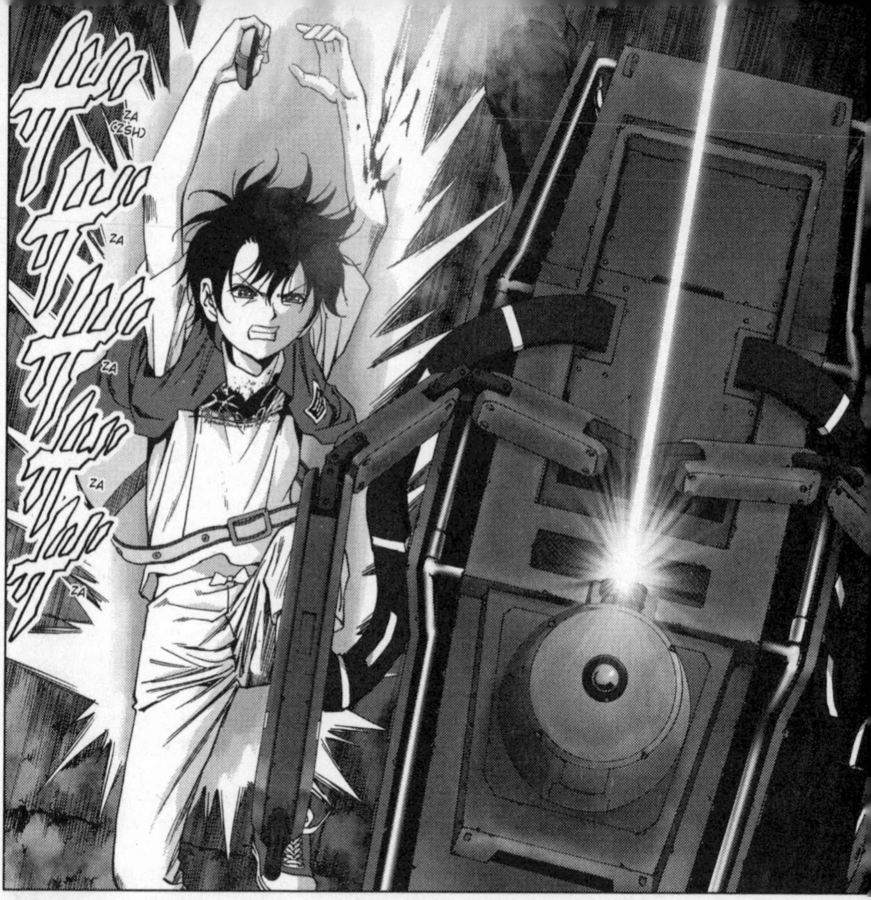
ZA
(ZSH)
ZA
ZA
ZA
ZA
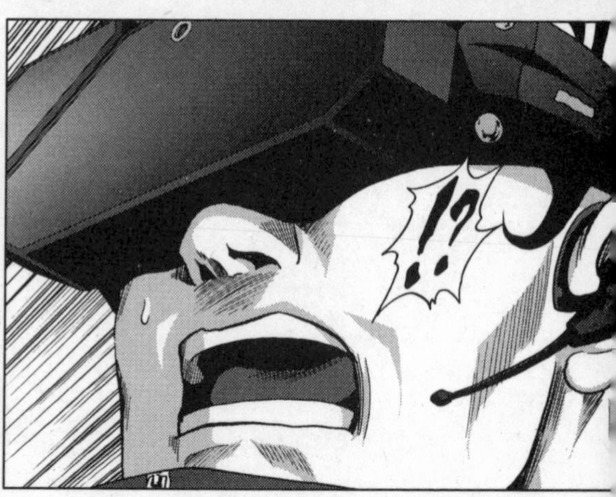
!?
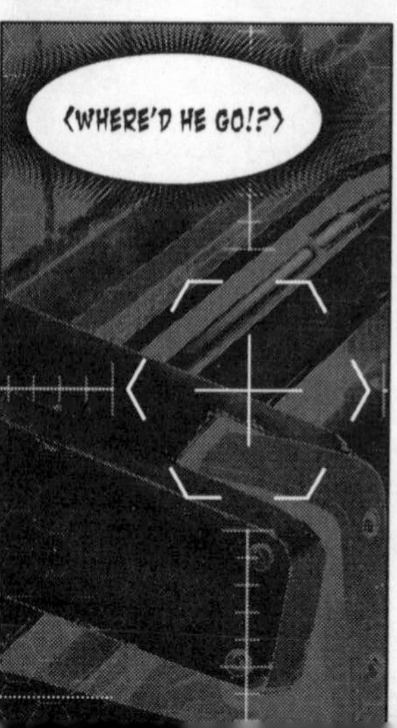
⟨WHERE'D HE GO!?⟩

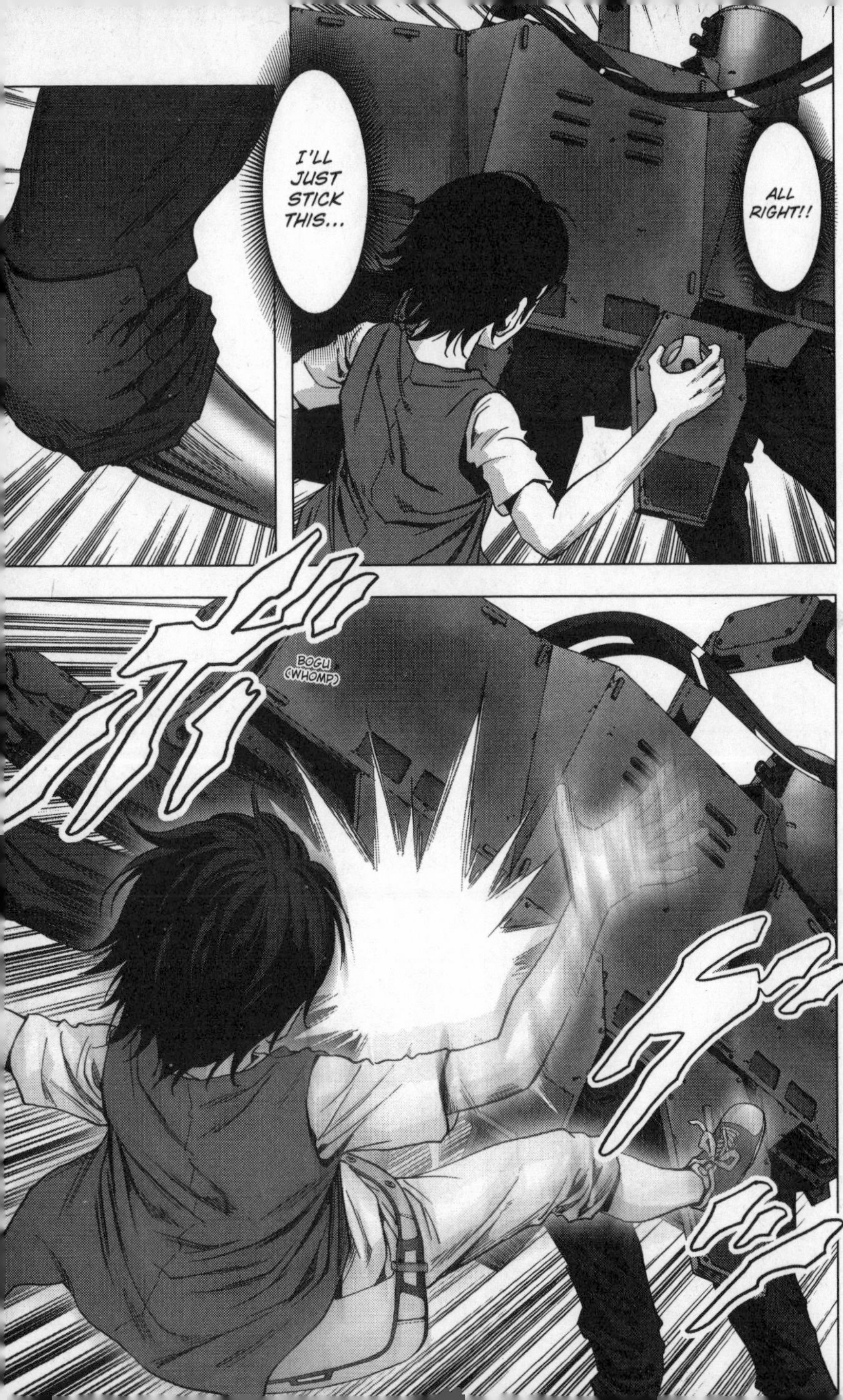
ALL RIGHT!!
I'LL JUST STICK THIS...
BOGU (WHOMP)

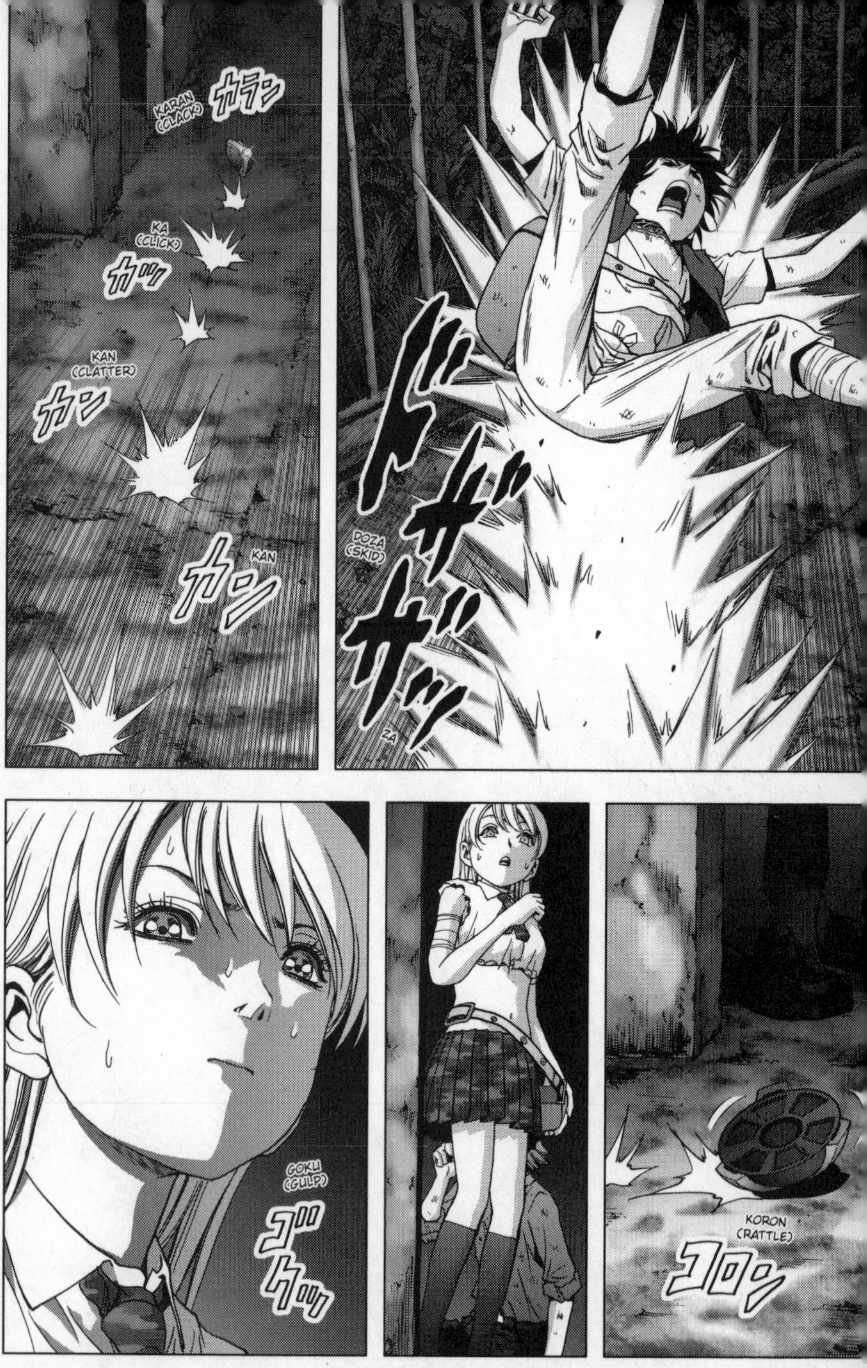
DOZA (SKID)
ドザザッ
ZA
KARAN (CLACK)
カラン
KA (CLICK)
カッ
KAN (CLATTER)
カン
KAN
カン
KORON (RATTLE)
コロン
GOKU (GULP)
ゴクッ

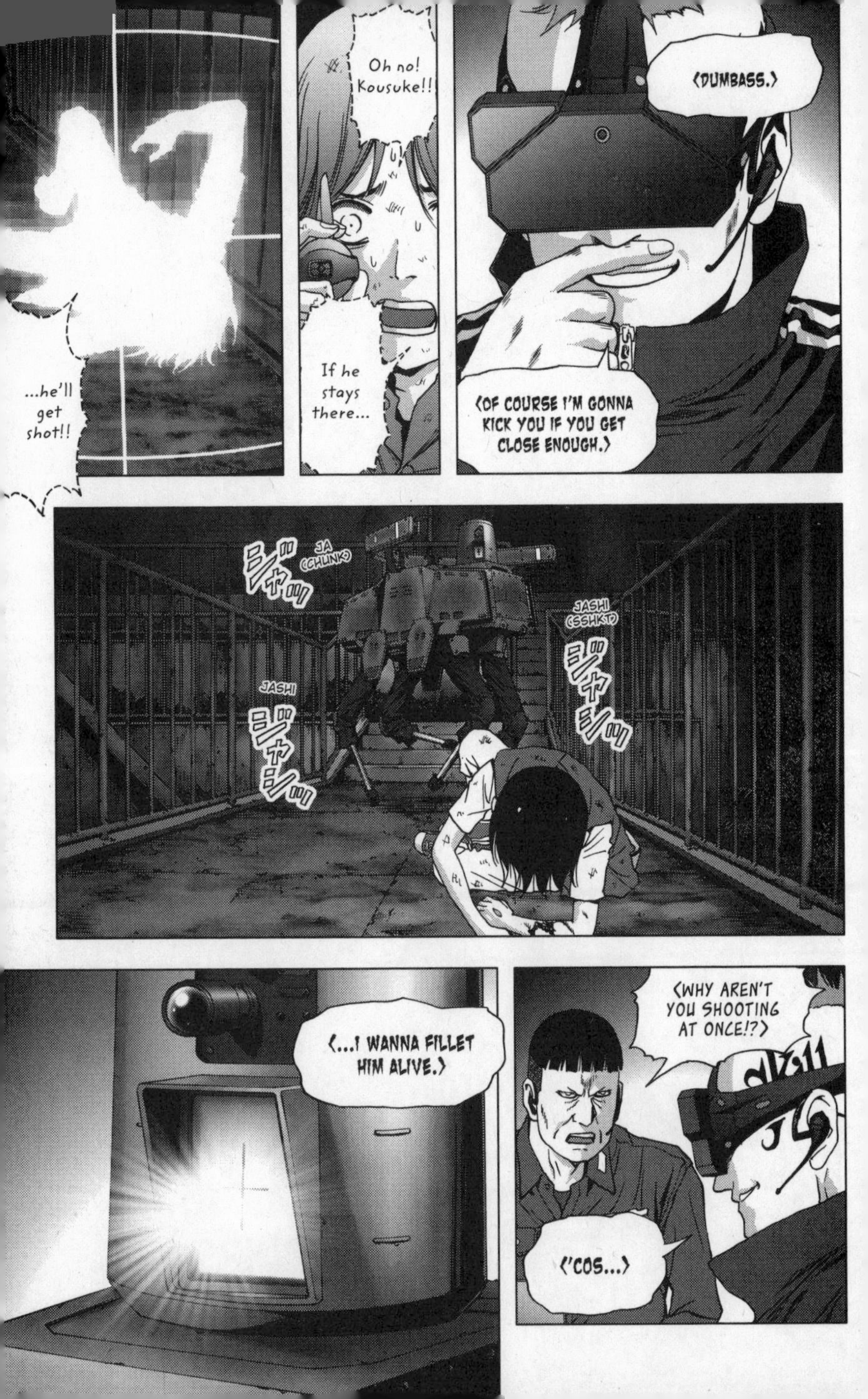
⟨DUMBASS.⟩
⟨OF COURSE I'M GONNA KICK YOU IF YOU GET CLOSE ENOUGH.⟩
Oh no! Kousuke!!
If he stays there...
...he'll get shot!!
JA (CHLUNK)
JASHI (SSHKT)
JASHI
⟨WHY AREN'T YOU SHOOTING AT ONCE!?⟩
⟨'COS...⟩
⟨...I WANNA FILLET HIM ALIVE.⟩

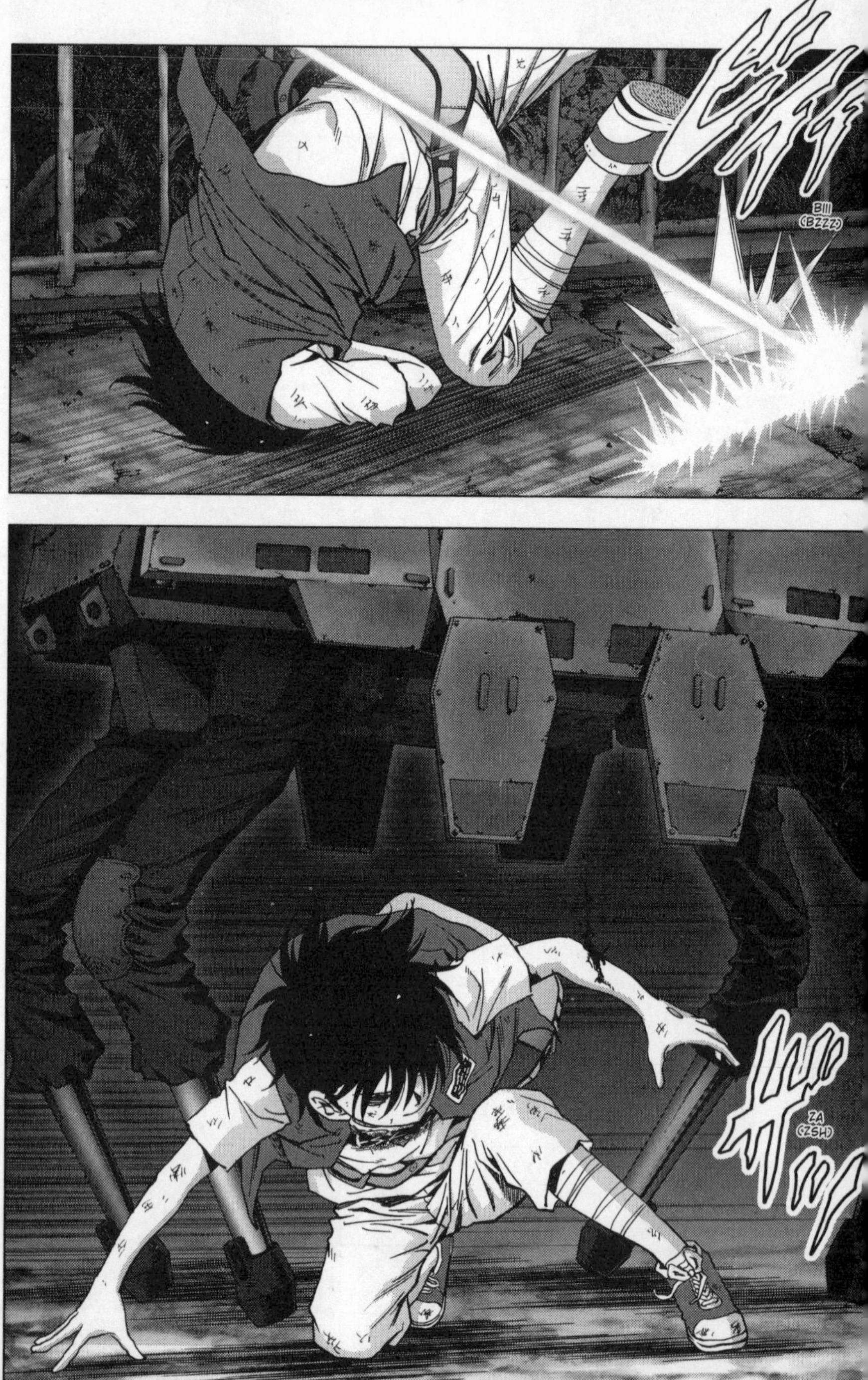
BIII
(BZZZ)
ZA
(ZSH)

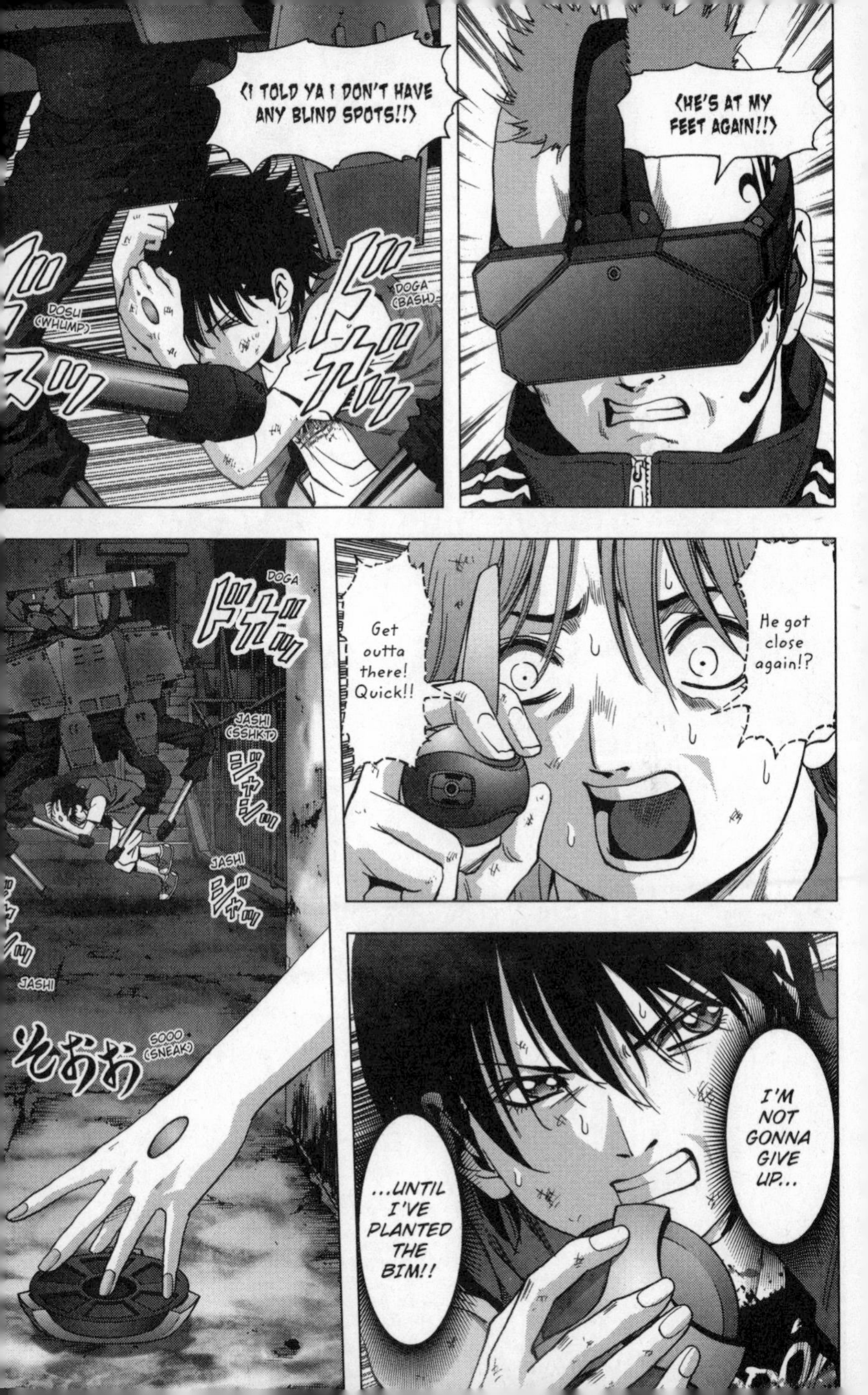
‹HE'S AT MY FEET AGAIN!!›
‹I TOLD YA I DON'T HAVE ANY BLIND SPOTS!!›
DOGA (BASH)
DOSU (WHUMP)
He got close again!?
Get outta there! Quick!!
I'M NOT GONNA GIVE UP...
...UNTIL I'VE PLANTED THE BIM!!
DOGA
JASHI (SSHKT)
JASHI
JASHI
SOOO (SNEAK)

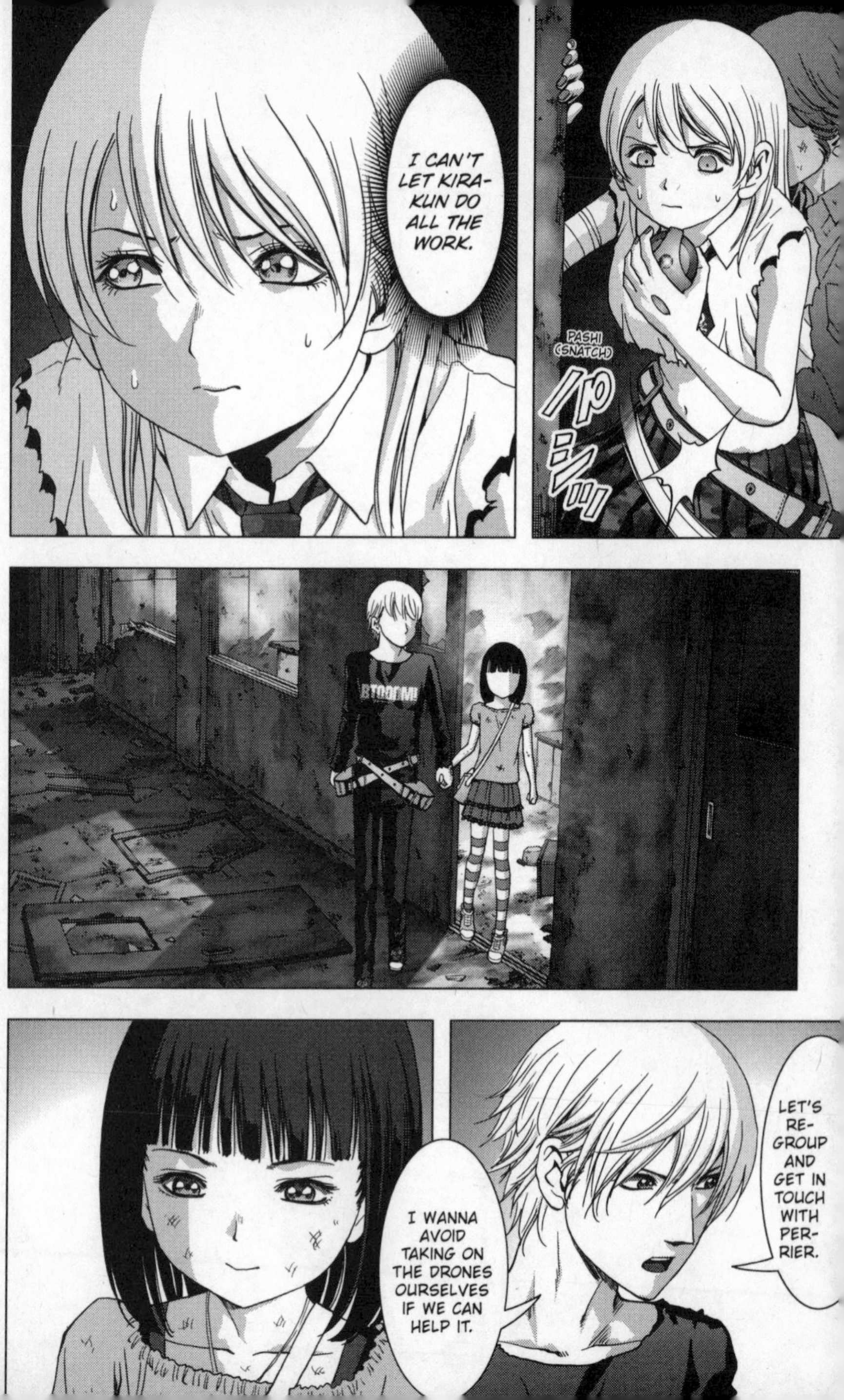
PASHI (SNATCH)
パッ
I CAN'T LET KIRA-KUN DO ALL THE WORK.
LET'S RE-GROUP AND GET IN TOUCH WITH PER-RIER.
I WANNA AVOID TAKING ON THE DRONES OURSELVES IF WE CAN HELP IT.

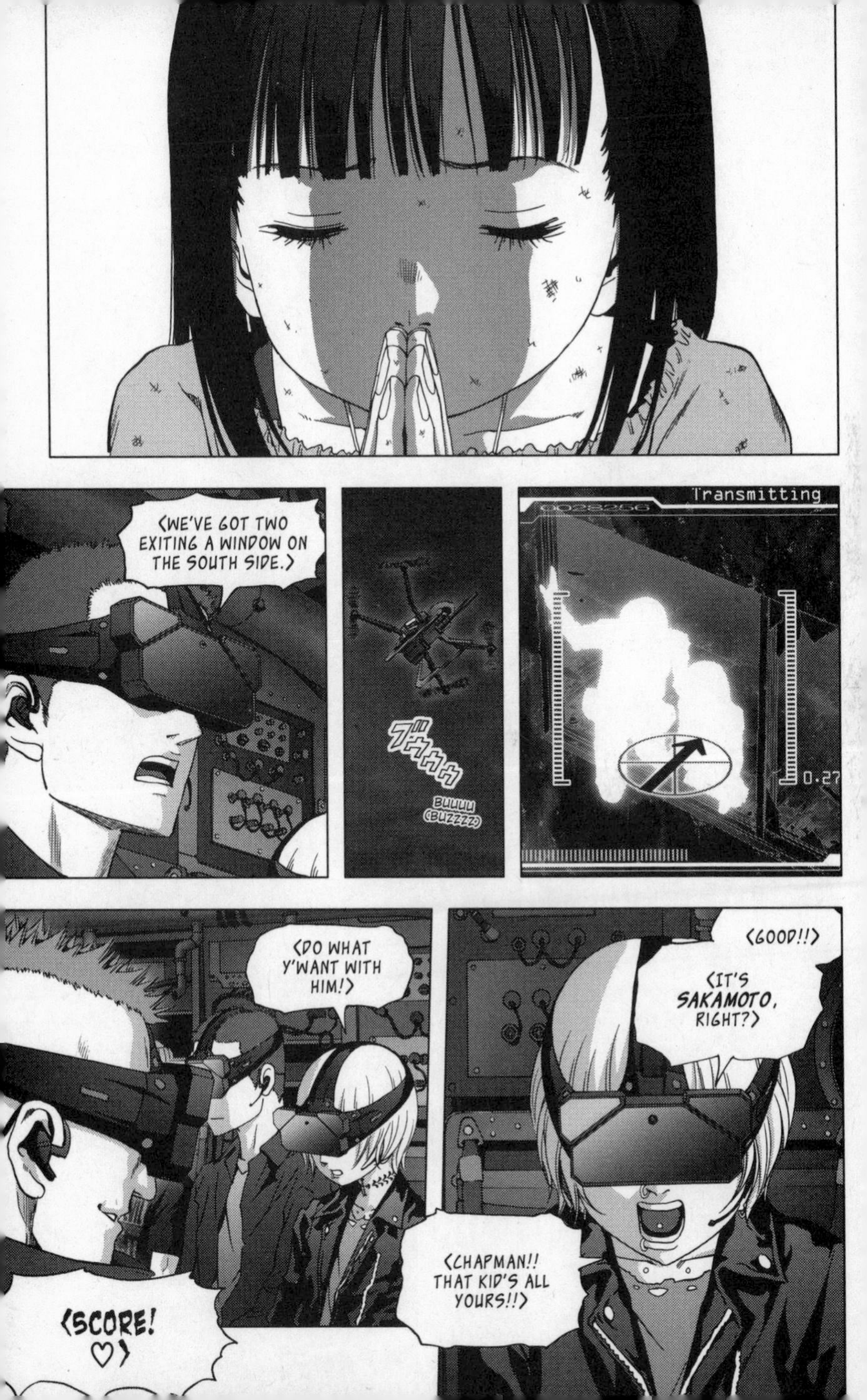
Transmitting
0.27
ブウウウ
Buuuu (BUZZZZ)
〈WE'VE GOT TWO EXITING A WINDOW ON THE SOUTH SIDE.〉
〈GOOD!!〉
〈IT'S SAKAMOTO, RIGHT?〉
〈CHAPMAN!! THAT KID'S ALL YOURS!!〉
〈DO WHAT Y'WANT WITH HIM!〉
〈SCORE! ♡〉

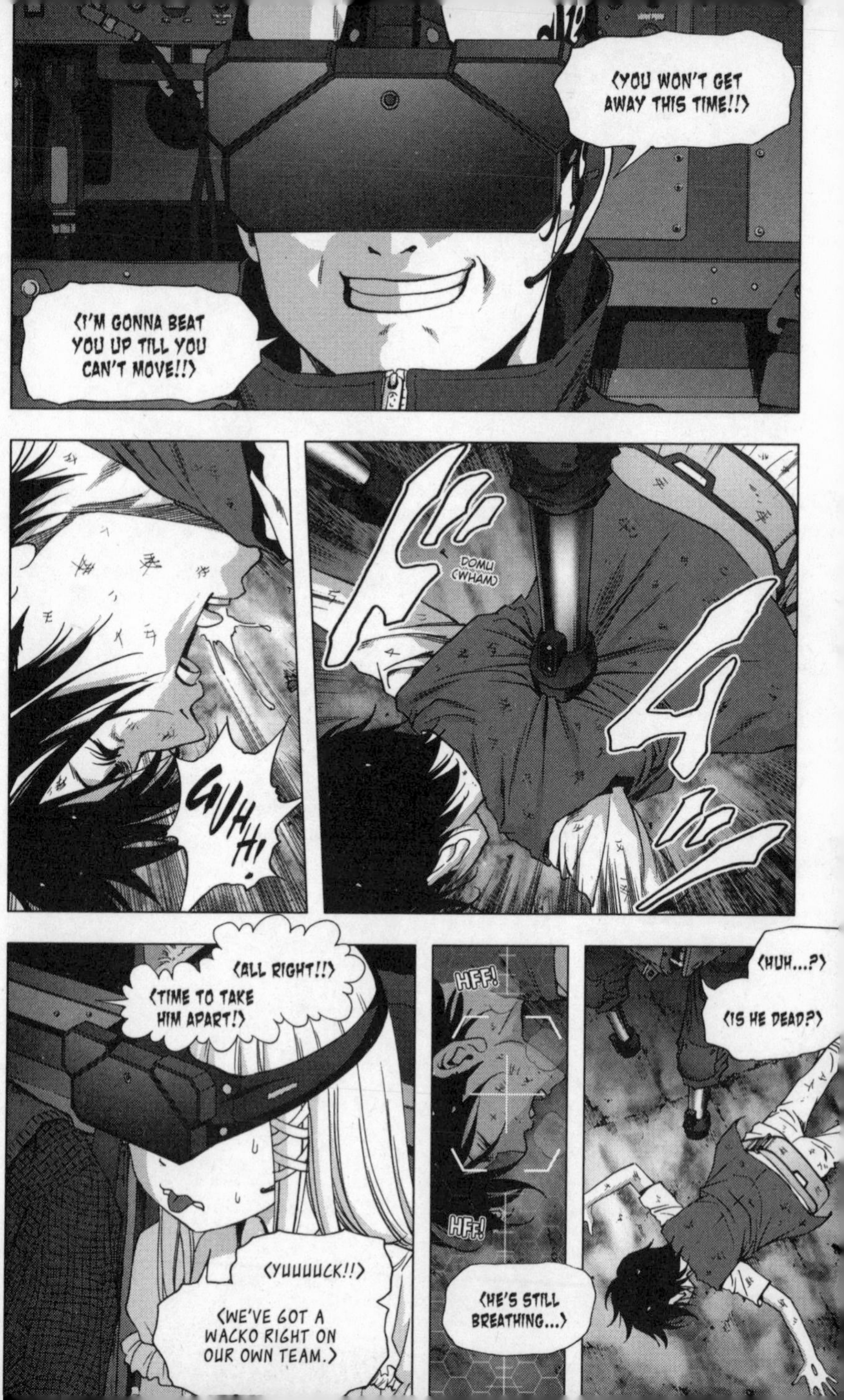

<YOU WON'T GET AWAY THIS TIME!!>
<I'M GONNA BEAT YOU UP TILL YOU CAN'T MOVE!!>
DOMU (WHAM)
GUHH!
<HUH...?>
<IS HE DEAD?>
HFF!
HFF!
<HE'S STILL BREATHING...>
<ALL RIGHT!!>
<TIME TO TAKE HIM APART!>
<YUUUUCK!!>
<WE'VE GOT A WACKO RIGHT ON OUR OWN TEAM.>

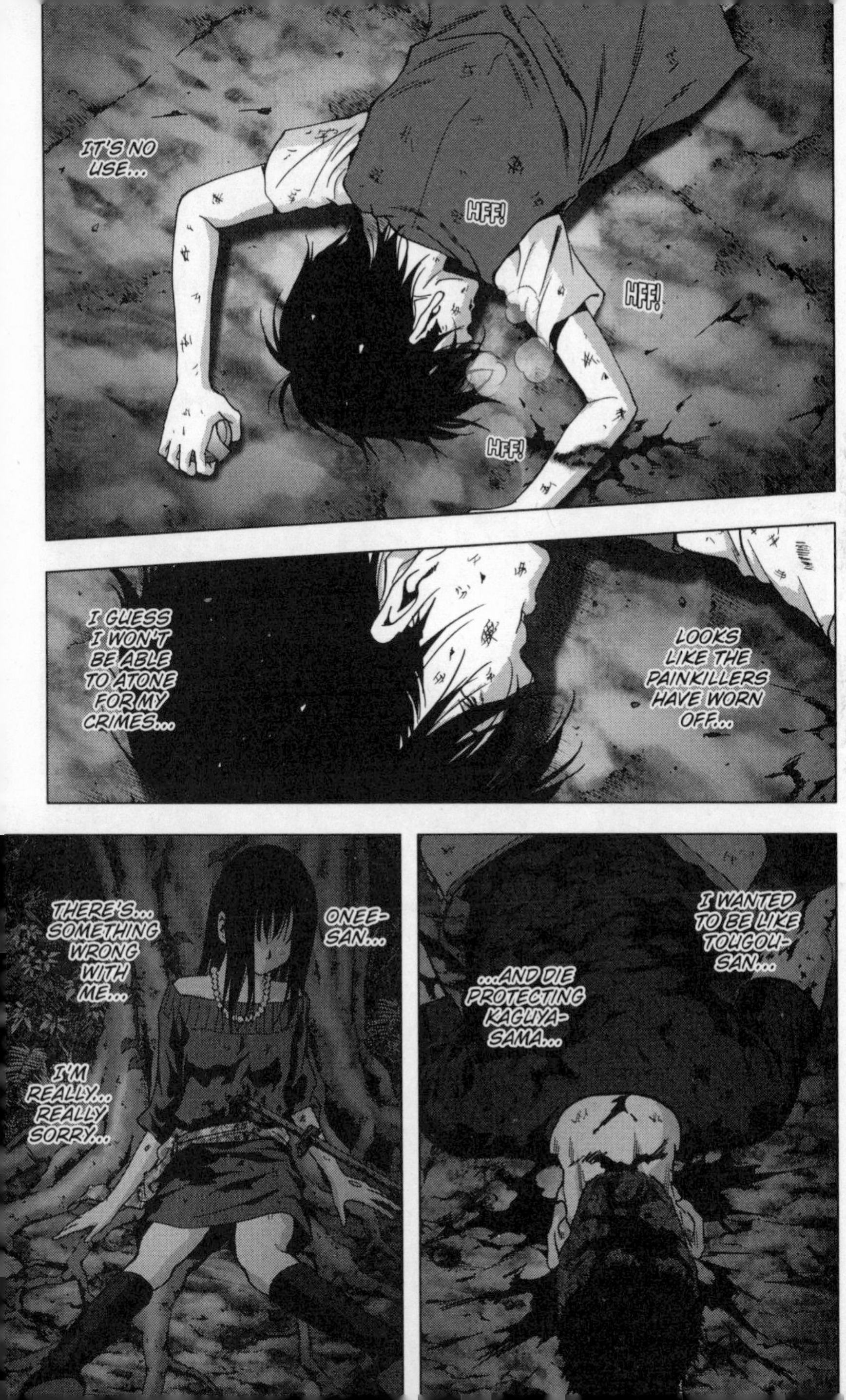
HFF!
HFF!
HFF!
IT'S NO USE...
LOOKS LIKE THE PAINKILLERS HAVE WORN OFF...
I GUESS I WON'T BE ABLE TO ATONE FOR MY CRIMES...
I WANTED TO BE LIKE TOUGOU-SAN...
...AND DIE PROTECTING KAGUYA-SAMA...
ONEE-SAN...
THERE'S... SOMETHING WRONG WITH ME...
I'M REALLY... REALLY SORRY...

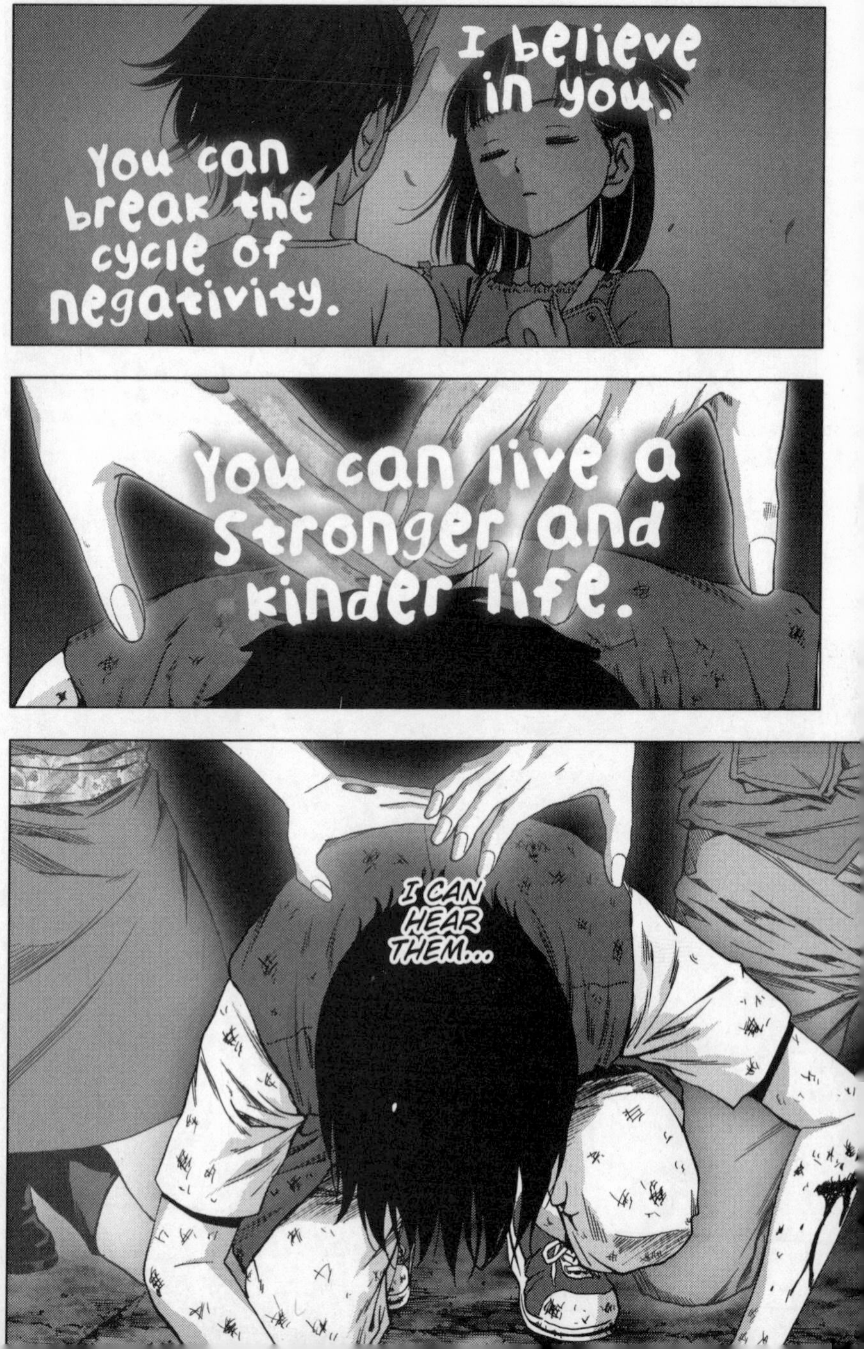
I believe in you.
You can break the cycle of negativity.
You can live a stronger and kinder life.
I CAN HEAR THEM...

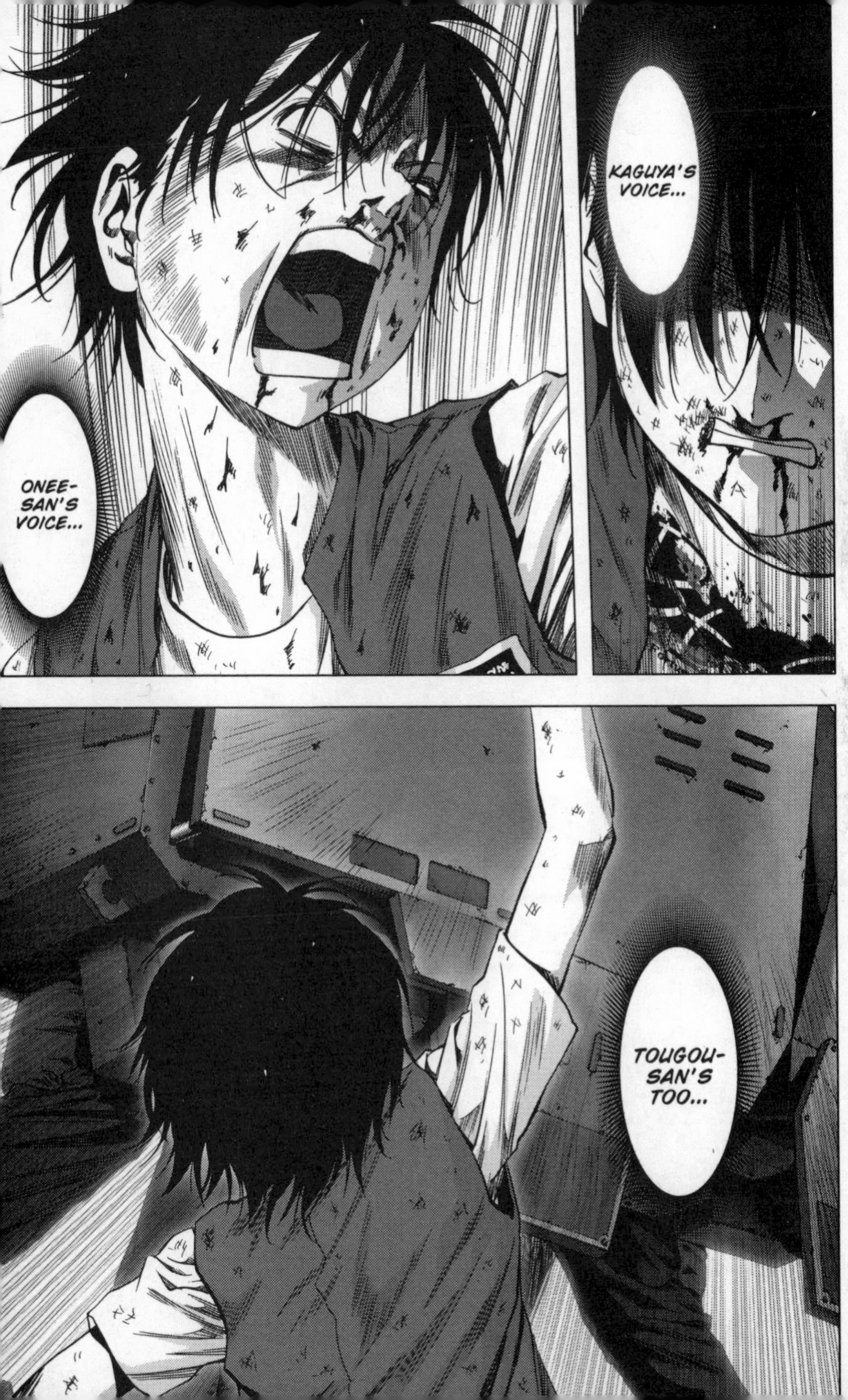
KAGUYA'S VOICE...
ONEE-SAN'S VOICE...
TOUGOU-SAN'S TOO...

BAN
(BAM)

!?

〈WH...WHAT...〉

〈...DID HE DO...?〉

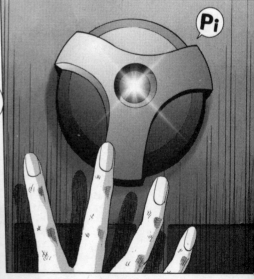

Pi

PIKO

PIKO
(PANG)

PIKOOON

PIIIN
(STIIING)

A
TRIPLE
ECHO!?

PIIIN

PIIIN
(STIIING)

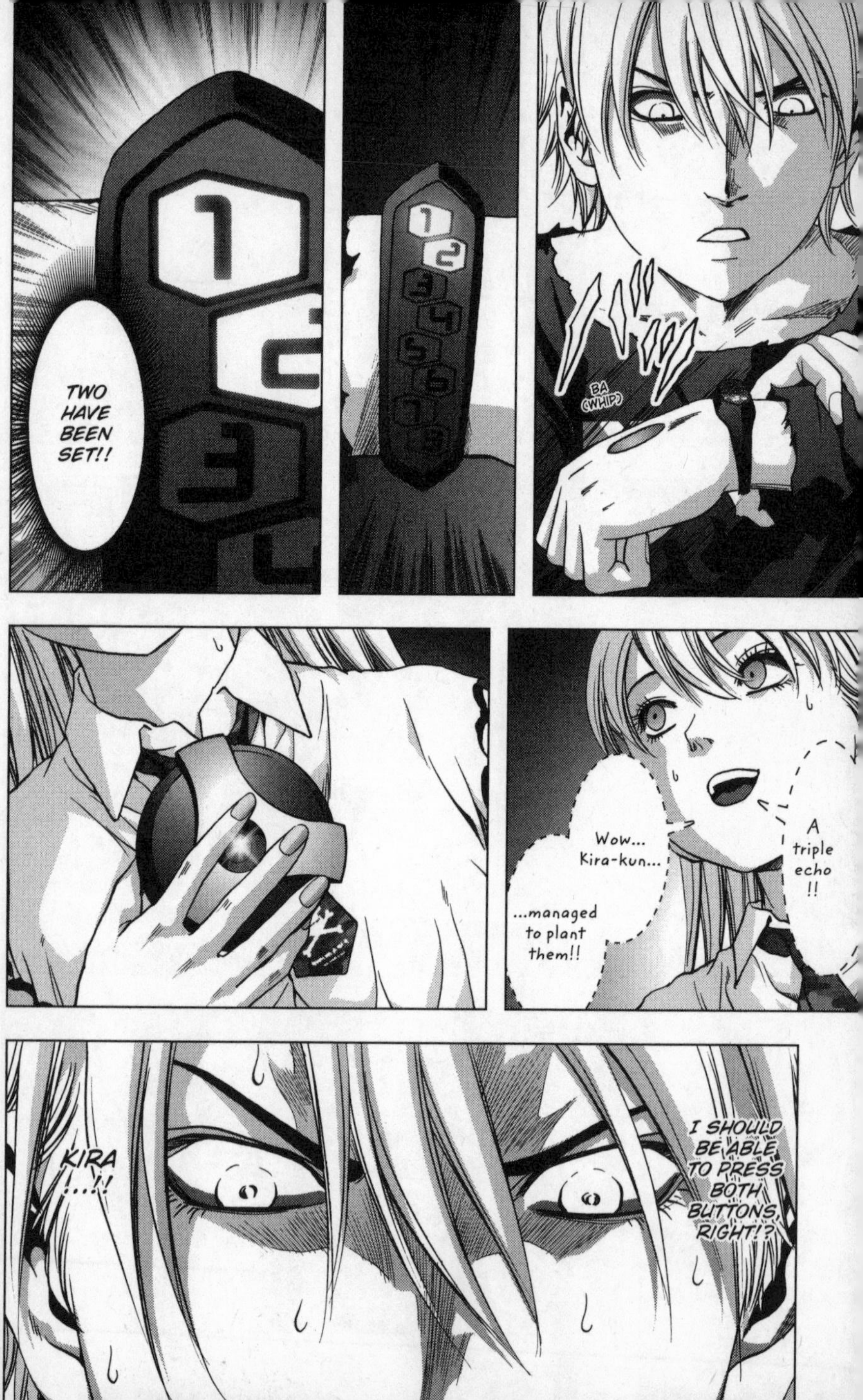
BA (WHIP)
TWO HAVE BEEN SET!!
A triple echo!!
Wow... Kira-kun...
...managed to plant them!!
I SHOULD BE ABLE TO PRESS BOTH BUTTONS, RIGHT!?
KIRA ...!!

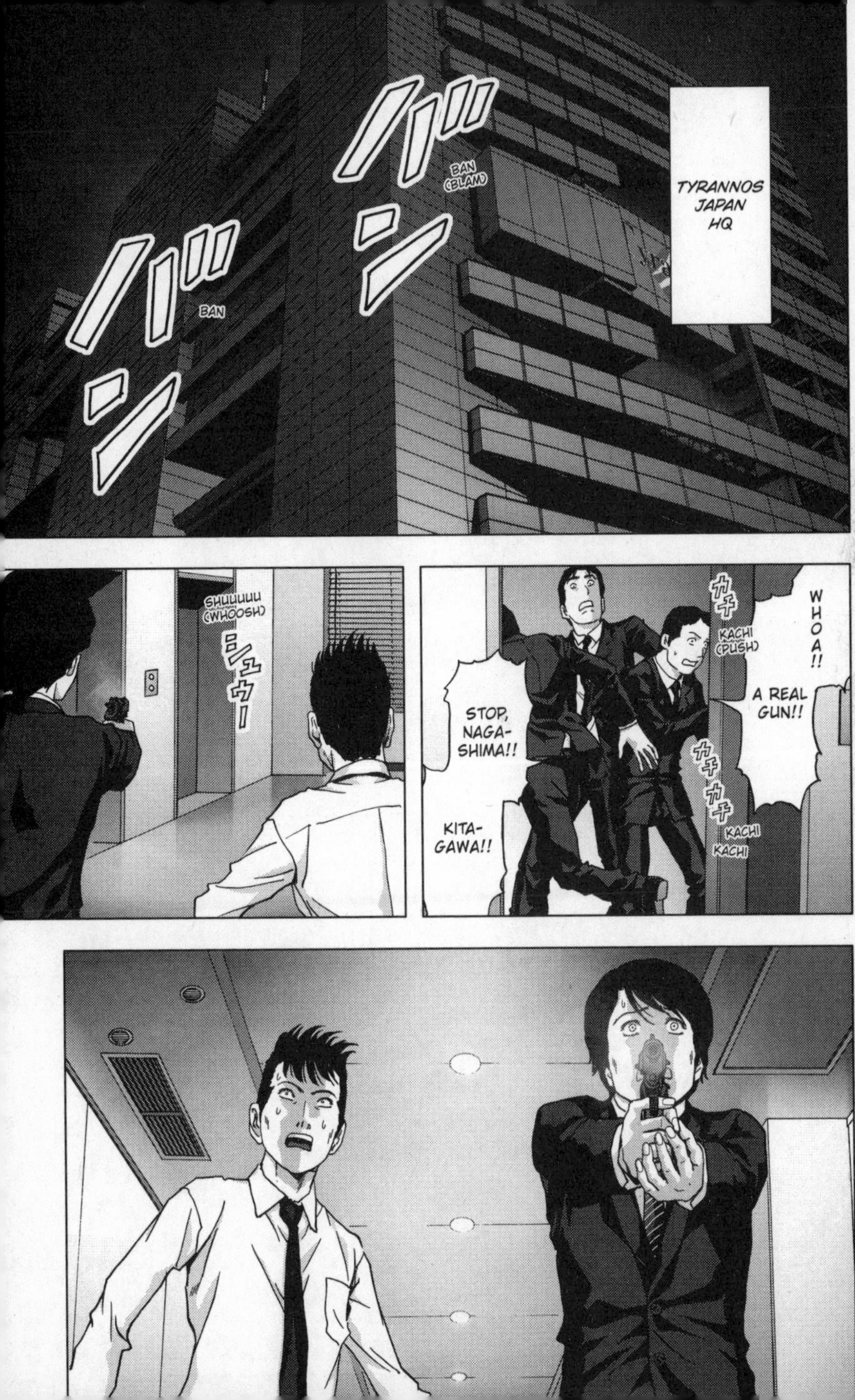

TYRANNOS JAPAN HQ
バン
BAN (BLAM)
バン
BAN
WHOA!!
A REAL GUN!!
カチ
KACHI (PUSH)
STOP, NAGA-SHIMA!!
KITA-GAWA!!
カチカチ
KACHI KACHI
SHUUUUU (WHOOSH)
シュウー

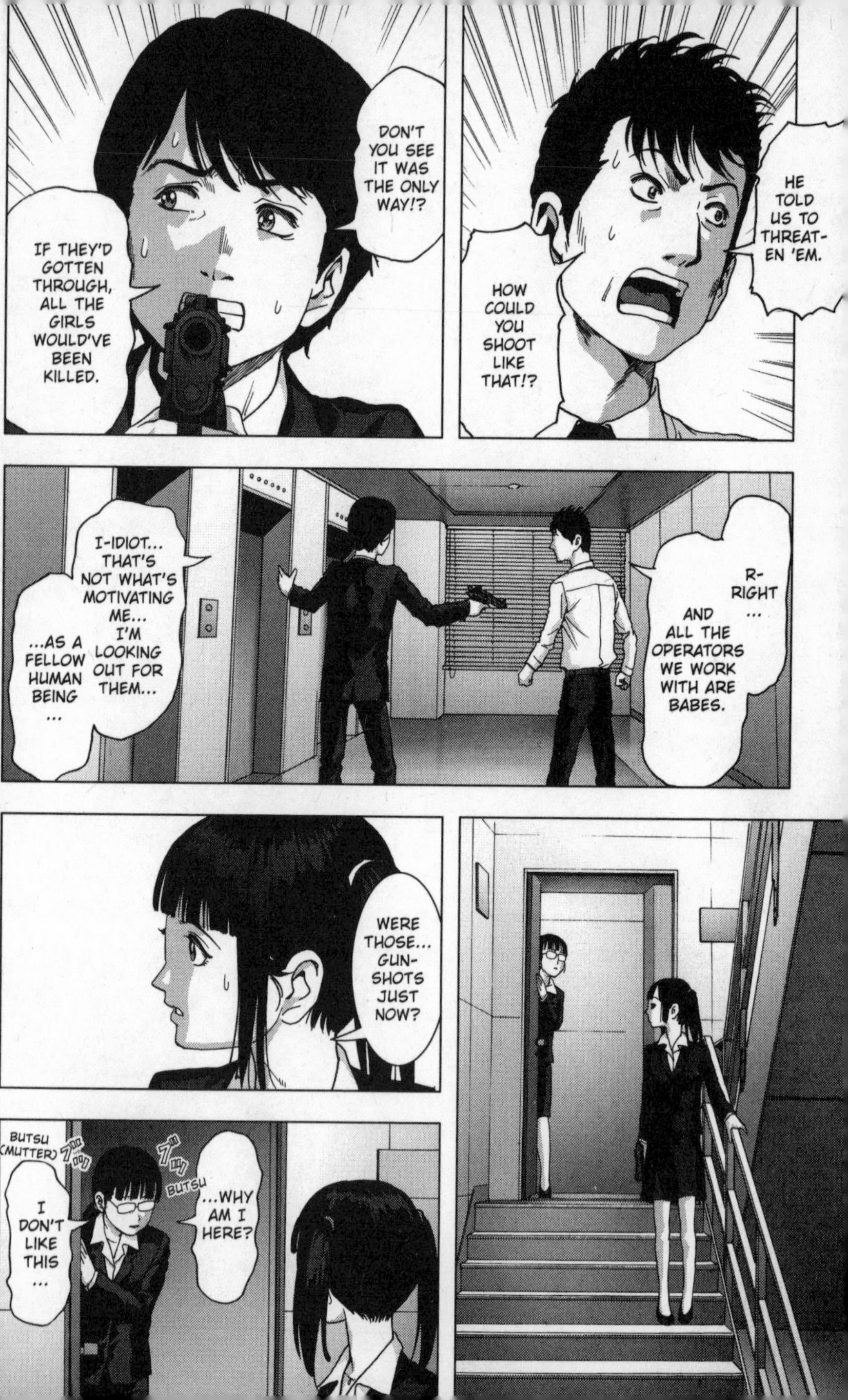
HE TOLD US TO THREAT-EN 'EM.
HOW COULD YOU SHOOT LIKE THAT!?
DON'T YOU SEE IT WAS THE ONLY WAY!?
IF THEY'D GOTTEN THROUGH, ALL THE GIRLS WOULD'VE BEEN KILLED.
R-RIGHT ...
AND ALL THE OPERATORS WE WORK WITH ARE BABES.
I-IDIOT... THAT'S NOT WHAT'S MOTIVATING ME... I'M LOOKING OUT FOR THEM...
...AS A FELLOW HUMAN BEING ...
WERE THOSE... GUN-SHOTS JUST NOW?
BUTSU
...WHY AM I HERE?
BUTSU (MUTTER)
I DON'T LIKE THIS ...

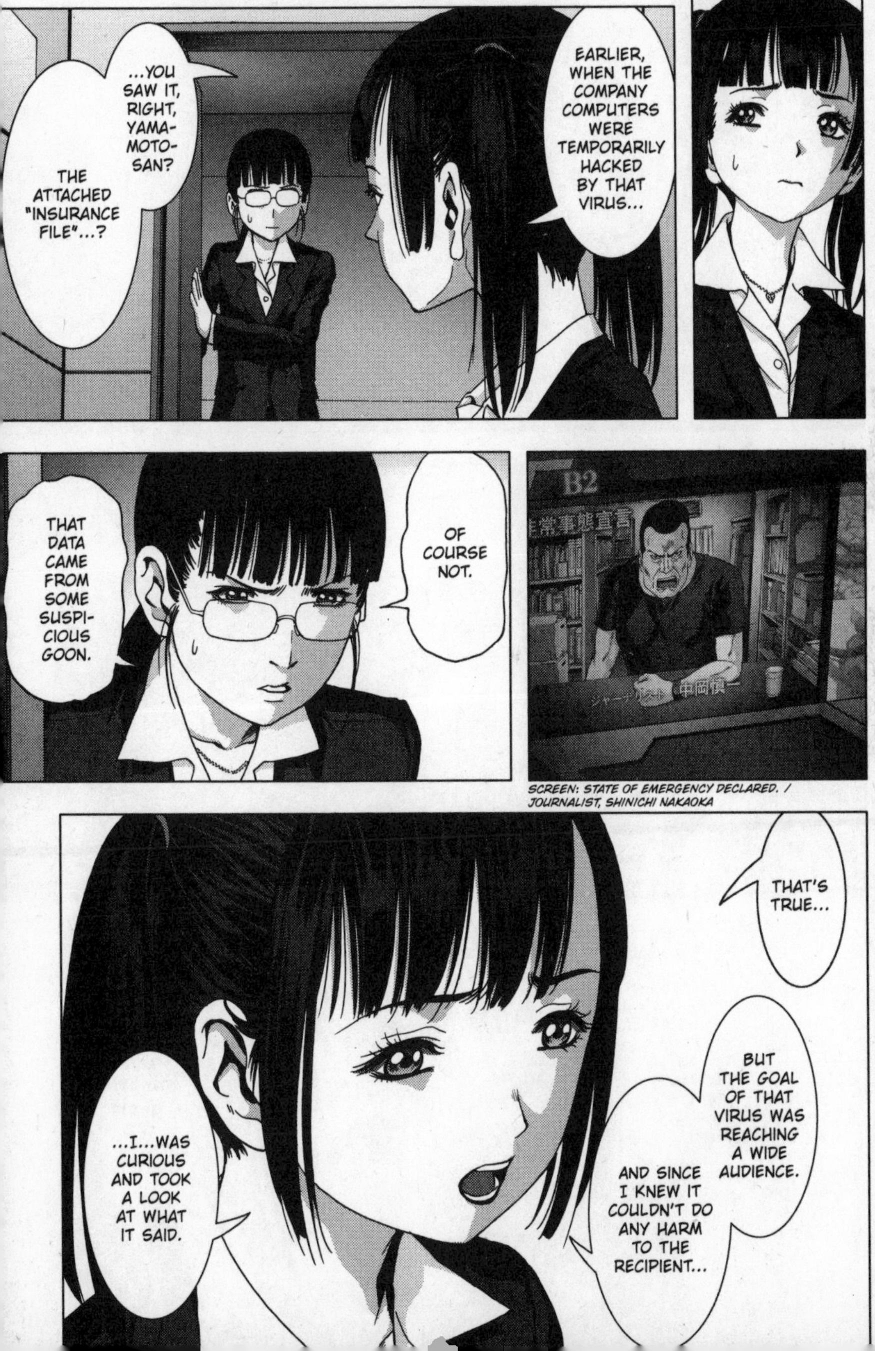
EARLIER, WHEN THE COMPANY COMPUTERS WERE TEMPORARILY HACKED BY THAT VIRUS...
...YOU SAW IT, RIGHT, YAMA-MOTO-SAN?
THE ATTACHED "INSURANCE FILE"...?
SCREEN: STATE OF EMERGENCY DECLARED. / JOURNALIST, SHINICHI NAKAOKA
OF COURSE NOT.
THAT DATA CAME FROM SOME SUSPI-CIOUS GOON.
THAT'S TRUE...
BUT THE GOAL OF THAT VIRUS WAS REACHING A WIDE AUDIENCE.
AND SINCE I KNEW IT COULDN'T DO ANY HARM TO THE RECIPIENT...
...I...WAS CURIOUS AND TOOK A LOOK AT WHAT IT SAID.

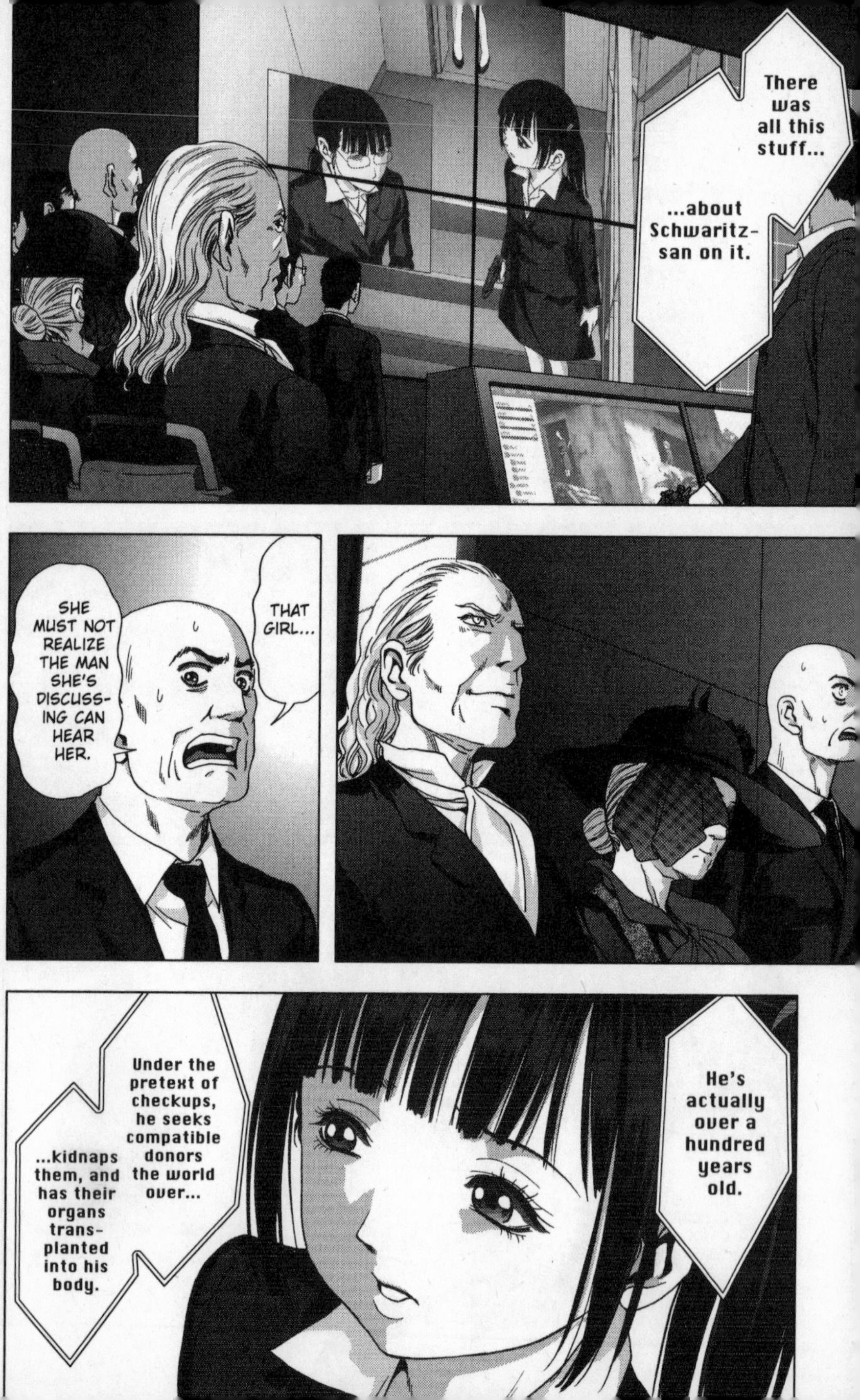
There was all this stuff...
...about Schwaritz-san on it.
THAT GIRL...
SHE MUST NOT REALIZE THE MAN SHE'S DISCUSSING CAN HEAR HER.
He's actually over a hundred years old.
Under the pretext of checkups, he seeks compatible donors the world over...
...kidnaps them, and has their organs transplanted into his body.

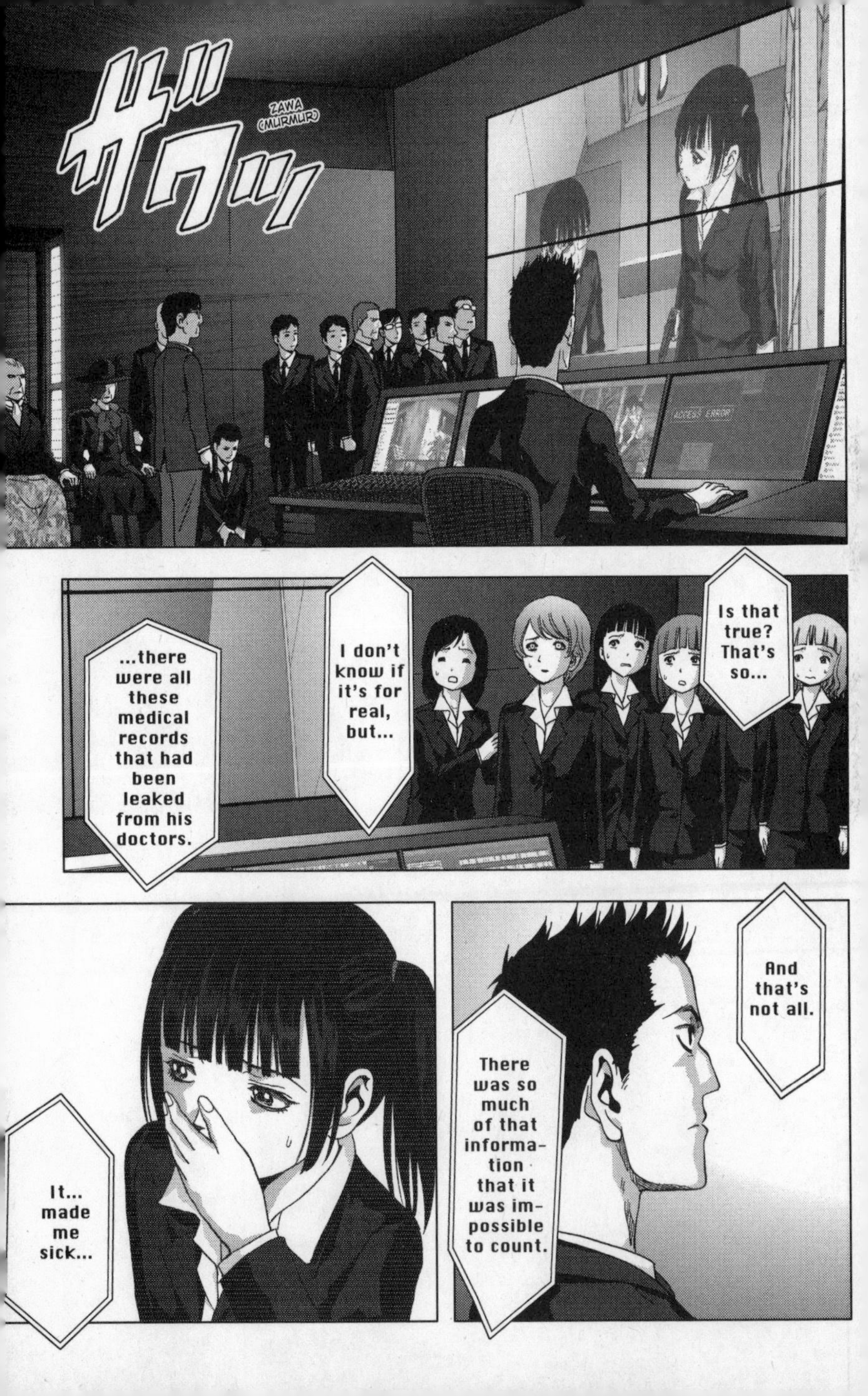
ザワッ
ZAWA (MURMUR)
ACCESS ERROR
Is that true? That's so...
I don't know if it's for real, but...
...there were all these medical records that had been leaked from his doctors.
And that's not all.
There was so much of that information that it was impossible to count.
It... made me sick...

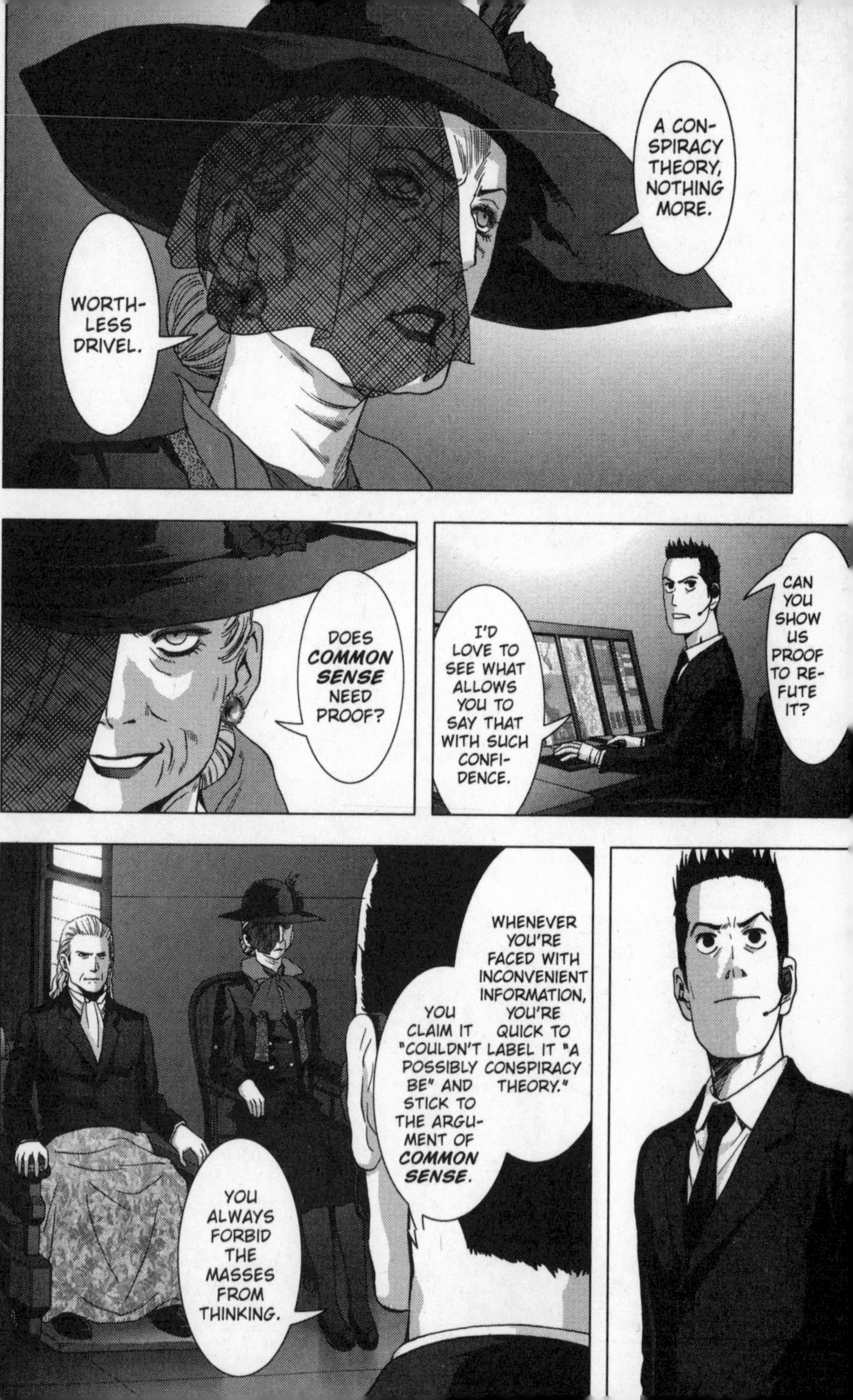
A CON-SPIRACY THEORY, NOTHING MORE.
WORTH-LESS DRIVEL.
CAN YOU SHOW US PROOF TO RE-FUTE IT?
I'D LOVE TO SEE WHAT ALLOWS YOU TO SAY THAT WITH SUCH CONFI-DENCE.
DOES COMMON SENSE NEED PROOF?
WHENEVER YOU'RE FACED WITH INCONVENIENT INFORMATION, YOU'RE QUICK TO LABEL IT "A CONSPIRACY THEORY."
YOU CLAIM IT "COULDN'T POSSIBLY BE" AND STICK TO THE ARGU-MENT OF COMMON SENSE.
YOU ALWAYS FORBID THE MASSES FROM THINKING.

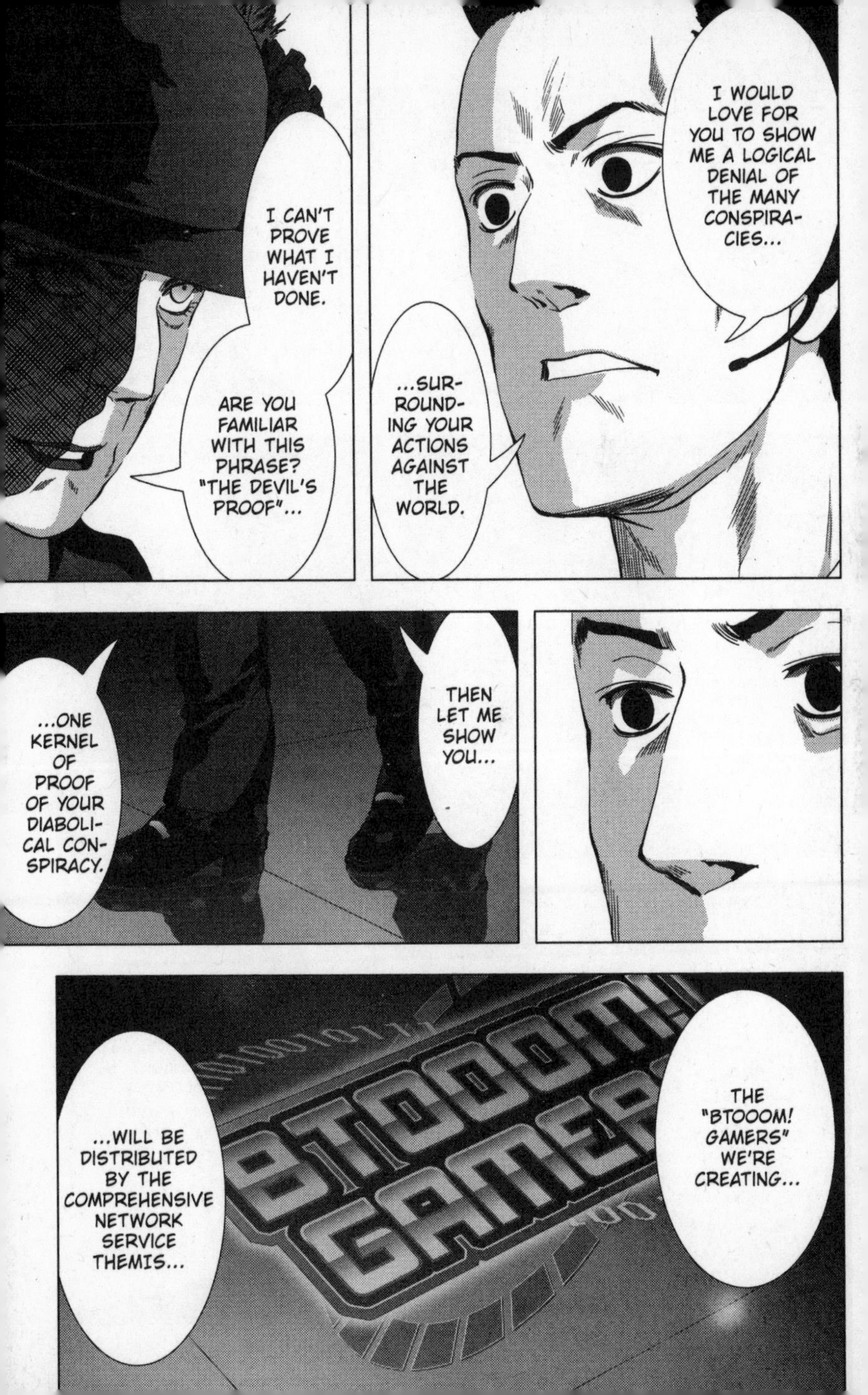
I WOULD LOVE FOR YOU TO SHOW ME A LOGICAL DENIAL OF THE MANY CONSPIRACIES...
...SURROUNDING YOUR ACTIONS AGAINST THE WORLD.
I CAN'T PROVE WHAT I HAVEN'T DONE.
ARE YOU FAMILIAR WITH THIS PHRASE? "THE DEVIL'S PROOF"...
THEN LET ME SHOW YOU...
...ONE KERNEL OF PROOF OF YOUR DIABOLICAL CONSPIRACY.
THE "BTOOOM! GAMERS" WE'RE CREATING...
...WILL BE DISTRIBUTED BY THE COMPREHENSIVE NETWORK SERVICE THEMIS...

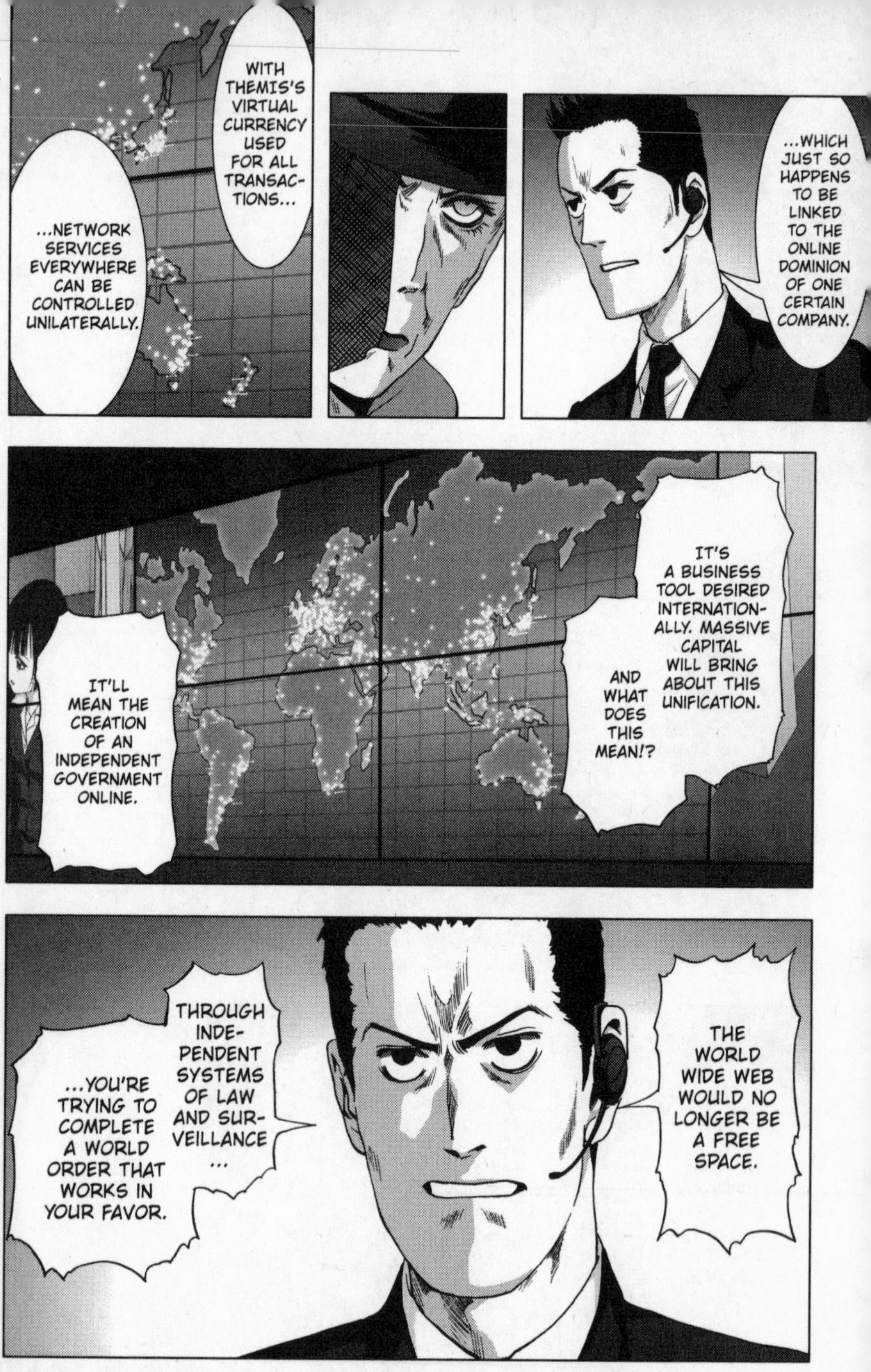
...WHICH JUST SO HAPPENS TO BE LINKED TO THE ONLINE DOMINION OF ONE CERTAIN COMPANY.
WITH THEMIS'S VIRTUAL CURRENCY USED FOR ALL TRANSACTIONS...
...NETWORK SERVICES EVERYWHERE CAN BE CONTROLLED UNILATERALLY.
IT'S A BUSINESS TOOL DESIRED INTERNATIONALLY. MASSIVE CAPITAL WILL BRING ABOUT THIS UNIFICATION.
AND WHAT DOES THIS MEAN!?
IT'LL MEAN THE CREATION OF AN INDEPENDENT GOVERNMENT ONLINE.
THE WORLD WIDE WEB WOULD NO LONGER BE A FREE SPACE.
THROUGH INDEPENDENT SYSTEMS OF LAW AND SURVEILLANCE...
...YOU'RE TRYING TO COMPLETE A WORLD ORDER THAT WORKS IN YOUR FAVOR.

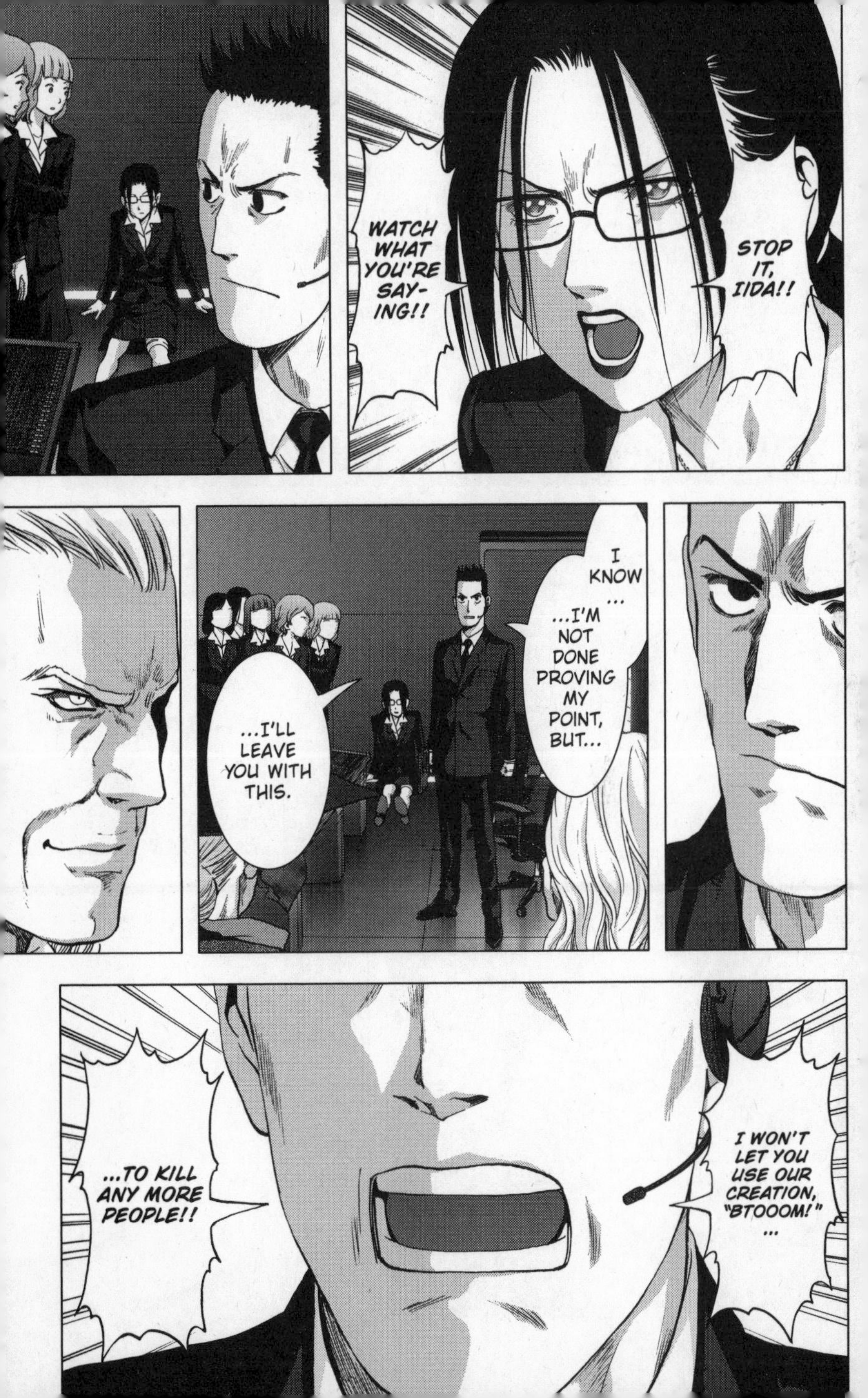
STOP IT, IIDA!!
WATCH WHAT YOU'RE SAYING!!
I KNOW...
...I'M NOT DONE PROVING MY POINT, BUT...
...I'LL LEAVE YOU WITH THIS.
I WON'T LET YOU USE OUR CREATION, "BTOOOM!"...
...TO KILL ANY MORE PEOPLE!!

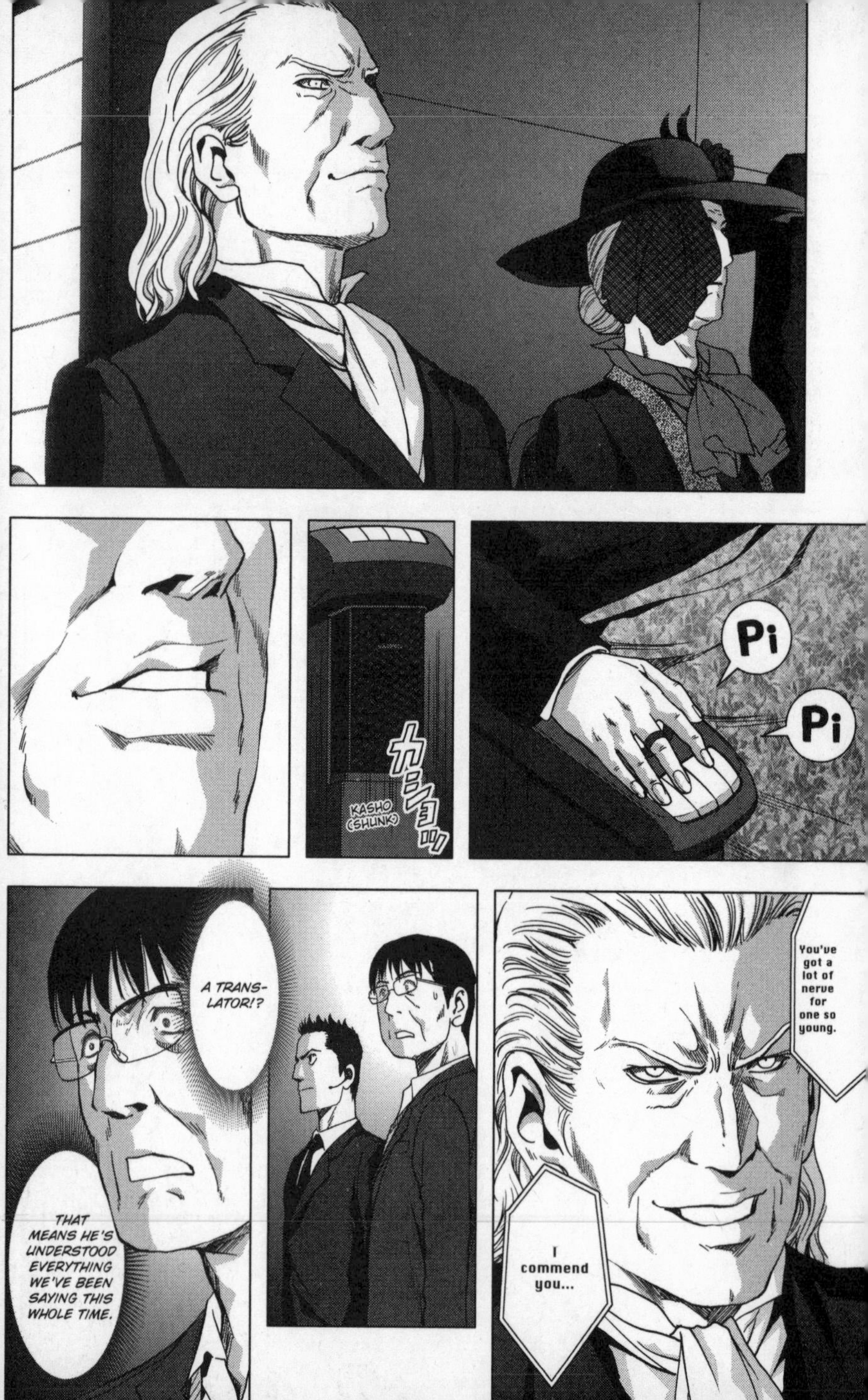
Pi
Pi
カショッ
KASHO (SHUNK)
You've got a lot of nerve for one so young.
I commend you...
A TRANSLATOR!?
THAT MEANS HE'S UNDERSTOOD EVERYTHING WE'VE BEEN SAYING THIS WHOLE TIME.

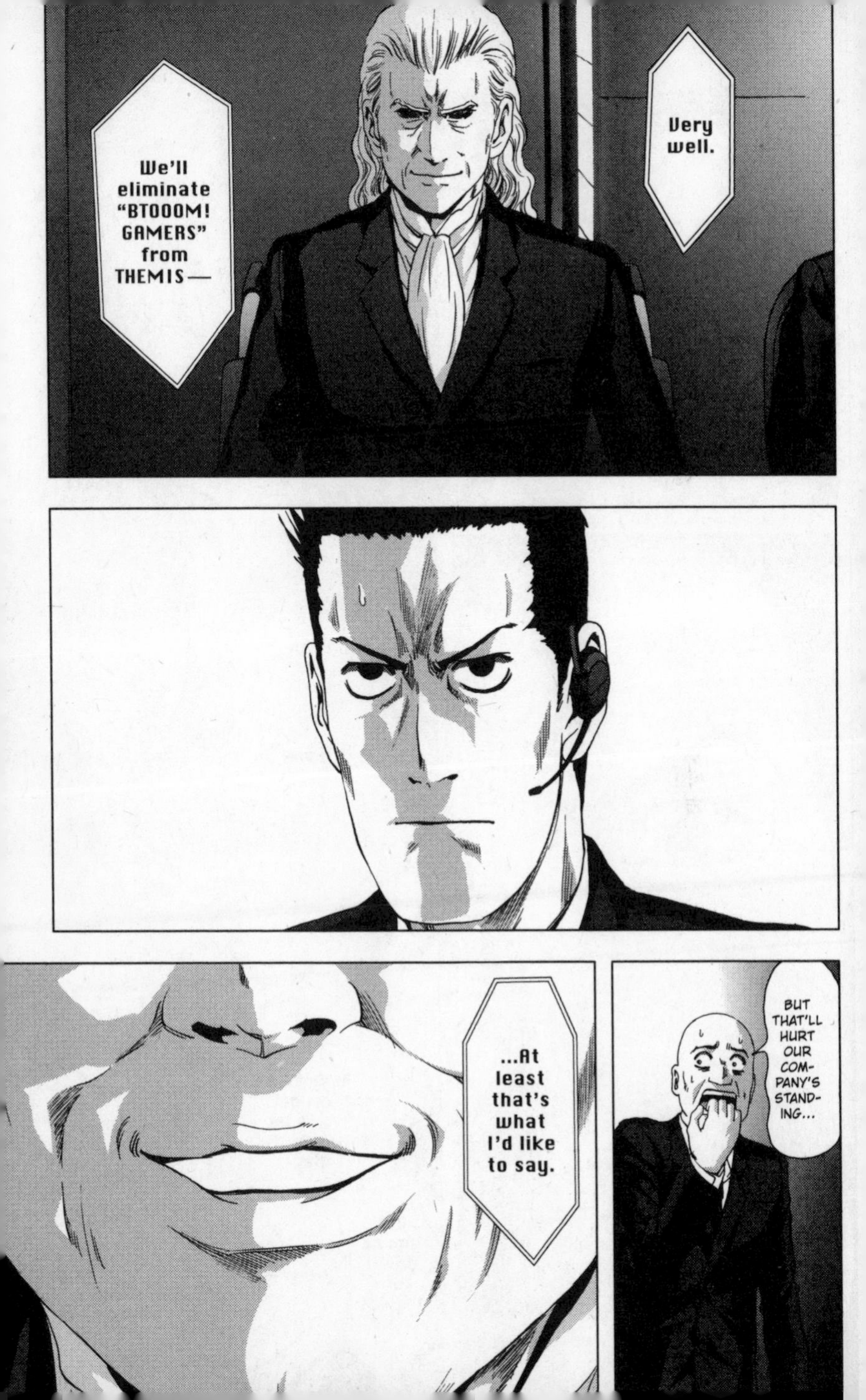
Very well.
We'll eliminate "BTOOOM! GAMERS" from THEMIS—
BUT THAT'LL HURT OUR COMPANY'S STANDING...
...At least that's what I'd like to say.

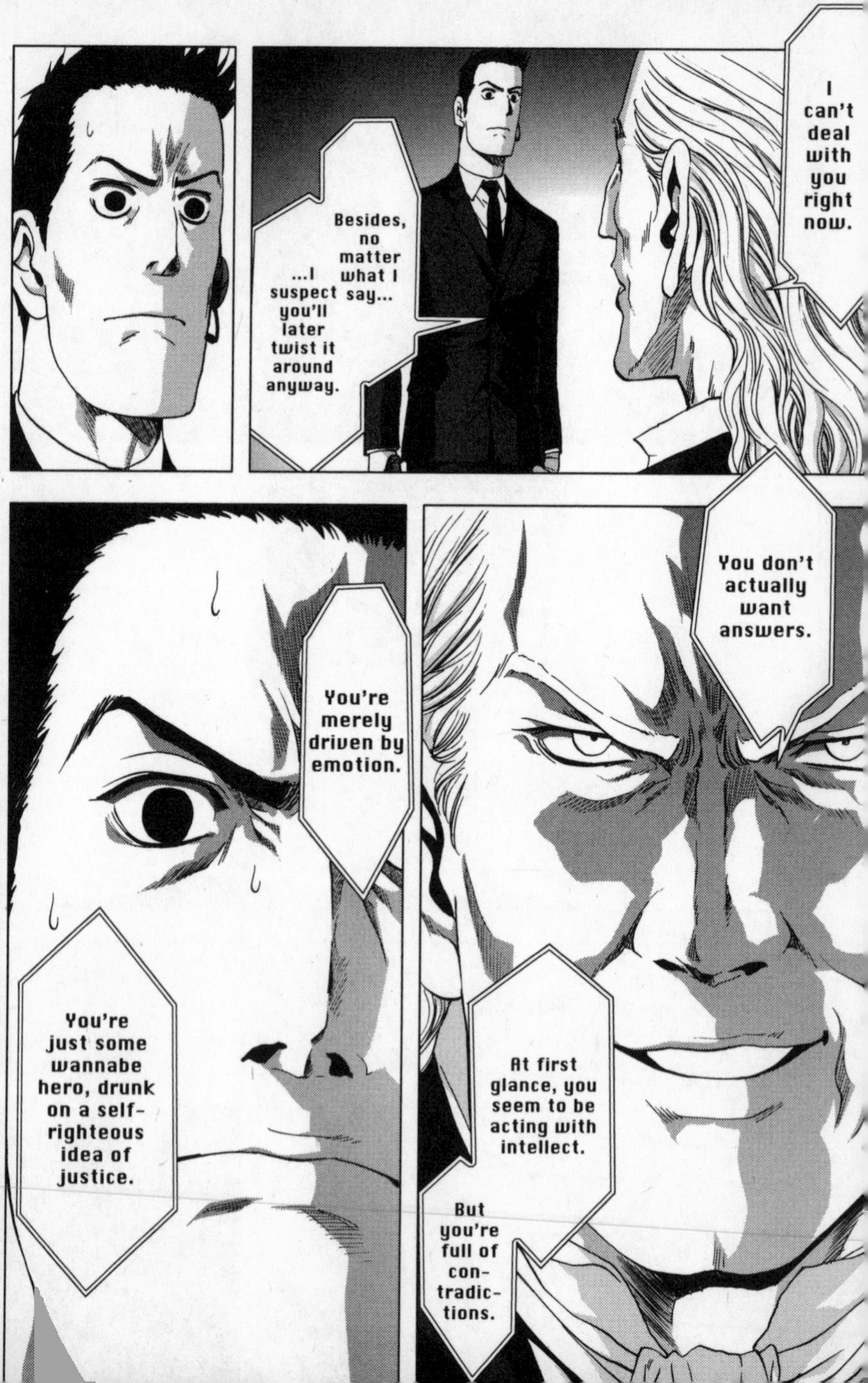
I can't deal with you right now.
Besides, no matter what I say...
...I suspect you'll later twist it around anyway.
You don't actually want answers.
At first glance, you seem to be acting with intellect.
But you're full of contradictions.
You're merely driven by emotion.
You're just some wannabe hero, drunk on a self-righteous idea of justice.

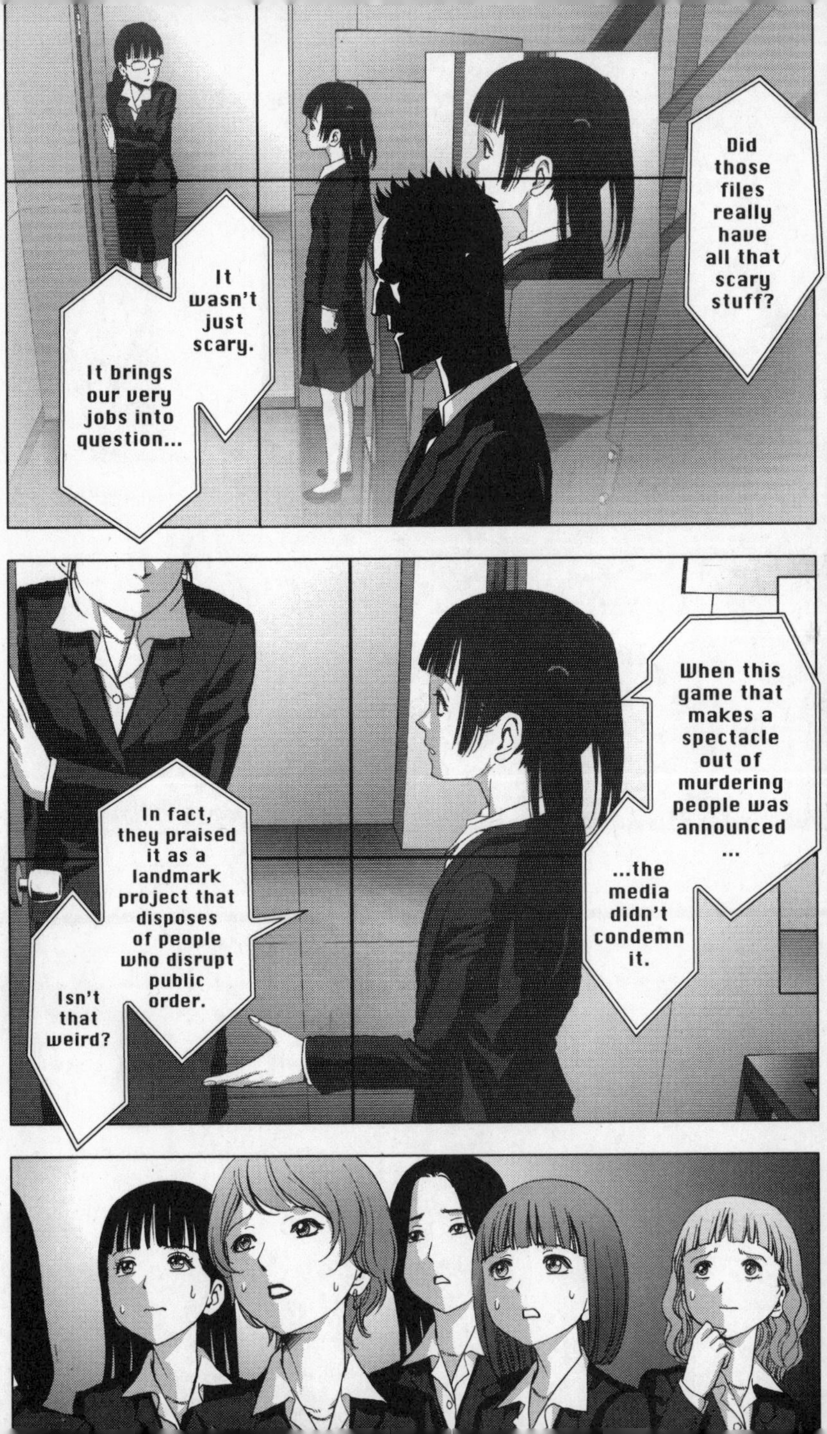
Did those files really have all that scary stuff?
It wasn't just scary.
It brings our very jobs into question...
When this game that makes a spectacle out of murdering people was announced...
...the media didn't condemn it.
In fact, they praised it as a landmark project that disposes of people who disrupt public order.
Isn't that weird?

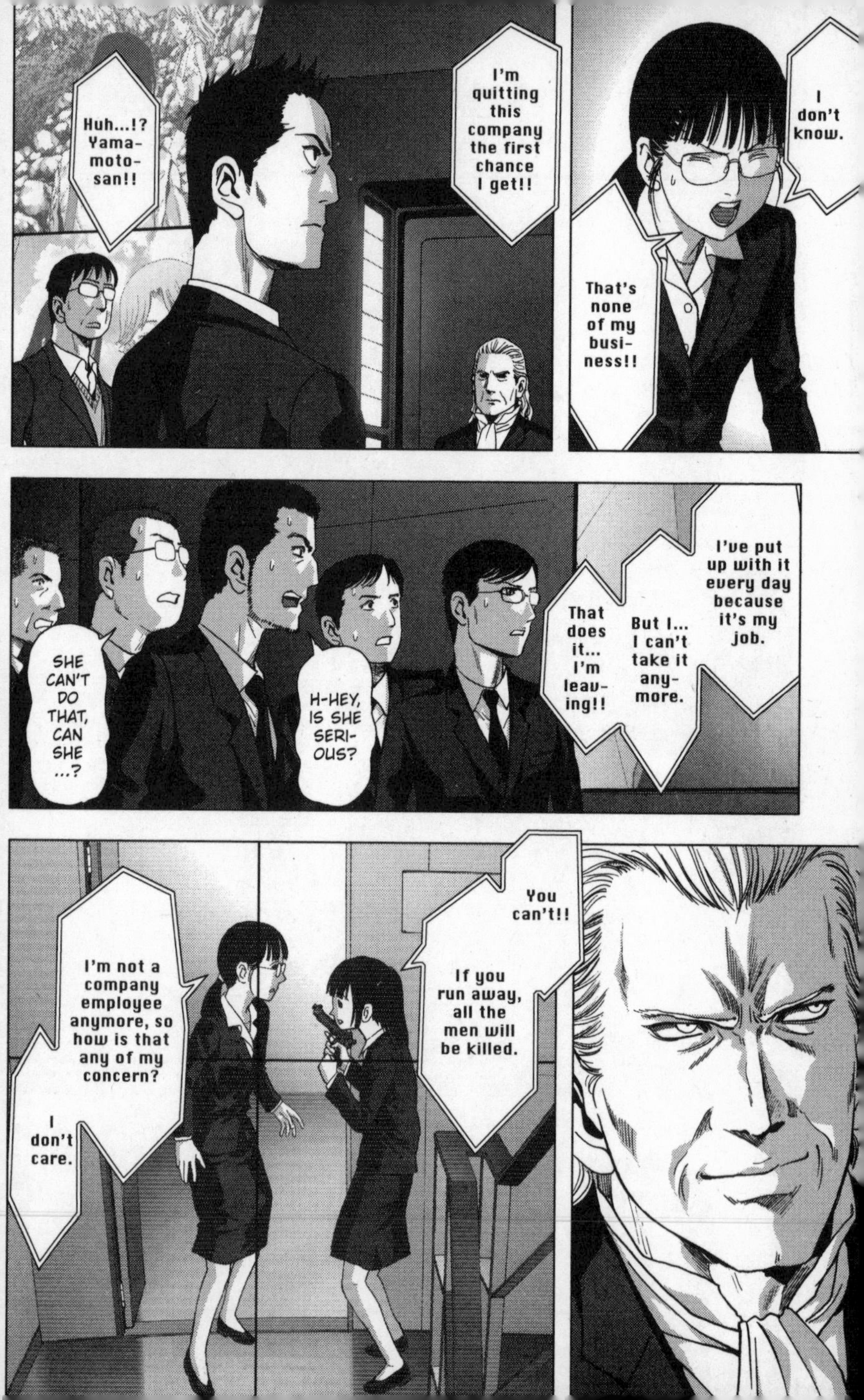
I don't know.
That's none of my business!!
I'm quitting this company the first chance I get!!
Huh...!? Yamamoto-san!!
I've put up with it every day because it's my job.
But I... I can't take it anymore.
That does it... I'm leaving!!
H-HEY, IS SHE SERIOUS?
SHE CAN'T DO THAT, CAN SHE...?
You can't!!
If you run away, all the men will be killed.
I'm not a company employee anymore, so how is that any of my concern?
I don't care.

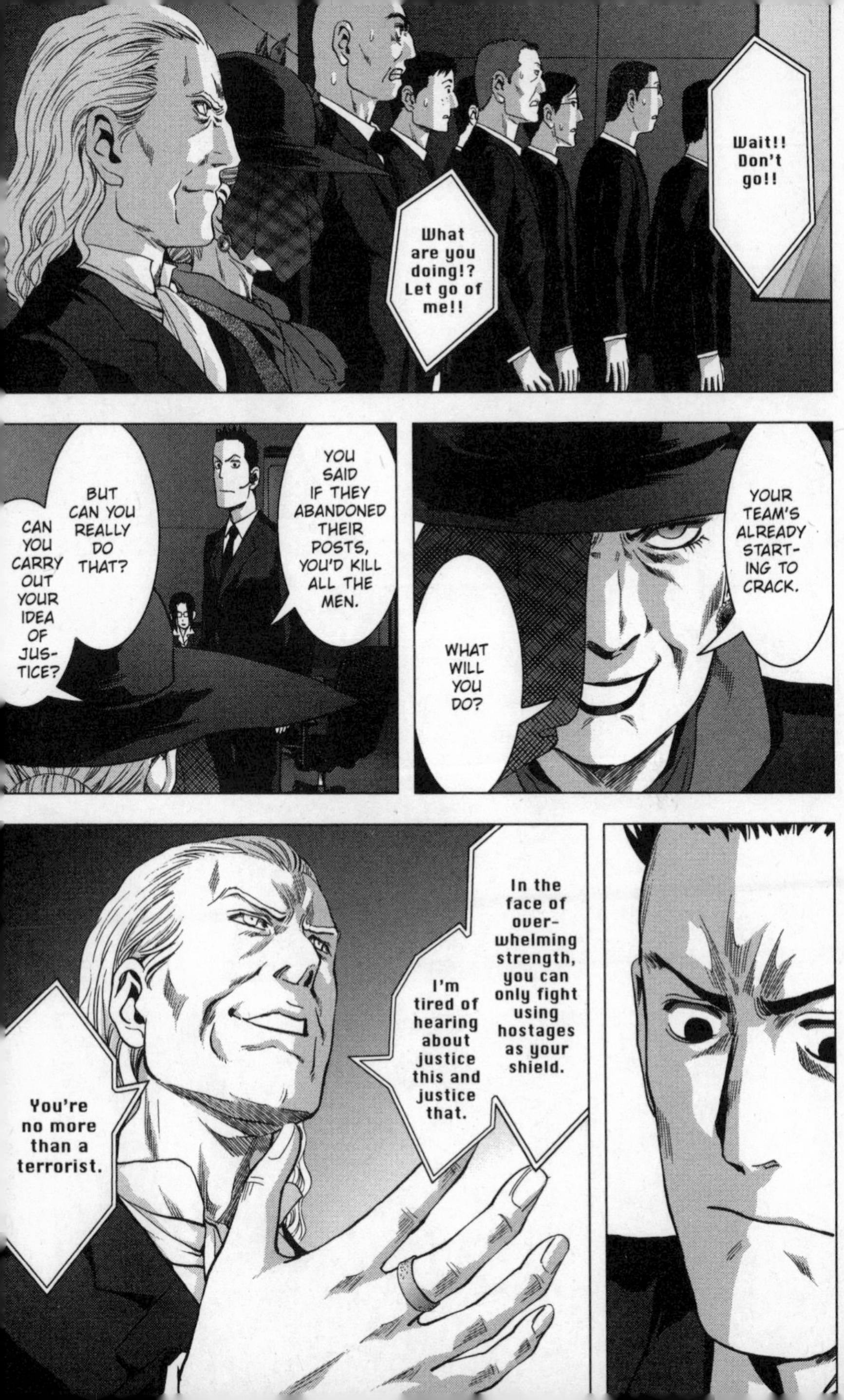
Wait!! Don't go!!
What are you doing!? Let go of me!!
YOUR TEAM'S ALREADY STARTING TO CRACK.
WHAT WILL YOU DO?
YOU SAID IF THEY ABANDONED THEIR POSTS, YOU'D KILL ALL THE MEN.
BUT CAN YOU REALLY DO THAT?
CAN YOU CARRY OUT YOUR IDEA OF JUSTICE?
In the face of overwhelming strength, you can only fight using hostages as your shield.
I'm tired of hearing about justice this and justice that.
You're no more than a terrorist.

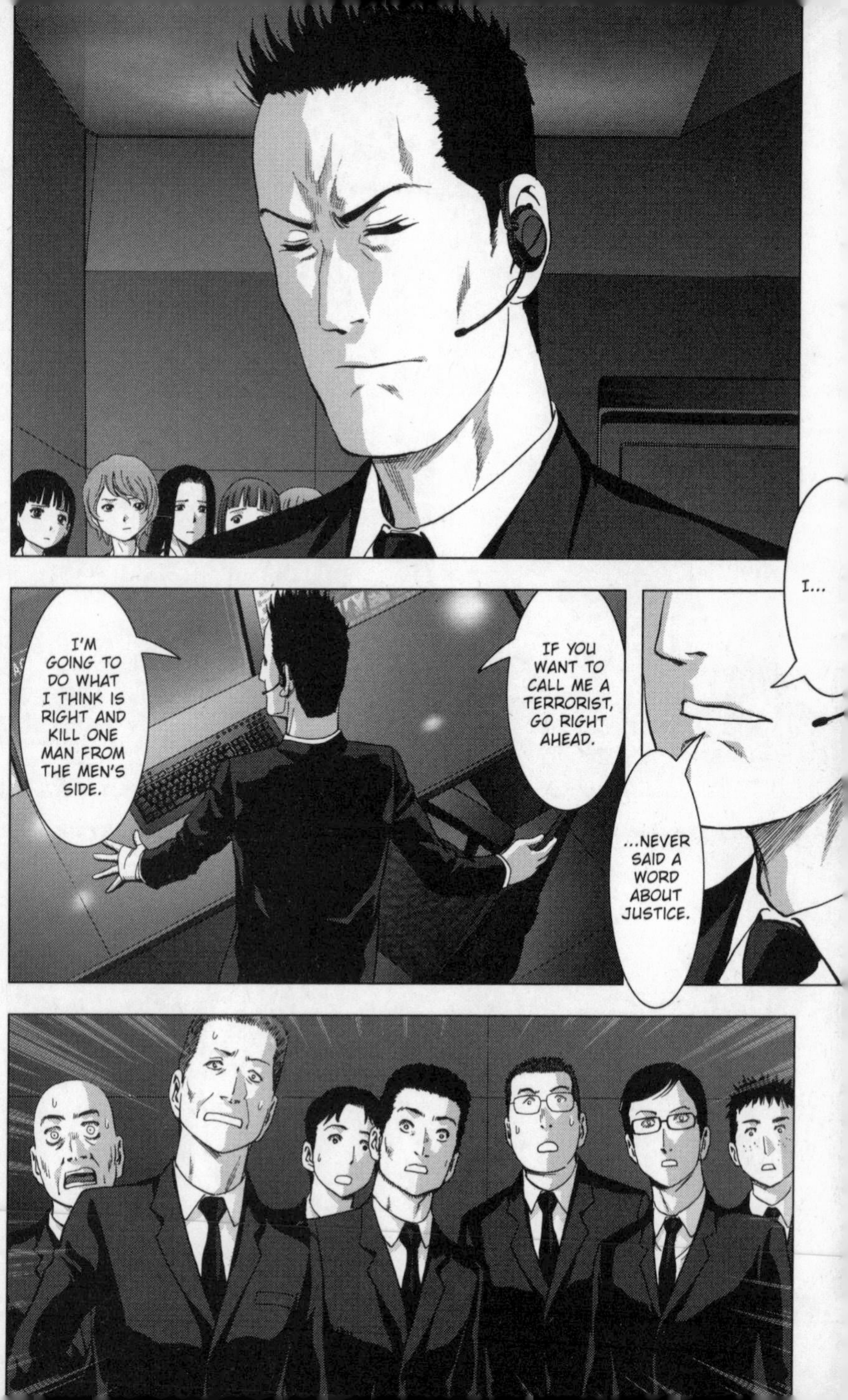
I...
...NEVER SAID A WORD ABOUT JUSTICE.
IF YOU WANT TO CALL ME A TERRORIST, GO RIGHT AHEAD.
I'M GOING TO DO WHAT I THINK IS RIGHT AND KILL ONE MAN FROM THE MEN'S SIDE.

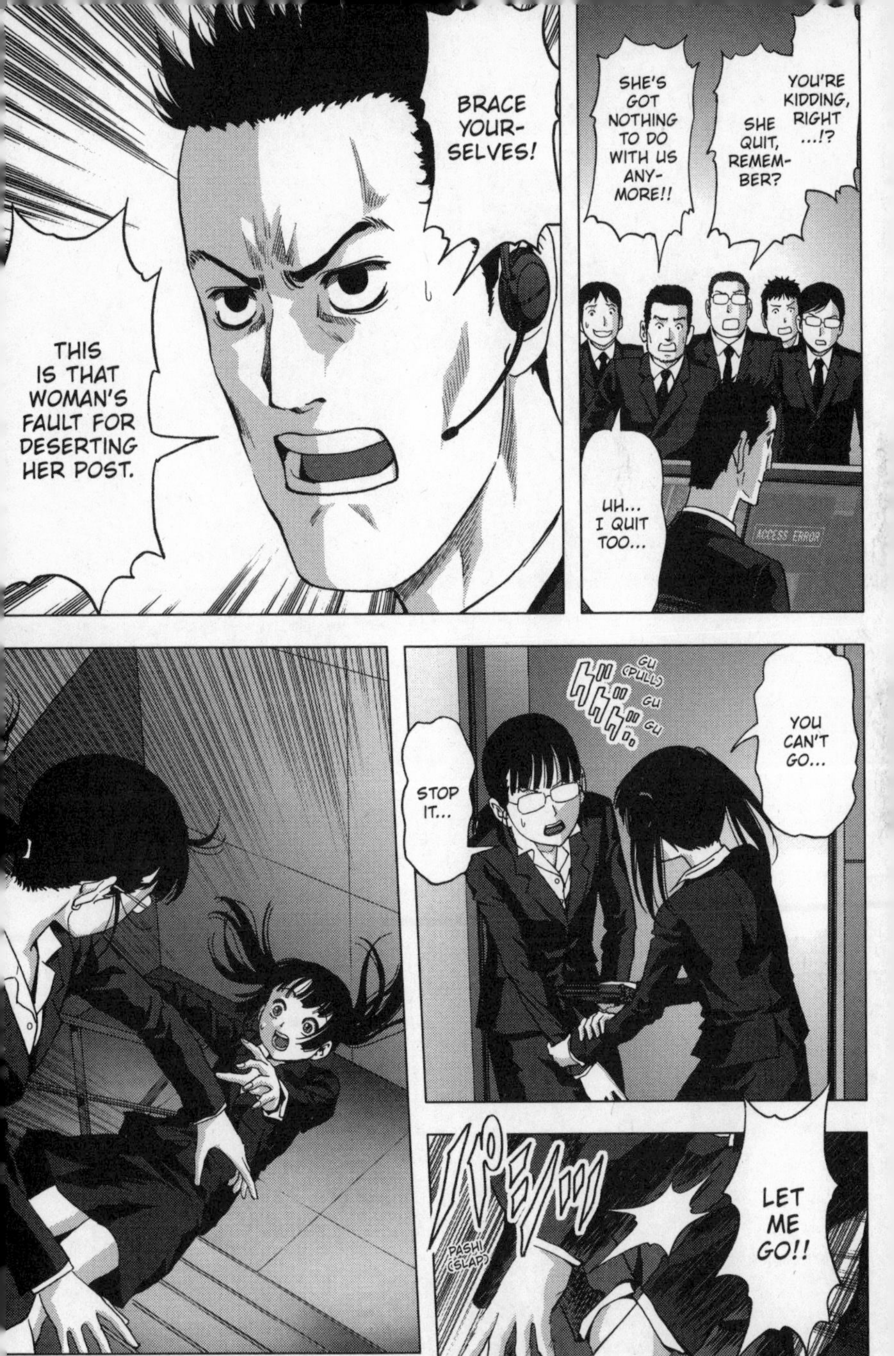
YOU'RE KIDDING, RIGHT ...!?
SHE QUIT, REMEMBER?
SHE'S GOT NOTHING TO DO WITH US ANYMORE!!
ACCESS ERROR
UH... I QUIT TOO...
BRACE YOUR-SELVES!
THIS IS THAT WOMAN'S FAULT FOR DESERTING HER POST.
YOU CAN'T GO...
GU (PULL) GU GU
STOP IT...
LET ME GO!!
PASHI (SLAP)

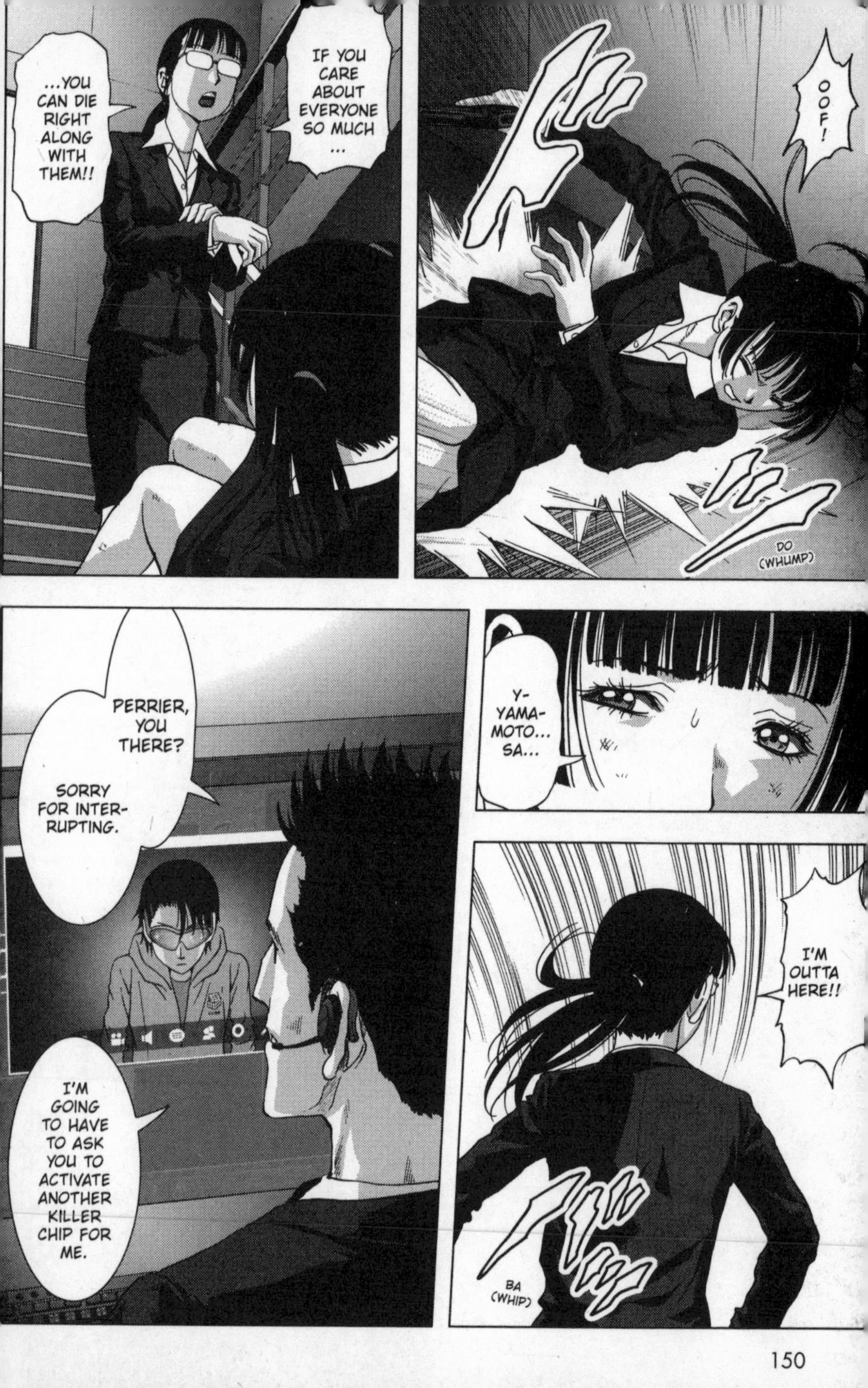
OOF!
DO (WHUMP)
IF YOU CARE ABOUT EVERYONE SO MUCH ...
...YOU CAN DIE RIGHT ALONG WITH THEM!!
Y-YAMAMOTO... SA...
I'M OUTTA HERE!!
BA (WHIP)
PERRIER, YOU THERE?
SORRY FOR INTERRUPTING.
I'M GOING TO HAVE TO ASK YOU TO ACTIVATE ANOTHER KILLER CHIP FOR ME.

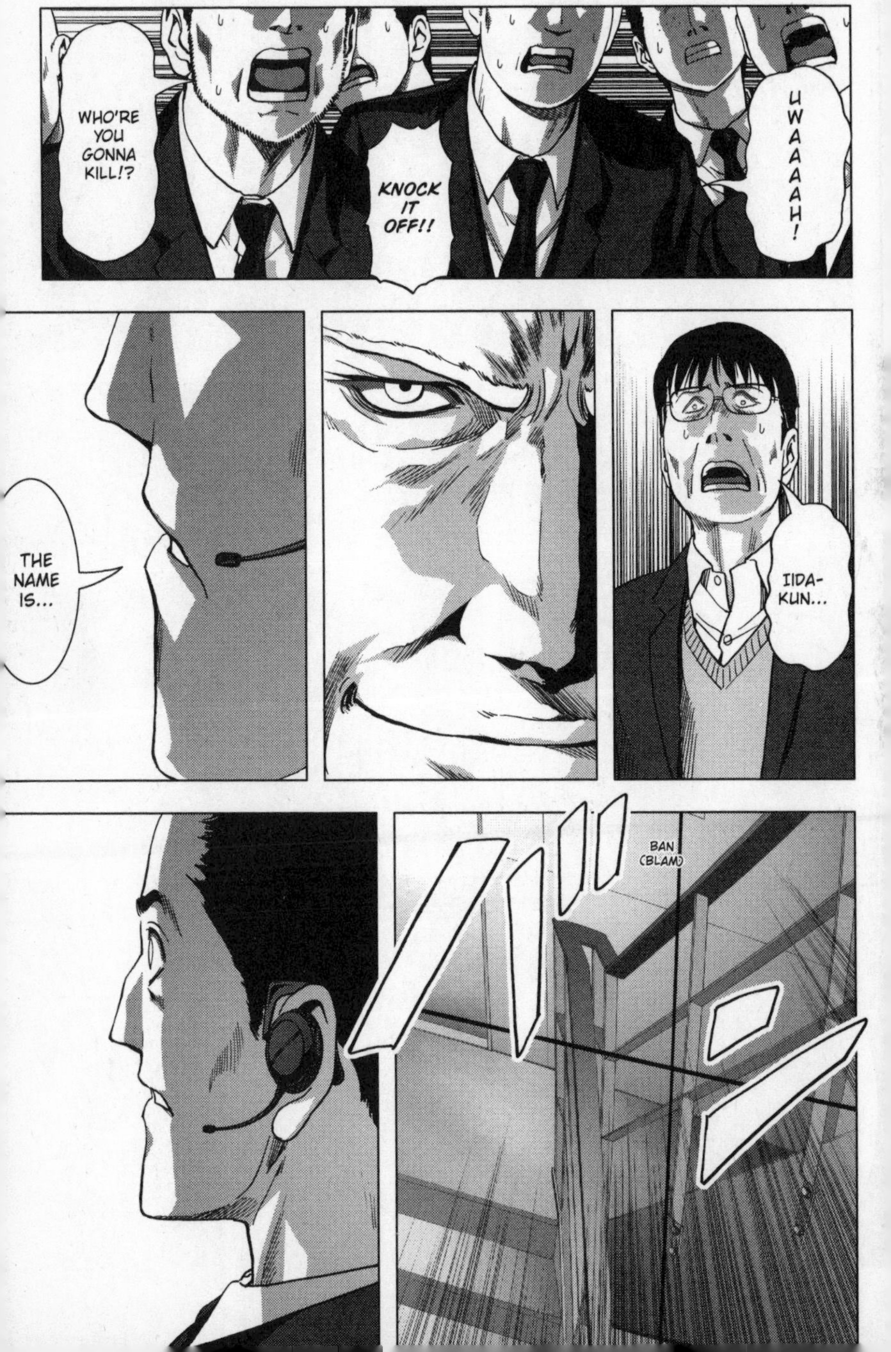
UWAAAAH!
KNOCK IT OFF!!
WHO'RE YOU GONNA KILL!?
IIDA-KUN...
THE NAME IS...
BAN
(BLAM)

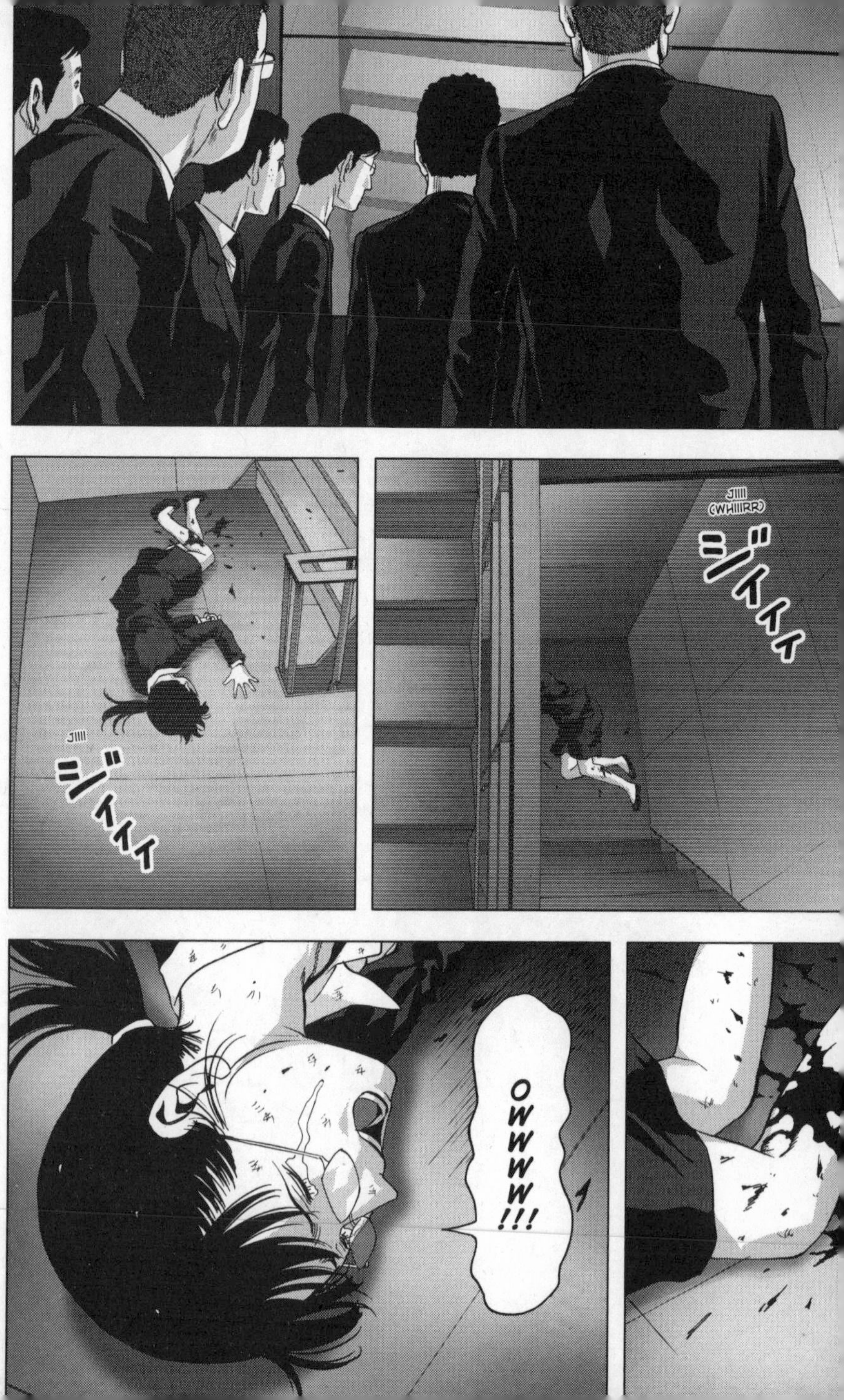
JIIII
(WHIIIRR)
ジイイイ
JIIII
ジイイイ
OWWWW!!!

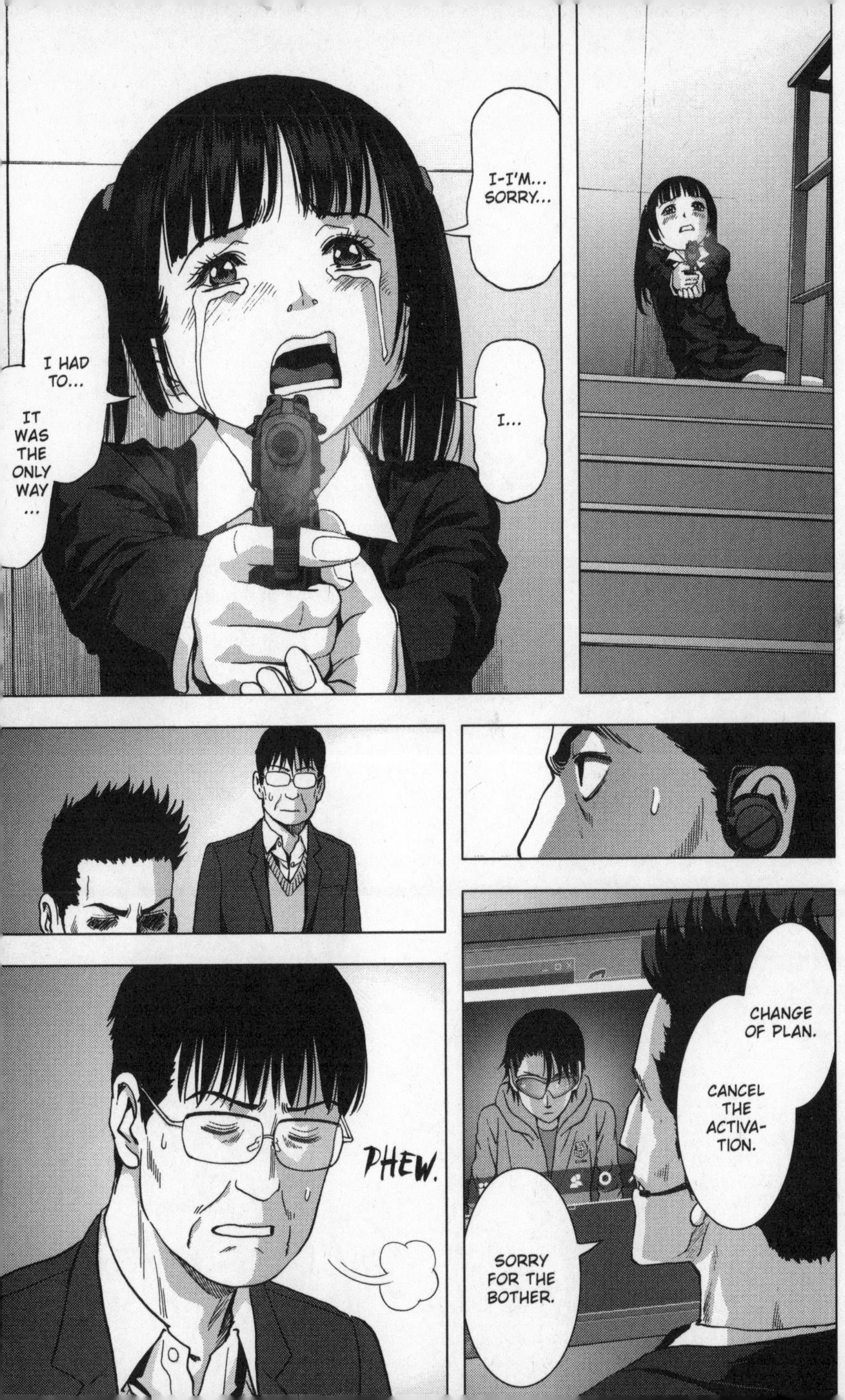
I-I'M... SORRY...
I...
I HAD TO...
IT WAS THE ONLY WAY...
CHANGE OF PLAN.
CANCEL THE ACTIVATION.
SORRY FOR THE BOTHER.
PHEW.

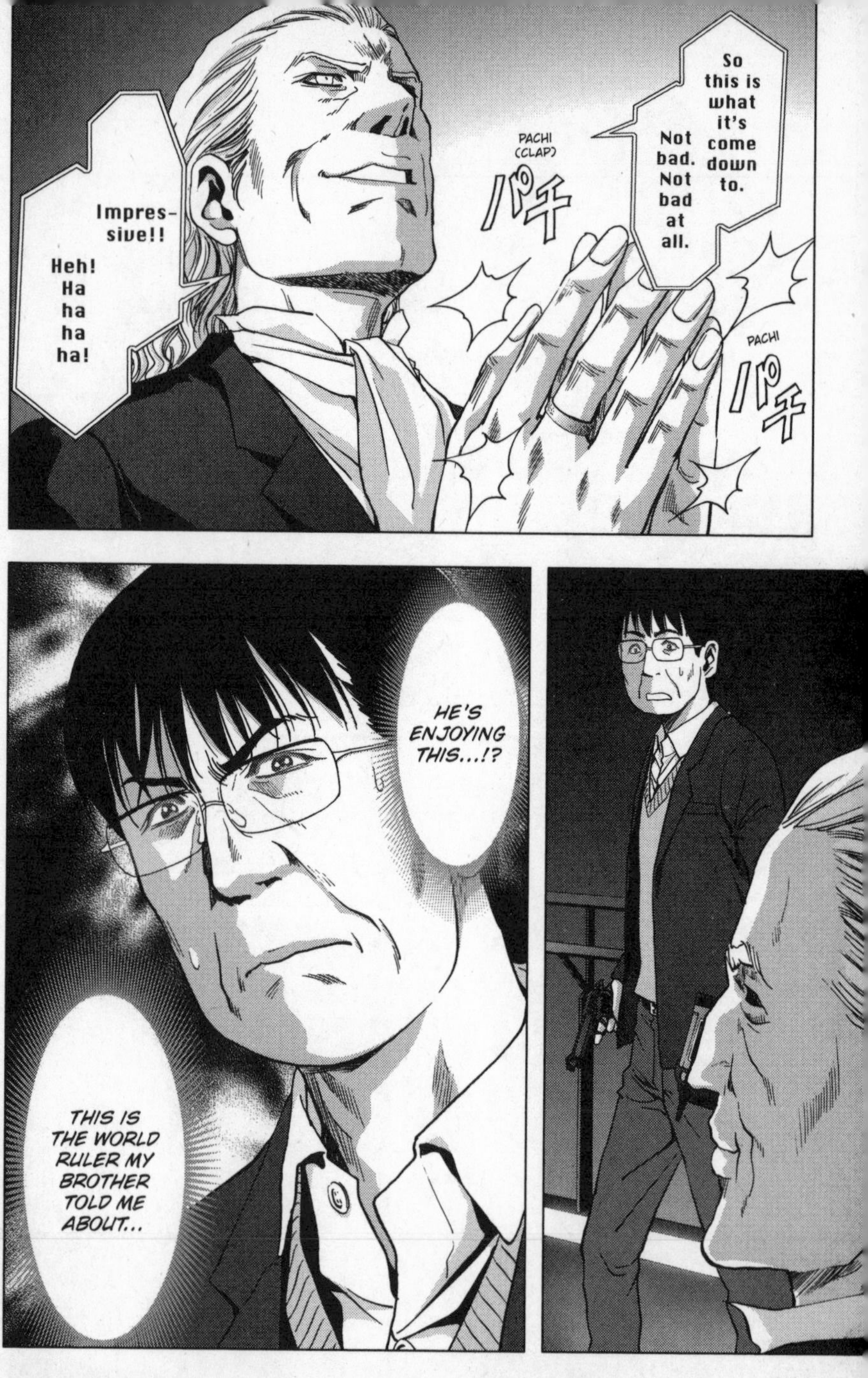

So this is what it's come down to.
Not bad. Not bad at all.
パチ
PACHI (CLAP)
パチ
PACHI
Impres-sive!!
Heh! Ha ha ha ha!
HE'S ENJOYING THIS...!?
THIS IS THE WORLD RULER MY BROTHER TOLD ME ABOUT...

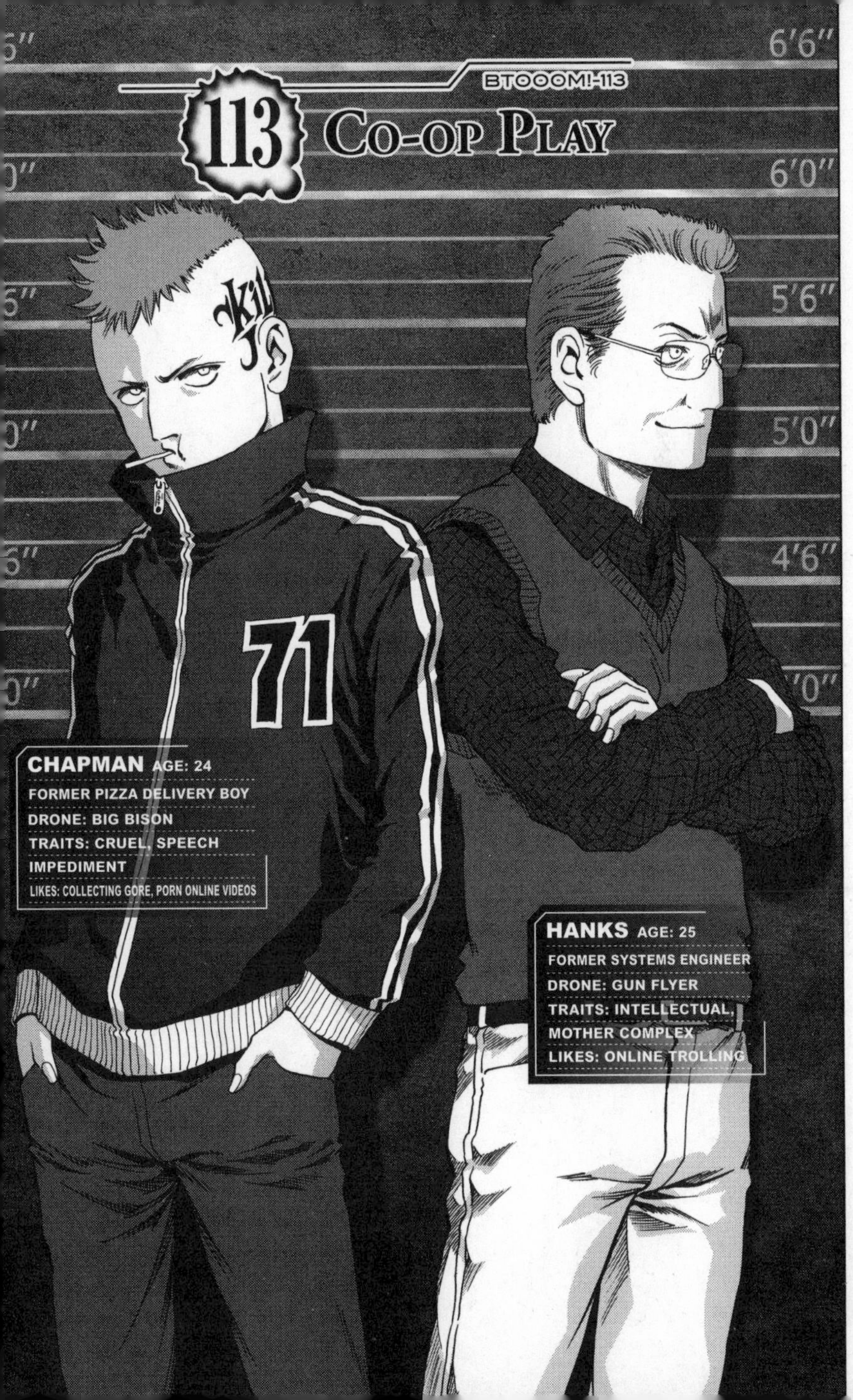

BTOOOM!-113
113 CO-OP PLAY
6'6"
6'0"
5'6"
5'0"
4'6"
71
CHAPMAN AGE: 24
FORMER PIZZA DELIVERY BOY
DRONE: BIG BISON
TRAITS: CRUEL, SPEECH IMPEDIMENT
LIKES: COLLECTING GORE, PORN ONLINE VIDEOS
HANKS AGE: 25
FORMER SYSTEMS ENGINEER
DRONE: GUN FLYER
TRAITS: INTELLECTUAL, MOTHER COMPLEX
LIKES: ONLINE TROLLING

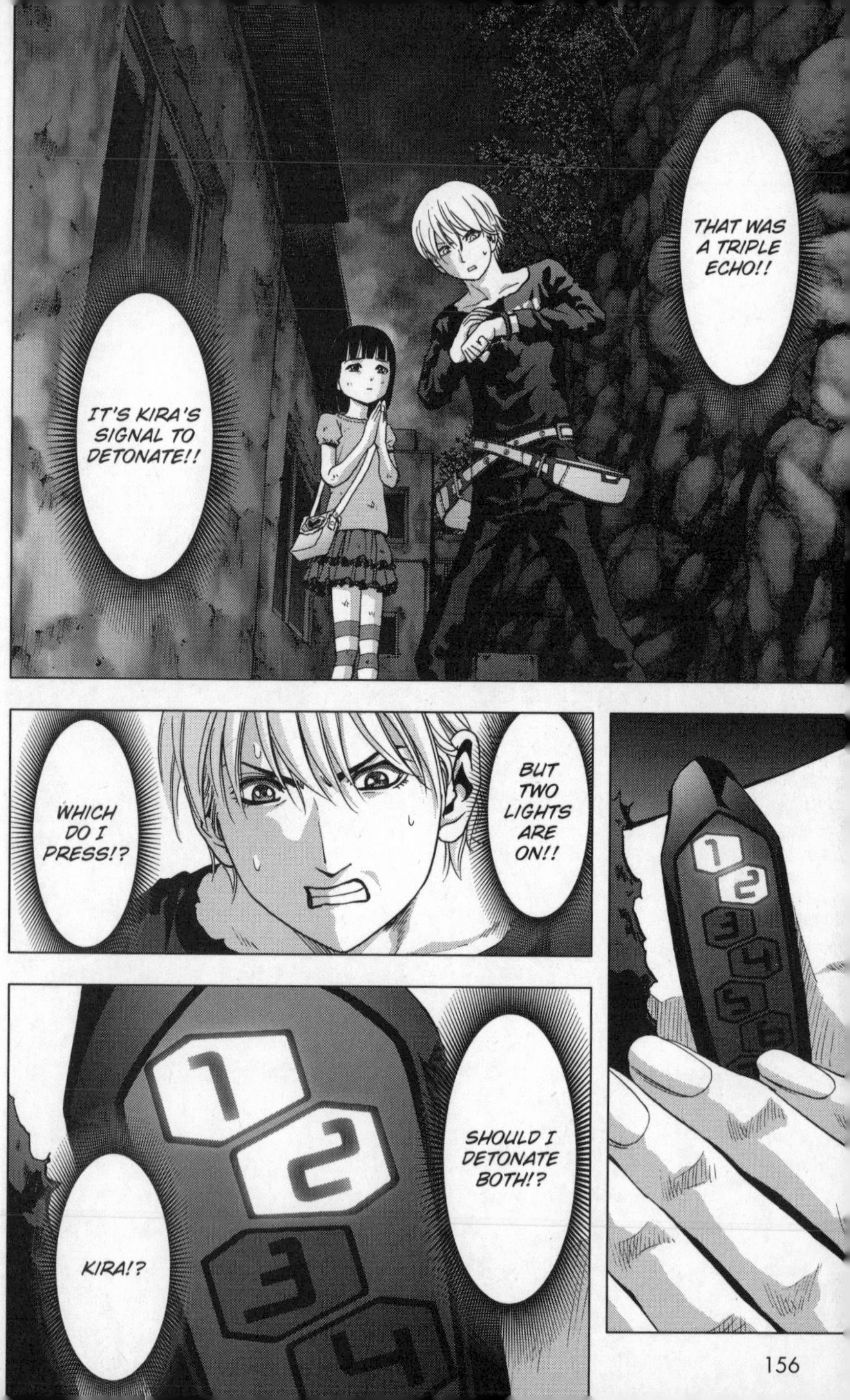
THAT WAS A TRIPLE ECHO!!
IT'S KIRA'S SIGNAL TO DETONATE!!
BUT TWO LIGHTS ARE ON!!
WHICH DO I PRESS!?
SHOULD I DETONATE BOTH!?
KIRA!?

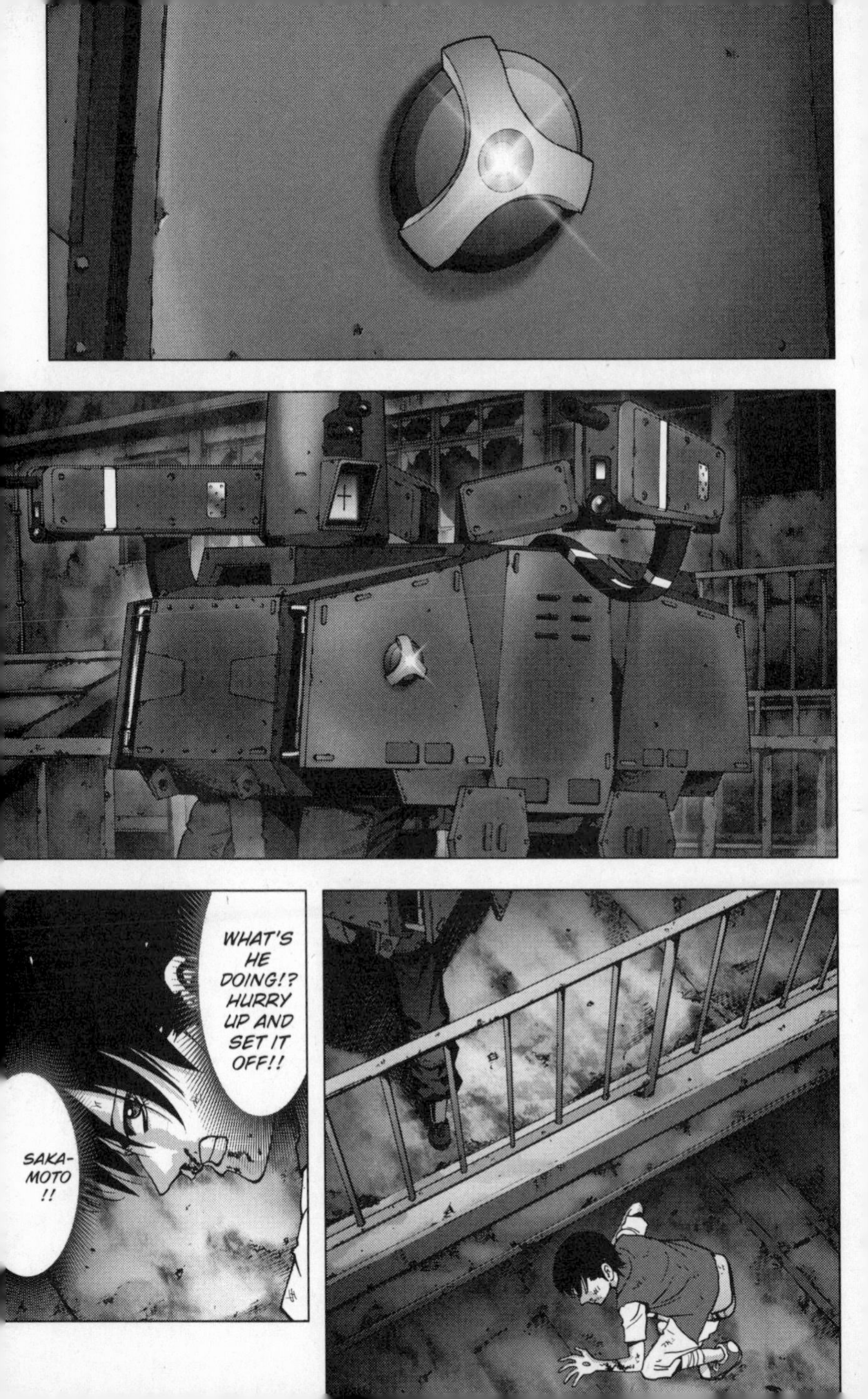
WHAT'S HE DOING!? HURRY UP AND SET IT OFF!!
SAKA-MOTO !!

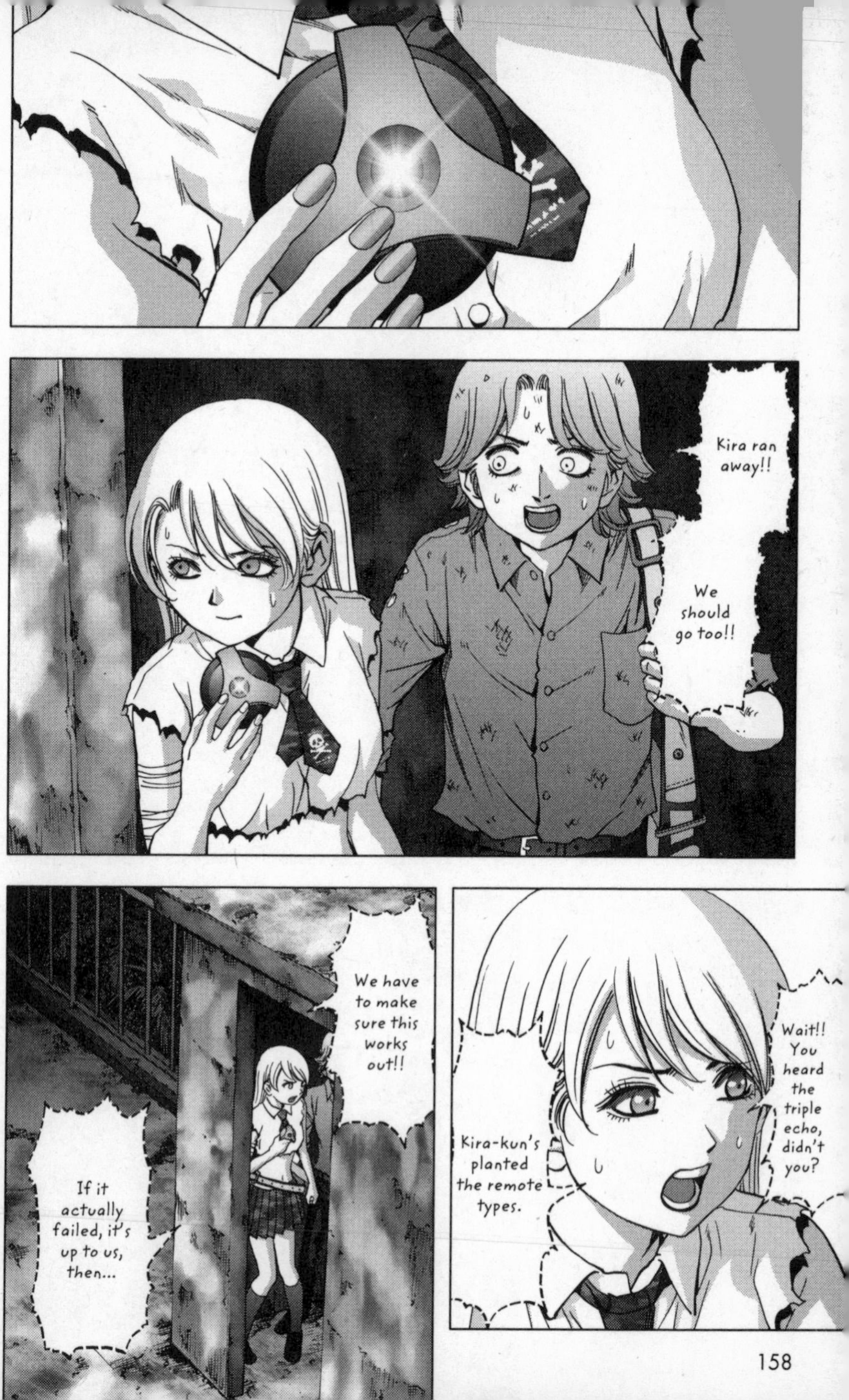
Kira ran away!!
We should go too!!
Wait!! You heard the triple echo, didn't you?
Kira-kun's planted the remote types.
We have to make sure this works out!!
If it actually failed, it's up to us, then...

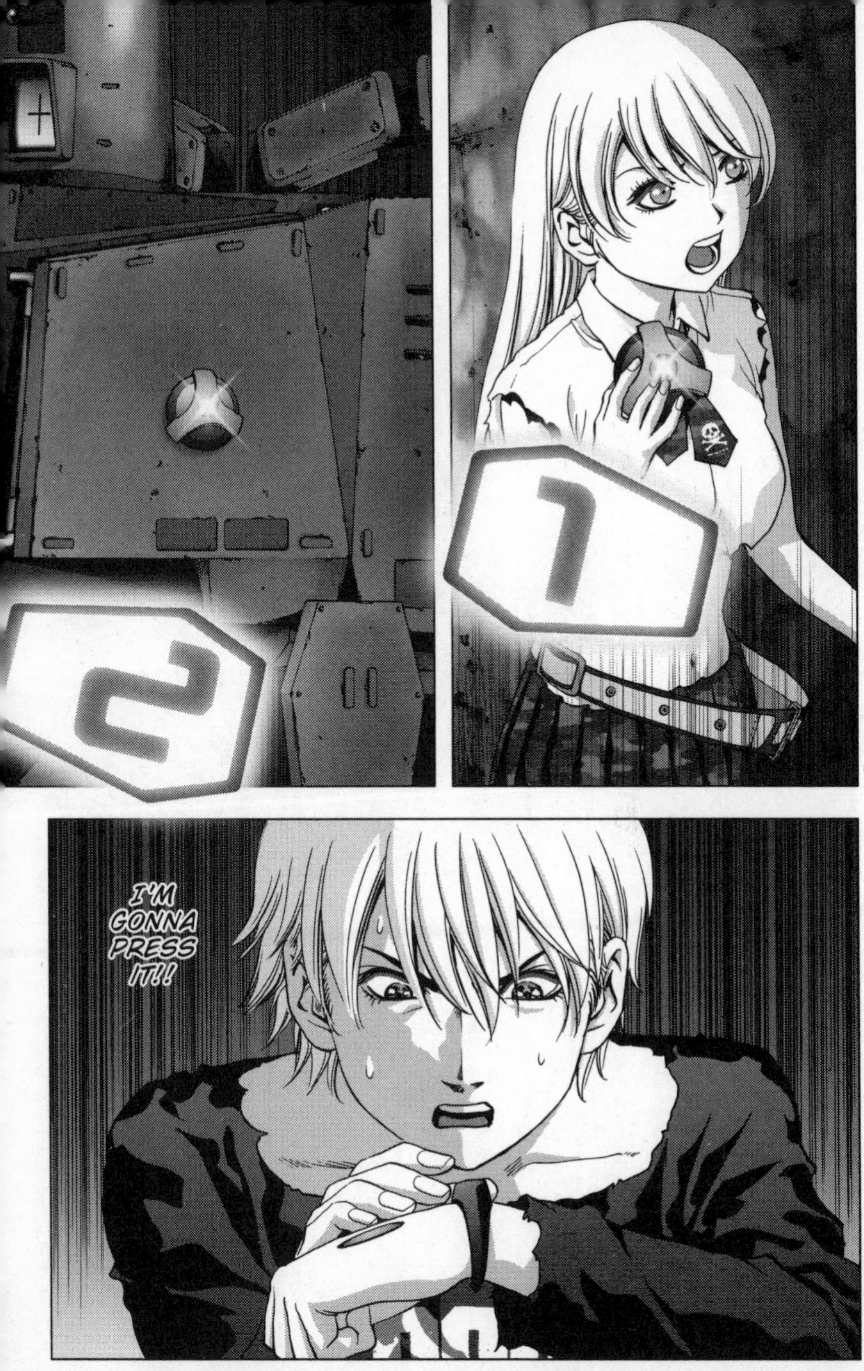
1
2
I'M GONNA PRESS IT!!

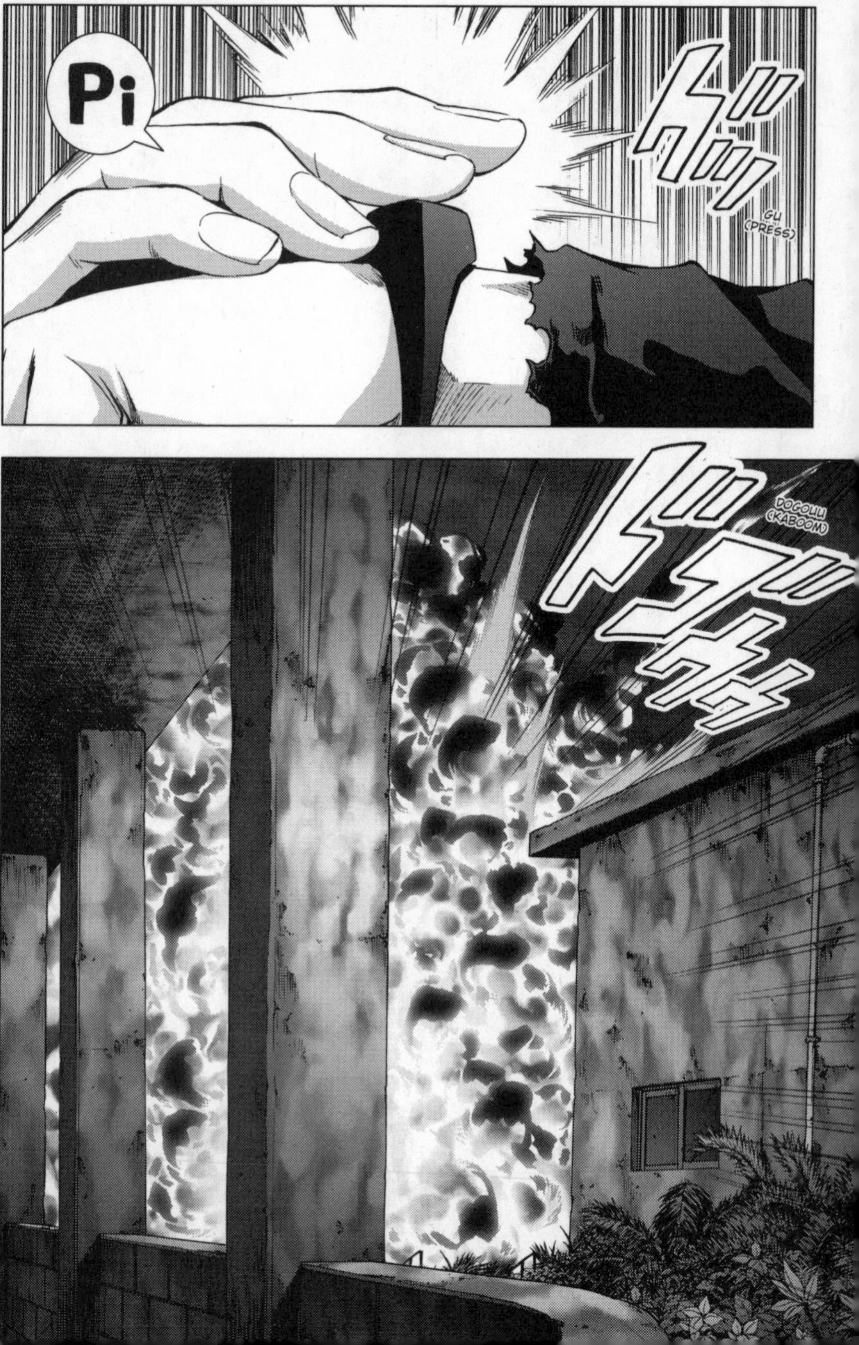
Pi
GU (PRESS)
DOGOUU (KABOOM)

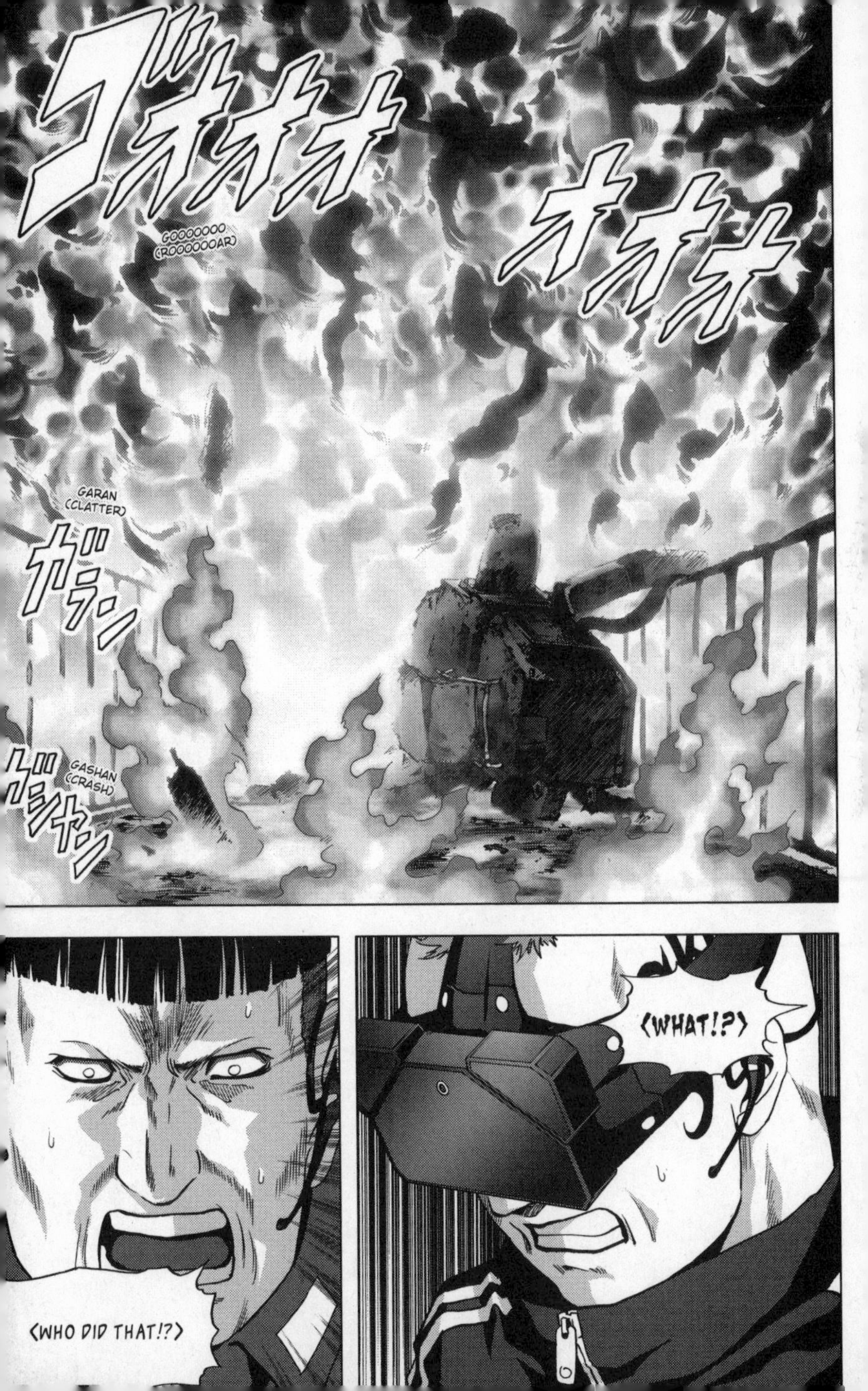
ゴオオオオオオ
GOOOOOOO (ROOOOOOAR)
ガラン
GARAN (CLATTER)
ガシャン
GASHAN (CRASH)
⟨WHAT!?⟩
⟨WHO DID THAT!?⟩

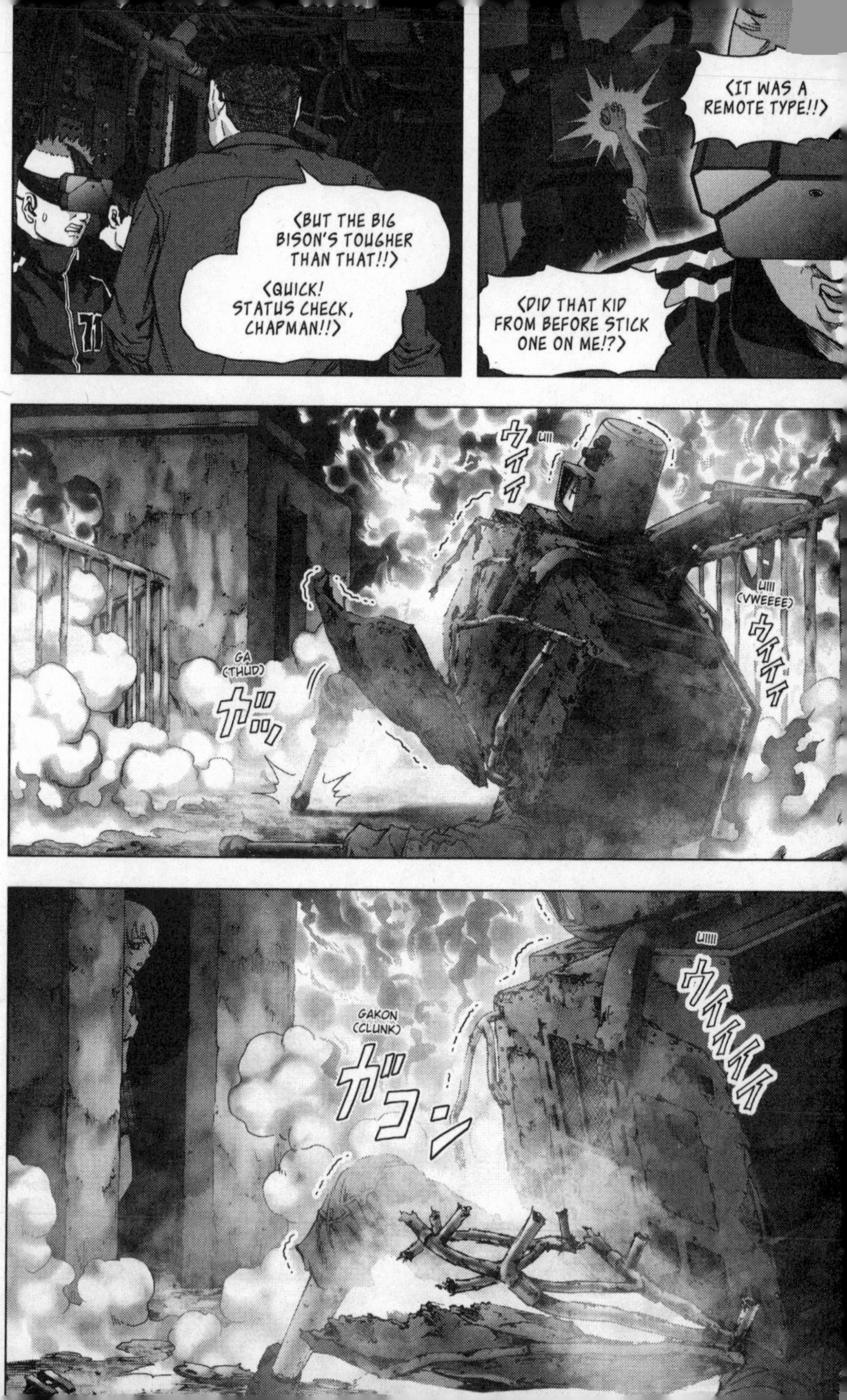
<IT WAS A REMOTE TYPE!!>
<DID THAT KID FROM BEFORE STICK ONE ON ME!?>
<BUT THE BIG BISON'S TOUGHER THAN THAT!!>
<QUICK! STATUS CHECK, CHAPMAN!!>
UIII (VWEEEE)
UII
GA (THUD)
UIIII
GAKON (CLUNK)

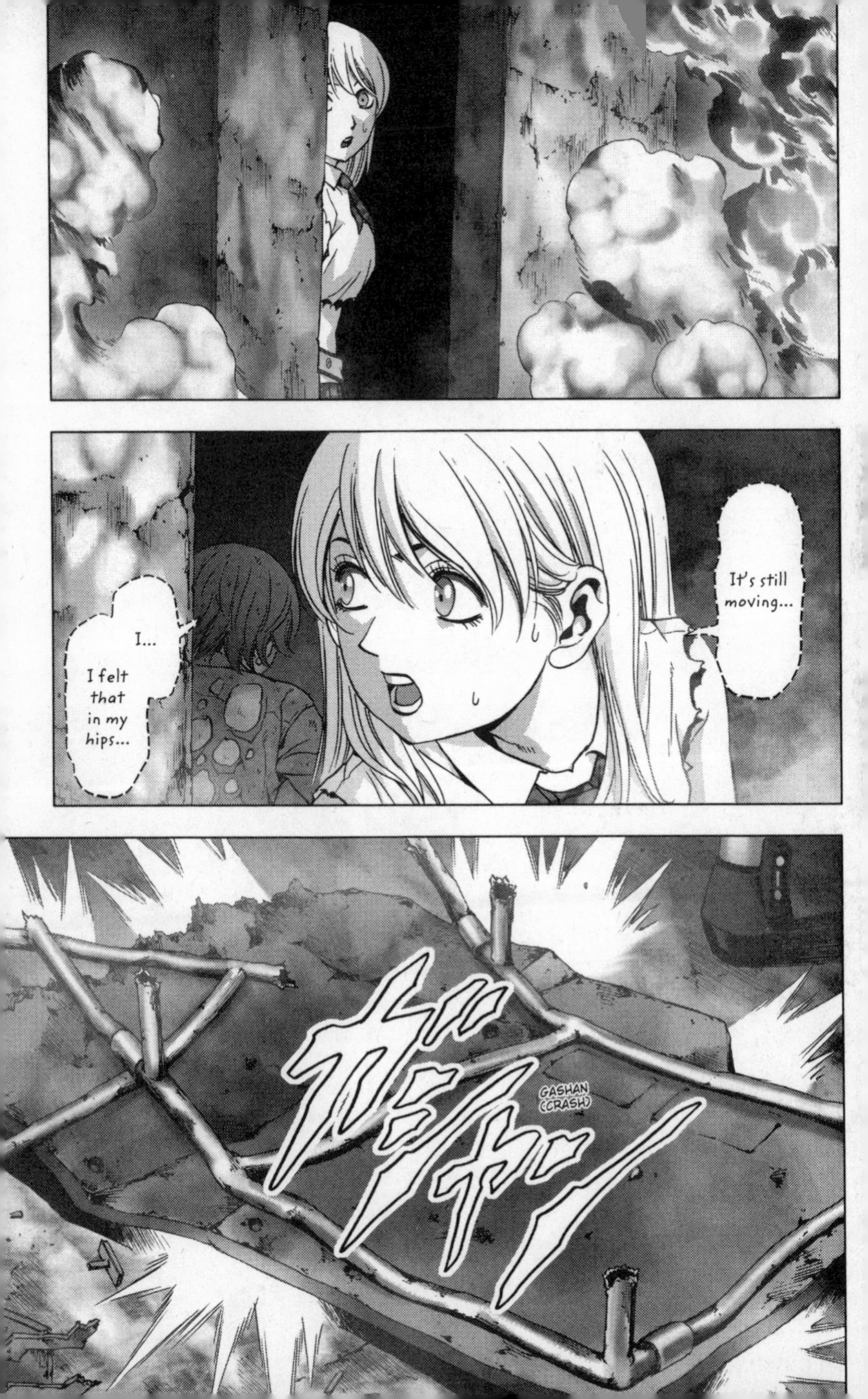
It's still moving...
I... I felt that in my hips...
GASHAN (CRASH)

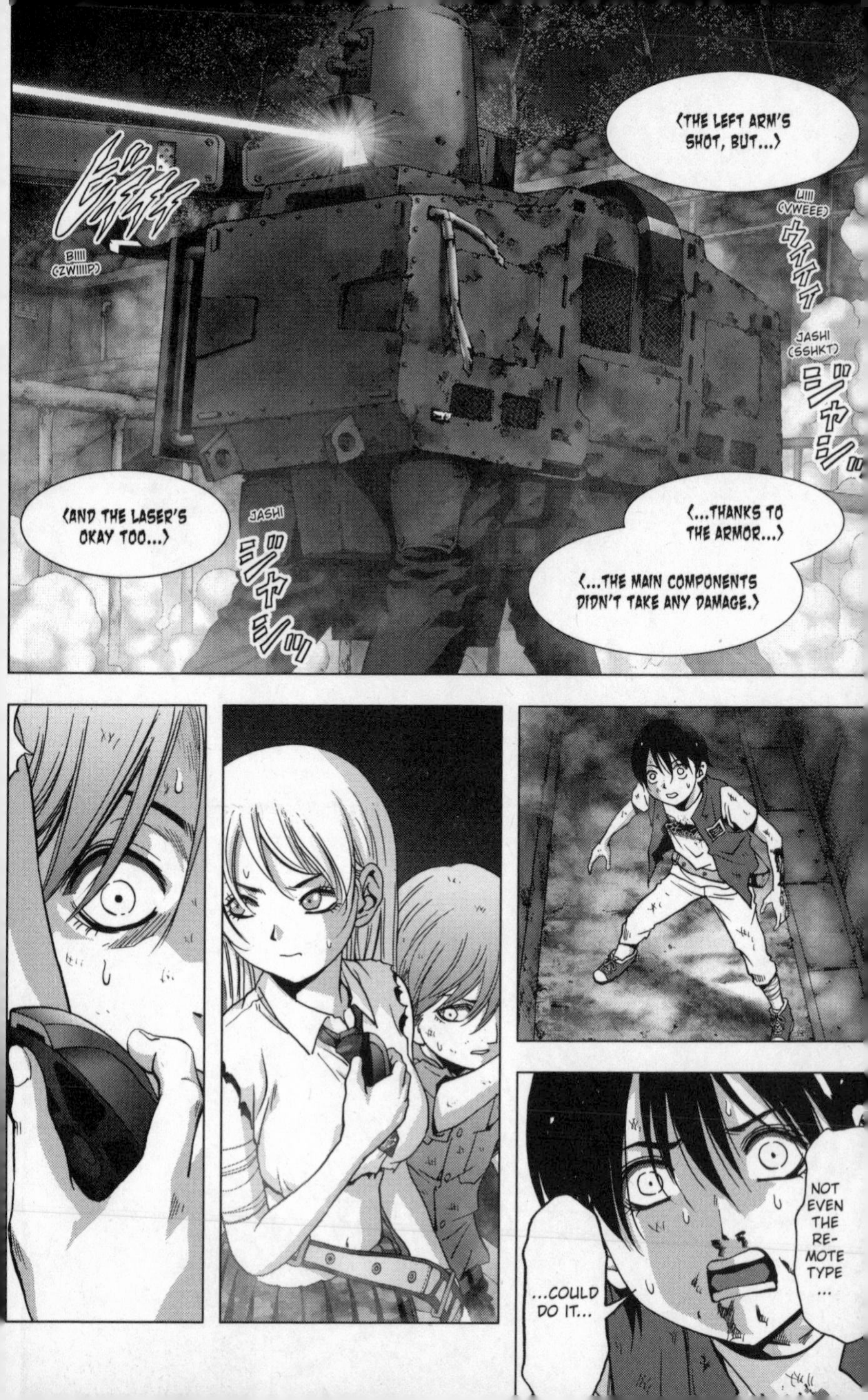
<THE LEFT ARM'S SHOT, BUT...>
UIII (VWEEE)
JASHI (SSHKT)
BIII (ZWIIIIP)
<...THANKS TO THE ARMOR...>
<...THE MAIN COMPONENTS DIDN'T TAKE ANY DAMAGE.>
JASHI
<AND THE LASER'S OKAY TOO...>
NOT EVEN THE RE-MOTE TYPE ...
...COULD DO IT...

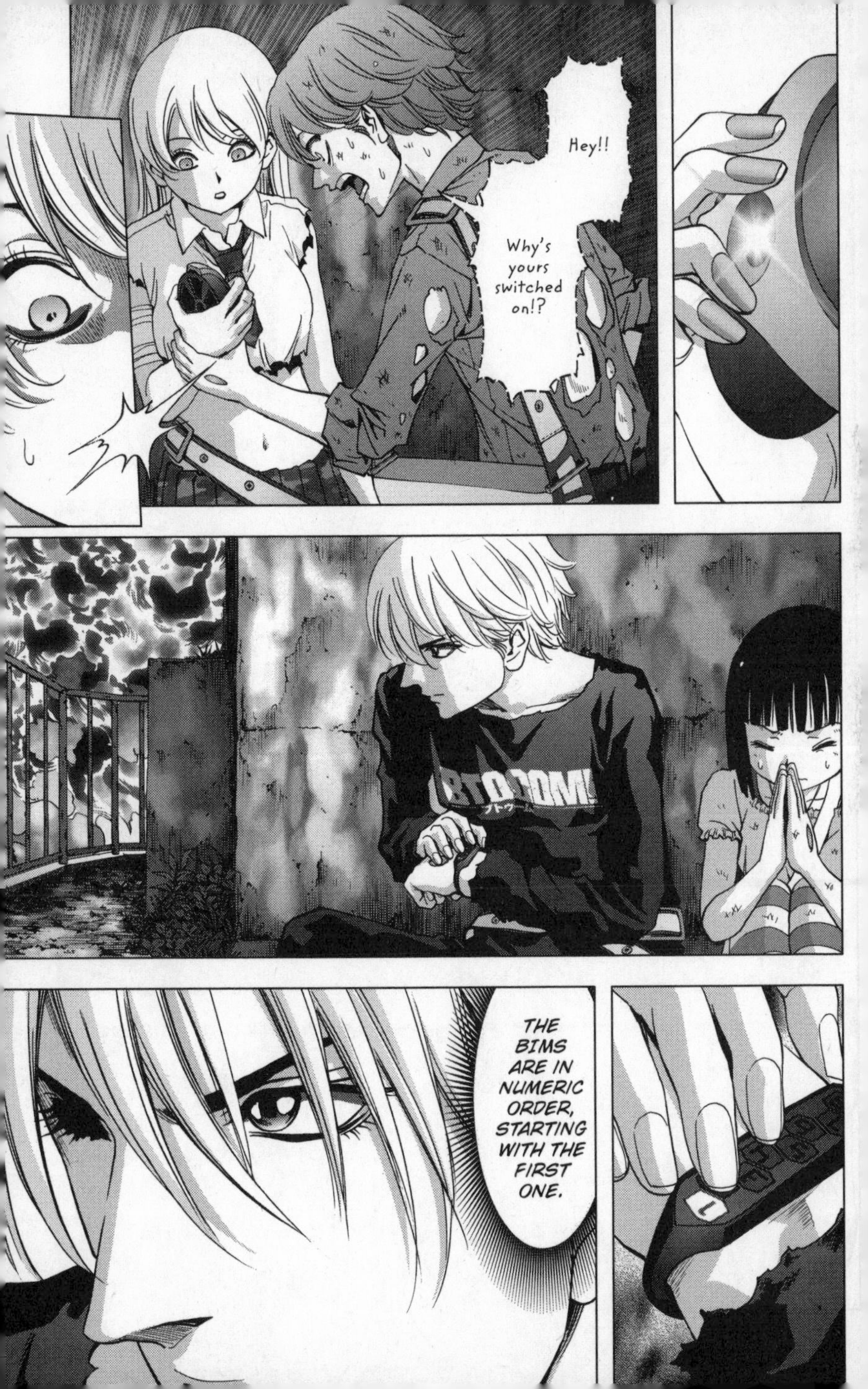
Hey!!
Why's yours switched on!?
THE BIMS ARE IN NUMERIC ORDER, STARTING WITH THE FIRST ONE.

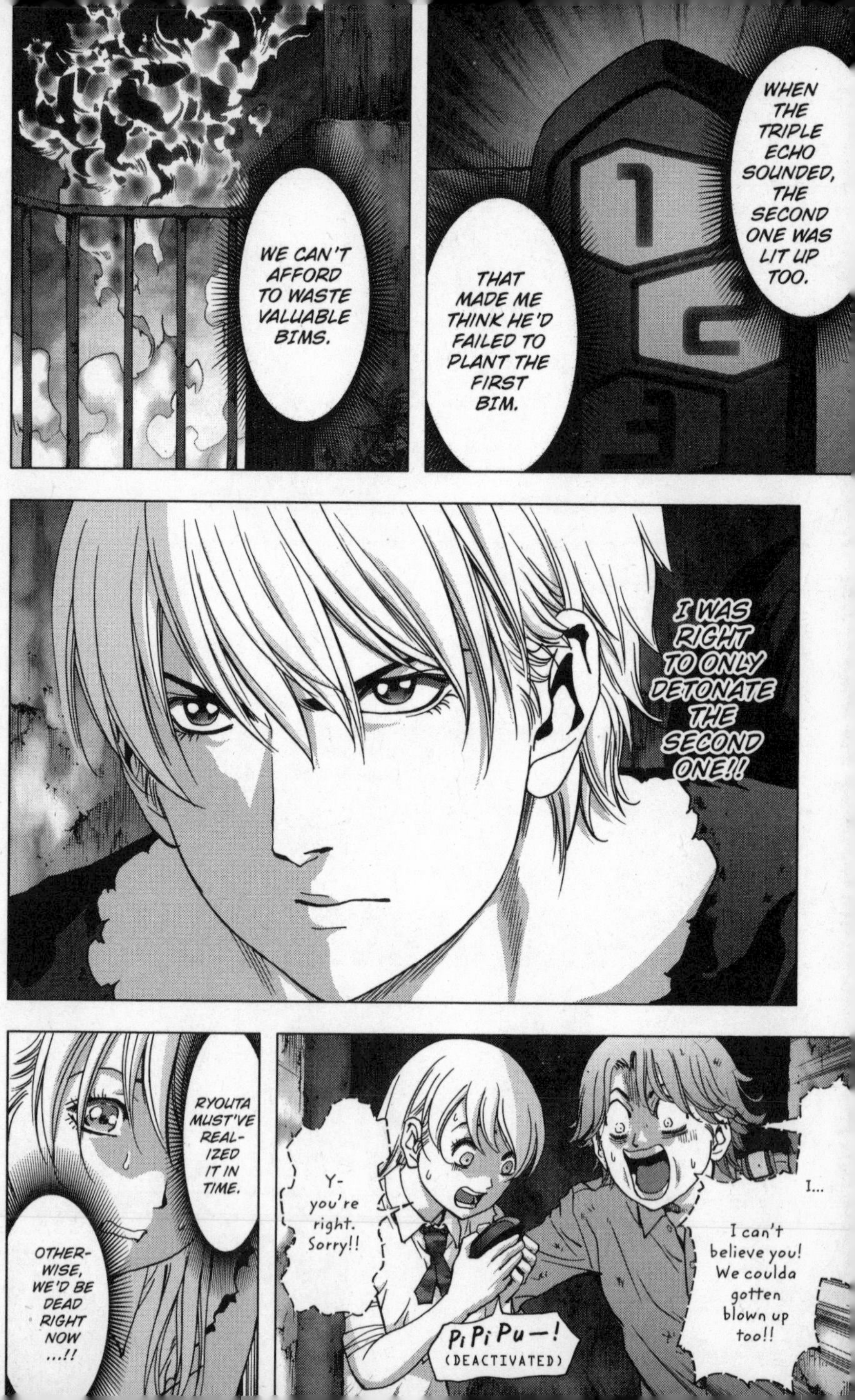
WHEN THE TRIPLE ECHO SOUNDED, THE SECOND ONE WAS LIT UP TOO.
THAT MADE ME THINK HE'D FAILED TO PLANT THE FIRST BIM.
WE CAN'T AFFORD TO WASTE VALUABLE BIMS.
I WAS RIGHT TO ONLY DETONATE THE SECOND ONE!!
I...
I can't believe you! We coulda gotten blown up too!!
Y-you're right. Sorry!!
PiPiPu—! (DEACTIVATED)
RYOUTA MUST'VE REALIZED IT IN TIME.
OTHERWISE, WE'D BE DEAD RIGHT NOW ...!!

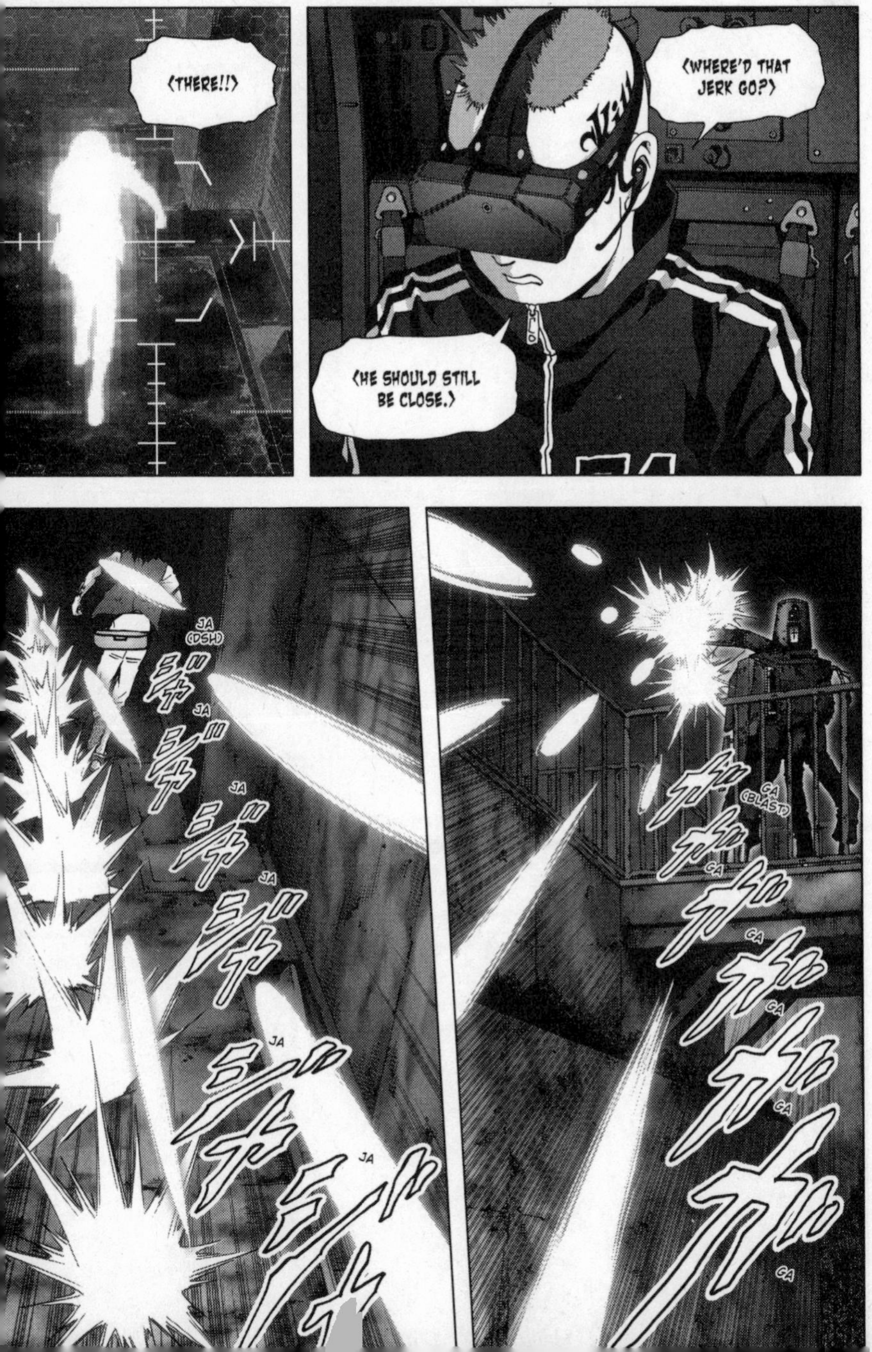
〈WHERE'D THAT JERK GO?〉
〈HE SHOULD STILL BE CLOSE.〉
〈THERE!!〉
GA (BLAST)
GA
GA
GA
GA
GA
JA (DSH)
JA
JA
JA
JA
JA

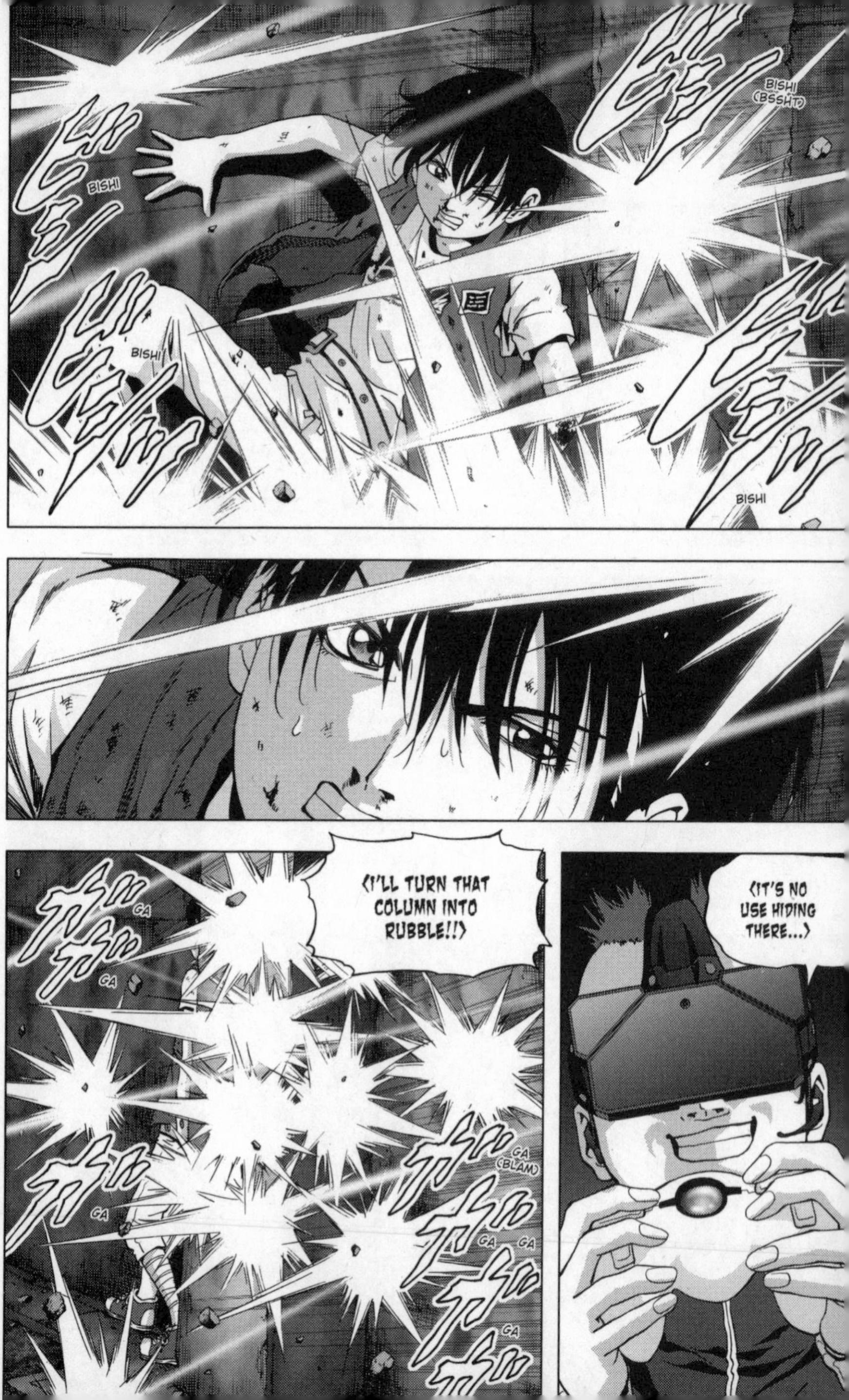
BISHI (BSSHT)
BISHI
BISHI
BISHI
⟨IT'S NO USE HIDING THERE...⟩
⟨I'LL TURN THAT COLUMN INTO RUBBLE!!⟩
GA (BLAM)
GA
GA
GA
GA
GA
GA

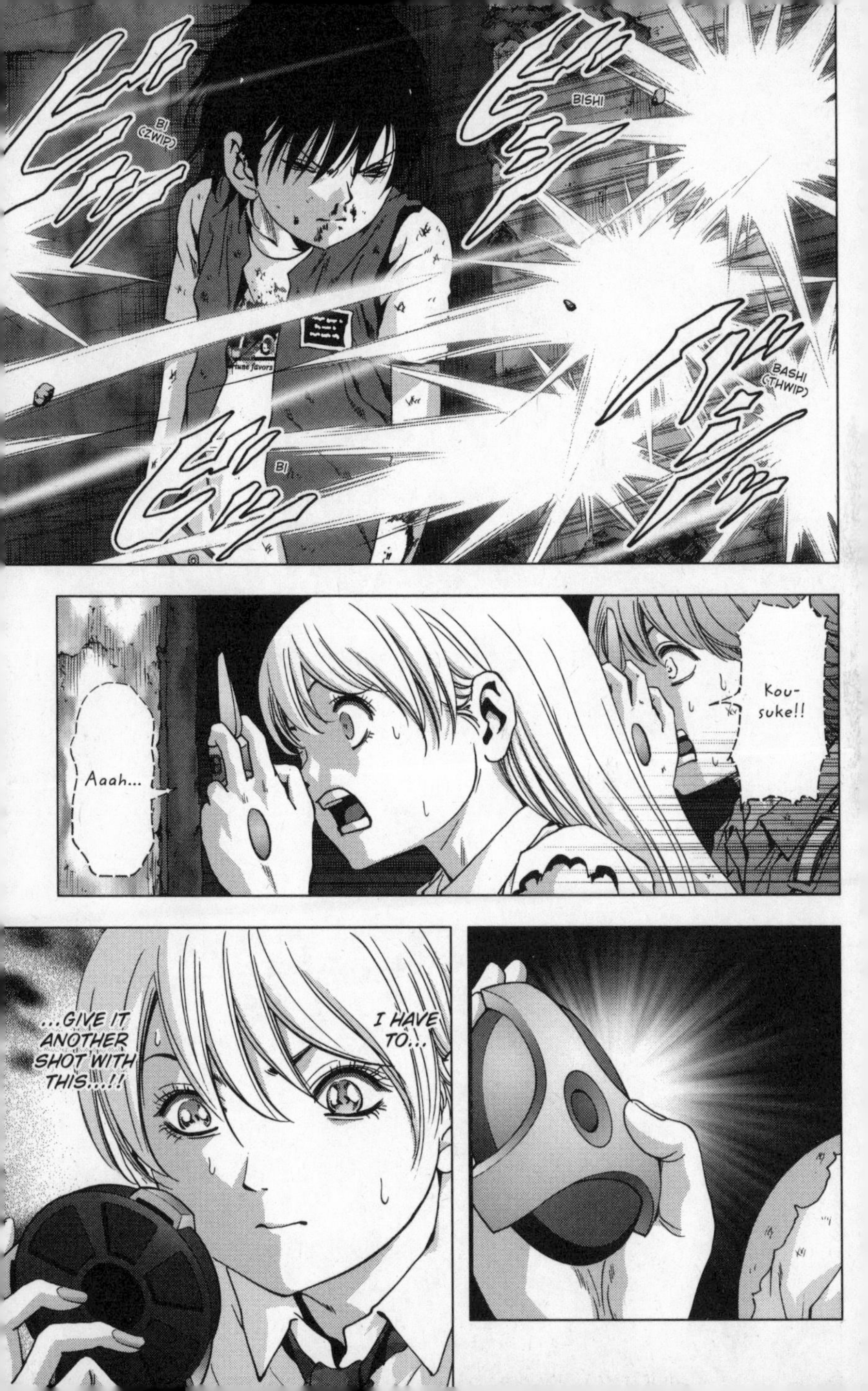
BISHI
BI (ZWIP)
BASHI (THWIP)
BI
Kou-suke!!
Aaah...
I HAVE TO...
...GIVE IT ANOTHER SHOT WITH THIS...!!

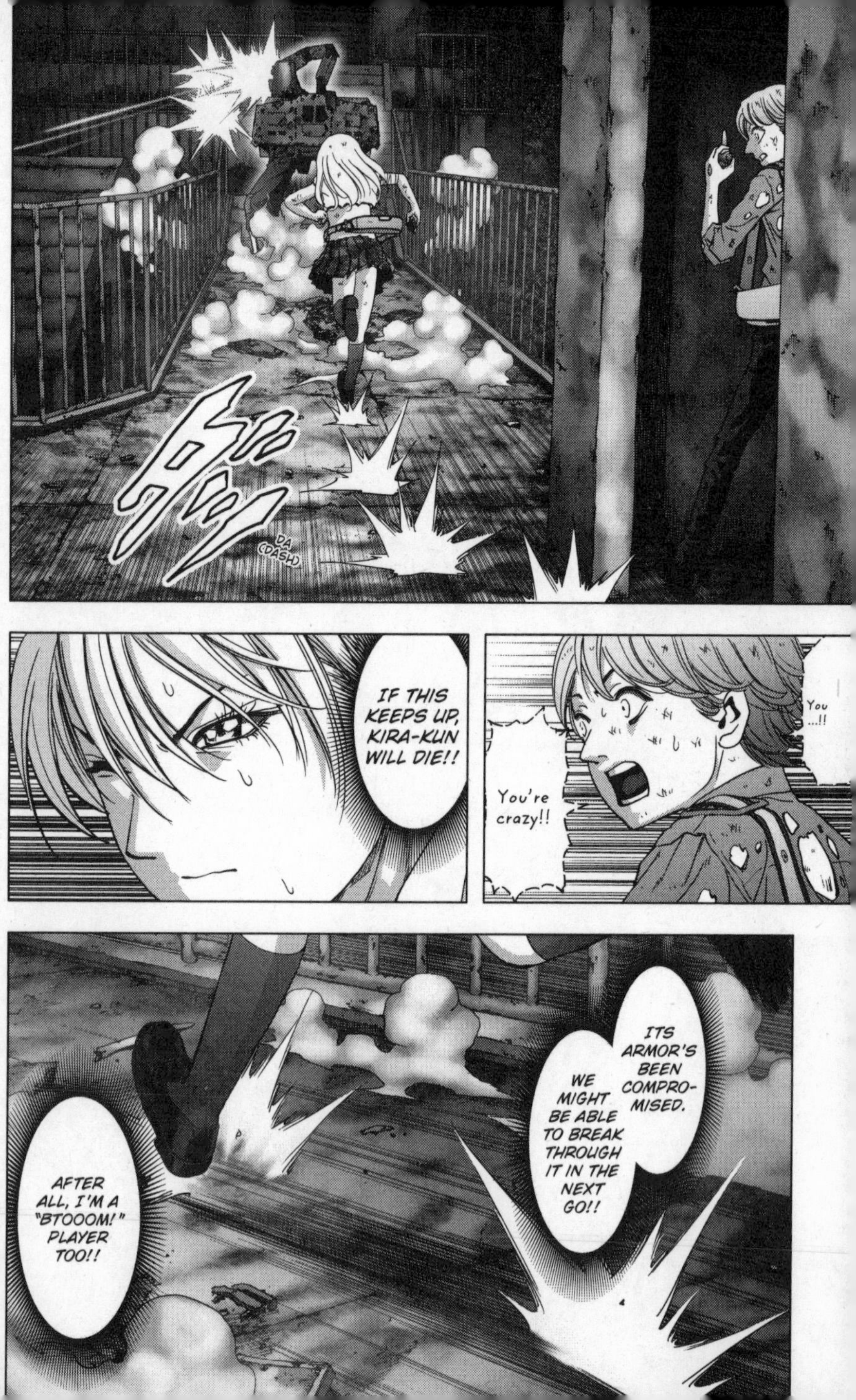
DA (DASH)
You ...!!
You're crazy!!
IF THIS KEEPS UP, KIRA-KUN WILL DIE!!
ITS ARMOR'S BEEN COMPRO-MISED.
WE MIGHT BE ABLE TO BREAK THROUGH IT IN THE NEXT GO!!
AFTER ALL, I'M A "BTOOOM!" PLAYER TOO!!

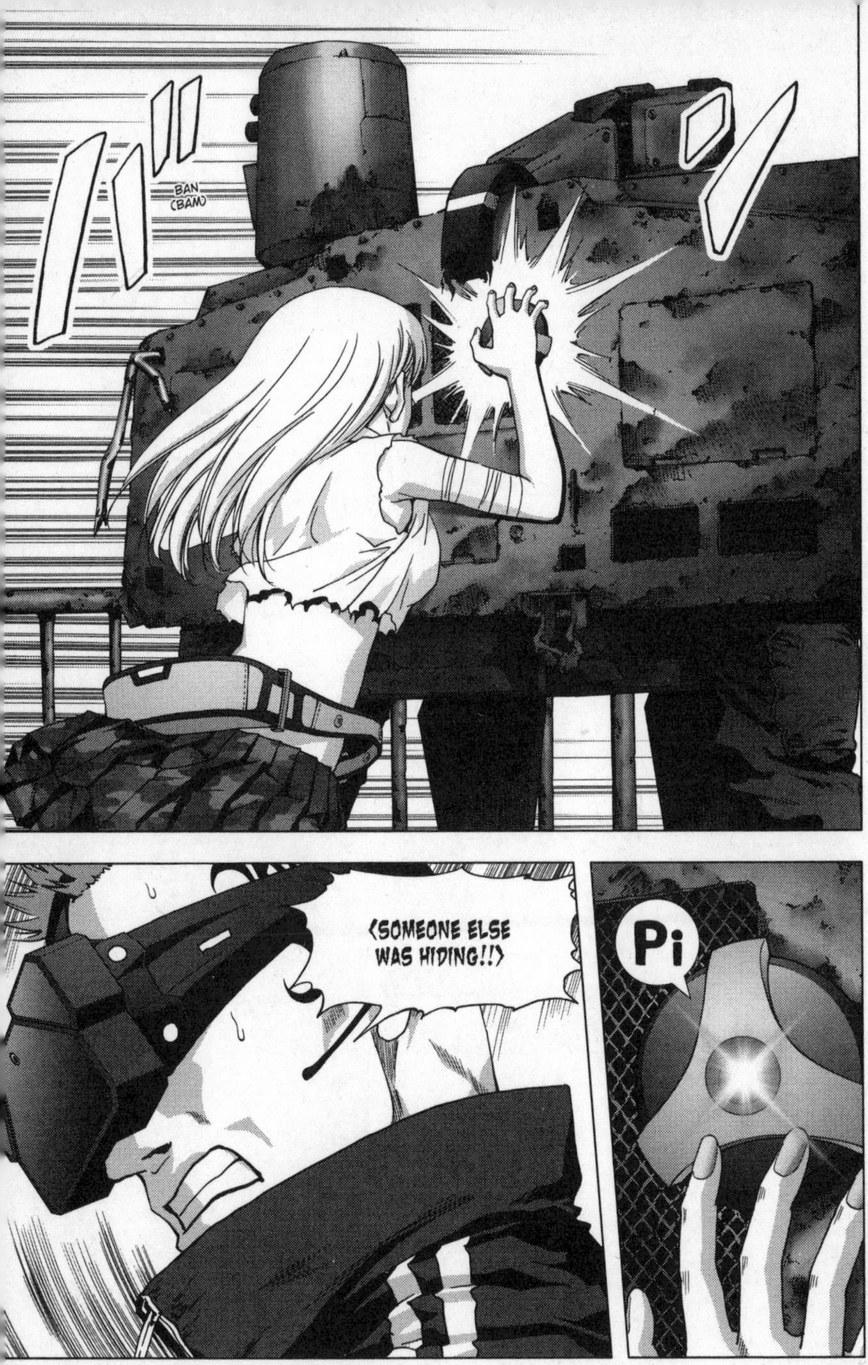
BAN
(BAM)
Pi
‹SOMEONE ELSE WAS HIDING!!›

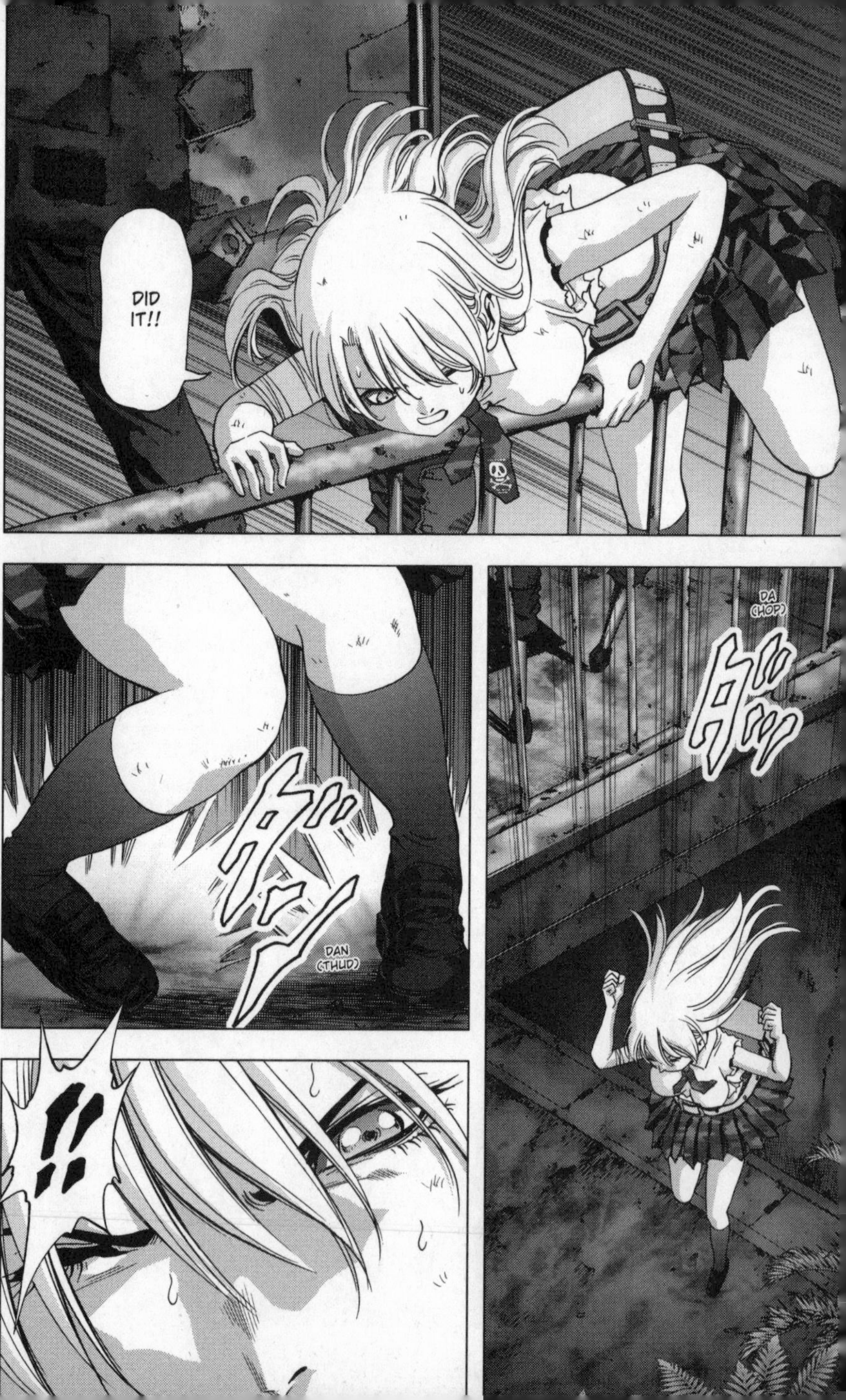
DID IT!!
DA (HOP)
DAN (THUD)
!!

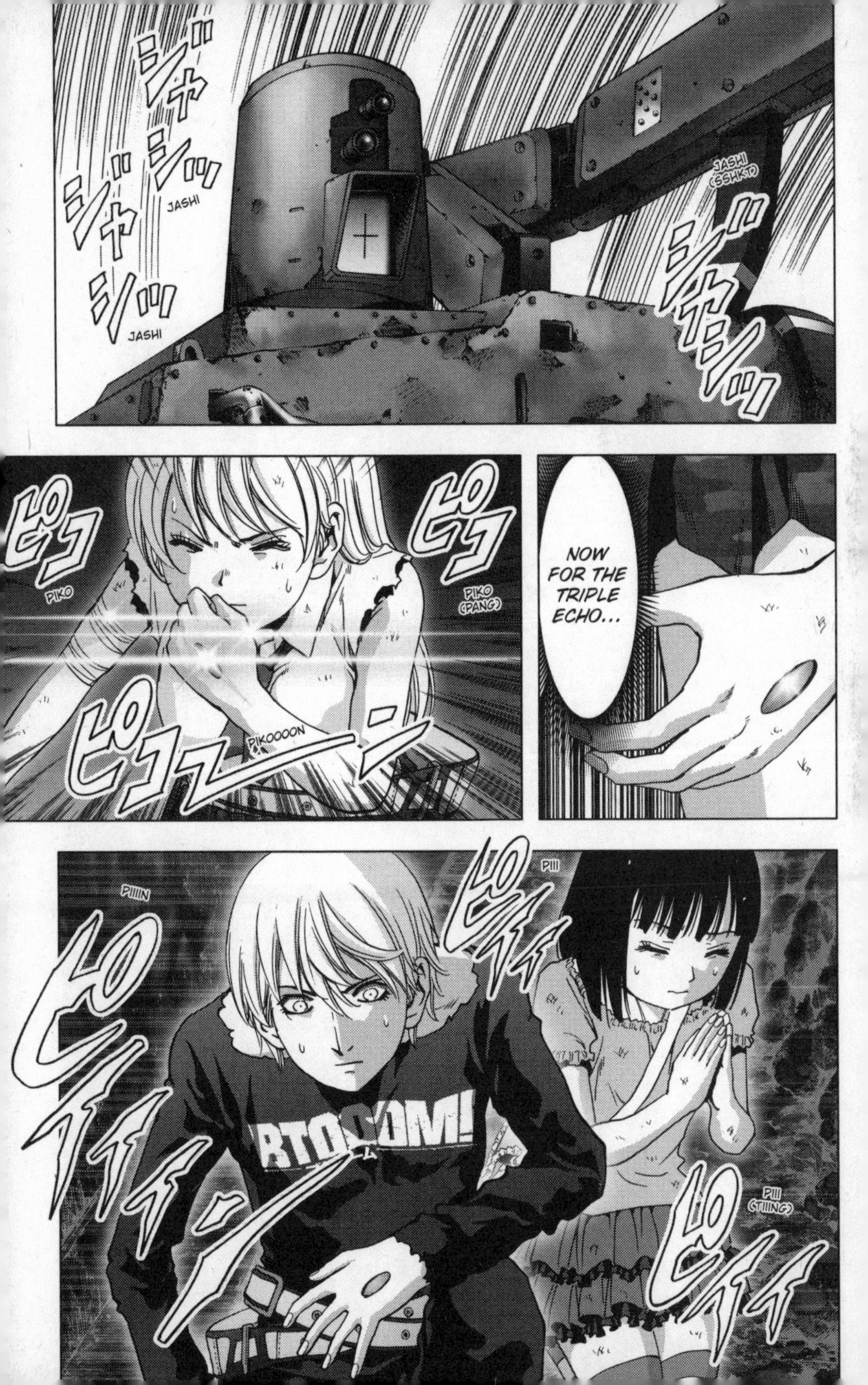
JASHI (SSHKT)
JASHI
JASHI
NOW FOR THE TRIPLE ECHO…
PIKO (PANG)
PIKO
PIKOOOON
PIII
PIII (TIIING)
PIIIN

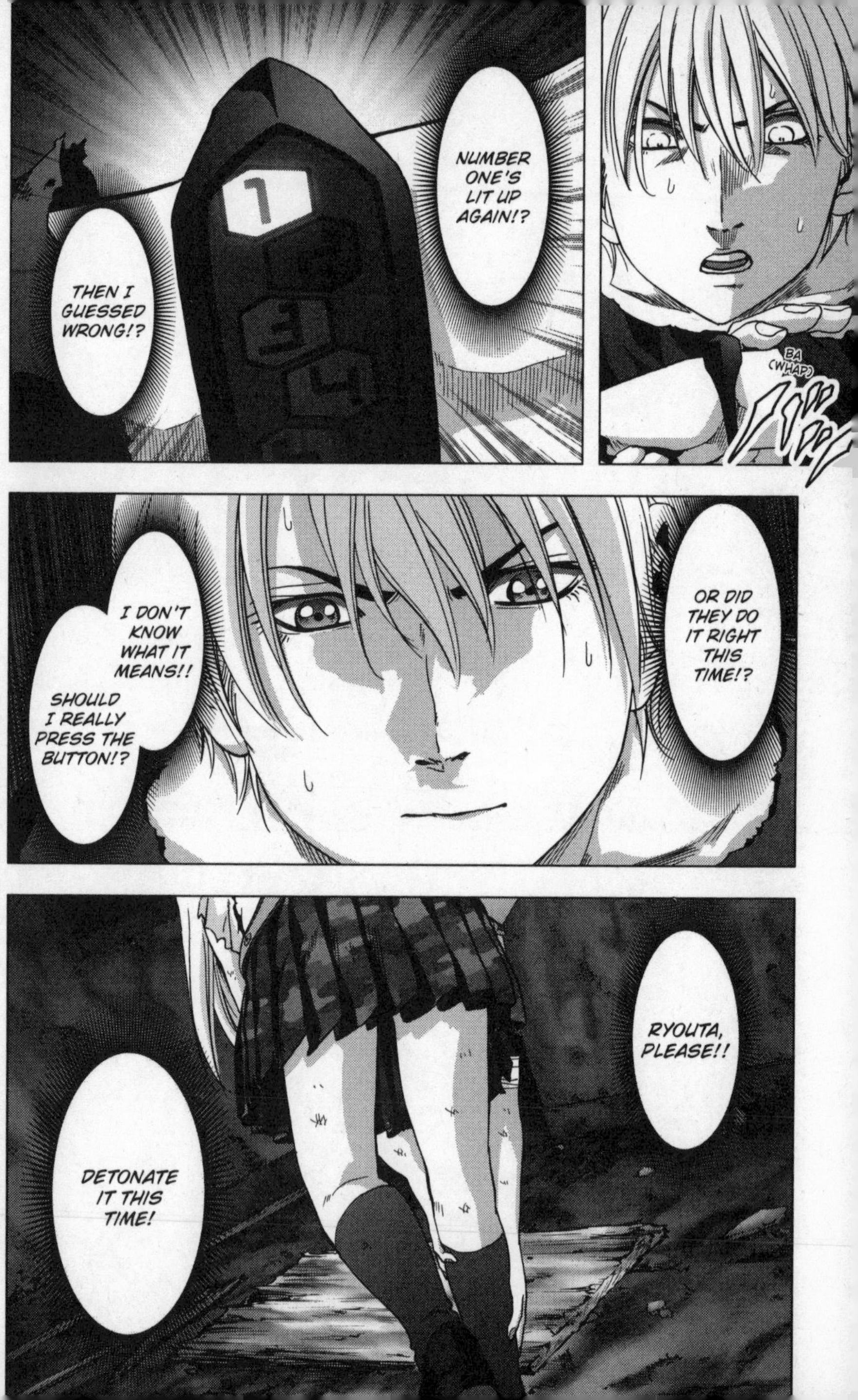
BA (WHAP)
NUMBER ONE'S LIT UP AGAIN!?
THEN I GUESSED WRONG!?
OR DID THEY DO IT RIGHT THIS TIME!?
I DON'T KNOW WHAT IT MEANS!! SHOULD I REALLY PRESS THE BUTTON!?
RYOUTA, PLEASE!!
DETONATE IT THIS TIME!

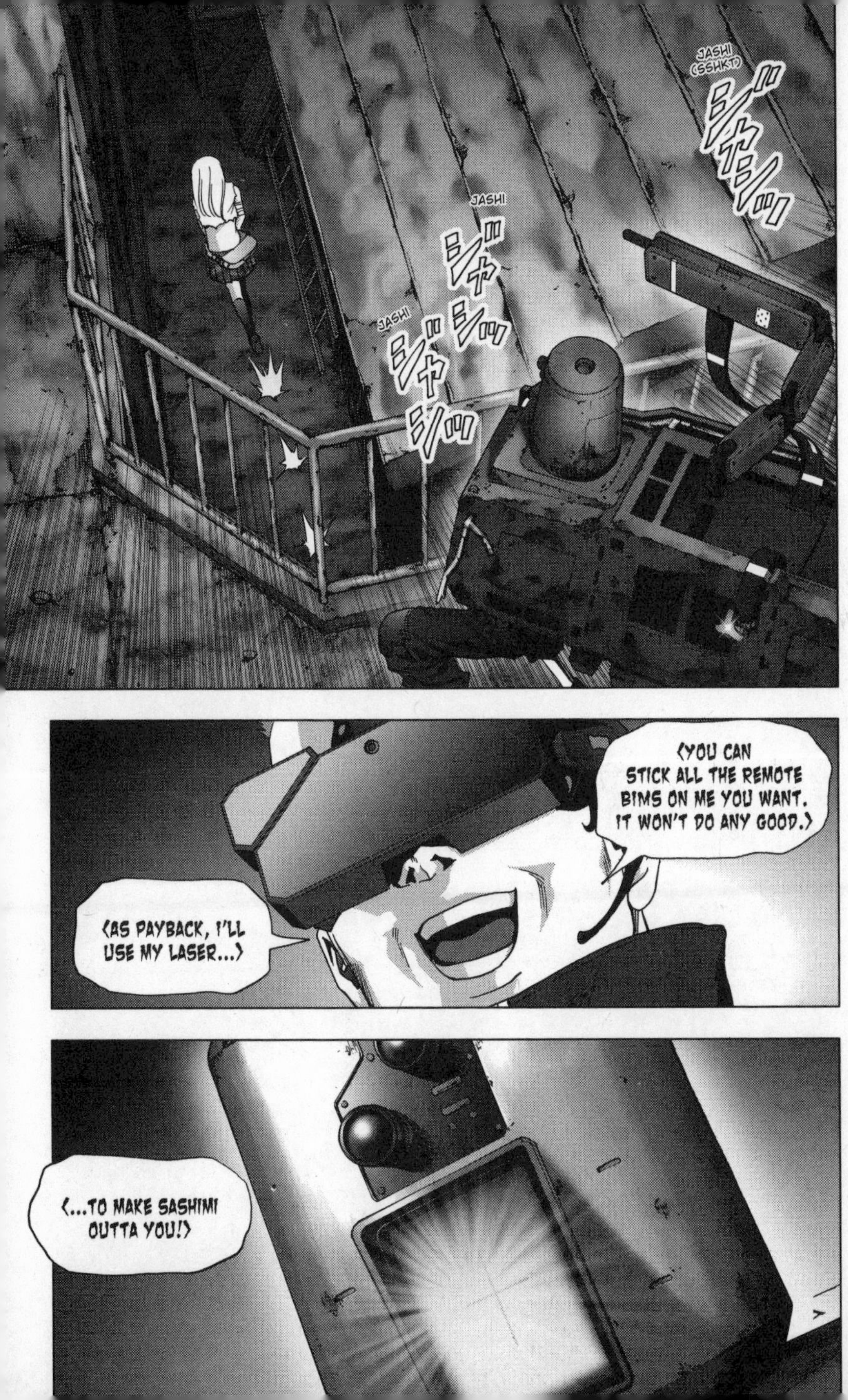
JASHI (SSHKT)
JASHI
JASHI
<YOU CAN STICK ALL THE REMOTE BIMS ON ME YOU WANT. IT WON'T DO ANY GOOD.>
<AS PAYBACK, I'LL USE MY LASER...>
<...TO MAKE SASHIMI OUTTA YOU!>

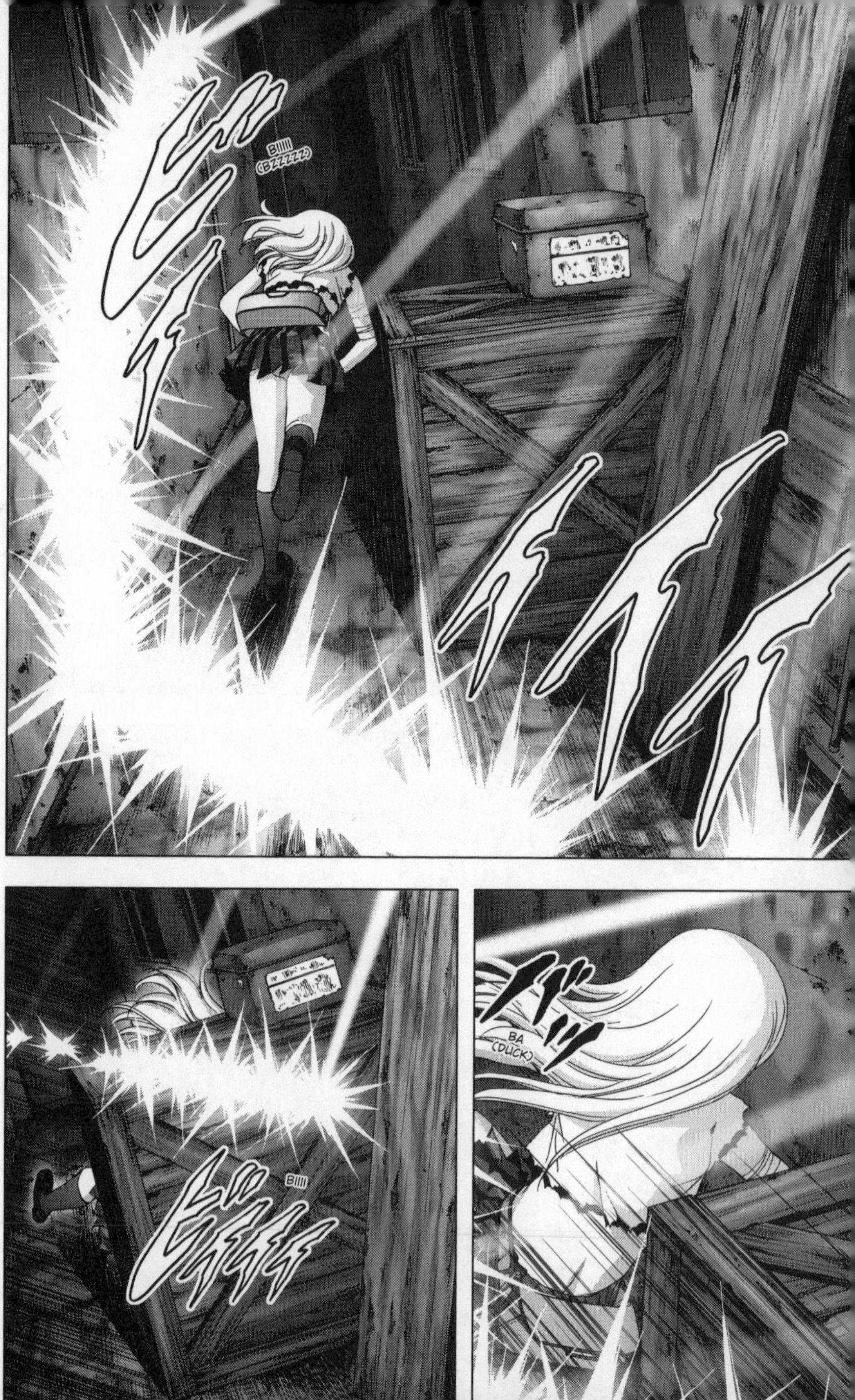
BIIIII
(BZZZZZZ)
BA
(DUCK)
BIIII

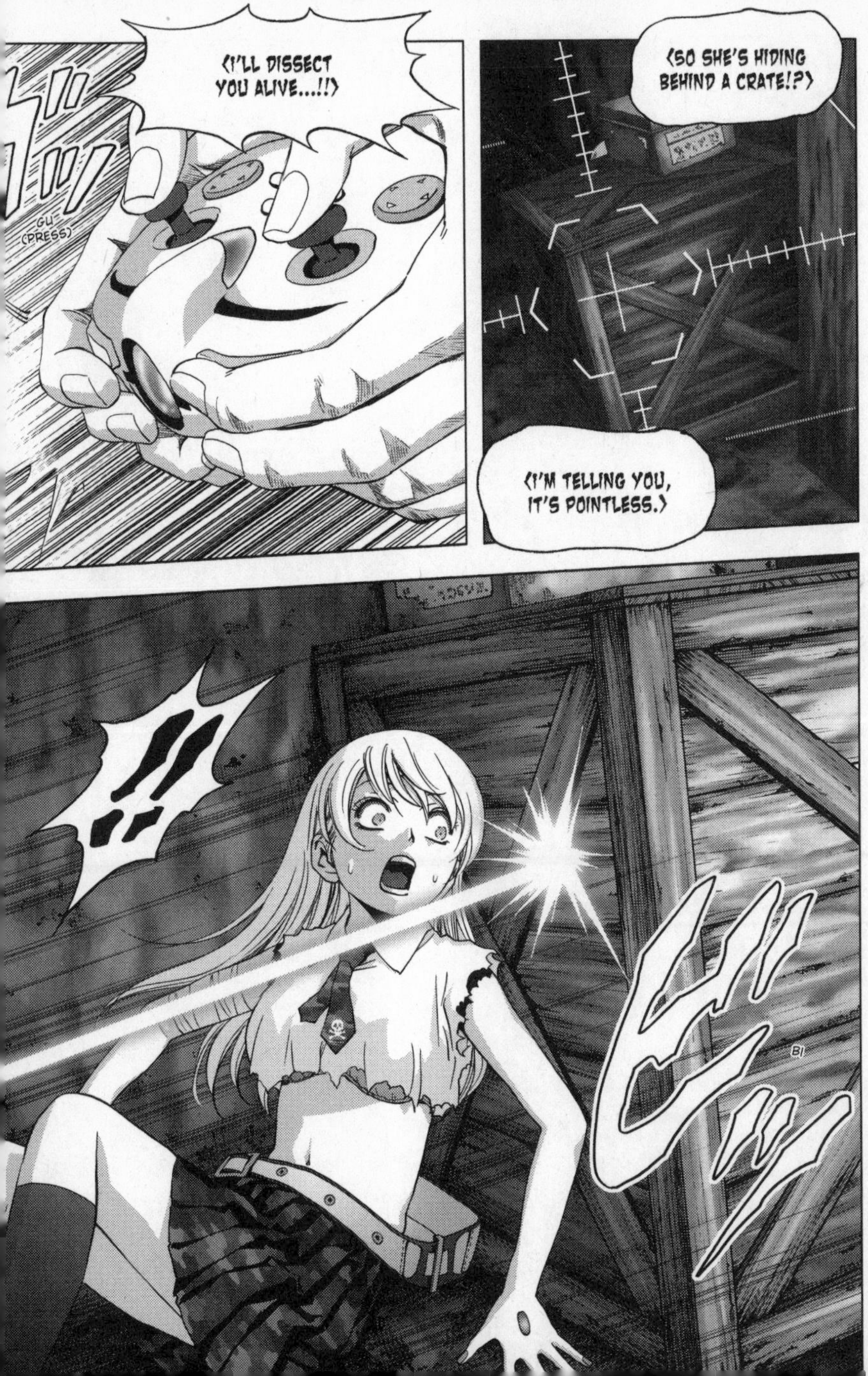
〈SO SHE'S HIDING BEHIND A CRATE!?〉
〈I'M TELLING YOU, IT'S POINTLESS.〉
〈I'LL DISSECT YOU ALIVE...!!〉
GU (PRESS)
!!
BI

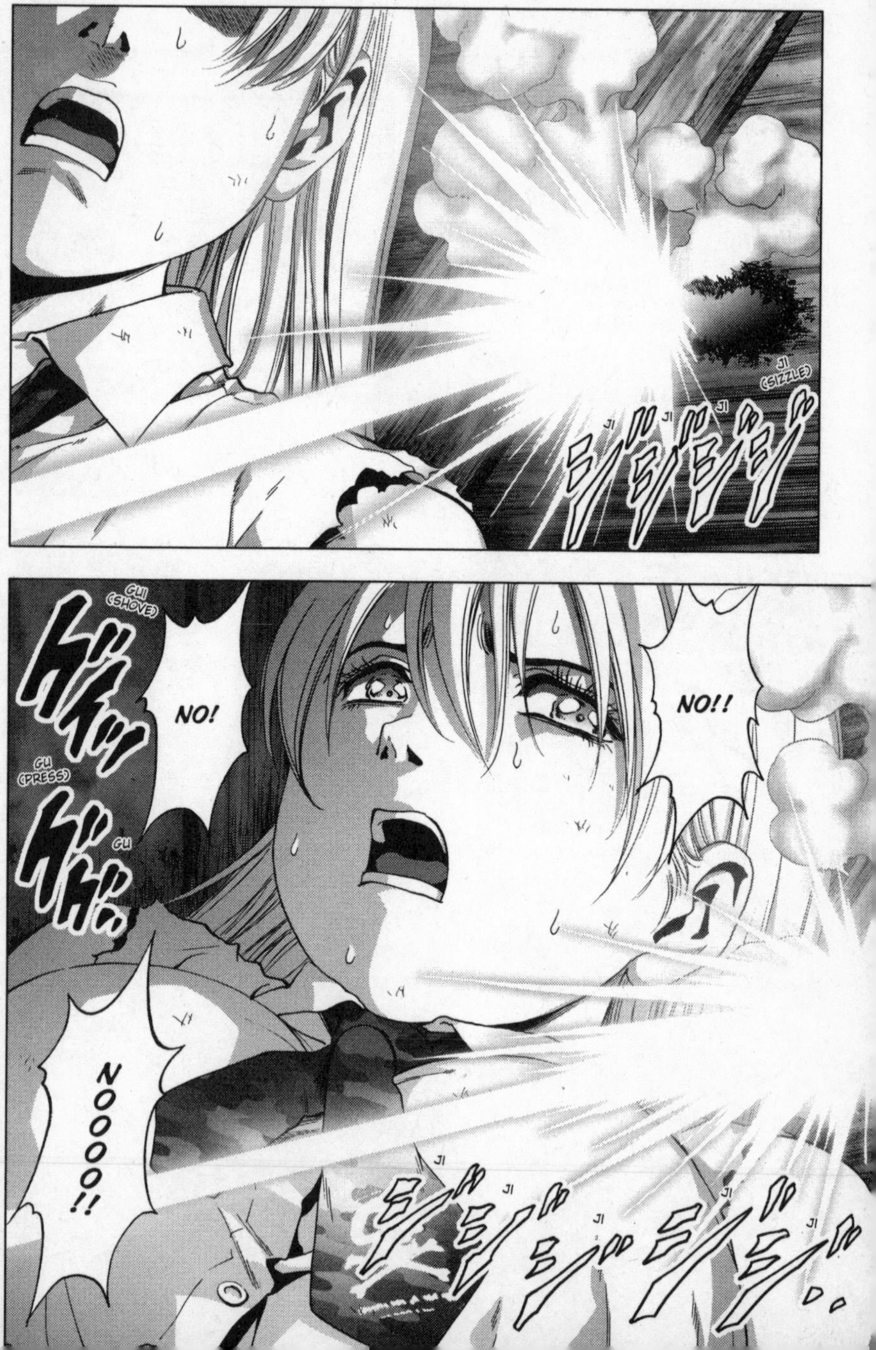
JI (SIZZLE)
JI
JI
JI
NO!!
NO!
GUI (SHOVE)
GU (PRESS)
GU
NOOOOO!!
JI
JI
JI
JI
JI

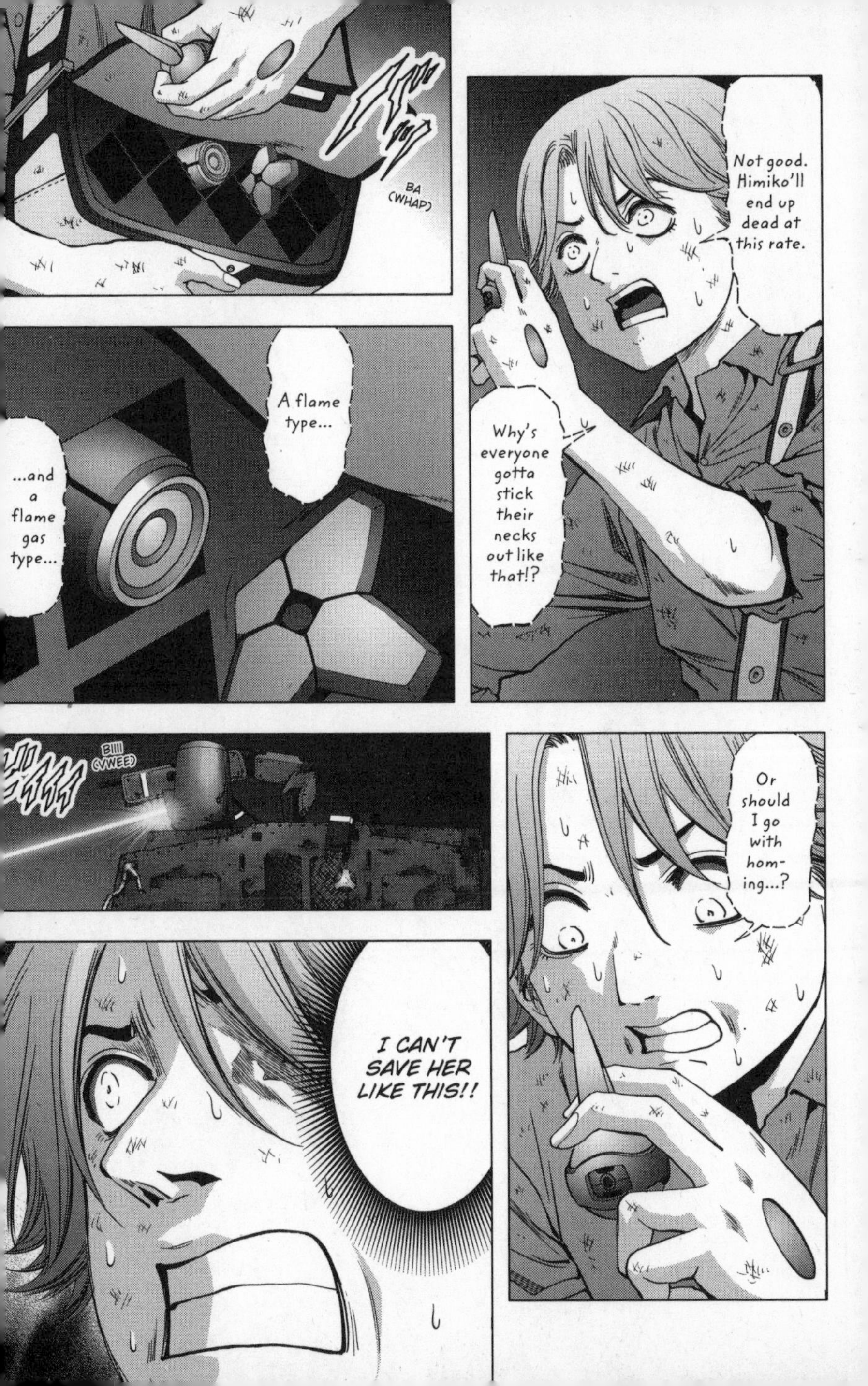
Not good. Himiko'll end up dead at this rate.
Why's everyone gotta stick their necks out like that!?
BA (WHAP)
A flame type...
...and a flame gas type...
Or should I go with hom-ing...?
BIIII (VWEE)
I CAN'T SAVE HER LIKE THIS!!

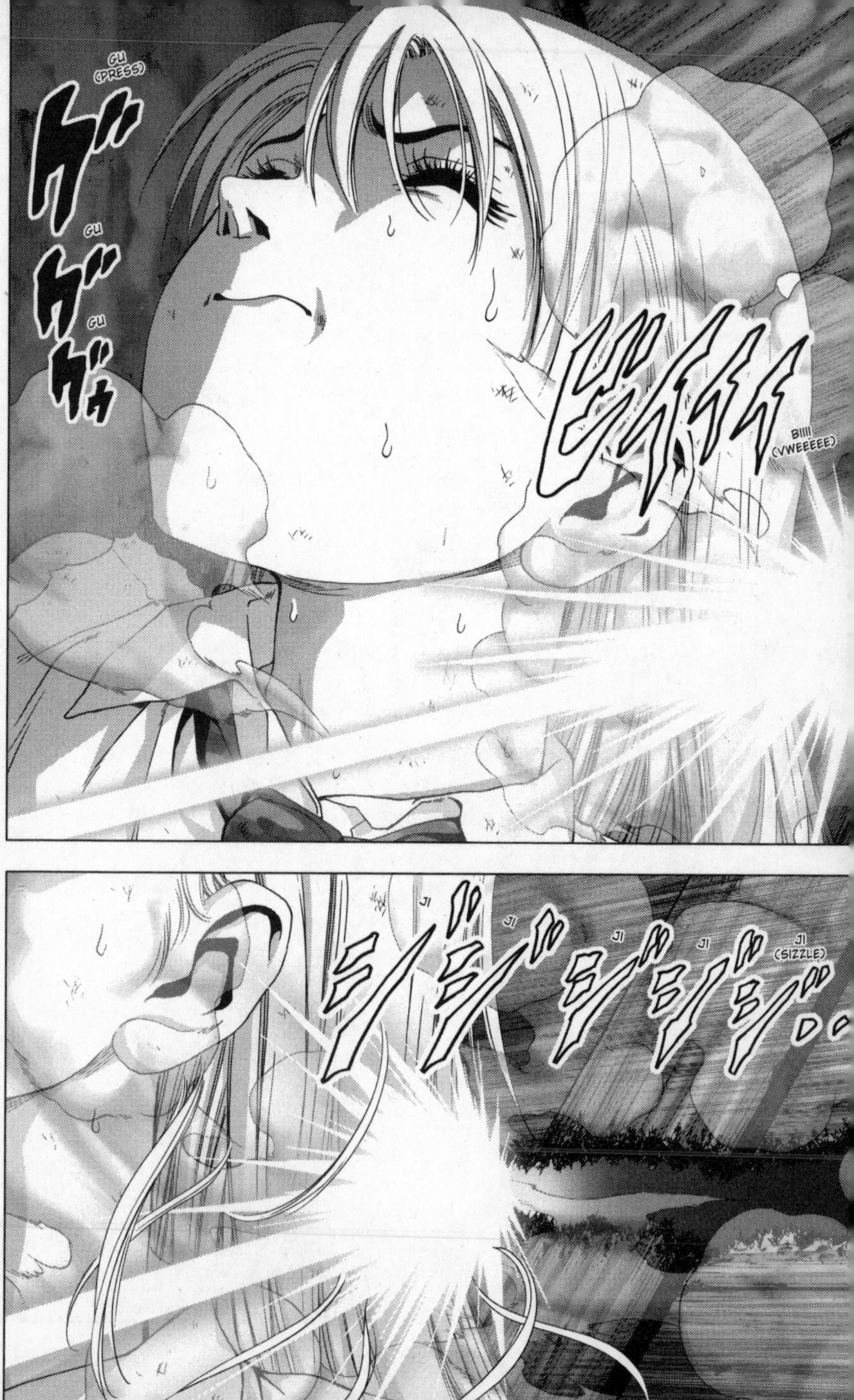
BIIII (VWEEEEE)
GU (PRESS)
GU
GU
JI
JI
JI
JI
JI (SIZZLE)

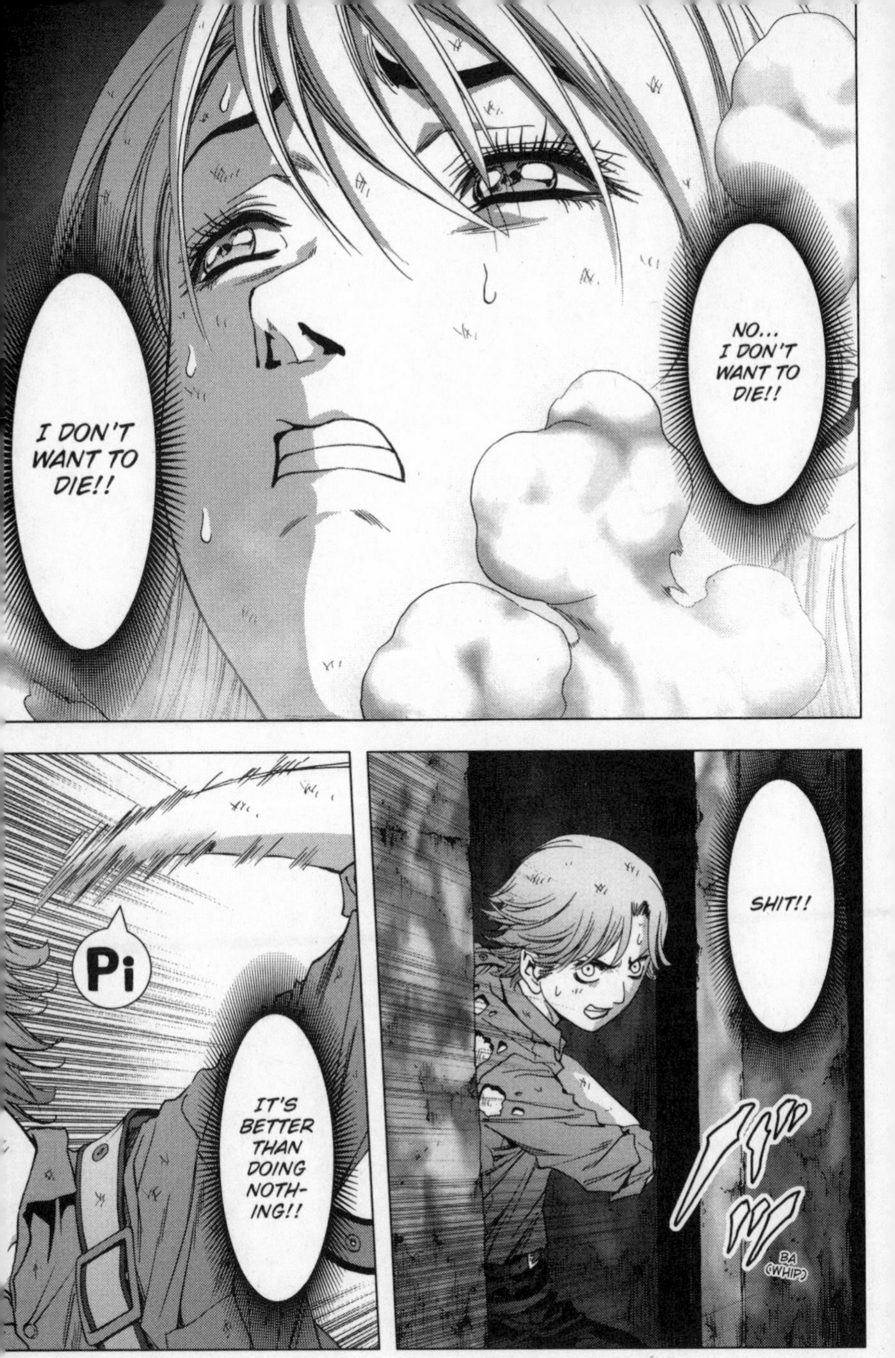
NO... I DON'T WANT TO DIE!!
I DON'T WANT TO DIE!!
SHIT!!
BA (WHIP)
Pi
IT'S BETTER THAN DOING NOTH-ING!!

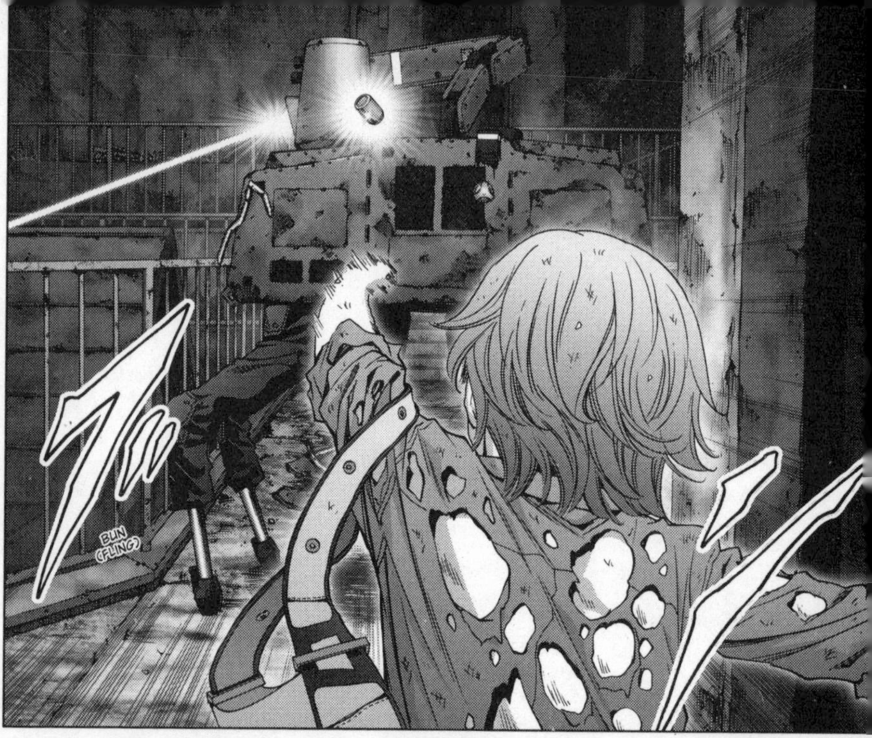
BUN
(FLING)

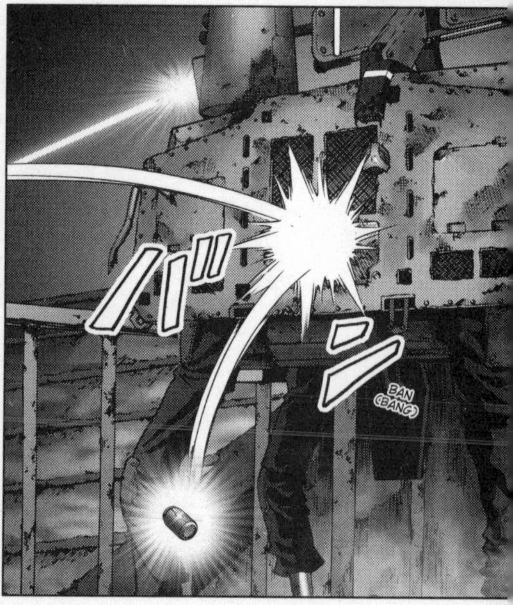
BAN
(BANG)

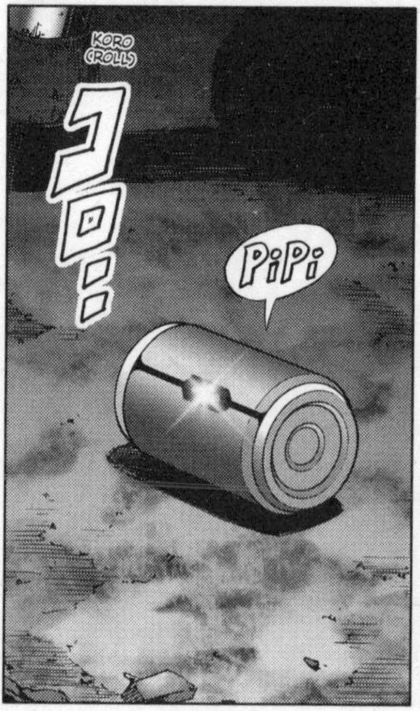
KORO
(ROLL)
PiPi

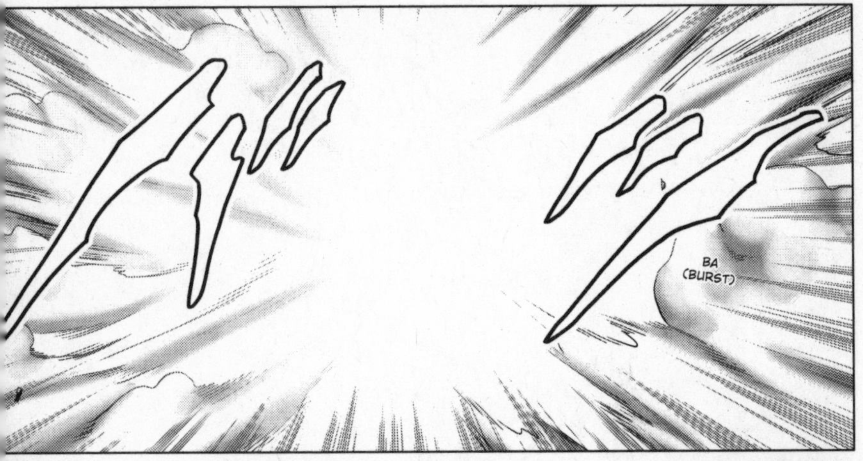
BA
(BURST)
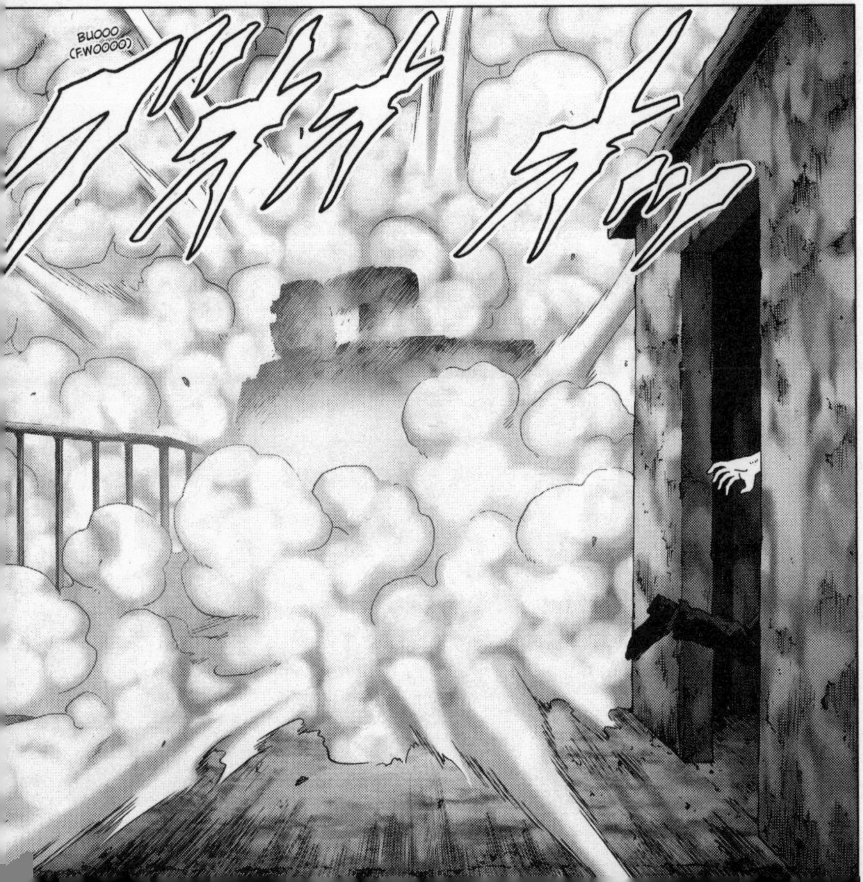
BUOOO
(F-WOOOO)

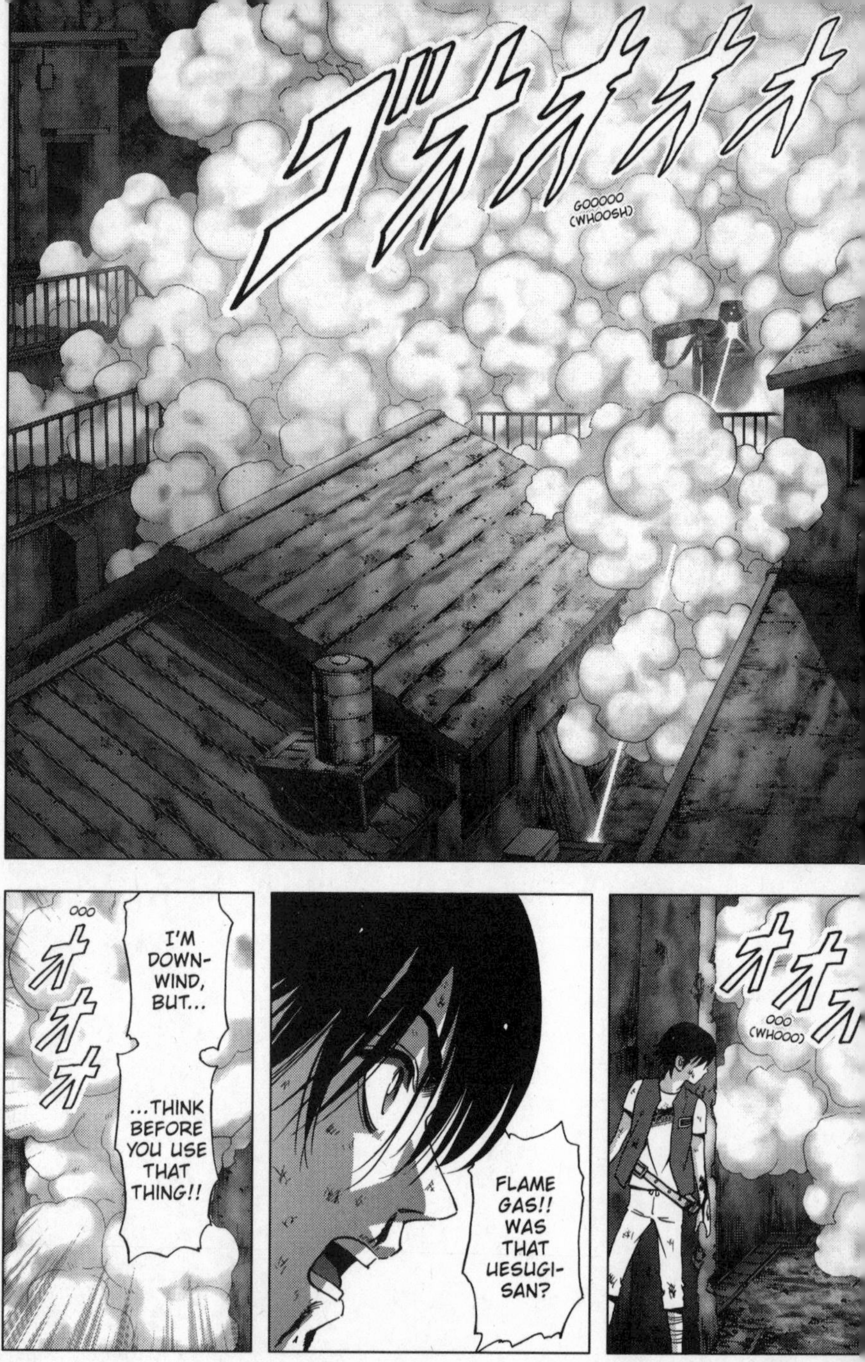
ゴォォオオ
GOOOOO (WHOOSH)
オオ
OOO (WHOOO)
FLAME GAS!! WAS THAT UESUGI-SAN?
OOO
オオオ
I'M DOWN-WIND, BUT...
...THINK BEFORE YOU USE THAT THING!!

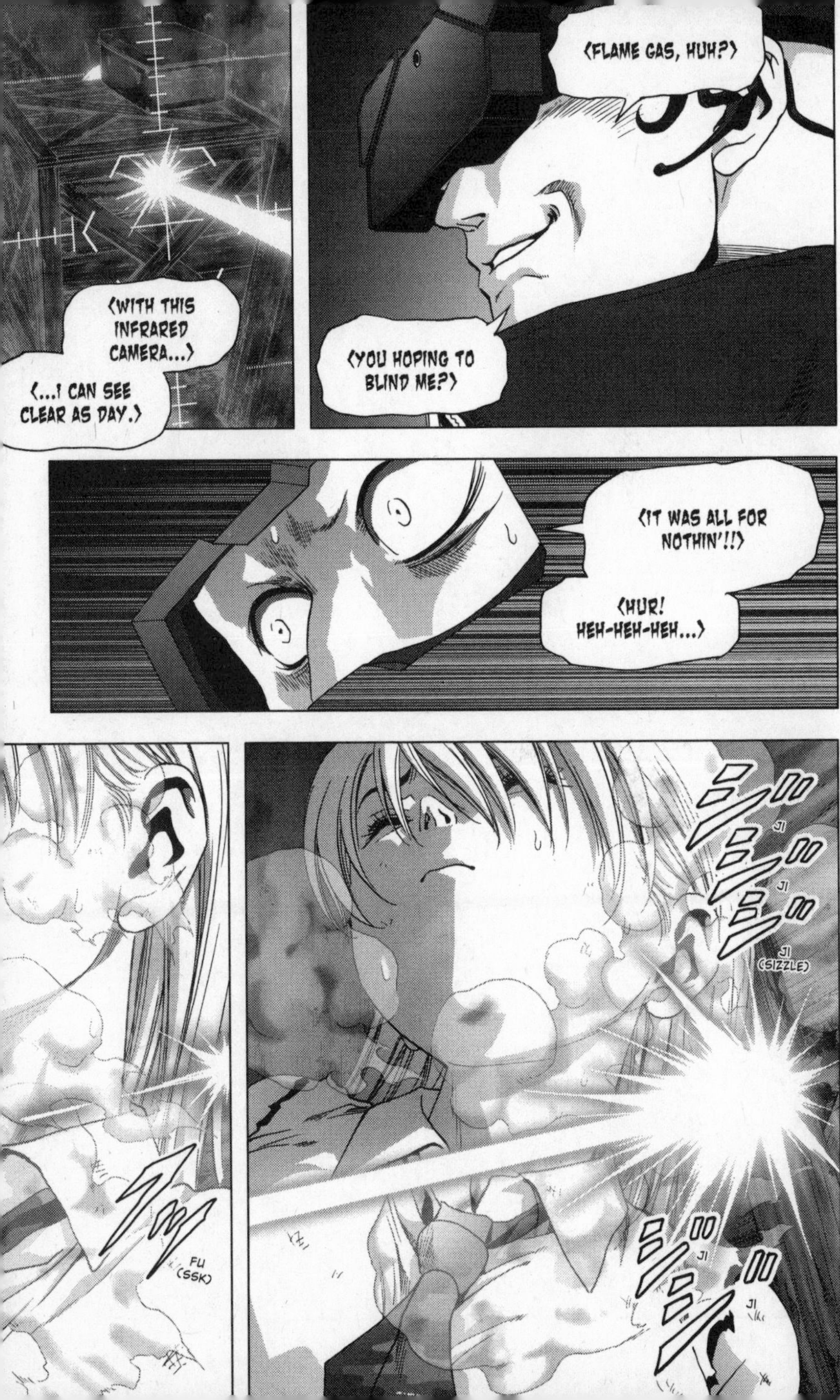

⟨FLAME GAS, HUH?⟩
⟨YOU HOPING TO BLIND ME?⟩
⟨WITH THIS INFRARED CAMERA...⟩
⟨...I CAN SEE CLEAR AS DAY.⟩
⟨IT WAS ALL FOR NOTHIN'!!⟩
⟨HUR! HEH-HEH-HEH...⟩
JI
JI
JI (SIZZLE)
JI
JI
FU (SSK)

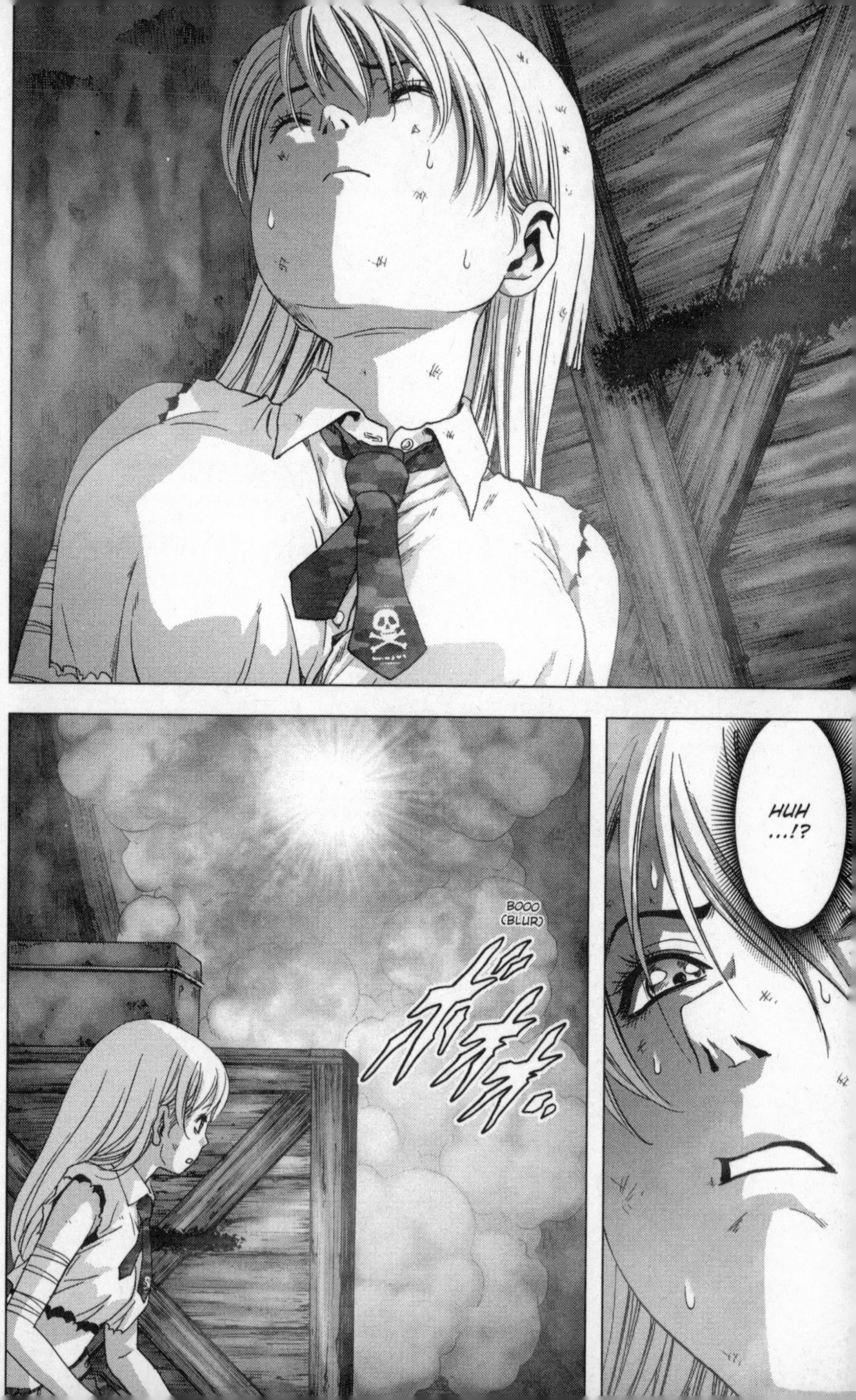
HUH ...!?
BOOO (BLUR)

BIIIIII
(VWEEEE)

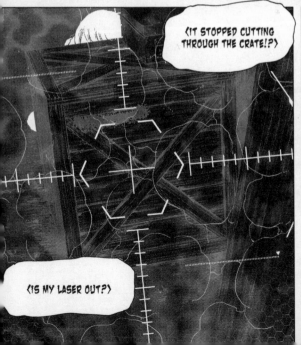

〈IT STOPPED CUTTING
THROUGH THE CRATE!?〉

〈IS MY LASER OUT?〉

〈HUH?〉

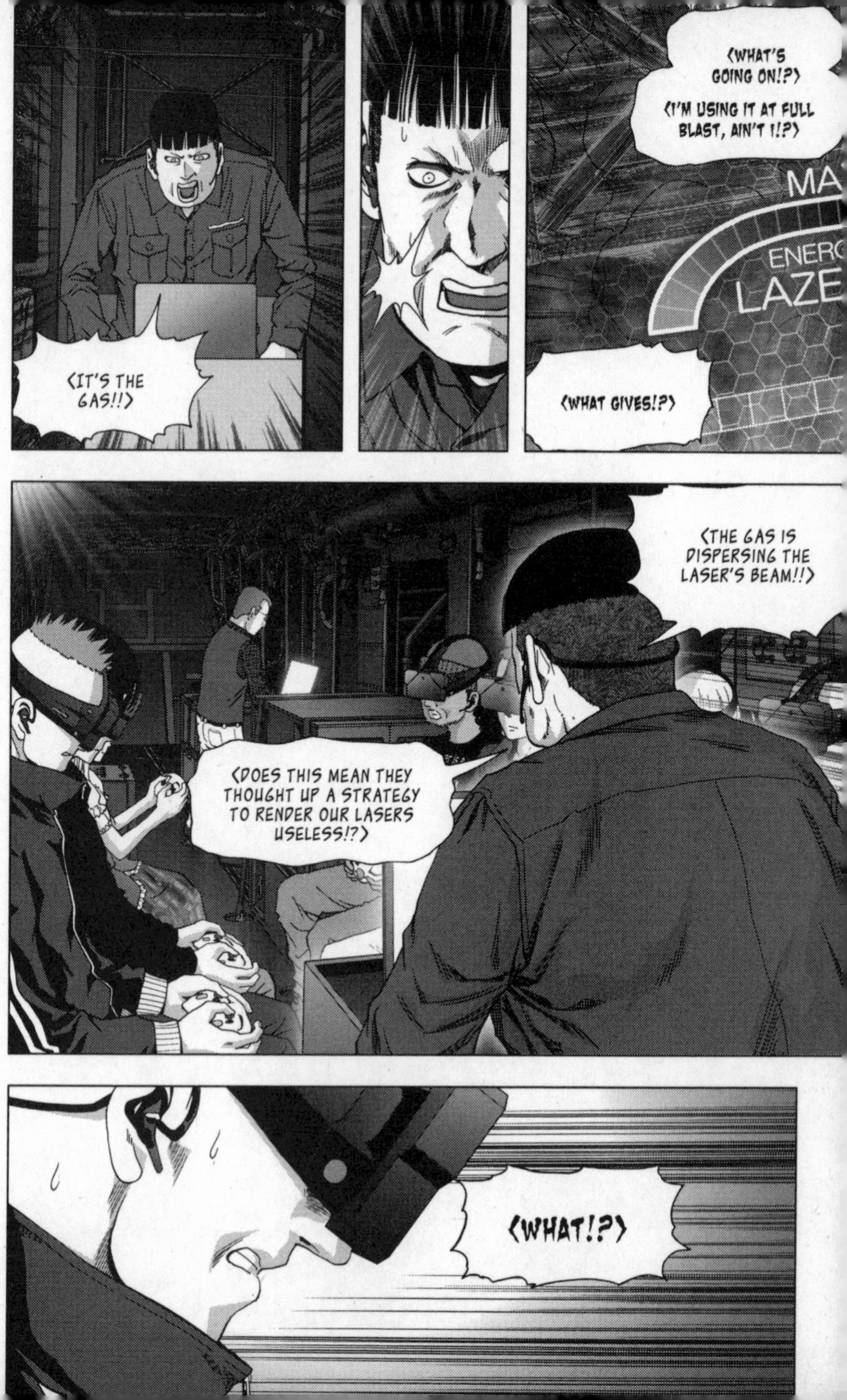
⟨WHAT'S GOING ON!?⟩
⟨I'M USING IT AT FULL BLAST, AIN'T I!?⟩
⟨WHAT GIVES!?⟩
⟨IT'S THE GAS!!⟩
⟨THE GAS IS DISPERSING THE LASER'S BEAM!!⟩
⟨DOES THIS MEAN THEY THOUGHT UP A STRATEGY TO RENDER OUR LASERS USELESS!?⟩
⟨WHAT!?⟩

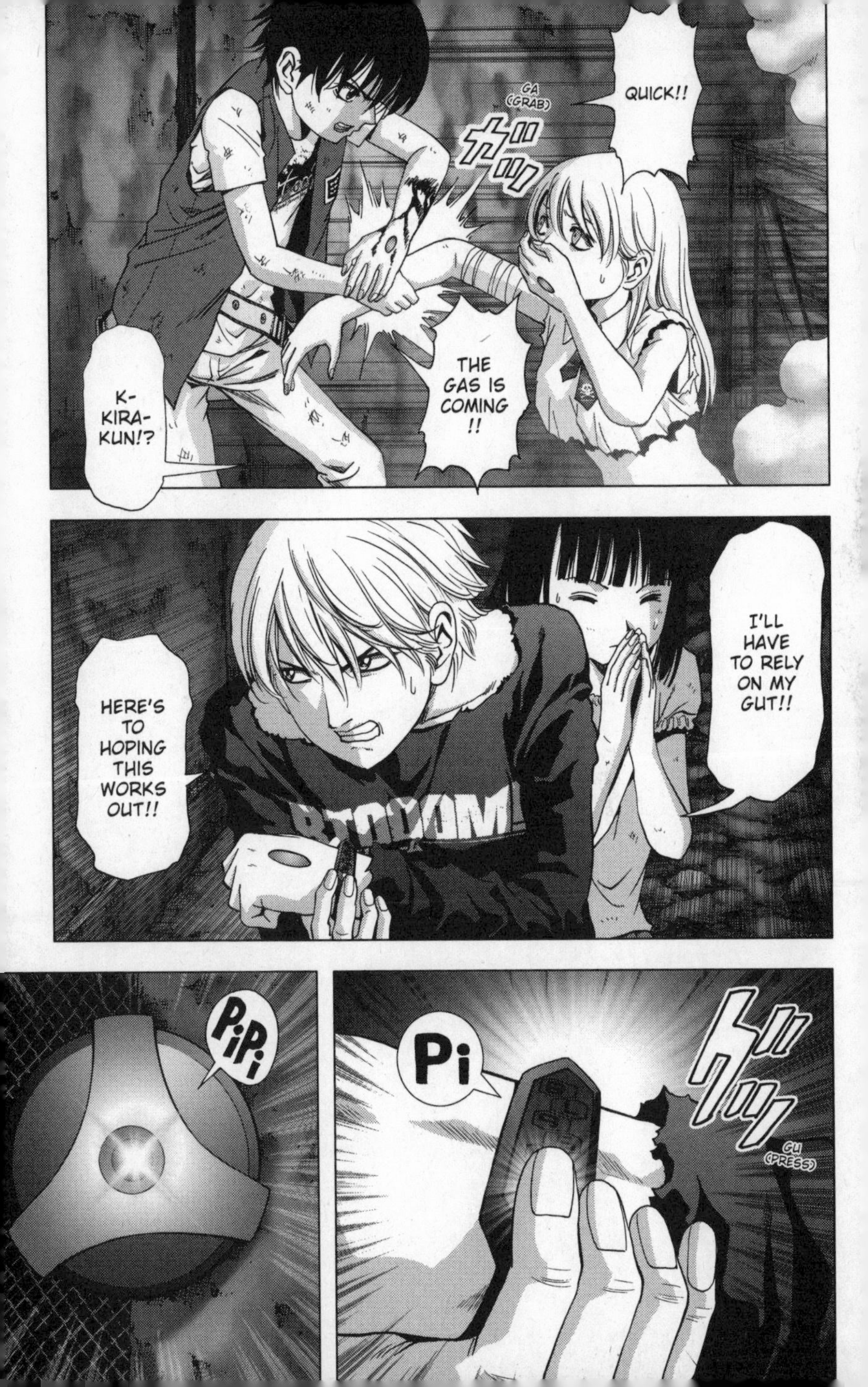
QUICK!!
GA (GRAB)
THE GAS IS COMING!!
K-KIRA-KUN!?
I'LL HAVE TO RELY ON MY GUT!!
HERE'S TO HOPING THIS WORKS OUT!!
GU (PRESS)
Pi
PiPi

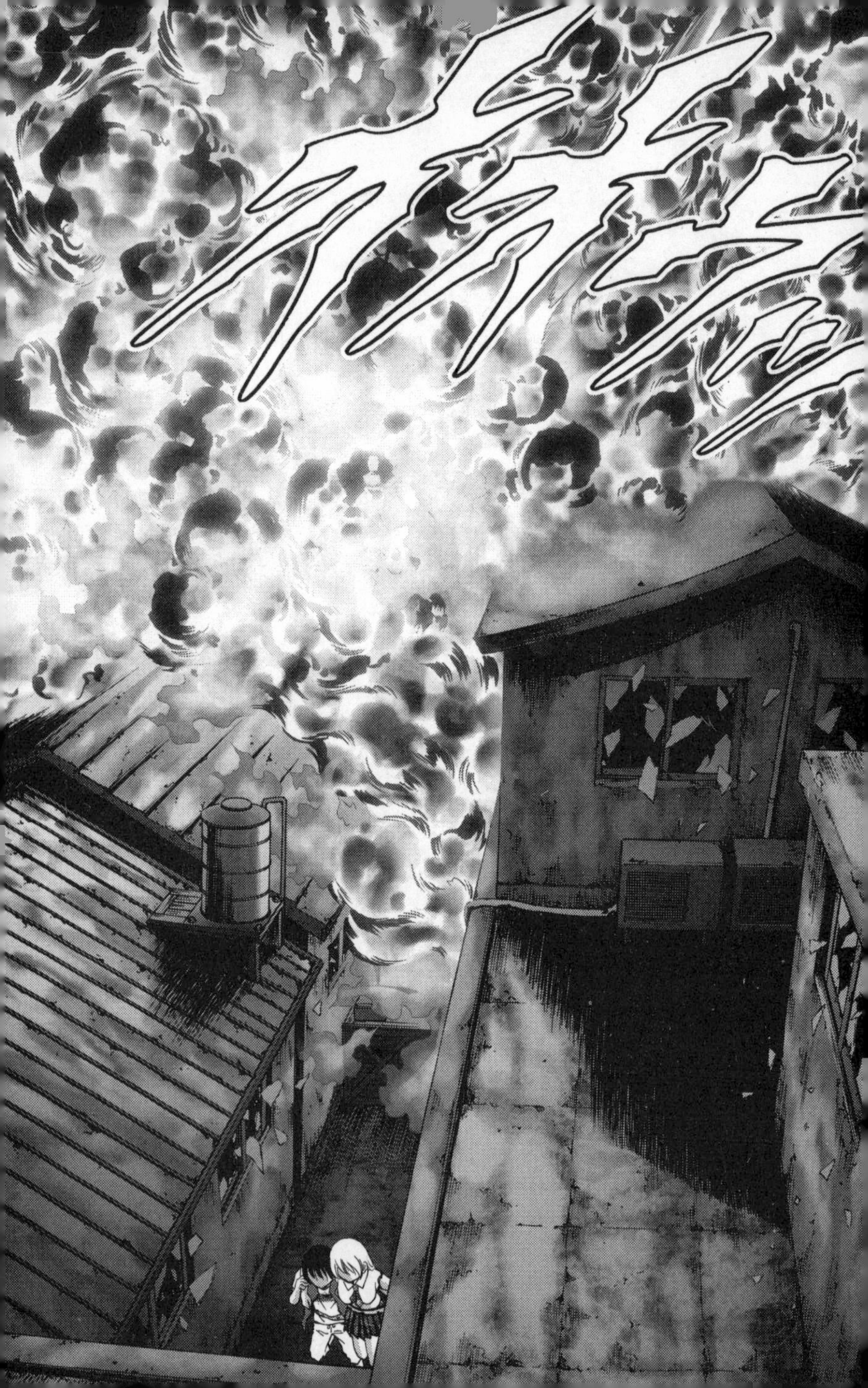

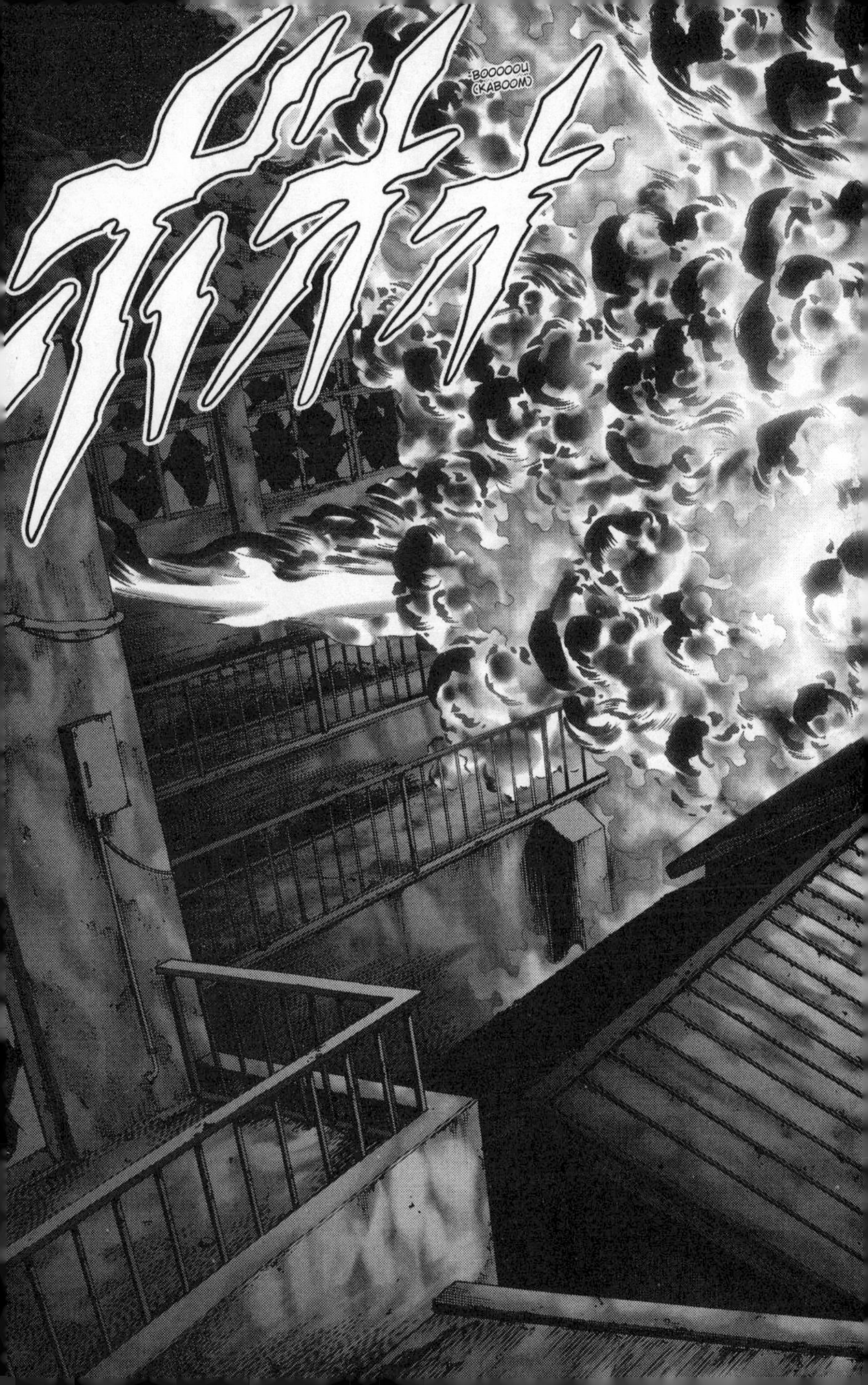
BOOOOOU (KABOOM)

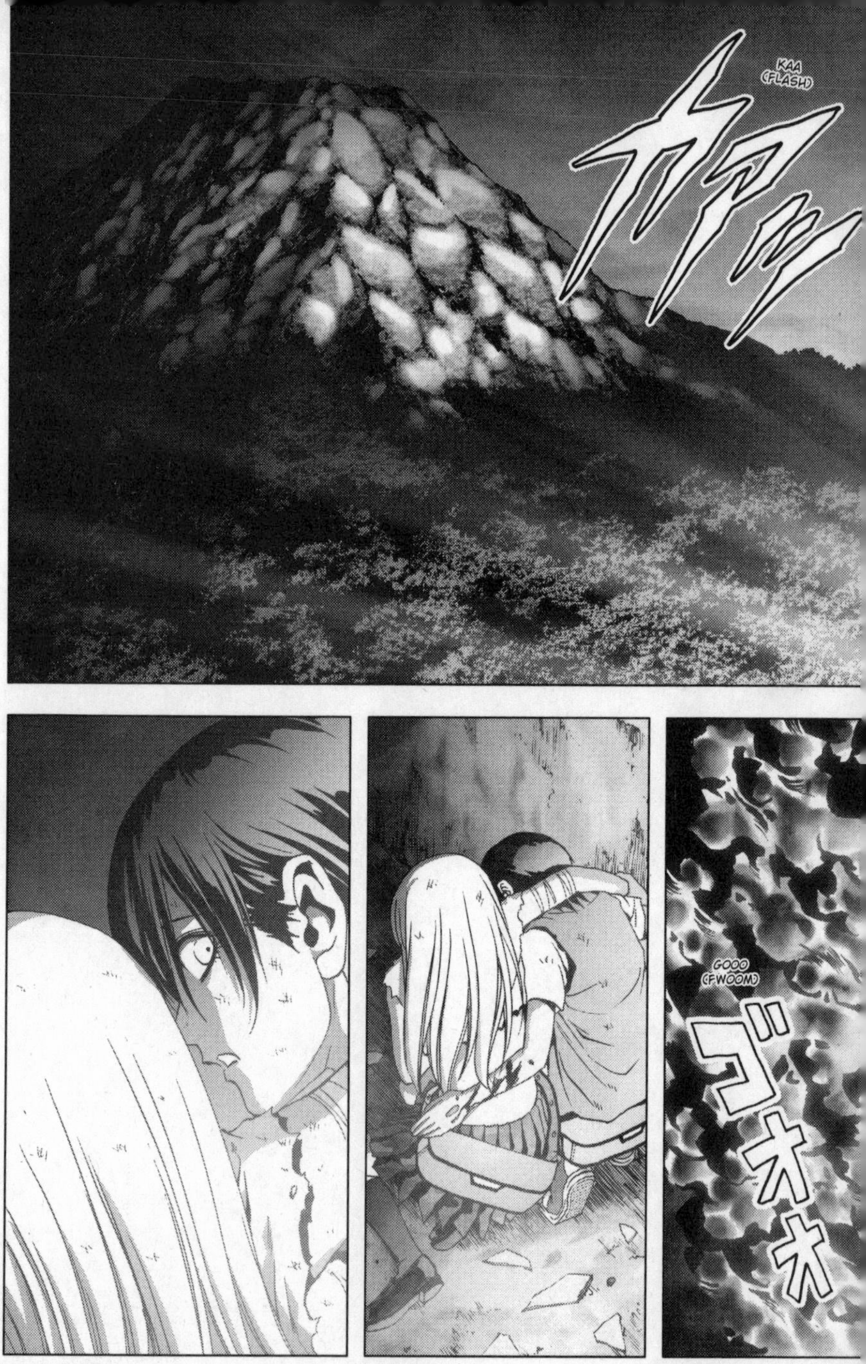
KAA
(FLASH)
カァッ
GOOO
(FWOOM)
ゴオオ

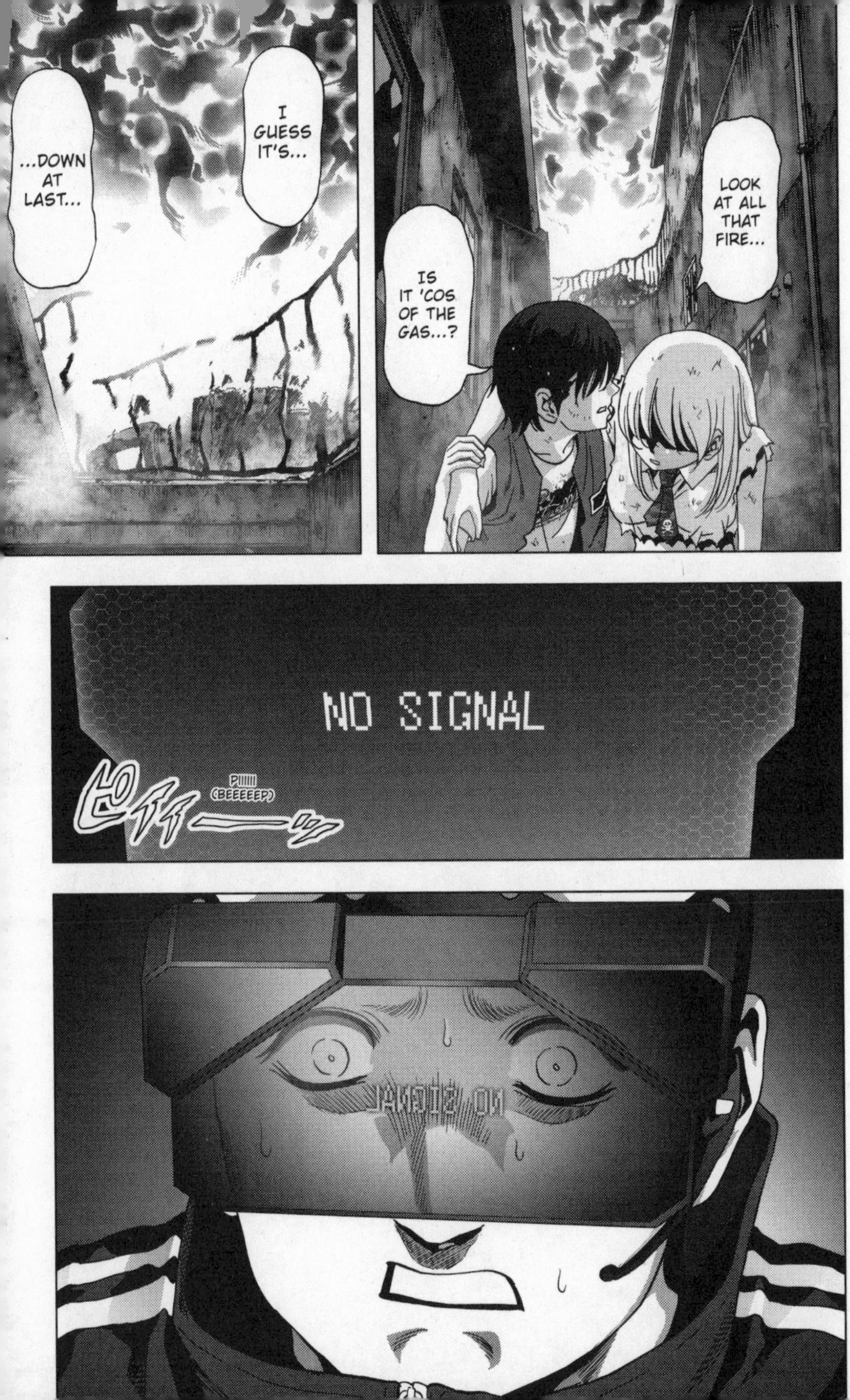
LOOK AT ALL THAT FIRE...
IS IT 'COS OF THE GAS...?
I GUESS IT'S...
...DOWN AT LAST...
NO SIGNAL
PIIIII (BEEEEEP)

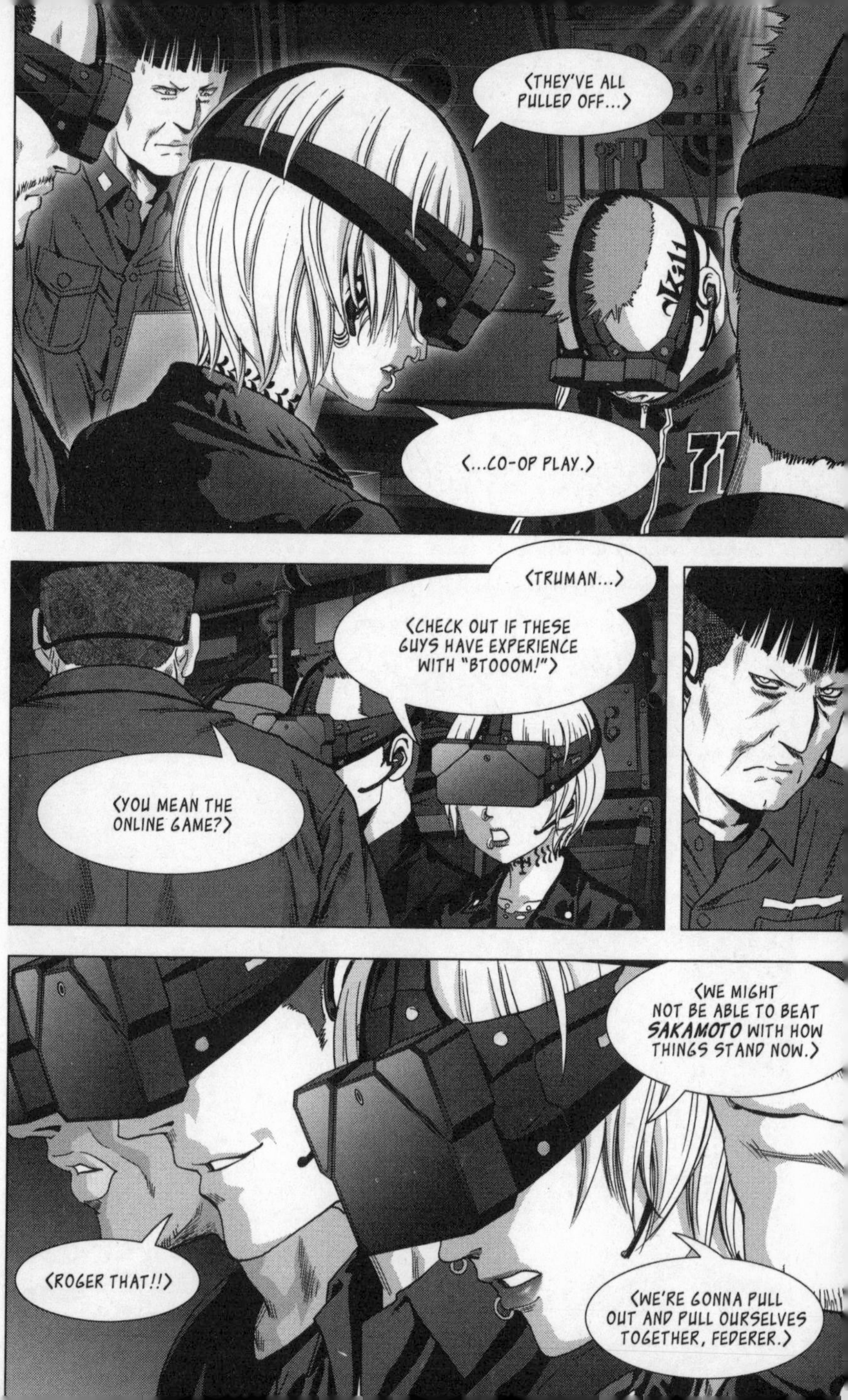
〈THEY'VE ALL PULLED OFF...〉
〈...CO-OP PLAY.〉
〈TRUMAN...〉
〈CHECK OUT IF THESE GUYS HAVE EXPERIENCE WITH "BTOOOM!"〉
〈YOU MEAN THE ONLINE GAME?〉
〈WE MIGHT NOT BE ABLE TO BEAT **SAKAMOTO** WITH HOW THINGS STAND NOW.〉
〈WE'RE GONNA PULL OUT AND PULL OURSELVES TOGETHER, FEDERER.〉
〈ROGER THAT!!〉

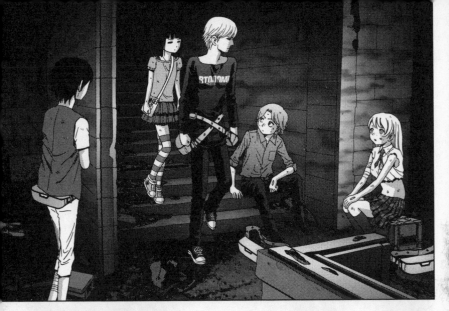

OH, GOOD ... YOU'RE ALL OKAY.

R-RYOUTA ...

YORO
(WOBBLE)

30,,,

DANG, THOSE WERE SOME CRAZY EXPLOSIONS.

FIGURED I WAS AS GOOD AS DEAD.

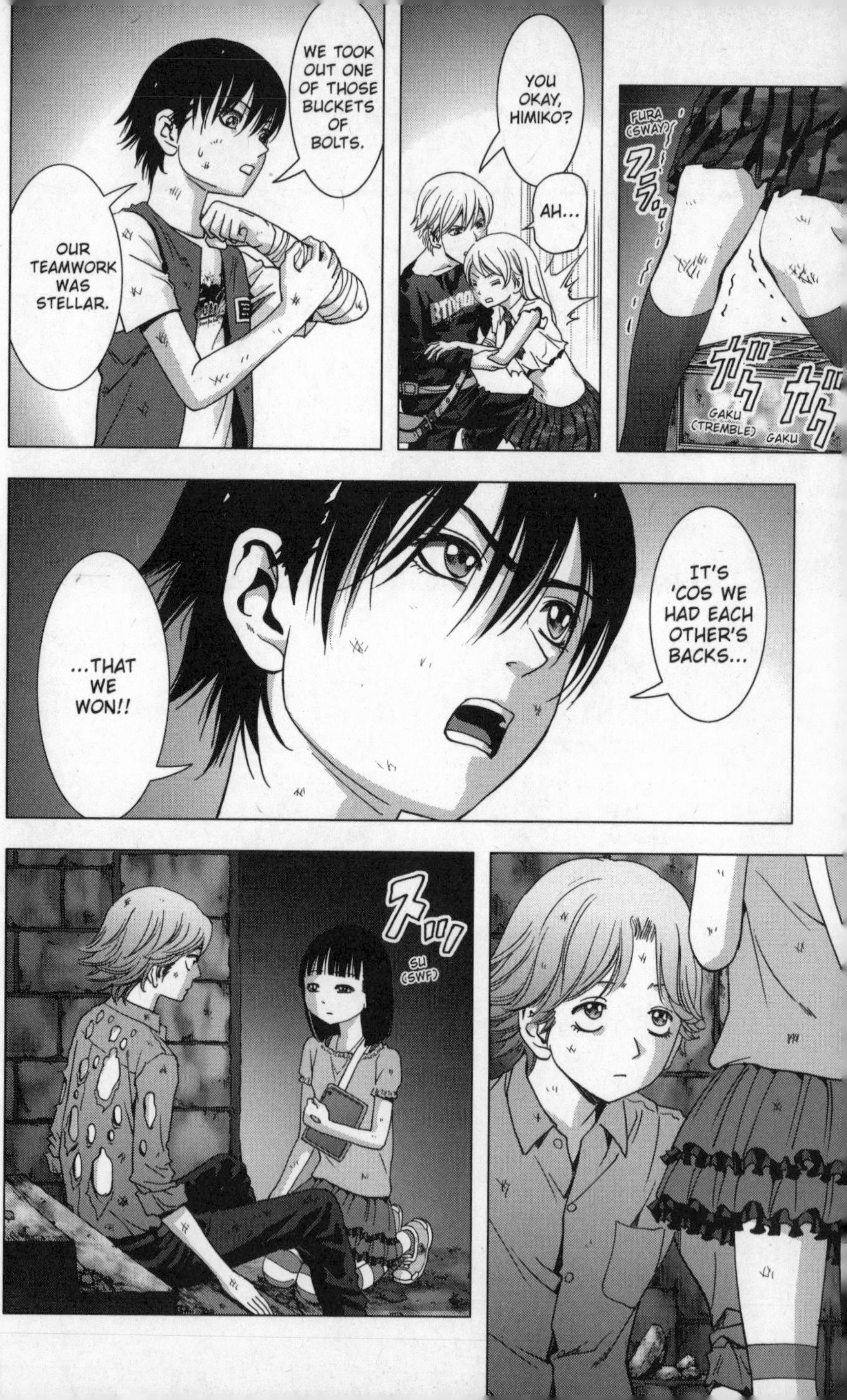
FURA (SWAY)
GAKU (TREMBLE) GAKU
YOU OKAY, HIMIKO?
AH...
WE TOOK OUT ONE OF THOSE BUCKETS OF BOLTS.
OUR TEAMWORK WAS STELLAR.
IT'S 'COS WE HAD EACH OTHER'S BACKS...
...THAT WE WON!!
SU (SWF)

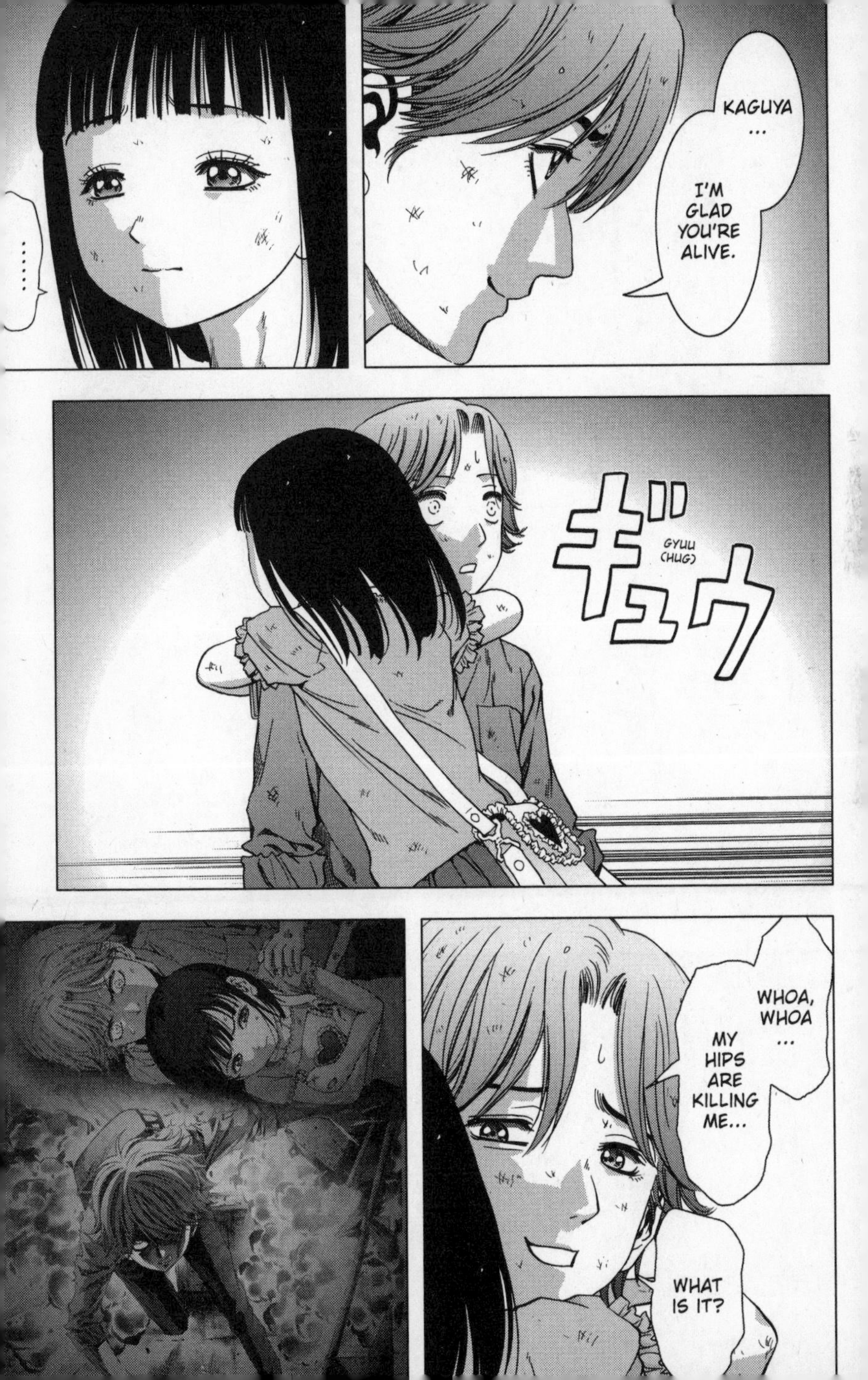
KAGUYA ...
I'M GLAD YOU'RE ALIVE.
......
ギュウ
GYUU (HUG)
WHOA, WHOA ...
MY HIPS ARE KILLING ME...
WHAT IS IT?

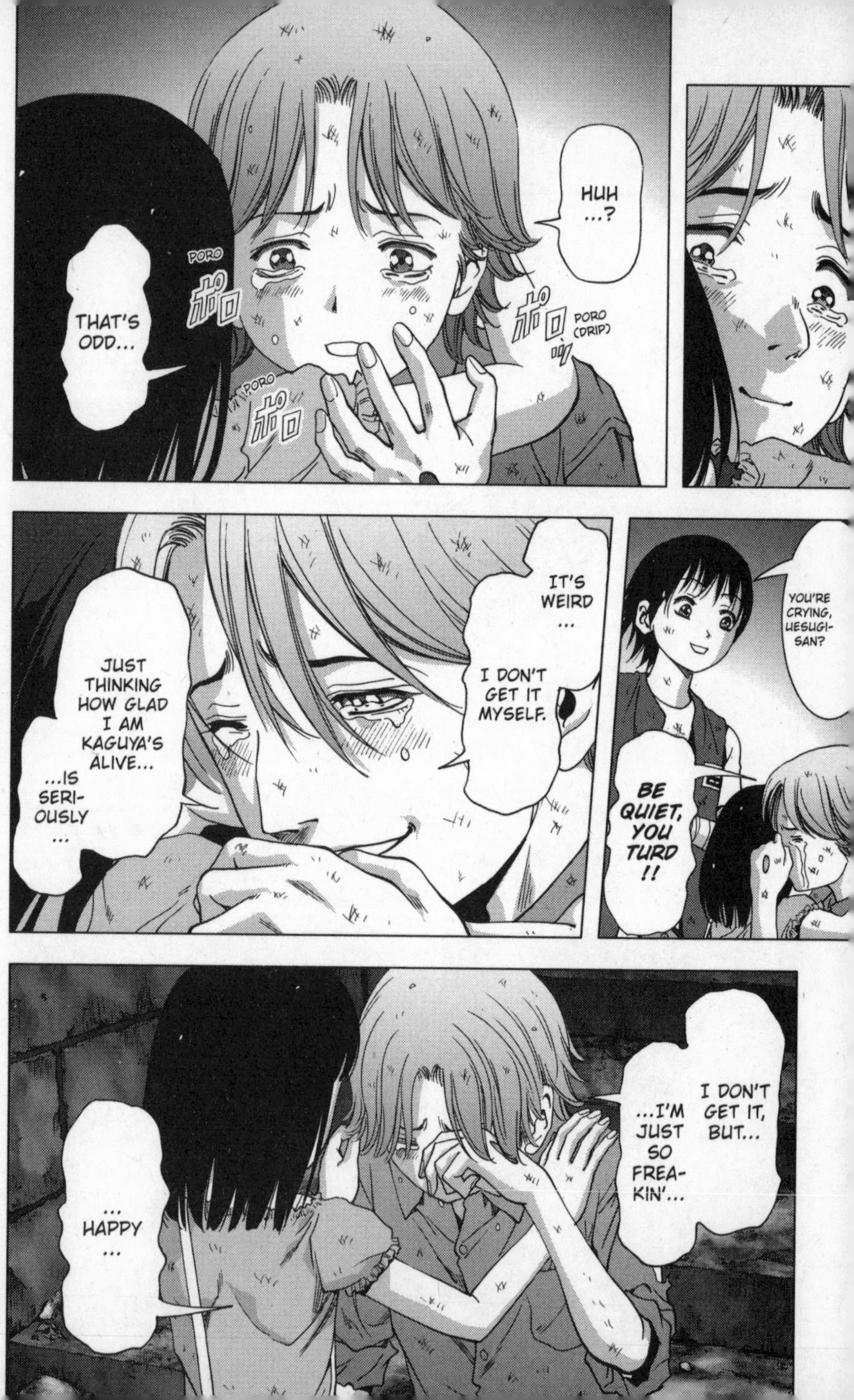
HUH ...?
ポロ PORO (DRIP)
PORO ポロ
THAT'S ODD...
PORO ポロ
YOU'RE CRYING, UESUGI-SAN?
BE QUIET, YOU TURD!!
IT'S WEIRD ...
I DON'T GET IT MYSELF.
JUST THINKING HOW GLAD I AM KAGUYA'S ALIVE...
...IS SERIOUSLY ...
I DON'T GET IT, BUT...
...I'M JUST SO FREAKIN'...
... HAPPY ...

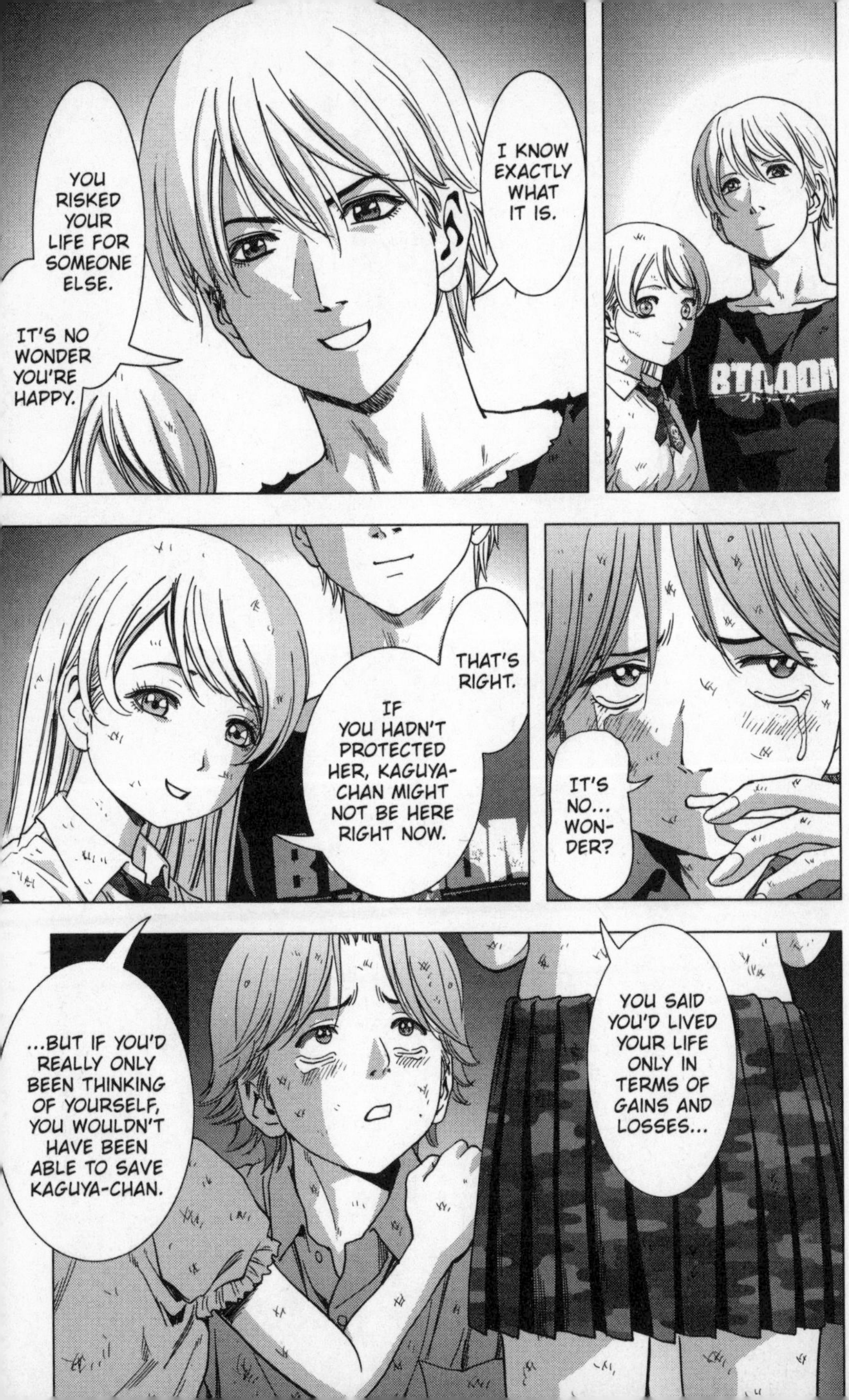
I KNOW EXACTLY WHAT IT IS.
YOU RISKED YOUR LIFE FOR SOMEONE ELSE.
IT'S NO WONDER YOU'RE HAPPY.
IT'S NO... WON-DER?
THAT'S RIGHT.
IF YOU HADN'T PROTECTED HER, KAGUYA-CHAN MIGHT NOT BE HERE RIGHT NOW.
YOU SAID YOU'D LIVED YOUR LIFE ONLY IN TERMS OF GAINS AND LOSSES...
...BUT IF YOU'D REALLY ONLY BEEN THINKING OF YOURSELF, YOU WOULDN'T HAVE BEEN ABLE TO SAVE KAGUYA-CHAN.

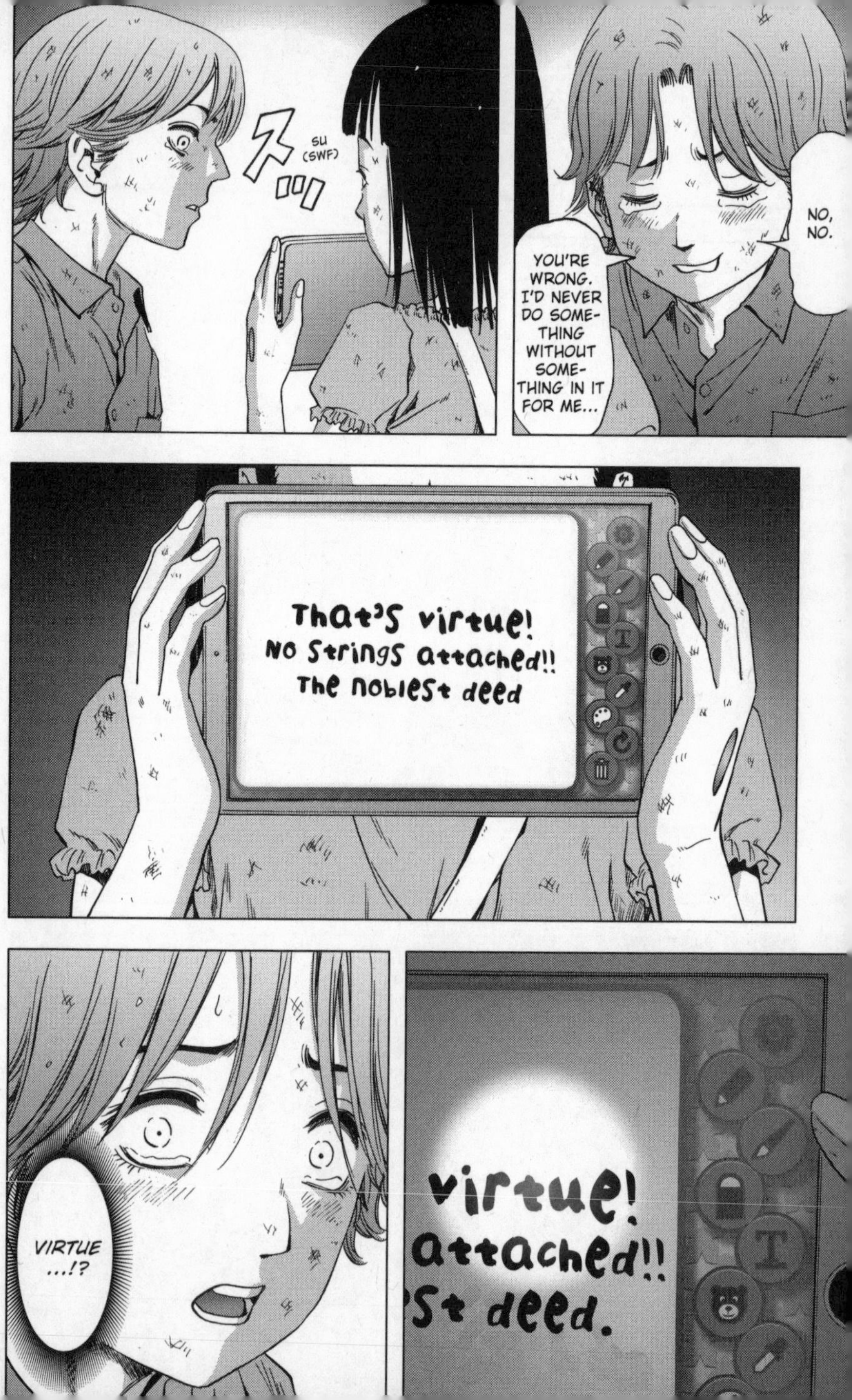
NO, NO.
YOU'RE WRONG. I'D NEVER DO SOMETHING WITHOUT SOMETHING IN IT FOR ME...
SU (SWF)
That's virtue! No strings attached!! The noblest deed
virtue! attached!! st deed.
VIRTUE ...!?

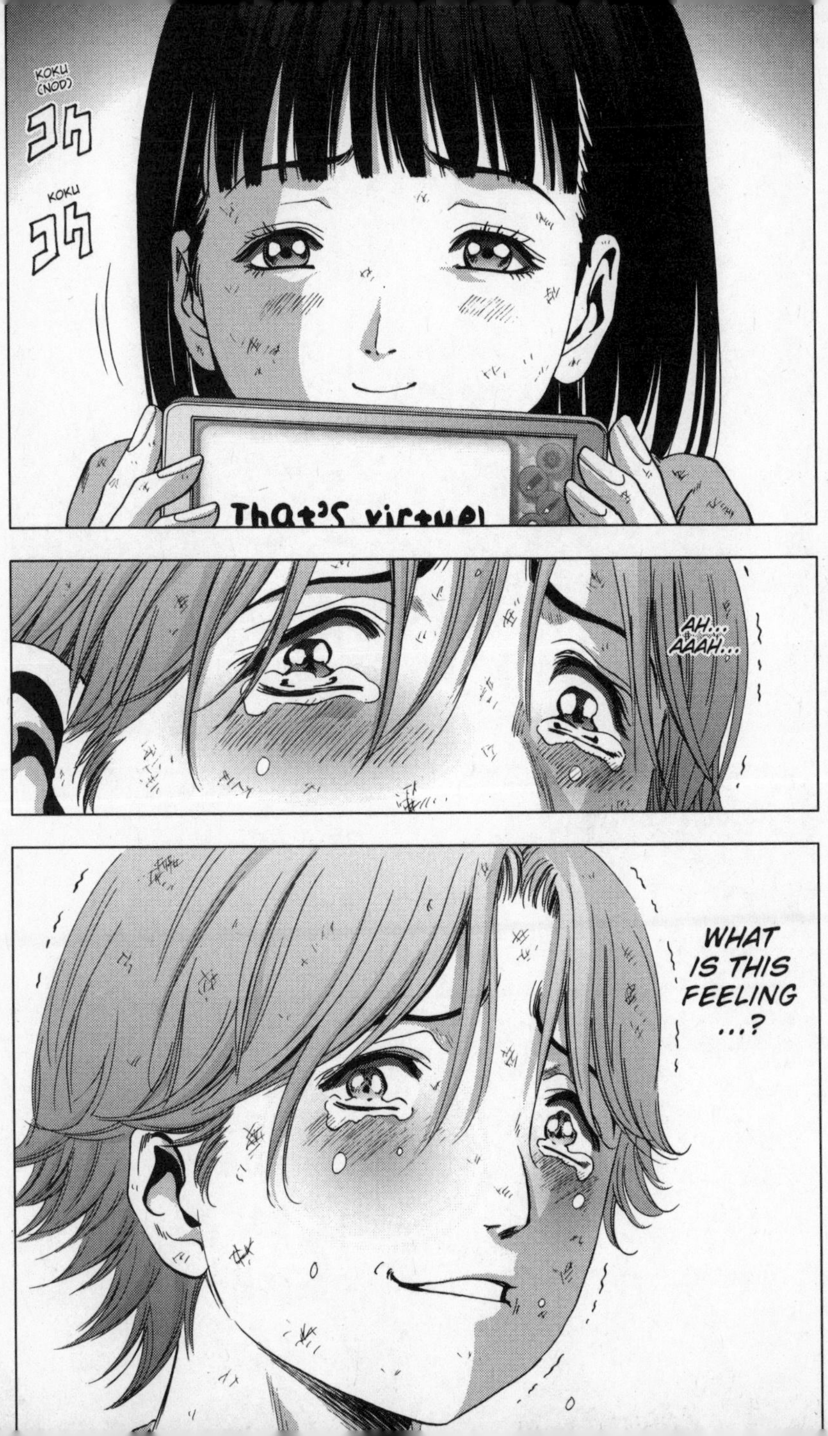
KOKU (NOD)
コク
KOKU
コク
That's virtue!
AH... AAAH...
WHAT IS THIS FEELING ...?

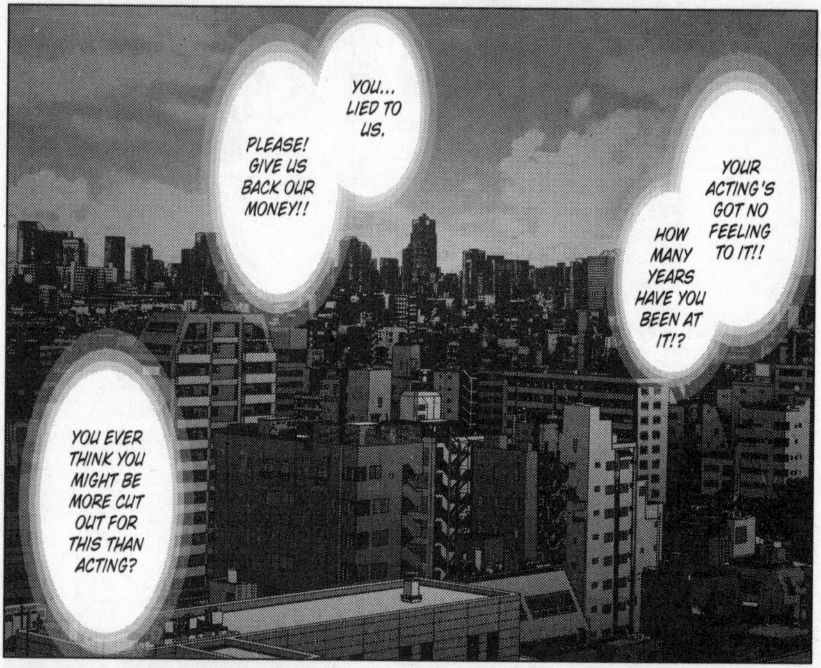
YOUR ACTING'S GOT NO FEELING TO IT!!
HOW MANY YEARS HAVE YOU BEEN AT IT!?
YOU... LIED TO US.
PLEASE! GIVE US BACK OUR MONEY!!
YOU EVER THINK YOU MIGHT BE MORE CUT OUT FOR THIS THAN ACTING?

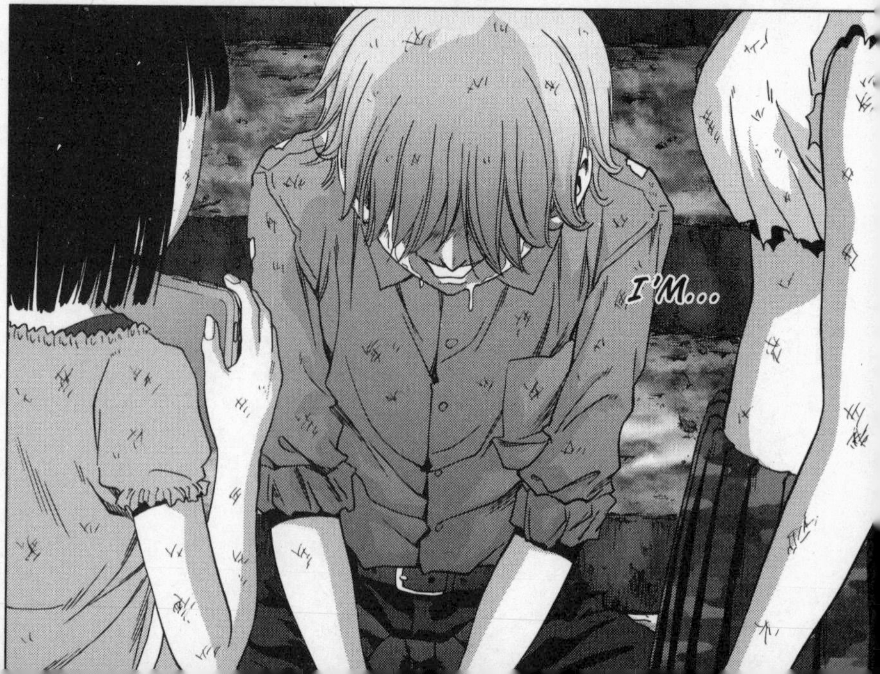
I'M...

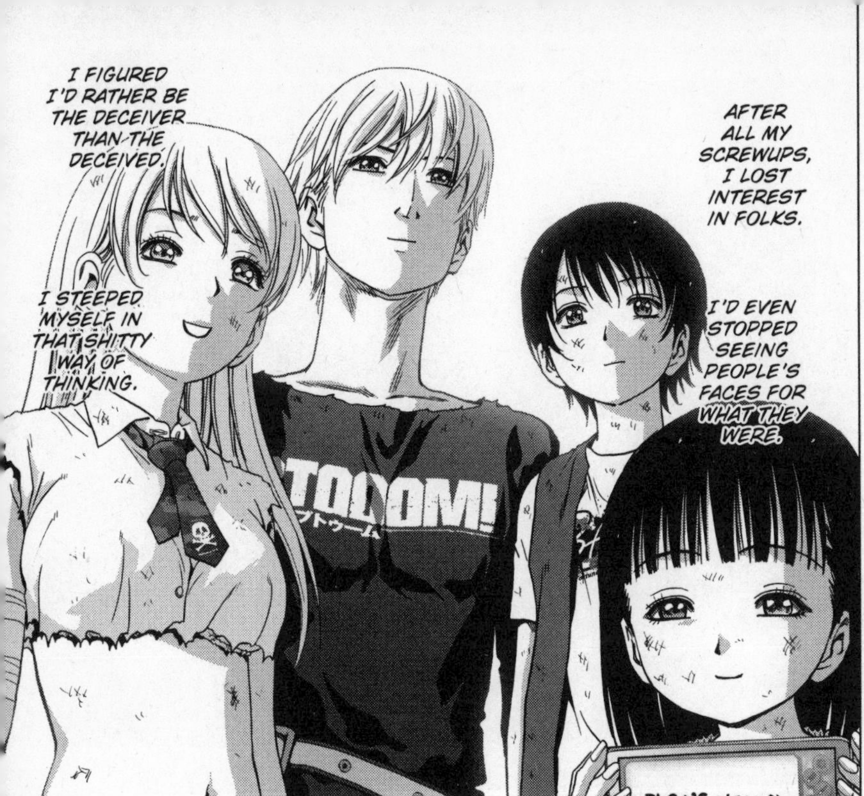
AFTER ALL MY SCREWUPS, I LOST INTEREST IN FOLKS.
I FIGURED I'D RATHER BE THE DECEIVER THAN THE DECEIVED.
I'D EVEN STOPPED SEEING PEOPLE'S FACES FOR WHAT THEY WERE.
I STEEPED MYSELF IN THAT SHITTY WAY OF THINKING.
That's virtue!

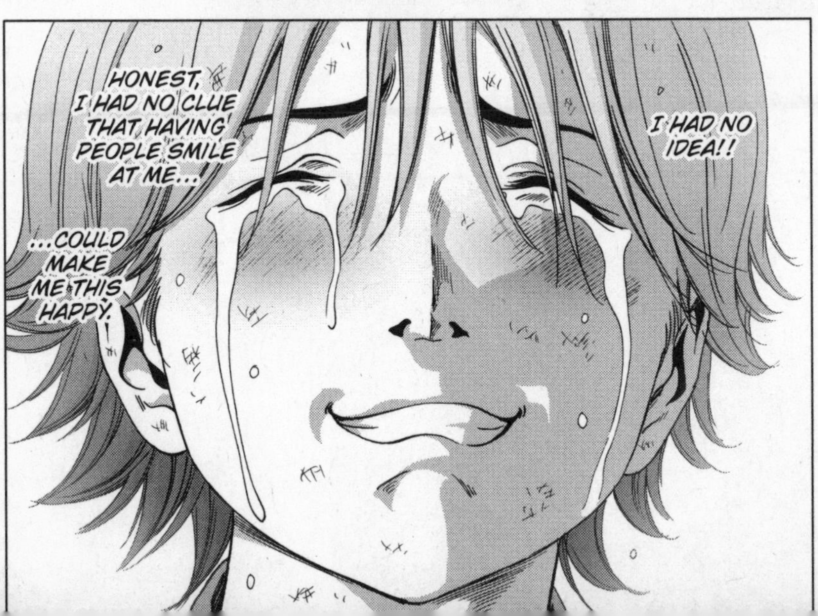
HONEST, I HAD NO CLUE THAT HAVING PEOPLE SMILE AT ME...
...COULD MAKE ME THIS HAPPY.
I HAD NO IDEA!!

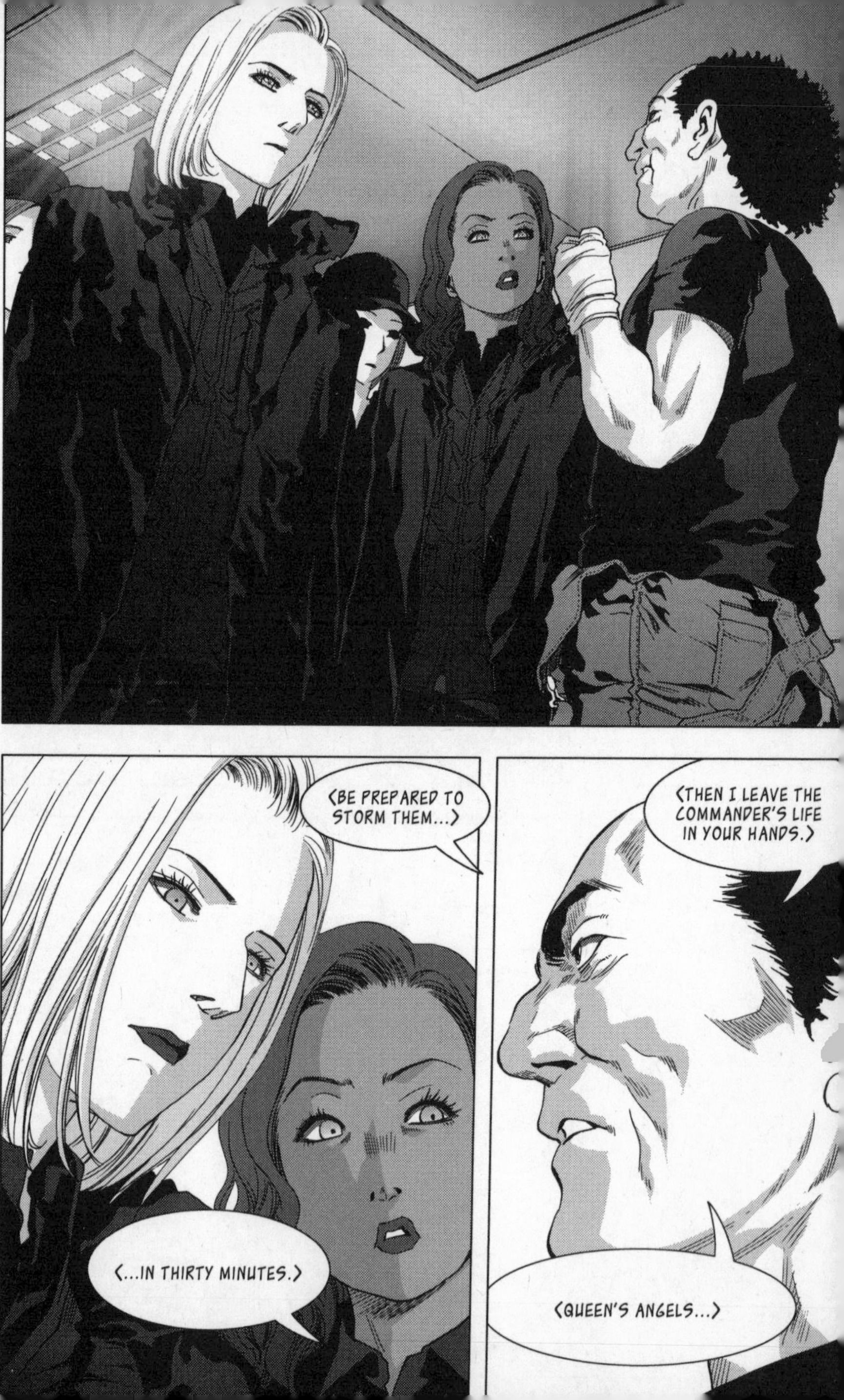
⟨THEN I LEAVE THE COMMANDER'S LIFE IN YOUR HANDS.⟩
⟨QUEEN'S ANGELS...⟩
⟨BE PREPARED TO STORM THEM...⟩
⟨...IN THIRTY MINUTES.⟩

TO BE CONTINUED IN BTOOOM! 25

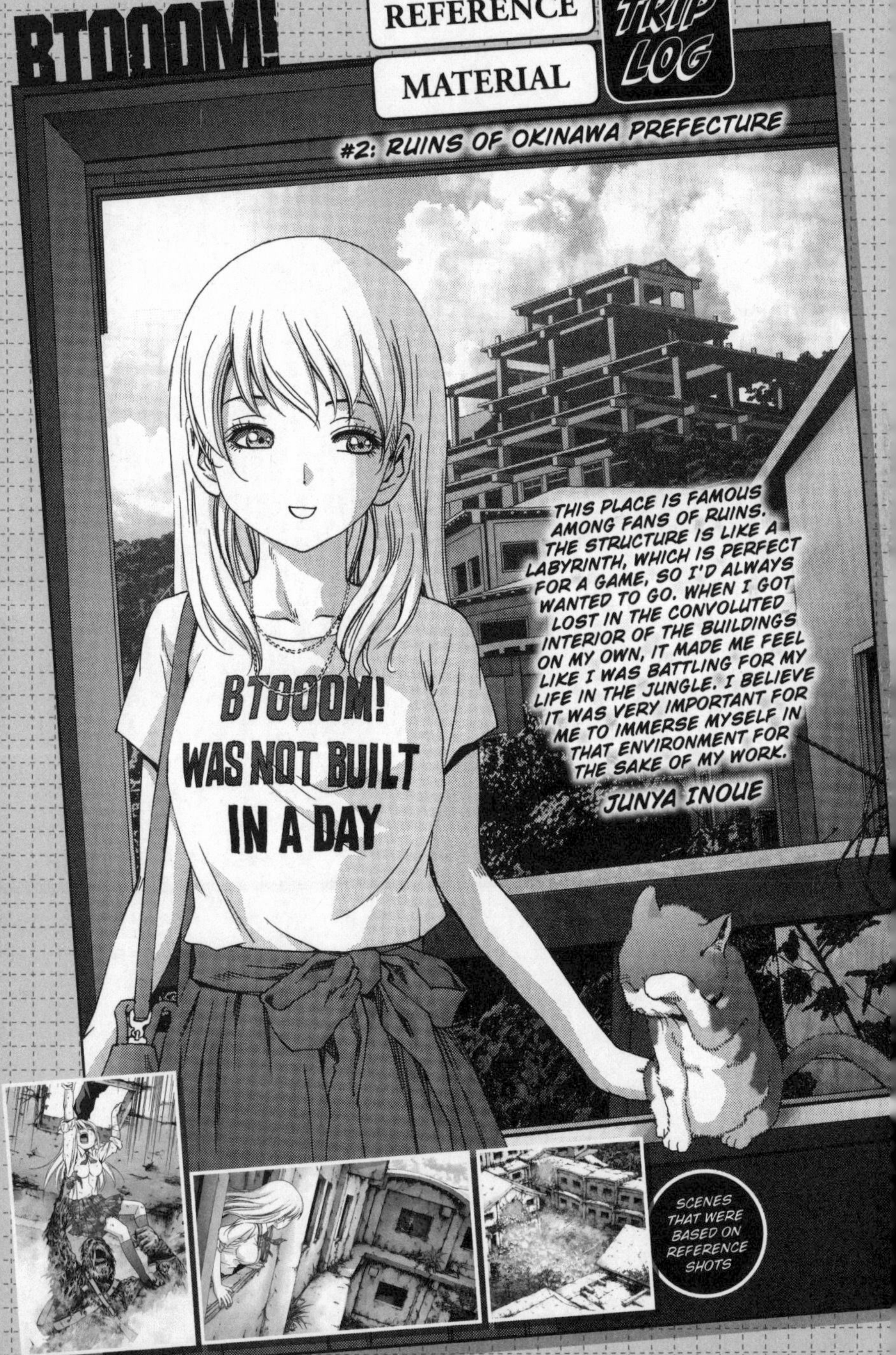

BTOOOM!
REFERENCE MATERIAL
TRIP LOG
#2: RUINS OF OKINAWA PREFECTURE
BTOOOM! WAS NOT BUILT IN A DAY
THIS PLACE IS FAMOUS AMONG FANS OF RUINS. THE STRUCTURE IS LIKE A LABYRINTH, WHICH IS PERFECT FOR A GAME, SO I'D ALWAYS WANTED TO GO. WHEN I GOT LOST IN THE CONVOLUTED INTERIOR OF THE BUILDINGS ON MY OWN, IT MADE ME FEEL LIKE I WAS BATTLING FOR MY LIFE IN THE JUNGLE. I BELIEVE IT WAS VERY IMPORTANT FOR ME TO IMMERSE MYSELF IN THAT ENVIRONMENT FOR THE SAKE OF MY WORK.
JUNYA INOUE
SCENES THAT WERE BASED ON REFERENCE SHOTS

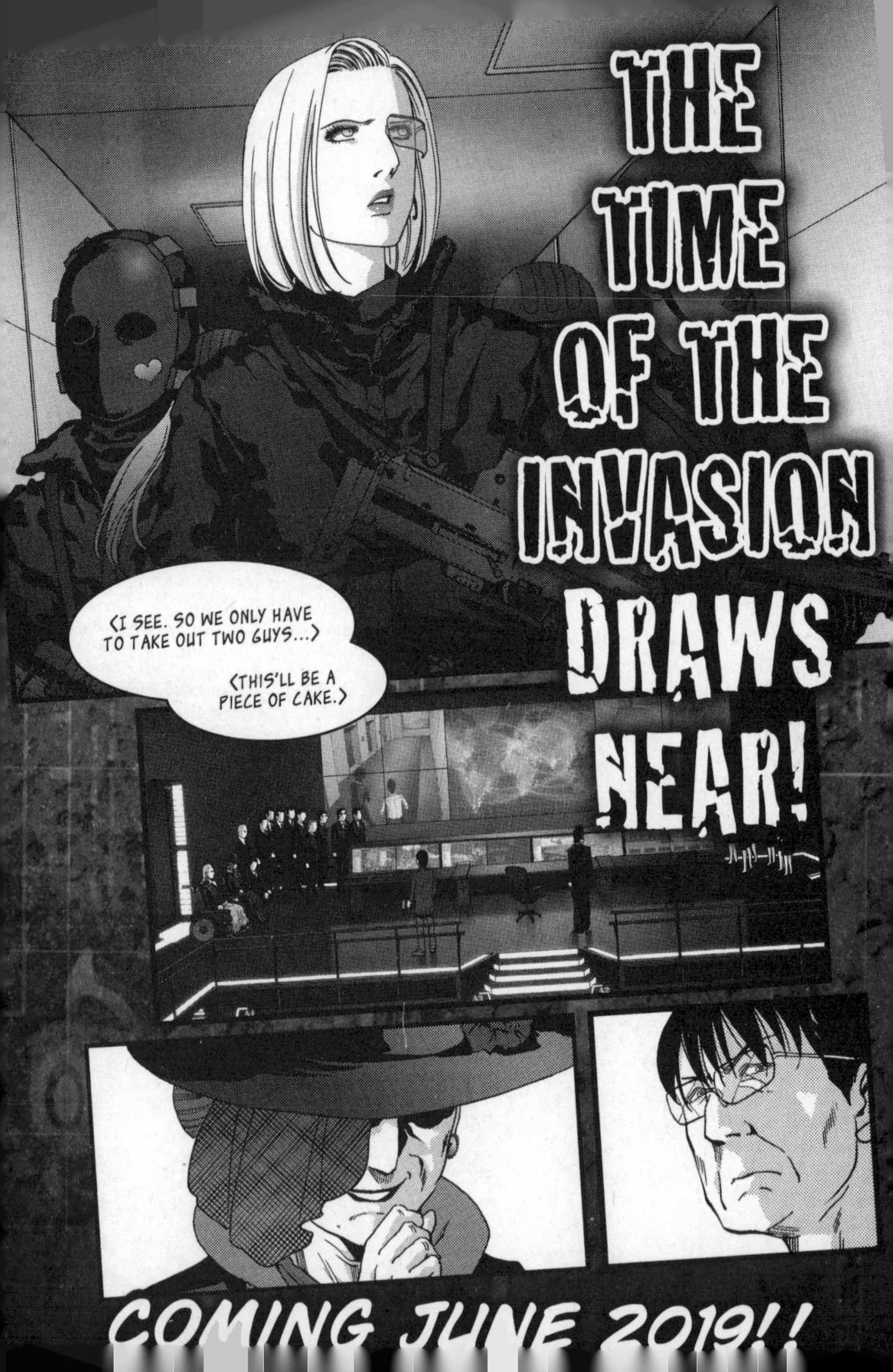
THE TIME OF THE INVASION DRAWS NEAR!
<I SEE. SO WE ONLY HAVE TO TAKE OUT TWO GUYS...>
<THIS'LL BE A PIECE OF CAKE.>
COMING JUNE 2019!!

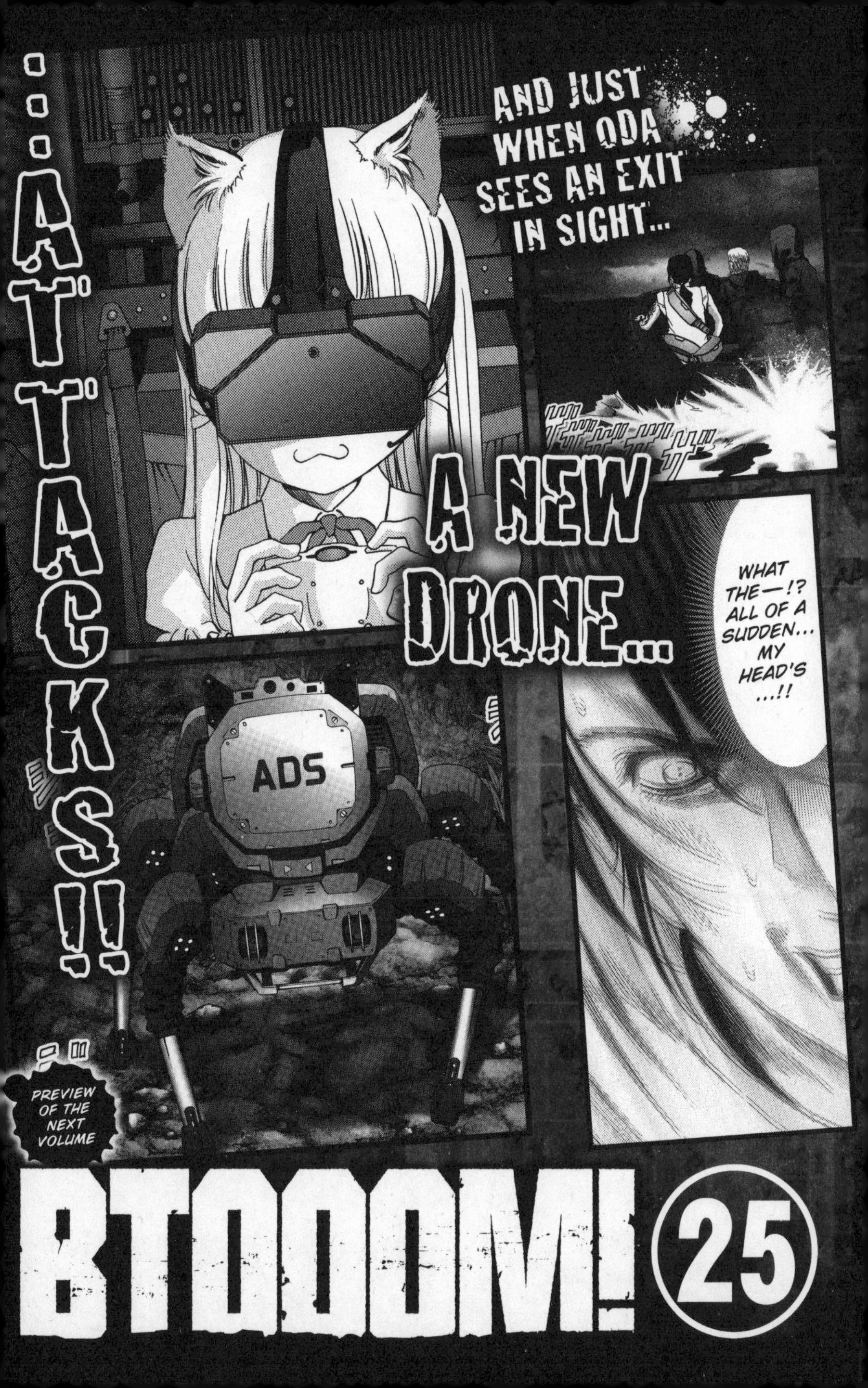
AND JUST WHEN ODA SEES AN EXIT IN SIGHT...
A NEW DRONE...
...ATTACKS!!
WHAT THE—!? ALL OF A SUDDEN... MY HEAD'S ...!!
ADS
PREVIEW OF THE NEXT VOLUME
BTOOOM! 25

baae

BTOOOM! 24

JUNYA INOUE

Translation: Christine Dashiell

Lettering: Brndn Blakeslee

BTOOOM! © Junya INOUE 2017. All rights reserved. English translation rights arranged with SHINCHOSHA PUBLISHING CO. through Tuttle-Mori Agency, Inc., Tokyo.

English translation © 2019 by Yen Press, LLC

Yen Press
1290 Avenue of the Americas
New York, NY 10104

Visit us at yenpress.com
facebook.com/yenpress
twitter.com/yenpress
yenpress.tumblr.com
instagram.com/yenpress

First Yen Press Edition: March 2019

Yen Press is an imprint of Yen Press, LLC.
The Yen Press name and logo are trademarks of Yen Press, LLC.

The publisher is not responsible for websites (or their content) that are not owned by the publisher.

Library of Congress Control Number: 2013497409

ISBNs: 978-1-9753-2895-5 (paperback)
       978-1-9753-2896-2 (ebook)

10 9 8 7 6 5 4 3 2 1

WOR

APR -- 2019

Printed in the United States of America

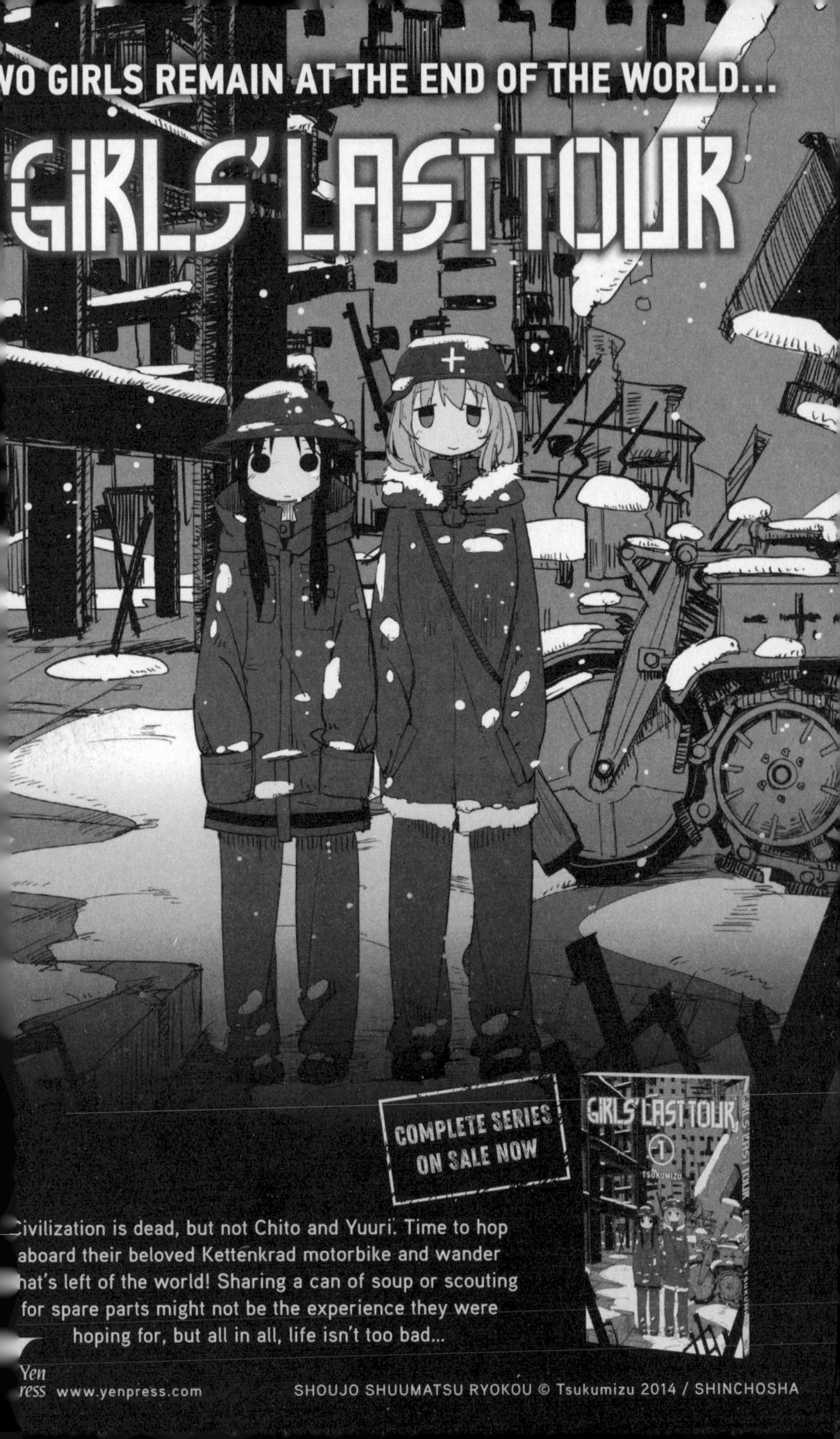

WO GIRLS REMAIN AT THE END OF THE WORLD...
GIRLS' LAST TOUR
COMPLETE SERIES ON SALE NOW
GIRLS' LAST TOUR 1
TSUKUMIZU
Civilization is dead, but not Chito and Yuuri. Time to hop
aboard their beloved Kettenkrad motorbike and wander
hat's left of the world! Sharing a can of soup or scouting
for spare parts might not be the experience they were
hoping for, but all in all, life isn't too bad...
Yen
ress www.yenpress.com
SHOUJO SHUUMATSU RYOKOU © Tsukumizu 2014 / SHINCHOSHA